T0321729

Fraud Prevention, Confidentiality, and Data Security for Modern Businesses

Arshi Naim
King Kalid University, Saudi Arabia

Praveen Kumar Malik
Lovely Professional University, India

Firasat Ali Zaidi
Tawuniya Insurance, Saudi Arabia

A volume in the Advances in
Information Security, Privacy, and
Ethics (AISPE) Book Series

Published in the United States of America by
IGI Global
Business Science Reference (an imprint of IGI Global)
701 E. Chocolate Avenue
Hershey PA, USA 17033
Tel: 717-533-8845
Fax: 717-533-8661
E-mail: cust@igi-global.com
Web site: http://www.igi-global.com

Library of Congress Cataloging-in-Publication Data

Names: Naim, Arshi, DATE- editor. | Malik, Praveen Kumar, editor. | Zaidi,
    Firasat, 1973- editor.
Title: Fraud prevention, confidentiality, and data security for modern
    businesses / Arshi Naim, Praveen Malik, Firasat Zaidi, editor.
Description: Hershey, PA : Business Science Reference, [2023] | Includes
    bibliographical references and index. | Summary: "The objective of this
    book is to provide an overview of the security challenges, practices,
    and blueprints for today's data storage and analysis systems to protect
    against current and emerging attackers in the modern business practices
    including the coverage of the organizational, strategic, and
    technological issues"-- Provided by publisher.
Identifiers: LCCN 2022027708 (print) | LCCN 2022027709 (ebook) | ISBN
    9781668465813 (hardcover) | ISBN 9781668465820 (paperback) | ISBN
    9781668465837 (ebook)
Subjects: LCSH: Data protection. | Fraud--Prevention. | Computer security.
    | Computer networks--Security measures.
Classification: LCC HF5548.37 F73 2023 (print) | LCC HF5548.37 (ebook) |
    DDC 005.8--dc23/eng/20220624
LC record available at https://lccn.loc.gov/2022027708
LC ebook record available at https://lccn.loc.gov/2022027709

This book is published in the IGI Global book series Advances in Information Security, Privacy,
and Ethics (AISPE) (ISSN: 1948-9730; eISSN: 1948-9749)

British Cataloguing in Publication Data
A Cataloguing in Publication record for this book is available from the British Library.

All work contributed to this book is new, previously-unpublished material.
The views expressed in this book are those of the authors, but not necessarily of the publisher.

For electronic access to this publication, please contact: eresources@igi-global.com.

Advances in Information Security, Privacy, and Ethics (AISPE) Book Series

Manish Gupta
State University of New York, USA

ISSN:1948-9730
EISSN:1948-9749

MISSION

As digital technologies become more pervasive in everyday life and the Internet is utilized in ever increasing ways by both private and public entities, concern over digital threats becomes more prevalent.

The **Advances in Information Security, Privacy, & Ethics (AISPE) Book Series** provides cutting-edge research on the protection and misuse of information and technology across various industries and settings. Comprised of scholarly research on topics such as identity management, cryptography, system security, authentication, and data protection, this book series is ideal for reference by IT professionals, academicians, and upper-level students.

COVERAGE

- Electronic Mail Security
- Data Storage of Minors
- CIA Triad of Information Security
- Technoethics
- Network Security Services
- Device Fingerprinting
- Internet Governance
- Cyberethics
- Tracking Cookies
- Access Control

IGI Global is currently accepting manuscripts for publication within this series. To submit a proposal for a volume in this series, please contact our Acquisition Editors at Acquisitions@igi-global.com or visit: http://www.igi-global.com/publish/.

Titles in this Series

For a list of additional titles in this series, please visit: *http://www.igi-global.com/book-series/*

Information Security and Privacy in Smart Devices Tools, Methods, and Applications
Carlos Rabadão (Computer Science and Communication Research Centre, Polytechnic of Leiria, Portugal) Leonel Santos (Computer Science and Communication Research Centre, Polytechnic of Leiria, Portugal) and Rogério Luís de Carvalho Costa (Polytechnic of Leiria, Portugal)
Information Science Reference • © 2023 • 310pp • H/C (ISBN: 9781668459911) • US $250.00

Handbook of Research on Cybersecurity Issues and Challenges for Business and FinTech Applications
Saqib Saeed (Department of Computer Information Systems, College of Computer Science and Information Technology, Imam Abdulrahman Bin Faisal University, Dammam, Saudi Arabia) Abdullah M. Almuhaideb (Department of Networks and Communications, College of Computer Science and Information Technology, Imam Abdulrahman Bin Faisal University, Dammam, Saudi Arabia) Neeraj Kumar (Thapar Institute of Engineering and Technology, India) Noor Zaman (Taylor's University, Malaysia) and Yousaf Bin Zikria (Yeungnam University, South Korea)
Business Science Reference • © 2023 • 552pp • H/C (ISBN: 9781668452844) • US $315.00

Cybersecurity Issues, Challenges, and Solutions in the Business World
Suhasini Verma (Manipal University Jaipur, India) Vidhisha Vyas (IILM University, Gurugram, India) and Keshav Kaushik (University of Petroleum and Energy Studies, India)
Information Science Reference • © 2023 • 288pp • H/C (ISBN: 9781668458273) • US $265.00

Handbook of Research on Technical, Privacy, and Security Challenges in a Modern World
Amit Kumar Tyagi (National Institute of Fashion Technology, New Delhi, India)
Information Science Reference • © 2022 • 474pp • H/C (ISBN: 9781668452509) • US $325.00

701 East Chocolate Avenue, Hershey, PA 17033, USA
Tel: 717-533-8845 x100 • Fax: 717-533-8661
E-Mail: cust@igi-global.com • www.igi-global.com

Table of Contents

Detailed Table of Contents

    Sérgio Sargo Lopes, Polytechnic Higher Institute of Gaya, Portugal &
        LE@D Open University, Portugal
    Mário Dias Lousã, Polytechnic Higher Institute of Gaya, Portugal
    Fernando Almeida, Polytechnic Higher Institute of Gaya, Portugal &
        INESC TEC, Portugal

Information security has become a necessity for all organizations. ITIL, designed for large organizations, has also been gradually adopted by smaller companies and has incorporated practices related to information security management (ISM). This study aims to understand the main risks associated with ISM, considering the context of micro companies. For this purpose, a qualitative model was built based on four case studies of micro companies in the information technology industry. The results show that companies are concerned about information security, given the growth of external threats. However, these companies have a lack of commitment, of resources, and of knowledge that hinder the implementation of an ISM policy. Therefore, it is evident that the challenge of ISM is demanding and should be addressed, considering that the security of an organization should be analyzed in a holistic context, where all perspectives should be considered to reflect the multidisciplinary nature of security.

Lemma Lessa, Addis Ababa University, Ethiopia
Antonyo George Etoribussi, Addis Ababa University, Ethiopia

Extant literature supports that e-health applications are developed with a proper set of security mechanisms in place. However, the majority of the security mechanisms were not considered from the users' point of view. As a result, the security of health information is becoming an important and growing concern. The objective of this study is to evaluate the usability of security mechanisms of e-Health applications functional at health facilities operating under the Addis Ababa Health Bureau, and identify the strengths and weaknesses of the usability of the security features of the e-Health applications. This study uses a qualitative research methodology. The findings revealed that out of the thirteen criteria, learnability, aesthetics and minimalist design, and user language complied; on the contrary, revocability and user suitability were not in compliance with security features according to all the experts' review of all e-Health applications. Finally, recommendations were given for practice, and suggestions were forwarded for future research.

Arshi Naim, King Khalid University, Saudi Arabia
Hamed Alqahtani, King Khalid University, Saudi Arabia
Anandhavalli Muniasamy, King Khalid University, Saudi Arabia
Syeda Meraj Bilfaqih, King Khalid University, Saudi Arabia
Ruheena Mahveen, King Khalid University, Saudi Arabia
Reshma Mahjabeen, King Khalid University, Saudi Arabia

This chapter is an extended research work showing the role of applications of Information Systems (IS) and importance of data security in Marketing Management. This research focuses on the application of Decision Support Systems (DSS) models of what-if analysis (WIA) for customer relationship management (CRM) at Analysis, Operational and Directional (AOD) level and also shows the dependence on the Information Success model (ISM). The second part of the chapter shows the role of data security in the growth of marketing for the companies. Hypothetical data are analyzed for (AOD) by three types of (WIA) to attain CRM and profit maximization. The results show that the analytical method based on the concepts of DSS can be used by all customer-oriented firms as a general model for achieving CRM and data security is a key to success for all firms.

    Arun Kumar Singh, Papua New Guinea University of Technology, Lae,
      Papua New Guinea

Python is a more powerful high-level language created by Guido van Rossum (first appeared in 20 February 1991; 31 years ago), and its language constructs and object-oriented approach aim to help programmers write clear, logical code for small- and large-scale projects. Its design philosophy emphasizes code readability with the use of significant indentation. Python is an object oriented, scripted, and interpreted language for both learning and real-world programming. First in this paper, Python is introduced as a language, and a summary given about data science, machine learning, and IoT. Then, details are provided about the packages that are popular in the data science and machine learning communities, such as NumPy, SciPy, TensorFlow, Keras, and Matplotlib. After that, the authors will show the working criteria of Python for building IOT applications. The authors will use different code examples throughout. The learning experience, and executed examples, contained in this paper interactively used Jupyter notebook (notebook: 6.4.11) with Python (v3.10.4:9d38120e33, Mar 23 2022) on macOS Catalina-Version 10.15.7.

    A. V. Senthil Kumar, Hindusthan College of Arts and Sciences, India
    Rahul Ramaswamy G., Hindusthan College of Arts and Science, India
    Ismail Bin Musirin, Universiti Teknologi Mara, Malaysia
    Indrarini Dyah Irawati, Telcom University, Indonesia
    Abdelmalek Amine, GeCoDe Laboratory, University of Saida Dr.
      Moulay Tahar, Algeria
    Seddik Bri, Moulay Ismail University, Morocco

A steganography approach is a beneficial approach for hiding and encrypting messages in text, audio, video, and image formats. After the original text file is first encrypted, this encrypted file is embedded with an image file, and that image will be transferred to the recipient. The motive of this method is easy communication and transferring of files to end users safely. The intruder is the only one who can view the unhidden message which is in text, audio, video, or image format. Thus, the message is encrypted successfully. Although there are many advantages for the steganography, which also has some limitations, these issues are mainly aimed in this paper. In this chapter, the challenges of steganography are rectified with the help of securing techniques. Finally, in the results section, findings in image size and the complexity of image quality at the sender side and receiver side in one-bit, two-bit, three-bit, and four-bit steganography images are stated. Thus, steganography methods are taking progressive steps to transform this capability into higher contributions.

Chapter 6

Srinivasa Rao Gundu, Department of Computer Science and
      Applications, Government Degree College Sitaphalmandi,
      Hyderabad, India
Panem Charanarur, Department of Cyber Security and Digital
      Forensics, National Forensic Sciences University, India
J.Vijaylaxmi, PVKK Degree and PG College, Anantapur, India

Talking about 'big data' refers to datasets that are either extraordinarily large or have a complex structure. These traits may sometimes be accompanied by more difficult data storage, processing, and application of following activities, or the extraction of discoveries. The practice of doing analytics on massive, complex datasets, sometimes known as 'big data,' is a method that may be utilized to discover links and patterns in these datasets that were previously undiscovered. However, attempts to protect the privacy and security of big data are undermined by its rapid spread.

Chapter 7

Awais Ashraf, Bahria University, Pakistan
Sehrish Aqeel, Universiti Malaysia Sarawak, Malaysia
Abdul Hafeez Muhammad, Bahria University, Pakistan

Online shopping platforms "Draz.pk," "Homesopping.pk," and "Telemart.pk," were the most often used online stores in Pakistan. E-commerce platforms have not achieved their complete objectives, because they are faced with many usability issues. It is recommended that an evaluation of the usability of e-commerce platforms should be explored through different usability scales. This research study evaluates the usability of e-commerce platforms in Pakistan. In this research study, three e-commerce platforms were selected for usability evaluation. For this purpose total of 15 users were selected and performed the System Usability Scale method of assessing the usability. The result of the System Usability Scale method indicated usability of the "Homesopping.pk" and "Telemart.pk" was less than below 70%, which indicated that these websites need to improve the user interface. Five expert evaluators were also selected for Heuristic evaluation to perform on "Homesopping. pk" to find out the usability issues.

    Amir Manzoor, Karachi School of Business and Leadership, Karachi,
      Pakistan

Blockchain technology enables online sharing of digital information. A blockchain acts as public ledger that everyone has access to but is not controlled by a central authority. It is a technology that empowers people and organizations to collaborate and transact in an online environment that is trusted and transparent. The blockchain technology provides many benefits, including increased transparency and traceability of transactions. However, the security and privacy issues of blockchain can outweigh its benefits. This literature-review based study explores the privacy and security challenges of blockchain technology and their solutions.

    Panem Charanarur, Department of Cyber Security and Digital
      Forensics, National Forensic Sciences University, India
    Srinivasa Rao Gundu, Government Degree College Sitaphalamandi,
      Hyderabad, India
    J. Vijaylaxmi, PVKK Degree and PG College, Anantapur, India

Every aspect of our life, from travel and healthcare to entertainment and governmental interactions, stands to benefit greatly from the advent of the internet of things. Despite this enormous potential, however, a number of significant obstacles must first be overcome. The race to create laws, rules, and governance that will lead this progress without strangling innovation has become more difficult because of the exponential expansion in the number of connected devices. Discover the origins of the IoT, its many definitions, and some of its most important uses in this in-depth read. Future fears and difficulties relating to security and privacy are taken into account, both generally and in the more specific context of individual applications.

    Mumtaz Hussain, NEDUET, Pakistan
    Samrina Siddiqui, NEDUET, Pakistan
    Noman Islam, KIET, Pakistan

This paper presents the concept of social engineering. The internet has completely changed the mode of operations of modern-day systems. There are billions of internet users and this number is rising every day. Hence, ensuring the security is very important for any cyber physical systems. This paper focuses on one of the very important aspects of cyber security, i.e., social engineering. It is defined as a set of techniques of human manipulation by exploitation of the basic emotions of human beings. Different institutions deploy state-of-the-art systems to protect the data housed in their datacenter. However, it is also essential that an individual must secure their personal information from the social engineers. Hence, this paper discusses the data privacy issues and various relevant techniques under the umbrella of social engineering. It discusses various social engineering techniques and summarizes those techniques, thus concluding the paper.

Chapter 11
   Aysha Abdulla, Ibn Rushd College For Management Sciences, Saudi Arabia

As cyberattacks have become common due to ubiquitous hyperconnectivity of devices, modern business is highly susceptible to data breaches. This chapter aims to investigate the relevance of cyber security in business models. It explains the business impact of cyber security and the various types of cyber threats that has devastating effects on businesses. It further elaborates the various layers of business models. The major security provisioning scenarios that can be effectively applied to them are deduced and the chapter henceforth advances into the explanation of various technological concepts of cyber security. By integrating the security provisioning scenarios with the help of various cyber security technologies and the different layers of business model, an integrated framework of business model options including the most opportunistic model is developed. This research finding provides pragmatic solutions for building lucrative business model options in cyber security with optimum performance.

Chapter 12
   Arshiya Begum Mohammed, King Khalid University, Saudi Arabia
   Asfia Sabahath, King Khalid University, Saudi Arabia

The term big data was started in the year of 2012 and since then it has emerged as one of the top trends in the business and technology world. Big data is referred to as massive amounts of data or information in business and technology. Many organizations are collecting, storing, and analyzing vast amounts of data in today's world. This data is commonly referred to as big data due to its volume, velocity, and variety of forms it takes. Businesses are recognizing the potentiality of big data and processing it to analyze the business. The development of big data tools has a significant impact on managerial decision-making in modern business. The key to success in big data implementation includes a clear business objective, a strong data infrastructure, skilled people, a strong decision-making team, and the correct analytical tools. The main objective of this chapter is to find the challenges, and implementation of big data, and how big data revolutionizes fraud detection and prevention methods in modern business.

Preface

The modern business world faces many new challenges in preserving its confidentiality and data from online attackers. Further, it also faces a struggle with preventing fraud. These challenges threaten businesses internally and externally and can cause huge losses. It is essential for business leaders to be up to date on the current fraud prevention, confidentiality, and data security to protect their businesses.

Fraud Prevention, Confidentiality, and Data Security for Modern Businesses provides examples and research on the security challenges, practices, and blueprints for today's data storage and analysis systems to protect against current and emerging attackers in the modern business world. It includes the organizational, strategic, and technological depth to design modern data security practices within any organization. Covering topics such as confidential communication, information security management, and social engineering, this premier reference source is an indispensable resource for business executives and leaders, entrepreneurs, IT managers, security specialists, students and educators of higher education, librarians, researchers, and academicians.

Chapter 1: The Risks Associated With ITIL Information Security Management in Micro Companies

Sérgio Lopes, Mário Lousã, Fernando Almeida

Information security has become a necessity for all organizations. ITIL, designed for large organizations, has also been gradually adopted by smaller companies and has incorporated practices related to information security management (ISM). This study aims to understand the main risks associated with ISM, considering the context of micro companies. For the purpose, a qualitative model was built based on four case studies of micro companies in the information technology industry. The results show that companies are concerned about information security, given the growth of external threats. However, these companies have a lack of commitment, of resources, and of knowledge that hinder the implementation of an ISM policy. Therefore, it is evident that the challenge of ISM is demanding and should be addressed, considering that the security of an organization should be analyzed in a holistic context, where all perspectives should be considered to reflect the multidisciplinary nature of security.

Chapter 2: Usability of Security Mechanisms of E-Health Application – Cases From Ethiopia

Lemma Lessa, Antonyo Etoribussi

Extant literature support that e-health applications are developed with a proper set of security mechanisms in place. However, the majority of the security mechanisms were not considered from the users' point of view. As a result, the security of health information is becoming an important and growing concern. The objective of this study is to evaluate the usability of security mechanisms of e-Health applications functional at health facilities operating under the Addis Ababa Health Bureau and identify strengths and weaknesses of the usability of the security features of the e-Health applications. This study uses a qualitative research methodology. The finding reviled that out of the thirteen criteria, learnability, aesthetics and minimalist design, and user language complied, on the contrary revocability and user suitability were not in compliance with security features according to all the experts' review of all e-Health applications. Finally, recommendations were given for practice, and suggestions were forwarded for future research.

Chapter 3: Applications of Information Systems and Data Security in Marketing Management

Arshi Naim, Hamed Alqahtani, Anandhavalli Muniasamy, Syeda Meraj Bilfaqih, Ruheena Mahveen, Reshma Mahjabeen

This chapter is an extended research work showing the role of applications of Information Systems (IS) and importance of data security in Marketing Management. This research focuses on the application of Decision Support Systems (DSS) models of what-if analysis (WIA) for customer relationship management (CRM) at Analysis, Operational and Directional (AOD) level and also shows the dependence on the Information Success model (ISM). The second part of the chapter shows the role of data security in the growth of marketing for the companies. Hypothetical data are analyzed for (AOD) by three types of (WIA) to attain CRM and profit maximization. The results show that the analytical method based on the concepts of DSS can be used by all customer-oriented firms as a general model for achieving CRM and data security is a key to success for all firms.

Chapter 4: A Basic Process of Python Use for IOTAP, Data Science, and Rapid Machine Learning Model Development

Arun Singh

Python is a more powerful high-level language created by Guido van Rossum (First appeared in 20 February 1991; 31 years ago) and Its language constructs and object-oriented approach aim to help programmers write clear, logical code for small- and large-scale projects. Its design philosophy emphasizes code readability with the use of significant indentation. Python is an object oriented, scripted and interpreted language for both learning and real world programming. Work in this paper first we introduce Python as a language, and give summary about Data science, Machine learning and IOT, and then details about the packages that are popular in the Data science and Machine learning communities, such as NumPy, SciPy, TensorFlow, Keras, Matplotlib. After that, we will go to show the working criteria of python for building IOT applications. We will use different code examples throughout. The learning experience, execute examples contained in this paper interactively using Jupyter notebook (notebook: 6.4.11) with python (v3.10.4:9d38120e33, Mar 23 2022) on macOS Catalina-Version 10.15.7.

Chapter 5: A Study of Steganography Approach for Securing Data in a Confidential Communication Using Encryption

A.V. Senthil Kumar, Rahul Ramaswamy G, Ismail Bin Musirin, Indrarini Dyah Irawati, Abdelmalek Amine, Seddik Bri

A steganography approach is a beneficial approach for hiding and encrypting messages in text, audio, video and image formats. At first the original text file is encrypted, this encrypted file is embedded with an image file and that image will be transferred to the recipient. The motive of this method is easy to communicate and transfer files to end users safely. The intruder is the only one who can view the unhidden message which is in text, audio, video, or image format. Thus the message is encrypted successfully. Although there are many advantages for the steganography, which also has some limitations, these issues are mainly aimed in this paper. In this chapter, the challenges of steganography are rectified with the help of securing techniques. Finally, in the results section, findings in image size and the complexity of image quality at the sender side and receiver side in one-bit, two-bit, three-bit, and four-bit steganography images are stated. Thus steganography methods are taking progressive steps to transform this capability into higher contributions.

Chapter 6: Deception Preclusion, Discretion, and Data Safety for Contemporary Business

Srinivasa Gundu, Charan Panem, Vijaylaxmi J.

When we talk about "big data," we're referring to datasets that are either extraordinarily large or have a complex structure. These traits may sometimes be accompanied by more difficult data storage, processing, and application of following activities, or the extraction of discoveries. The practice of doing analytics on massive, complex datasets, sometimes known as "big data," is a method that may be utilized to discover links and patterns in these datasets that were previously undiscovered. However, attempts to protect the privacy and security of big data are undermined by its rapid spread.

Chapter 7: Evaluation of Usability of E-Commerce Websites in Pakistan Using System Usability Scale and Heuristics Methods

Awais Ashraf, Sehrish Aqeel, Abdul Hafeez Muhammad

Online shopping platforms "Draz.pk", "Homesopping.pk" and "Telemart.pk" were the most often used online store in Pakistan. E-commerce platforms have not to gain their complete objectives, because they are faced with many usability issues. It is recommended that evaluate the usability of e-commerce platforms should be explored through different usability scales. This research study evaluates the usability of e-commerce platforms in Pakistan. In this research study, three e-commerce platforms were selected for usability evaluation. For this purpose total of 15 users were selected and performed the System Usability Scale method of assessing the usability. The result of the System Usability Scale method indicated usability of the "Homesopping.pk" and "Telemart.pk" was less than below 70% which indicated that these websites need to improve the user interface. Five Expert Evaluators were also selected for Heuristic evaluation to perform on "Homesopping.pk" to find out the usability issues.

Chapter 8: Privacy and Security Under Blockchain Technology – Challenges and Solutions

Amir Manzoor

Blockchain technology enables online sharing of digital information. A blockchain acts as public ledger that everyone has access to but is not controlled by a central authority. It is a technology that empowers people and organizations to collaborate and transact in an online environment that is trusted and transparent. The blockchain technology provides many benefits including increased transparency and traceability of transactions. However, the security and privacy issues of blockchain can outweigh its benefits. This literature-review based study explores the privacy and security challenges of blockchain technology and their solutions.

Chapter 9: Protection of Personal Data and Internet of Things Security

Srinivasa Gundu, Charan Panem, Vijaylaxmi J.

Every aspect of our life, from travel and healthcare to entertainment and governmental interactions, stands to benefit greatly from the advent of the Internet of Things. Despite this enormous potential, however, a number of significant obstacles must first be overcome. The race to create laws, rules, and governance that will lead this progress without strangling innovation has become more difficult because to the exponential expansion in the number of connected devices. Discover the origins of the IoT, its many definitions, and some of its most important uses in this in-depth read. Future fears and difficulties relating to security and privacy are taken into account, both generally and in the more specific context of individual applications.

Chapter 10: Social Engineering And Data Privacy

Mumtaz Hussain, Samrina Siddiqui, Noman Islam

This paper presents the concept of social engineering. Internet has completely changed the mode of operations of modern day systems. There are billions of users of internet and this number is rising every day. Hence, ensuring the security is very important for any cyber physical systems. This paper focuses on one of the very important aspects of cyber security i.e. social engineering. It is defined as a set of techniques of human manipulation by exploitation of the basic emotions of human beings. Different institutions deploy state-of-the-art systems to protect the data housed in their datacenter. However, it is also essential that individual must secure his personal information from the social engineers. Hence, this paper discusses the data privacy issues and various relevant techniques under the umbrella of social engineering. It discusses various social engineering techniques and summarizes those techniques thus concluding the paper.

Chapter 11: Relevance of Cybersecurity in the Business Models

Aysha Abdulla

As cyberattacks have become common due to ubiquitous hyperconnectivity of devices, modern business is highly susceptible to data breaches. This chapter aims to investigate the relevance of cyber security in business models. It explains the business impact of cyber security and the various types of cyber threats that has devastating effects on businesses. It further elaborates the various layers of business models. The major security provisioning scenarios that can be effectively applied to them are deduced and the chapter henceforth advances into the explanation of various technological concepts of cyber security. By integrating the security provisioning scenarios with the help of various cyber security technologies and the different layers of business model, an integrated framework of business model options including the most opportunistic model is developed. This research finding provides pragmatic solutions for building lucrative business model options in cyber security with optimum performance.

Chapter 12: Implementation of Big Data in Modern Business – Fraud Detection and Prevention Techniques

Arshiya Mohammed, Asfia Sabahath

The big data term was started in the year of 2012 and since then it has emerged as one of the top trends in the business and technology world. Big data is referred to as massive data or information in business and technology. Many organizations are collecting, storing, and analyzing vast data in today's world. This data is commonly referred to as big data due to its volume, velocity, and variety of forms it takes. Businesses are recognizing the potentiality of big data and processing it to analyze the business. The development of Bigdata tools has a significant impact on managerial decisions making in modern business. The key to success in big data implementation includes a clear business objective, a strong data infrastructure, skilled people, a strong decision-making team, and the correct analytical tools. The main objective of this chapter is to find the challenges, and implementation of big data, and how big data revolutionizes fraud detection and prevention methods in modern business.

Arshi Naim
King Kalid University, Saudi Arabia

Praveen Kumar Malik
Lovely Professional University, India

Firasat Ali Zaidi
Tawuniya Insurance, Saudi Arabia

Acknowledgment

We are delighted to welcome the readers of our new book *"Fraud Prevention, Confidentiality, and Data Security for Modern Businesses"*. We congratulate all chapter authors for their valuable submissions and keeping patience during critical review process. We wish to thank all reviewers as well who spared their precious time for the review process.

We are thankful to our family members and friends for giving me eternal happiness and support during the entire process.

Last but not the least, we express our gratitude to the almighty god for blessing us with wonderful life and showing us right paths in our all ups and downs during the so far journey of life.

Arshi Naim
Praveen Kumar Malik
Firasat Ali Zaidi

Chapter 1

The Risks Associated With ITIL Information Security Management in Micro Companies

Sérgio Sargo Lopes
ⓘ https://orcid.org/0000-0003-4039-9979
Polytechnic Higher Institute of Gaya, Portugal & LE@D Open University, Portugal

Mário Dias Lousã
Polytechnic Higher Institute of Gaya, Portugal

Fernando Almeida
ⓘ https://orcid.org/0000-0002-6758-4843
Polytechnic Higher Institute of Gaya, Portugal & INESC TEC, Portugal

ABSTRACT

Information security has become a necessity for all organizations. ITIL, designed for large organizations, has also been gradually adopted by smaller companies and has incorporated practices related to information security management (ISM). This study aims to understand the main risks associated with ISM, considering the context of micro companies. For this purpose, a qualitative model was built based on four case studies of micro companies in the information technology industry. The results show that companies are concerned about information security, given the growth of external threats. However, these companies have a lack of commitment, of resources, and of knowledge that hinder the implementation of an ISM policy. Therefore, it is evident that the challenge of ISM is demanding and should be addressed, considering that the security of an organization should be analyzed in a holistic context, where all perspectives should be considered to reflect the multidisciplinary nature of security.

DOI: 10.4018/978-1-6684-6581-3.ch001

INTRODUCTION

Information is nowadays a key element for the competitiveness of organizations. As studies (Chung et al., 2016; Grander et al., 2021; Phillips-Wren et al., 2021) demonstrate, information satisfies the needs of organizations to recognize the characteristics of a given context and support the decision-making process. Information can be materialized in many different formats. Not all media are digital, although the increasing role of digitization processes is recognized (Ellström et al., 2021; Kraus et al., 2022). Managing all this information effectively has become essential for the sustainability of a business (Etzion & Aragon-Correa, 2016; Serban, 2017). Consequently, information security, as a potentially valuable asset, should no longer be seen as a minor activity in the context of organizations. The protection of these valuable assets associated with information is referred to as information security.

Information security is the protection of information, the systems and devices that use, store, and transmit that information (Kim & Solomon, 2021). Therefore, the goal of information security is to adequately protect information assets to ensure business continuity or operation, minimizing potential losses and maximizing the return on investment. To achieve this purpose, the literature reveals the need to protect three critical aspects of information: confidentiality, integrity, and availability (Qadir & Quadri, 2016; Yee & Zolkipli, 2021). Confidentiality ensures that only authorized people have access to the data; integrity looks at protecting the information from unauthorized changes; and availability seeks to ensure that all information is accessible when it is required. The correct presentation of these three aspects of information ensures credibility and trust in organizations and businesses and can be achieved through the application of controls. Controls can be more or less sophisticated and are the result of a combination of policies, procedures, and organizational structures.

Since it is not possible to ensure total protection of information from all current and potential threats, it is necessary to perform an information security risk analysis to determine the potential threats and vulnerabilities. Furthermore, this knowledge is important for defining the necessary countermeasures to be applied to mitigate the impact of these risks to an acceptable level. In this way, risk analysis is seen by Eling et al. (2021) as a process of identifying the assets, the risks to those assets, and the procedures to mitigate the risks to those assets. It is from the risk analysis that management can make proper decisions regarding information security.

Information security management (ISM) is currently an indispensable element in the various silos of corporate and business management. The Information Technology Infrastructure Library (ITIL), created with the goal of increasing maturity in the management of its processes in information technology, offers a set of best practices for project management in areas such as support, services, infrastructure management, application management, and security management (Soomro & Wahba, 2011). This last component concerning security management only emerged explicitly in 2018 with the publication of ITIL v.4. Furthermore, ITIL v.4 states that organizations must ensure that security aspects are integrated into all other IT Service Management (ITSM) processes. Because it is an IT service-oriented methodology, based on market best practices, the ITIL methodology has been widely used by companies with this focus and business.

The ITIL methodology defines various elements of information security related to information security policies (e.g., definition of security policies and who is responsible for them), information security plans (e.g., definition of how policies should be implemented for a particular information system or business unit), and information security manuals (e.g., operational documents for daily use with detailed instructions on information security). One of the most attractive factors for a security manager in adopting the ITIL methodology is the perception that the other disciplines in the set must adopt security techniques within their processes. According to Yamakawa et al. (2012), this leads to organizational leaders (e.g., change management, asset management) being directly responsible for implementing security within their own area. This makes for a global perception of security within the entire organization and has contributed to the reduction of organizational silos (Cusick, 2018). As recognized in Jäntti and Cater-Steel (2017) and Marrone and Kolbe (2011), ITIL was initially aimed at large organizations with the goal of establishing an agenda that managed information technology services should adopt to provide the best results for an organization. However, this is a principle that should be independent of the number of people, the technology, or the turnover of an organization. Having a set of good practices in this area ensures that organizations can provide quality service and minimize the occurrence of failures (Gil-Gómez et al., 2014). Allied to this, we also have the benefit of finding solutions more quickly when problems arise. It is in this direction that studies have emerged exploring the risks and benefits of ITIL adoption by Small and medium-sized enterprises (SMEs) (Dávila et al., 2020; El Yamami et al., 2018; Levstek et al., 2022). However, these studies do not specifically explore the risks and difficulties of adopting the ITIL Information Security Management framework. Moreover, and specifically considering the Portuguese business context in which this study was developed, SMEs represent 99.9% of the population, and 96% of them are micro companies (Andrade, 2020). The objective of this study addresses this research gap by looking specifically at the risks and mitigation measures that micro companies face by adopting ITIL Information Security Management as these companies have fewer resources available for business process analysis and service improvement implementation. This study offers relevant implications for micro companies, especially in the context where cybersecurity attacks have been multiplying and is currently assumed as a challenge for the operation of these companies (Brooks, 2022; Sausalito, 2021). This study also contributes for micro companies to establish a strategy for growth and sustainability of their operations and supports one of the major goals of ITIL implementation, which is the continuous improvement of their services.

This manuscript is organized as follows: in the background, a theoretical review of information security, information security policies, and ITIL is performed; after that, the main risks of information security management are identified and the research questions for the empirical study are formulated; next, the methodology of the study is presented, and the case studies and the methods adopted for their analysis are characterized; subsequently, the results are analyzed and discussed, considering their conceptual and practical relevance; finally, the main contributions of the study are enumerated, and the limitations of the study are explored, and some suggestions for future work are given.

BACKGROUND

The information obtained and/or generated in the corporate environment, especially those existing in digital environments, are considered a high-value asset for companies, and in general terms, it covers fundamental factors for business management, which go far beyond purely technological issues (Jassim, 2022). These factors are related to issues around the credibility of companies, legal aspects, and qualitative increment of the services provided to their clients (Jia, 2020), whether in data protection or in the preservation of the information of the company itself, its partners, and clients.

The challenges of maintaining an adequate Information Security (IS) management system are high (Whitman & Mattord, 2017) and are continuously growing in complexity, especially in network environments of high availability and large dimensions in terms of technological resources of software, hardware, and human resources, which are fundamental assets for the maintenance of information management systems in small, medium, and large companies. However, in order to perform adequate work around the IS, it is necessary to implement a series of standardized and widely tested and validated procedures in the business environment, and for this purpose, we have the ISO/IEC 27000 family of standards, of which ISO/IEC 27001 is the starting point to define the necessary requirements for an adequate IS management and consequent elevation of the maturity degree (Lopez-Leyva et al, 2020) in the practical implementation of the IS in companies.

In the search for the qualitative increment of IS management, companies usually develop an Information Security Policy (ISP), based on the ISO/IEC 27000 family standards, in the form of a digital and/or physical document, which should be easily accessible by employees and widely disclosed in the company, which will contain a series of IS guidelines (Chin & Chua, 2021), adapted to the most varied departments and business rules of the company. The ISP is the result generated through several processes and controls that involve asset inventory, asset risk analysis, return on investment (ROI), among other reasons specific to each company, which must be carefully analyzed so that the ISP is efficient, effective, and aligned with the requirements listed mainly by the ISO/IEC 27001 standard, which indicates a series of procedures to establish, implement, maintain, and continuously improve (International Organization for Standardization [IOS], 2013) an Information Security Management System (ISMS).

Chin & Chua (2021) state that it is important to analyze the behavioral factors that lead the employees in the scope of the companies to adhere to the ISP in accordance with what is foreseen and judged as adequate in IS, because in practice it is the employees who will be the driving force of the effective operation of the ISMS. Some studies (Ormond et al., 2019) indicate that the behavioral aspects of employees in relation to the implementation (or not) of the ISP are closely linked to affective issues and that negative affective flows directly influence the decision making of employees, which may result in non-compliance actions, misapplication, or disregard regarding the implementation of good practices proposed in the ISP, being necessary to better understand the factors that lead employees to not want to comply with the ISP and be resistant to the IS processes proposed within companies. Meanwhile, other authors (D'Arcy & Lowry, 2019) present a multilevel model that aims to verify employee compliance with ISP, which in brief: i) attempts to explain behaviors based on employees' beliefs, encompassing moods, whether positive, negative, or episodic; and ii) aspects related to moral issues, facing the influence of the norms that employees should follow, according to what is foreseen in the ISP, having the affective perception of employees as the central element of the model, adjusted in everyday behavioral constructs so that the model developed, can explain the differences and affective nuances of employees. The practical application of the model showed that affective aspects influence employees' decision making (Hina & Dominic, 2017) to deliberately violate ISP, but other aspects related to personal beliefs should also be considered, and that employees' daily relationship with the professional environment, company norms, including ISP, should be considered, and worked affectively with employees.

It is important to note that many previously existing and/or new models can be implemented within the development of an ISP. This will require the execution of many steps and numerous processes, many of these being supported by digital resources and other IT management frameworks, and it is not a simple process (Ismail et al., 2017) to implement, either by the level of complexity involved, the huge amount of controls required, as the specificities of each company around its business rules (Lima et al., 2020; Paananen et al., 2020), but having as a good starting point the standards of the ISO/IEC 27000 family, which will provide the necessary basis for the creation of an ISP that is within the best IS practices. Therefore, as we mentioned before, among several aspects, those directly related to credibility are a strong motivator for companies and their employees to adopt more secure practices (Alkhurayyif & Weir, 2017; Rantao & Njenga, 2020), either in the control of internal activities, processes, and the development of their products, or in the provision of services to their customers, and in the latter case, to adopt other frameworks for service delivery management, which will raise the final quality of their product or service, which will involve risk and impact analysis for the business (Kitsios et al., 2022).

However, if we specifically consider the risks associated with the provision of information and communications technology (ICT) services (Bhatti et al., 2021), in addition to the elaboration of an ISP, it will possibly be necessary to implement a complementary framework that can meet the specificities of the business rules of companies in the ICT field, and for this, we have the ITIL framework as an example. For this, we have as an example the ITIL structure, currently in version 4, whose framework is widely applied with the intention of qualitatively elevating the provision of ICT services, generating value for the customer, which includes the need to consider how the IS management will be performed (Berger et al., 2020) so that the service is provided within the requirements of quality previously determined (Reiter & Miklošík, 2020). Table 1 shows the value chain generated by ITIL in the various tasks performed to increase the level of efficiency of ICT services.

Risk analysis can be performed with the support of ITIL processes (Spasic & Markovic, 2013), within the context of generating value for the customer through the adoption of good practices in the management of IS incidents within the scope of ICT.

Table 1. Value chain of ICT Services

Engage	The service desk is the main channel for tactical and operational engagement with users.
Design and Transition	The service desk provides a channel for communicating with users about new and changed services. Service desk staff participate in release planning, testing, and early life support.
Obtain/Build	Service desk staff can be involved in acquiring service components used to fulfil service requests and resolve incidents.
Deliver and Support	The service desk is the coordination point for managing incidents and service requests.
Improve	Service desk activities are constantly monitored and evaluated to support continual improvement, alignment, and value creation. Feedback from users is collected by the service desk to support continual improvement.

Source: (Mathenge et al., 2019)

Regarding incident management, which is defined in the ITIL framework, it considers that incidents are disturbances or effects that were not planned in the ICT services and that consequently will reduce the quality of the service provided (Clarke, 2021). Incident management and risk reduction will be accomplished by adopting some techniques that involve performing, i) incident logging; ii) resolution; iii) prioritization; iv) monitoring; and v) reporting, i.e., ITIL has a particular framework for analyzing data and information (Müller & de Lichtenberg, 2018) and then implementing procedures for risk resolution. Therefore, within the philosophy of best practices in ICT service delivery, ITIL presents techniques in its processes, which allow to verify and analyze the strengths and weaknesses (Cronholm & Persson, 2016) of the service provided to adopt a preventive posture in the management of possible incidents.

In the context of ITIL, incident handling and risk analysis and its other processes are, in the current version of the framework, based on a new conceptual model that has some key aspects (Lopes, 2021), such as the Service Value System (SVS), the Service Value Chain (SVC), and the four dimensions of service management that involve: i) organizations and people; ii) information and technology; iii) partners and suppliers; and iv) value streams and processes. The SVS contains the SVC which is an operational model with the flexibility for the creation, delivery, and continuous improvement of services (Axelos, 2022), including risk management itself. The SVC defines six main activities involving i) plan; ii) improve; iii) engage; iv) design and transition; v) procure and build; and vi) deliver and support.

ITIL has another group of processes that the authors consider important and that have real potential to mitigate risks, that is, the processes of change management, which together with the processes of incident management, tend to enhance decision-making around the planning and preparation of the ISP, including bringing closer the governance of companies in relation to IT operations (Mahalle et al., 2020). ITIL change management processes can help companies adopt a more effective preventive posture towards potential IS incidents, allowing them to react to changes more efficiently and effectively (Eikebrokk & Iden, 2017), mitigating potential negative impacts around the business. Change management has focused on what ITIL refers to as "continuous service improvement" (Arisenta et al., 2020) and among the techniques used we can mention SWOT analysis (Granulo & Tanovic, 2020), whose name is an acronym for Strengths, Weaknesses, Opportunities, and Threats, being a very popular method to evaluate a given context of the business rules of companies. SWOT can be implemented in a generic way, such as to assess the ITIL processes themselves in a given business context, or in a specific way to assess a particular process, such as the incident management and change management processes, within the scope of business risk analysis and consequent ISP.

It is important to note, that in the scientific literature we find studies that present the implementation of ITIL in conjunction with other ICT management frameworks (Galup et al., 2020; Rios et al., 2017), which allow the potentization of techniques and procedures for asset identification and analysis, risk/threat identification and analysis, such as, for example, i) COBIT; ii) DevOps; iii) DevSecOps; iv) Lean; v) Agile. However, the implementation of IT management frameworks brings with it a series of challenges that by themselves are already configured as risks, both in the implementation and the subsequent adoption of the processes set forth in the ISP. Among these challenges we can mention, for example, i) the need for a culture change within the company, both among employees and in top management (Monica et al., 2020); ii) implementation at various and different organizational levels; iii) decentralized business organization; iv) dependence on resources not controlled by the company; v) focus only on details to the detriment of the company's project scope objectives.

In ITIL (version 4), the approach around its system of generating value for customers (Axelos, 2022) is based on several practices, categorized into: i) general management practices; ii) service management practices; and iii) technical management practices. Among these practices, the framework presents us some relevant to IS management and the consequent development of an ISP, which can be considered to increase the maturity level of companies, whether small, medium, or large, in the risk and threat mitigation strategy. This strategy involves the implementation of controls and metrics that allow increasing the visibility of the company's constraints and opportunities, contributing to the decision-making process, if we consider the risks in a double perspective, i.e., risks that might compromise the business, but risks understood as opportunities that can leverage the business, either by the qualitative increment of processes, as in the delivery of services and products to customers.

RESEARCH QUESTIONS FORMULATION AND DEVELOPMENT

The preservation of the confidentiality, integrity, and availability of information requires security measures to prevent and protect the organization's information systems (Kim & Solomon, 2021). The prevention consists of a set of measures that aim to reduce the probability of existing threats materializing (Axelos, 2022). In turn, protection involves measures that aim to provide information systems with the ability to inspect, detect, and react, allowing them to reduce and limit the impact of threats when they happen (Silva et al., 2003).

Organizational information systems are subject to threats and vulnerabilities of different origins. Threats can result from natural causes (e.g., water, fire, climate catastrophe) or human causes (accidental (e.g., fire, floods, incorrect configuration of systems) or intentional (e.g., sabotage, destruction, deactivations, computer viruses, theft, fraud)) (Dokuchaev et al., 2020). These threats can affect the information systems in different ways. For example, sabotage, destruction, and deactivations can affect confidentiality, integrity, and availability of information (Corallo et al., 2020; Sarala et al., 2015). Fires, floods, climate catastrophes, computer viruses, theft, and fraud can also affect the availability of information (Mathur et al., 2015). In turn, vulnerabilities are the organizational characteristics that enable the materialization of a threat. These vulnerabilities can be rooted in the organizational structure (e.g. lack of traceability or accountability leading to the potential use of falsifications, malware insertion); in the use of external providers, which may result in a loss of visibility and control over how systems, system elements, and services are developed, deployed, and maintained; on the computer network (e.g. insecure password protection); or in software (e.g. use of untrusted frameworks, unlicensed software) (Hameed et al., 2019; Ross, 2018). In addition, untrained or insufficiently motivated staff can be a major vulnerability (Axelos, 2022). Human Resources properly trained and paying attention to information security policies and other controls can help detect, prevent, and correct information security incidents. Therefore, information security is critically dependent on the behavior of the human resources of the organization (Glaspie & Karwowski, 2018).

Beyond the responsibility to protect organizational assets from threats, organizations also have an obligation to manage risks to individuals (clients and collaborators) when information systems process personally identifiable information (Ross, 2018). Thus, it is critical that organizations establish and maintain robust security programs to prevent and protect the company's information systems and ensure compliance with privacy requirements (Deane et al., 2020). Furthermore, the occurrence of a disaster may pose several impacts on the organization, such as, for example, damaged reputation, lost income and competitive advantage, risk to personal safety, breach of law, health and safety, and immediate and long-term loss of market share (Axelos, 2022). Therefore, it is essential that companies remain vigilant, and that each element of the organization understands their responsibilities and is accountable for protecting organizational assets and managing risk (Corallo et al., 2020).

The security programs seek to guarantee the safety of the organization through the introduction of measures that allow reducing exposure to all risks (Silva et al., 2003). For this purpose, it is necessary to define the strategy that leads to the security of the organization, identifying and analyzing the risks and defining prevention and protection actions (Deane et al., 2020; Glaspie & Karwowski, 2018; Hameed et al., 2019; Ross, 2018). Thus, information security management involves the definition of policies, processes, behaviors, risk management, and controls that must: ensure that security incidents do not occur (prevention); quickly and reliably identify incidents (detection); and recover from incidents once detected (correction).

In this sense, the management of information security, according to ITIL, must be guided from the highest level of the organization, based on clearly understood governance requirements and organizational policies (Schinagl & Shahim, 2020). For this purpose, within a global plan, large organizations have teams dedicated to information security that carry out risk assessments and define policies, norms, procedures, and security controls. The global security plan contains the organization's risk analysis, strategy, and action plan for the implementation of the measures. The security policy integrates a reduced set of rules that define, in general terms, what is considered by the organization as acceptable or unacceptable. The security norms contain all the organization's security rules, setting out in detail the guidelines established in the security policy. The procedures describe the operations in a very detailed way, indicating all their steps in compliance with security norms. Controls aim to minimize the risks to which the company is subject, and can be deterrent, preventive, detective, and corrective. Thus, according to ITIL v.4, several processes and procedures are required to support information security management (e.g., information security incident management process; risk management process; control review and audit process; identity and access management process; event management; procedures for penetration testing and vulnerability scanning; procedures for managing information security related changes; configuration changes).

In case of disaster (a sudden, unforeseen event that causes losses and difficulties for the organization, negatively affecting its ability to perform essential services), the organization must be prepared to allow the business to continue its activities. For this purpose, organizations must have a service continuity plan, which describes the procedures to be implemented and the human, technical, and material resources necessary for their execution in the case of a disaster, ensuring the continuity of its activities, safeguarding the interests of stakeholders and the organization's reputation and value-creating activities (Silva et al., 2003). ITIL v.4 states, the disaster recovery plans, must ensure that the recovery of the organization's critical functions occurs quickly, ensuring that their viability is not compromised, considering the four dimensions of service management (organizations and people, information and technology, partners and suppliers, value streams and processes). However, to define initial responses to an incident (an unplanned interruption of a service or a reduction in the quality of a service), it will be important that organizations have a contingency plan, including, for example, emergency procedures and the description of the teams that execute them according to the implementation of an action plan (Aldawood & Skinner, 2019). According to the scope and severity of the incident, it may be necessary to implement a crisis management plan which can be activated by the contingency team during the execution of its contingency plan.

This plan, through service continuity management, seeks to ensure control during the disaster according to the policies, strategies, and recovery options defined by the organization, including for this purpose, for example, the description of the organization's command and control structure during a disaster, the communications plan, and auxiliary information (e.g., contracts, supplier contacts).

ITIL v.4 offers a set of best practices for security management in organizations that require the availability of human, technical, financial, and material resources, with teams dedicated to information security that carry out risk assessments and define policies, norms, procedures, and security controls. With the aim of supporting micro companies in security management, the focus of this study is on the assessment of the risks and mitigation measures faced by adopting ITIL Information Security Management. For this purpose, the following research questions are addressed:

- **RQ1.** What are the main threats that micro companies face in the current context regarding information security?
- **RQ2.** What are the main challenges that a micro company faces in terms of information security management?
- **RQ3.** How are prevention and protection measures defined to ensure information security?
- **RQ4.** Who defines security policies, norms, procedures, and controls?
- **RQ5.** In the context of information security management, what roles are assigned to the company's human resources?
- **RQ6.** How do companies manage an unplanned service interruption (incident)?
- **RQ7.** How does the micro company ensure that service availability and performance are maintained at a sufficient level in case of a disaster?
- **RQ8.** Is information security management a priority for micro companies?

MATERIALS AND METHODS

The growth of cloud computing has reduced infrastructure management costs and allowed many small companies to effectively start managing their IT processes (Izquierdo, 2022). ITIL offers a set of best practices that are important for the daily life of an IT team. These practices have been widely disseminated and validated, mainly in the context of large organizations. However, the business fabric in Portugal is mainly made up of micro companies that often see these practices as inaccessible and expensive. Apparently, and due to their small size, these organizations would escape cyberattacks. However, the reality is quite different. As reported in Virani (2022), smaller organizations are the most vulnerable to the growing cybersecurity threats, mainly because they have fewer robust protection mechanisms and can be used as intermediate elements for a larger-scale attack.

The European Commission's benchmark (European Commission [EC], 2022) defines a micro company as a small company that employs less than 10 workers and has a turnover of not exceeding two million euros. Its small size means that there is a plethora of organizations of this type with unique and extremely diverse characteristics. Quantitative studies on this phenomenon would not allow us to capture these characteristics in depth when interpreting the data. In this sense, this study adopts a qualitative methodology by conducting four case studies to explore and typify the risks associated with ITIL Information Security Management in these organizations. Four micro companies working in the information technology sector and incubated in technology parks in Portugal were selected. According to Rashid et al. (2019), the case study should necessarily be systematic, detailed, intensive, and interactive. Furthermore, it is recommended that the researcher ensure construct validity, internal validity, external validity, and reliability (Yin, 2017). In this sense, this study collects multiple sources of evidence and adopts the same interview script across them to allow for replication across multiple cases.

The profile of the four micro companies is presented in Table 1. All companies work in the information technology field, mainly in system administration, development of technological solutions, and computer consulting. All companies operate in a niche market, although they implement different business strategies. CS1 and CS4 focus on a specific market area, such as Enterprise Resource Planning (ERP) and blockchain technology solutions; CS2 focuses on the needs of its clients, regardless of their size; and CS3 focuses on the less technically specialized profile of its clients.

The interviews were conducted in person and using Google Meet, in view of the limitations of some companies in receiving external guests on their company premises due to the COVID-19 pandemic. In both scenarios, the interview duration was identical and had an allocated time of between 30 and 45 minutes. The interviews were conducted between April 11, 2022, and May 18, 2022. The interviews were conducted with the Chief Technology Officer (CTO) of each company. However, since CS3 does not formally have this position, the co-founder of that company was interviewed. All companies are implementing ITIL v.4. However, not all have the same level of maturity since the implementation was only carried out in CS1 in 2020 and in CS3 in 2021. The other two companies (i.e., CS2 and CS4) have adopted ITIL since its inception, especially in CS2 which has adopted ITIL since 2005.

The interview script followed the research questions established in the previous section of this manuscript. Accordingly, eight questions were asked, adopting a semi-structured questionnaire model in which the eight questions previously established define the interview script, but which allows, however, the inclusion of new questions for further exploration. Horton et al. (2004) recognize that this approach is flexible enough to be adopted in qualitative studies, since it brings pre-defined questions but allows for adaptation according to the directions of the dialog between you and the interviewee.

For each interview, an individual cognitive map was developed that was validated by each interviewee and allowed to build a Strategic Options Development and Analysis (SODA). This is a method that is mostly adopted to model complex problems and that allows the aggregation of the individual vision of each case study and facilitates the understanding of the system and its multiple dependencies (Abuabara & Paucar-Caceres, 2021). Furthermore, a thematic analysis was performed on the individual reports of each interviewee to allow the identification of the main convergent and divergent themes between the case studies. According to Braun & Clarke (2006), thematic analysis offers great flexibility that can be applied in the analysis, interpretation, and systematization of the results of a qualitative analysis. Therefore, although the patterns individually found in each case study are relatively basic, they can represent a rich and detailed set when properly aggregated, considering multiple sources of evidence.

Table 2. Profile of the case studies

ID	Description
CS1	The company provides software engineering and business consulting services. The main characteristic of this company is the customization of solutions tailored to customer needs. In this sense, the company follows the clients from strategic planning to the implementation of solutions. The company does not focus on a sector of activity nor on a specific type of solution, although it focuses on the implementation of ERP solutions for SMEs.
CS2	The company provides cloud solutions through the design, remodeling, and renovation of data centers. The service offer begins with the design and conception of the solution, adapting it to the existing physical space on the client's premises, to ensure the necessary conditions for the proper functioning of the systems. Subsequently, the company implements production systems that are based on convergent infrastructures of processing, data storage, and other technological components. The company's strategy focuses on a niche market. However, there is no restriction on the technologies adopted nor in the size of the clients.
CS3	The company retails computer hardware and peripherals. Despite its focus, the company also offers other activities related to information technology and computing. Also of note is the acquisition of electronic, audiovisual and telecommunications equipment. In addition to the sales area, the company provides internet, multimedia, consulting, and computer programming services. The company's focus is mainly on providing a high follow-up service for clients less familiar with information and communication technologies.
CS4	The company was established just one year before the emergence of the COVID-19 pandemic and is dedicated to developing innovative solutions and exploring disruptive business models in fintech. Thus, the company has mainly developed efforts for the application of blockchain technology, mainly in the context of financial services. The company's focus is on the application of an emerging technology that involves highly specialized knowledge, and therefore, the collaboration and proximity with universities and research centers is a key point.

RESULTS AND DISCUSSION

Overview

Initially, a schematic representation of ITIL Information Security Management Risks for micro companies was developed by aggregating the information from the four conceptual maps. Three main risks emerge: i) lack of commitment; ii) lack of resources; and iii) lack of knowledge. To respond to the first risk, the role of establishing guidelines is highlighted. However, the absence of standards specifically developed for micro companies is an added difficulty that these companies face. In any case, the guidelines should take into consideration the current information security scenario of these organizations and their targets. Given the need for these organizations to deliver short-term results, it is fundamental that the proposed metrics consider both short- and long-term results. To respond to the challenges of lack of a resource, it is fundamental that microenterprises identify critical assets. The lack of human resources leads to the proposal of cross-security teams. In both situations, the objective is to present a risk management approach, in which process automation is an important element to reduce and systematize this process. Finally, the lack of knowledge is easily identifiable in these organizations due to the high unpredictability of the business of a micro company and the lack of IT expertise. Combined with these factors, we have the constant emergence of technologies and a high interdependence between various technological solutions. Combined with these factors, we have the constant emergence of technologies and a high interdependence between various technological solutions. The answer to these challenges is to provide training for employees in this field and the need to look at information security as a holistic approach.

In a second step, the webQDA software was used to identify the themes associated with each research question in the case studies, as shown in Table 2. A theme is considered convergent if it appears in more than 50% of the case studies and divergent otherwise. Despite the unique characteristics of each micro company, the number of convergent themes is much higher than the number of divergent themes, indicating that the information security challenges faced by micro companies are relatively common. Only divergent themes related to technology failures emerge in RQ1, the role of the CEO replacing the CTO/CIO in RQ4, and the creation of a lessons learned report in RQ6.

Figure 1. Representation of the problem and its dependencies in a SODA diagram

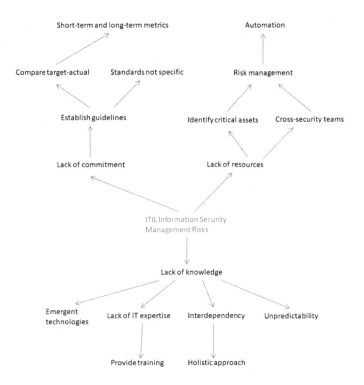

Table 3. Final themes identified by webQDA

Themes	Case Studies				Type
	CS1	CS2	CS3	CS4	
RQ1					
External attacks	X	X	X	X	Convergent
Human errors	X	X	X		Convergent
Technology failures	X		X		Divergent
RQ2					
Low awareness	X	X	X	X	Convergent
Low budget	X	X	X	X	Convergent
Lack of guidelines	X	X	X		Convergent
BYOD	X	X	X		Convergent
RQ3					
Definition of policy	X	X	X	X	Convergent
Establishment of goals	X	X	X	X	Convergent

continues on following page

Table 3. Continued

Themes	Case Studies				Type
	CS1	CS2	CS3	CS4	
Compliance monitoring	X	X	X	X	Convergent
RQ4					
CTO/CIO	X	X		X	Convergent
CEO			X		Divergent
Partners	X	X	X		Convergent
RQ5					
IS compliance	X	X	X	X	Convergent
Training	X	X	X	X	Convergent
RQ6					
Initial response	X	X	X	X	Convergent
Response strategy	X	X	X	X	Convergent
Third-party services	X	X	X	X	Convergent
Lesson learned report		X			Divergent
RQ7					
Incident response plan	X	X	X	X	Convergent
Business continuity	X	X	X	X	Convergent
Mitigating spread	X	X	X	X	Convergent
Document the incident	X	X		X	Convergent
RQ8					
High concern	X	X	X	X	Convergent
Business's goals priority	X	X	X	X	Convergent
Cloud services	X	X		X	Convergent
GDPR alignment	X	X	X		Convergent

RQ1. What Are the Main Threats That Micro Companies Face in The Current Context Regarding Information Security?

An external attack can be seen as a deliberate attempt by an individual or organization to breach the information system of another organization in which it seeks to obtain some benefit, even if it is not financially motivated. In general, it is perceptible that, considering a cost/benefit ratio, smaller organizations are more unprotected and, consequently, more vulnerable. This view is not specific to the Portuguese reality of micro companies but can also be found in other economies such as the USA or the UK. As reported in Bowcut (2021), cyber-attacks are a growing threat to smaller organizations. They can be a tempting target because they do not have the same infrastructure capabilities as large companies.

Investment in security infrastructure is essential for the protection of a micro company but will be insufficient if human errors are not properly mitigated. In a computer security context, human error comprises the unintentional actions performed by employees and users that cause or cause a security breach. This category covers a very diverse set of actions, such as downloading an infected file or using a weak password. CS1 reports "the increasing number of services available to the company meant that our employees had to memorize a very large set of passwords. Initially, we did not adopt a password management system and left this management to each employee. The problem is that each user used his or her own strategies to memorize passwords, many of them insecure, and that opened new security breaches".

The emergence of technological errors is a less common situation and is only reported in CS1 and CS3. The main reasons for its occurrence are the adoption of technological solutions from multiple manufacturers and the non-adoption of open standards, which hinder the interconnection between the various services. This vision is aligned with Percivall's (2010) recommendations, which state that the more standardized the interoperability mechanisms are, less effort will be demanded for the creation of interoperability interfaces and, consequently, communication will occur in a faster and more agile way.

RQ2. What Are the Main Challenges That a Micro Company Faces in Terms of Information Security Management?

Micro companies may not be able to eliminate complementary cybersecurity risks. However, if the decision makers are aware and capable of dealing with these issues, they can more easily manage the risk and make decisions about the necessary investment to mitigate that risk. However, also as recognized in Berger (2017) and Kabanda et al. (2018), the budget available to invest in cybersecurity is very small in small organizations, and that is aggravated in companies with a family structure and whose hierarchical structure is not very solid and defined. In this sense, it is recommended that organizations should not only infuse technology into their business models but also keep up with digital evolution, so that they can consider the inclusion of cybersecurity measures as a differentiating factor for success and risk reduction. ITIL should be seen as an approach to make the organization more efficient rather than as a bureaucratic element that increases complexity in managing the processes associated with information security management.

The CEO in a small organization plays a fundamental role that is not limited to the strategic and financial management of his company. As recognized by Shojaifar and Jarvinen (2021), the CEO has a crucial role in defining information security-oriented policies and guidelines that should be written, known, and implemented by the employees daily. However, this apparently easy mission is in practice much more complex to implement since, as highlighted in Grandi et al. (2021), these organizations have difficulties in finding specific guidelines oriented to the size of their organization. The lack of resources, combined with the lower financial availability, makes it frequent that employees adopt the "Bring your own device (BYOD)" paradigm, which adds cybersecurity problems in terms of data loss, malware, and legal problems, among others (Annansingh, 2021).

RQ3. How Are Prevention and Protection Measures Defined to Ensure Information Security?

In all four case studies, the existence of prevention and protection measures is reported. Security is a task for everyone and is not limited to the IT department, because in micro-companies this autonomous department does not exist. Therefore, security crosses boundaries within the organization. The definition of an information security policy is assumed to be a primary activity for organizations regardless of their size and typology. This policy aims to ensure the protection of the company's assets, business continuity, and the mitigation of its risks by preventing security incidents and reducing their potential impact. Nevertheless, and as reported by CS3, there are difficulties, namely "although we have an information security policy with the definition of clear goals, we are not always able to guarantee preventive measures in the face of daily business activities that require dedicated human resources". In CS2 it is also highlighted that "not all incidents related to information security are reported and properly investigated". Nevertheless, there is a concern about analyzing infrastructure and service risks from an information security perspective and according to the criteria of confidentiality, integrity, and availability. It is also recognized in CS2 that "it is important that the solutions adopted in our organization not only identify the problems but provide tools to correct the vulnerabilities". This is an important point for micro enterprises as the proposed solutions should not only give detailed insight into the risks but should also provide effective mechanisms to block the risks.

Continuous monitoring of security risks enables organizations to respond to threats before they occur. Its implementation requires the fulfillment of a set of steps such as collecting and analyzing data on the network, defining types of threats that require attention, applying mitigation measures against threats and generating reports for compliance analysis (Rieke et al., 2014). This is an effort that has been developed by micro companies, although not all these steps are effectively implemented in full, especially the last step concerning compliance analysis.

RQ4. Who Defines Security Policies, Norms, Procedures, And Controls?

The person responsible for defining the security policy was not the same in all the companies interviewed. In large companies, the studies carried out by Whitten (2008) and Karanja (2017) point out the need for a Chief Information Security Officer (CISO) who is responsible for information security. They report the necessity of a leader dedicated to the information security commitments and needs of any organization that involves technical, managerial, and leadership activities. In the micro companies interviewed, there is no person dedicated to the CISO role, and this role is mostly performed by the CTO or CIO. Despite the similarities between the roles of a CIO and a CISO, Hiter (2021) points out some differences since the CIO is mainly a generalist in the information management area, while the CISO is specialized in the security domain. In CS3 this role is performed by the CEO. It is evident that in the smaller micro companies, several positions are often occupied by the same person. In addition, there is a significant presence of owners, partners, and employees with family ties, which is one of the major differences in relation to an SME-type structure.

Partnerships are a relevant element to mitigate the reduced internal resources of micro-organizations in the information security field. The establishment of partnerships is a strategy in which smaller organizations have significant experience, especially to increase the visibility of their business and be able to attract new customers and address new markets (Benhayoun et al., 2021). In micro-enterprises, these partnerships are fundamental, but the choice of partners is often dictated by family ties within the management structure. Therefore, the low level of outsourcing pointed out to micro companies is not found in these case studies. In the information security field, there are no scientific studies evidencing its role, although it is recognized that the role of IT outsourcing can play for SMEs (Oliveira et al., 2021) or strategic decisions that large organizations should make regarding the outsourcing or insourcing of security services (Sivaraman, 2019).

RQ5. In the Context of Information Security Management, What Roles Are Assigned to The Company's Human Resources?

Human resources in a micro company tend to be more versatile, dynamic, and less specialized. Information security is often one more activity that the CTO, CIO, or CEO has to develop. However, it is not the main activity of these organizations. In recent years, as Kim et al. (2016) acknowledge, there has been an accelerated growth of information security compliance with current security policies and standards. In micro companies, information security compliance is fundamental to protect the critical information of the organization. However, the processes are not always properly formalized. As acknowledged by CS3, "we have difficulties identifying the critical information of our business, especially when it is distributed with our partners. Consequently, we have made investments in migrating to cloud solutions".

The training of human resources is an aspect that micro companies consider important, although in practice it is not always easy to find systematic and continuous evidence of such investment. It is true that in recent years, awareness has grown in these organizations of the need to manage cybersecurity risks. This awareness is because practically all organizations have evolved to a business model based on digital (Almeida et al., 2020; Bogavac et al., 2020). However, contrary to what happened in large companies, these organizations have not invested in hiring their own cybersecurity experts. Instead, there has been an expansion of cybersecurity services provided by third parties.

The perspective of investment in cybersecurity can be carried out in the education or training component. Both models are important and complementary. But micro businesses are more likely to invest in training with the aim of acquiring and developing new skills to keep up with rapidly changing technology. However, the investment in continuing education is smaller and often takes place with special intensity on the trainee's own initiative. A good example of this occurrence is given by CS4 when highlighting "we have two employees who are enrolled in a Massive Open Online Course (MOOC) on blockchain and smart contract security". This approach of attending MOOCs seems to be a good alternative to the gaps in continuing education that exist in this area in Portugal.

RQ6. How Do Companies Manage an Unplanned Service Interruption (Incident)?

When faced with a security incident, the priority for micro businesses is to provide an initial response to the challenge and minimize the scope of this incident. The establishment of a response plan to a security incident is also an element that companies highlighted, since having an initial response to this incident is insufficient. Rid & Buchanan (2014) establish that the information security incident response plan is a complete file produced to detect and outline the activities to be implemented in the case of any cybersecurity event that has a negative impact on the company. This plan is mainly relevant for information security groups to have the ability to deal with unforeseen events effectively. The main goal of an incident response strategy is to minimize loss and damage by effectively countering threats, which means responding to an attack in the shortest period of time and in the best way possible (Van der Kleij et al., 2017). However, in the context of micro companies, this plan has several weaknesses, especially in the definition of responsibilities that are often excessively focused on the management team of these companies, and that often do not have the necessary skills to implement this plan.

Outsourcing services in the field of information security is a path that has been progressively adopted by smaller organizations. This is a journey that was mainly initiated by organizations with a high percentage of technological solutions hosted in the cloud. One of the main reasons for the exponential increase in outsourcing services is presented in Makris (2021, p. 1) "Chief information security officers and CIOs/CTOs are finding it extremely difficult to hire and retain qualified cybersecurity staff. As a result, they are forced to look elsewhere for talent.". This challenge that is posed to large organizations is even more visible in the context of micro companies. Finally, the existence of a lesson learned report, as stated in Quader & Janeja (2021) is a practice that in micro companies is not widely spread. However, CS2 recognizes significant advantages in its application: "when faced with a security incident, we prepare a lesson-learned report which allows us to update our risk management models and mitigation measures".

RQ7. How Does the Micro Company Ensure That Service Availability and Performance Are Maintained at A Sufficient Level in Case of a Disaster?

An Incident Response Plan (IRP) is considered by micro companies as a key element to help them outline instructions that help detect, respond to, and limit the effects of cyber security incidents. CS2 highlights that there are several types of events that justify the activation of the IRP, such as data breaches, viruses, malware, DoS or DDoS type attacks, and other types of external or internal threats. The perception of the importance of an IRP is shared in the literature where one can find studies that explore its main benefits, such as faster incident response, early threat mitigation, better communication for faster action, and good business continuity (Nyre-Yu et al., 2019). IRP is considered an essential element in these organizations to ensure business continuity and mitigate the spread. However, incident documentation is not a regular practice in CS3. This result confirms the studies by Calvo-Manzano et al. (2015) that highlight that smaller companies see challenges related to information security management, problem management, and knowledge management as less of a priority.

RQ8. Is Information Security Management a Priority for Micro Companies?

All the companies participating in the case study recognize a high concern for information security and ensure that it is a priority for their business. ITIL is not designed to be a one-size-fits-all tool that allows an identical implementation for all organizations but should be tailored to the organization that is implementing it. The International Security Trust and Privacy Alliance (ISTPA) confirms this view by arguing that security should be looked at holistically, considering various dimensions such as accountability, disclosure, relevance, or participation (International Security, Trust, and Privacy Alliance [ISTPA], 2001). Micro businesses have a closer relationship with their customers and suppliers, which allows them to have more direct, personalized, and differentiating contact. This greater proximity with stakeholders is important when defining an information security management policy.

The recent security attacks on large companies in Portugal have raised awareness of this phenomenon. However, they were not the only elements that contributed to the increase in this awareness. Migration to cloud computing has become a must for many micro companies seeking to accelerate innovation and collaboration. As Abdul-Jabbar et al. (2020) recognize, cloud security and security management best practices designed to prevent unauthorized access are necessary to keep cloud data and applications protected from current cybersecurity threats. These companies recognize that for the process of digital transformation and transitioning to the cloud to be done right, a robust cloud security system is a must. Therefore, the cloud has helped micro companies to meet the challenge of low investment in technological innovation. Another relevant factor is the General Data Protection Regulation (GDPR). To ensure compliance with the GDPR, it is essential to establish an IRP to handle the situation and minimize the damage to data subjects. The GDPR states that ensuring the security of personal data is an obligation of those involved in data processing (Stepenko et al., 2022). Therefore, the GDPR has changed the policies and ways for companies to access and process personal data (Leite et al., 2022).

LIMITATIONS AND FUTURE RESEARCH DIRECTIONS

This study has some limitations that need to be addressed. First, only four case studies were included. Despite the richness of analysis that the case studies present, it is difficult to generalize their results to other organizations. The study considered the implementation of ITIL v.4 in a generalist way, without considering its various phases of implementation. Thus, it becomes relevant as future work to propose a longitudinal study to understand the risks and challenges of cybersecurity considering the various phases of ITIL implementation. It would also be relevant to explore the role COVID-19 has played in the digitalization of micro companies and how the pandemic has contributed to micro companies' being more exposed to internal and external security risks.

CONCLUSION

This study presents both theoretical and practical contributions. In the conceptual dimension, it is relevant to extend the literature on information security management, considering the specific context of a small-sized company. It is recognized that most of the studies in the field have addressed large companies and that it is necessary to deepen the adoption processes of ITIL Information Security Management in SMEs. However, the group of SMEs is extremely heterogeneous, including organizations with up to 250 employees and a turnover of up to 50 million euros. In the lowest segment are the micro companies, which represent more than 90% of the business sector in Portugal and, consequently, require in-depth and specific studies. This study contributes to looking at the risks associated with the process of implementing ITIL Information Security Management in micro companies, which allowed us to understand the challenges that are posed to these organizations and the response strategies that have been implemented.

In the practical dimension, this study provides important insights for micro companies to ensure a more complete and effective information security management process through the implementation of ITIL. This process is characterized by considering the policies, standards, procedures, and human resources involved in the information management processes. It also discusses the differences in the management of these processes in relation to large companies and larger SMEs. It also provides indications of how these companies can use ITIL to more fully and thoroughly address the challenges posed by information security management.

ITIL is a set of best practices in information technology management that aims to support organizations in developing a framework to control the quality and cost of managing the technological infrastructure of an organization. The application of this standard to all internal processes of an organization requires combining different types of information, from the inventory of the infrastructure, the impact of technological occurrences on services and business processes, to the repetition of occurrences associated with a particular component. ITIL v.4 specifically addresses information security management processes, which has become an increasingly important issue for organizations considering the growing number of security threats and incidents. This is a challenge that cannot be addressed exclusively by large companies, and smaller companies are progressively more exposed to internal and external threats that must be properly managed and mitigated. While a full ITIL deployment cycle may be too time-consuming and costly, it can contribute to helping smaller organizations, such as micro companies, define, organize, and measure the policies and processes involved with information security.

Micro companies have specific characteristics that raise risks related to the implementation of an information security management policy, namely a lack of commitment, a lack of resources, and a lack of knowledge. Despite this, and given the increasing security risks, these organizations look at this process with concern, although their social and economic environment may be more vulnerable when compared to a large company. The small size of micro companies means that the management of these processes is done by the CTO, CIO or CEO, and there is no specific position allocated to this area. Training in this area is recognized as a priority, although typically there is no training plan in this area, but it is attended informally by employees. Partners are seen as important elements for the increase in information security, and cloud computing and GDPR have contributed to the increase in awareness and maturity of these processes among micro companies.

REFERENCES

Abdul-Jabbar, S., Aldujaili, A., Mohammed, S. G., & Saeed, H. S. (2020). Integrity and Security in Cloud Computing Environment: A Review. *Journal of Southwest Jiaotong University*, *55*(1), 1–15. doi:10.35741/issn.0258-2724.55.1.11

Abuabara, L., & Paucar-Caceres, A. (2021). Surveying applications of Strategic Options Development and Analysis (SODA) from 1989 to 2018. *European Journal of Operational Research*, *292*(3), 1051–1065. doi:10.1016/j.ejor.2020.11.032

Aldawood, H., & Skinner, G. (2019). Reviewing cyber security social engineering training and awareness programs—Pitfalls and ongoing issues. *Future Internet*, *11*(3), 73. doi:10.3390/fi11030073

Alkhurayyif, Y., & Weir, G. R. S. (2017). Readability as a Basis for Information Security Policy Assessment. *Seventh International Conference on Emerging Security Technologies (EST)*, (pp. 114–121). IEEE. 10.1109/EST.2017.8090409

Almeida, F., Santos, J. D., & Monteiro, J. (2020). The Challenges and Opportunities in the Digitalization of Companies in a Post-COVID-19 World. *IEEE Engineering Management Review*, *48*(3), 97–103. doi:10.1109/EMR.2020.3013206

Andrade, V. (2020). Assim se vê a força da PME [This is how you can see the strength of the PME]. *Expresso*. https://expresso.pt/economia/2020-06-27-Assim-se-ve-a-forca-da-PME

Annansingh, F. (2021). Bring your own device to work: How serious is the risk? *The Journal of Business Strategy*, *42*(6), 392–398. doi:10.1108/JBS-04-2020-0069

Arisenta, R., Suharjito, & Sukmandhani, A. A. (2020). Evaluation Model of Success Change Management in Banking Institution Based on ITIL V3 (Case Study). *2020 International Conference on Information Management and Technology (ICIMTech)*, (pp. 470–475). IEEE. 10.1109/ICIMTech50083.2020.9211191

Axelos (2022). *ITIL® 4: the framework for the management of IT-enabled services.* Axelos. https://www.axelos.com/certifications/itil-service-management

Benhayoun, L., Ayala, N. F., & Le Dain, M. A. (2021). SMEs innovating in collaborative networks: How does absorptive capacity matter for innovation performance in times of good partnership quality? *Journal of Manufacturing Technology Management*, *32*(8), 1578–1598. doi:10.1108/JMTM-11-2020-0439

Berger, B. (2017). The Small and Medium Business' False Sense of Cybersecurity. *Security Magazine.* https://www.securitymagazine.com/blogs/14-security-blog/post/88373-the-small-and-medium-business-false-sense-of-cybersecurity

Berger, D., Shashidhar, N., & Varol, C. (2020). Using ITIL 4 in Security Management. *8th International Symposium on Digital Forensics and Security (ISDFS)*, (pp. 1–6). IEEE. 10.1109/ISDFS49300.2020.9116257

Bhatti, B. M., Mubarak, S., & Nagalingam, S. (2021). Information Security Risk Management in IT Outsourcing – A Quarter-Century Systematic Literature Review. *Journal of Global Information Technology Management*, *24*(4), 259–298. doi:10.1080/1097198X.2021.1993725

Bogavac, M., Prigoda, L., & Cekerevac, Z. P. (2020). SMEs Digitalization and the Sharing Economy. *MEST Journal*, *8*(1), 36–47. doi:10.12709/mest.08.08.01.05

Bowcut, S. (2021). Cybersecurity guide for small business. *Cybersecurity Guide.* https://cybersecurityguide.org/resources/small-business/

Braun, V., & Clarke, V. (2006). Using thematic analysis in psychology. *Qualitative Research in Psychology*, *3*(2), 77–101. doi:10.1191/1478088706qp063oa

Brooks, C. (2022). Cybersecurity in 2022 – A Fresh Look at Some Very Alarming Stats. *Forbes.* https://www.forbes.com/sites/chuckbrooks/2022/01/21/cybersecurity-in-2022--a-fresh-look-at-some-very-alarming-stats/?sh=1c40f4406b61

Calvo-Manzano, J. A., Lema-Moreta, L., Arcilla-Cabián, M., & Rubio-Sánchez, J. L. (2015). How small and medium enterprises can begin their implementation of ITIL? *Revista Facultad de Ingenieria Universidad de Antioquia (Medellín)*, *77*(77), 127–136. doi:10.17533/udea.redin.n77a15

Chin, W. Y., & Chua, H. N. (2021). Using the Theory of Interpersonal Behavior to Predict Information Security Policy Compliance. *Eighth International Conference on eDemocracy & eGovernment (ICEDEG)*, (pp. 80–87). IEEE. 10.1109/ICEDEG52154.2021.9530849

Chung, K., Boutaba, R., & Hariri, S. (2016). Knowledge based decision support system. *Information Technology Management, 17*(1), 1–3. doi:10.100710799-015-0251-3

Clarke, M. (2021). *ITIL Incident Management: What Are Best Practices? CIO Insight*. N.PAG-N.PAG.

Corallo, A., Lazoi, M., & Lezzi, M. (2020). Cybersecurity in the context of industry 4.0: A structured classification of critical assets and business impacts. *Computers in Industry, 114*, 103165. doi:10.1016/j.compind.2019.103165

Cronholm, S., & Persson, L. (2016). Best Practice in IT Service Management: Experienced Strengths and Weaknesses of Using ITIL. *Proceedings of the European Conference on Management, Leadership & Governance*, (pp. 60–67). IEEE.

Cusick, J. (2018). Organizational Design and Change Management for IT Transformation: A Case Study. *Journal of Computer Science and Information Technology, 6*, 10–25. doi:10.15640/jcsit.v6n1a2

D'Arcy, J., & Lowry, P. B. (2019). Cognitive-affective Drivers of Employees' Daily Compliance with Information Security Policies: A Multilevel, Longitudinal Study. *Information Systems Journal, 29*(1), 43–69. doi:10.1111/isj.12173

Dávila, A., Janampa, R., Angeleri, P., & Melendez, K. (2020). ITSM model for very small organisation: An empirical validation. *IET Software, 14*(2), 138–144. doi:10.1049/iet-sen.2019.0034

Deane, J. K., Goldberg, D. M., Rakes, T. R., & Rees, L. P. (2020). The effect of information security certification announcements on the market value of the firm. *Information Technology Management, 20*(3), 107–121. doi:10.100710799-018-00297-3

Dokuchaev, V. A., Maklachkova, V. V., & Statev, V. Y. (2020). Classification of personal data security threats in information systems. *Т-Сотт-Телекоммуникации и Транспорт, 14*(1), 56–60. doi:10.36724/2072-8735-2020-14-1-56-60

Eikebrokk, T. R., & Iden, J. (2017). Strategising IT Service Management through ITIL Implementation: Model and Empirical Test. *Total Quality Management & Business Excellence, 28*(3-4), 238–265. doi:10.1080/14783363.2015.1075872

El Yamami, A., Mansouri, K., Qbadou, M., & Illoussamen, E. H. (2018). Introducing ITIL Framework in Small Enterprises: Tailoring ITSM Practices to the Size of Company. *International Journal of Information Technologies and Systems Approach, 12*(1), 1–19. doi:10.4018/IJITSA.2019010101

Eling, M., McShane, M., & Nguyen, T. (2021). Cyber risk management: History and future research directions. *Risk Management & Insurance Review, 24*(1), 93–125. doi:10.1111/rmir.12169

Ellström, D., Holtström, J., Berg, E., & Josefsson, C. (2021). Dynamic capabilities for digital transformation. *Journal of Strategy and Management, 15*(2), 272–286. doi:10.1108/JSMA-04-2021-0089

Etzion, D., & Aragon-Correa, J. A. (2016). Big Data, Management, and Sustainability: Strategic Opportunities Ahead. *Organization & Environment, 29*(2), 147–155. doi:10.1177/1086026616650437

European Commission. (2022). *Internal Market, Industry, Entrepreneurship and SMEs.* European Commission. https://ec.europa.eu/growth/smes/sme-definition_pt

Galup, S., Dattero, R., & Quan, J. (2020). What Do Agile, Lean, and ITIL Mean to DevOps? *Communications of the ACM, 63*(10), 48–53. doi:10.1145/3372114

Gil-Gómez, H., Oltra-badenes, R., & Adarme-Jaimes, W. (2014). Service quality management based on the application of the ITIL standard. *Dyna, 81*(186), 1–6. doi:10.15446/dyna.v81n186.37953

Glaspie, H. W., & Karwowski, W. (2018). Human Factors in Information Security Culture: A Literature Review. In *International Conference on Applied Human Factors and Ergonomics* (pp. 269-280). Springer. 10.1007/978-3-319-60585-2_25

Grander, G., da Silva, L. F., & Gonzalez, E. D. R. S. (2021). Big data as a value generator in decision support systems: A literature review. *Rev. Gest., 28*(3), 205–222. doi:10.1108/REGE-03-2020-0014

Grandi, A. P., Sarri, A., & Paggio, V. (2021). What Europe's SMEs need to do for a cyber-secure future. *We Forum.* https://www.weforum.org/agenda/2021/06/cybersecurity-for-smes-europe/

Granulo, A., & Tanovic, A. (2020). The Advantage of Using SWOT Analysis for Companies with Implemented ITIL Framework Processes. *43rd International Convention on Information, Communication and Electronic Technology (MIPRO),* (pp. 1656–1661). IEEE, 10.23919/MIPRO48935.2020.9245393

Hameed, M. A., & Arachchilage, N. A. G. (2019). On the impact of perceived vulnerability in the adoption of information systems security innovations. *International Journal of Computer Network and Information Security*, *4*(4), 9–18. doi:10.5815/ijcnis.2019.04.02

Hina, S., & Dominic, D. D. (2017). Need for Information Security Policies Compliance: A Perspective in Higher Education Institutions. *International Conference on Research and Innovation in Information Systems (ICRIIS)*, (pp. 1–6). IEEE. 10.1109/ICRIIS.2017.8002439

Hiter, S. (2021). CIO vs CISO: What are the 5 Big Differences? *Coin Insight*. https://www.cioinsight.com/it-management/cio-vs-ciso/

Horton, J., Macve, R., & Struyven, G. (2004). Chapter 20 - Qualitative Research: Experiences in Using Semi-Structured Interviews. The Real Life Guide to Accounting Research, 339-357. doi:10.1016/B978-008043972-3/50022-0

International Organization for Standardization. (2013). *ISO/IEC 27001:2013*. ISO. https://www.iso.org/cms/render/live/en/sites/isoorg/contents/data/standard/05/45/54534.html

International Security, Trust, and Privacy Alliance (ISTPA) (2001). *The ISTPA Privacy Framework*. Columbia law. http://emoglen.law.columbia.edu/LIS/archive/privacy-legis/ISTPA-FrameworkWhitePaper013101.pdf

Ismail, W. B. W., Widyarto, S., Ahmad, R. A. T. R., & Ghani, K. A. A. (2017). Generic Framework for Information Security Policy Development. *4th International Conference on Electrical Engineering, Computer Science and Informatics (EECSI)*, (pp. 1–6). IEEE. 10.1109/EECSI.2017.8239132

Izquierdo, R. (2022). A Beginner's Guide to the ITIL Framework. *The Ascent.* https://www.fool.com/the-blueprint/itil-framework/

Jäntti, M., & Cater-Steel, A. (2017). Proactive Management of IT Operations to Improve IT Services. *Journal of Information Systems and Technology Management*, *14*(2), 191–218. doi:10.4301/S1807-17752017000200004

Jassim, N. A., Al-Zahir, B. A. M., & Khazraji, A. H. M. (2022). Diagnosing the Current Information Systems Security Department in the Information Technology Department According to the International Standard (Iso/Iec 27001: 2013). *Journal of Management Information & Decision Sciences*, *25*, 1–8.

Jia, L. (2020). Research on Information Security of Large Enterprises. *IEEE 8th International Conference on Information, Communication and Networks (ICICN)*, (pp. 219–223). IEEE. 10.1109/ICICN51133.2020.9205077

Kabanda, S., Tanner, M., & Kent, C. (2018). Exploring SME cybersecurity practices in developing countries. *Journal of Organizational Computing and Electronic Commerce*, *28*(3), 269–282. doi:10.1080/10919392.2018.1484598

Karanja, E. (2017). The role of the chief information security officer in the management of IT security. *Information and Computer Security*, *25*(3), 300–329. doi:10.1108/ICS-02-2016-0013

Kim, D., & Solomon, M. G. (2021). *Fundamentals of Information Systems Security*. Jones & Bartlett Learning.

Kim, D. J., Hwang, I. H., & Kim, J. S. (2016). A Study on Employee's Compliance Behavior towards Information Security Policy: A Modified Triandis Model. *Journal of Digital Convergence*, *14*(4), 209–220. doi:10.14400/JDC.2016.14.4.209

Kitsios, F., Chatzidimitriou, E., & Kamariotou, M. (2022). Developing a Risk Analysis Strategy Framework for Impact Assessment in Information Security Management Systems: A Case Study in IT Consulting Industry. *Sustainability*, *14*(3), 1269. doi:10.3390u14031269

Kraus, S., Durst, S., Ferreira, J. J., Veiga, P., Kailer, N., & Weinmann, A. (2022). Digital transformation in business and management research: An overview of the current status quo. *International Journal of Information Management*, *63*, 1–18. doi:10.1016/j.ijinfomgt.2021.102466

Leite, L., dos Santos, D. R., & Almeida, F. (2022). The impact of general data protection regulation on software engineering practices. *Information and Computer Security*, *30*(1), 79–96. doi:10.1108/ICS-03-2020-0043

Levstek, A., Pucihar, A., & Hovelja, T. (2022). Towards an Adaptive Strategic IT Governance Model for SMEs. *Journal of Theoretical and Applied Electronic Commerce Research*, *17*(1), 230–252. doi:10.3390/jtaer17010012

Lima, I., Pedrosa, I., & Rito, S. (2020). Information Security on Portuguese Statutory Auditors Firms. *15th Iberian Conference on Information Systems and Technologies (CISTI)*, (pp. 1–6). IEEE. 10.23919/CISTI49556.2020.9140820

Lopes, S. F. (2021). The Importance of the ITIL Framework in Managing Information and Communication Technology Services. *International Journal of Advanced Engineering Research and Science*, *8*(5), 292–296. doi:10.22161/ijaers.85.35

Lopez-Leyva, J. A., Kanter-Ramirez, C. A., & Morales-Martinez, J. P. (2020). Customized Diagnostic Tool for The Security Maturity Level of The Enterprise Information Based on ISO/IEC 27001. *8th International Conference in Software Engineering Research and Innovation (CONISOFT)*, (pp. 147–153). IEEE. 10.1109/CONISOFT50191.2020.00030

Mahalle, A., Yong, J., & Tao, X. (2020). ITIL Process Management to Mitigate Operations Risk in Cloud Architecture Infrastructure for Banking and Financial Services Industry. *Web Intell.*, *18*(3), 229–238. doi:10.3233/WEB-200444

Makris, C. (2021). Why enterprises are massively subcontracting cybersecurity work. *Venture Beat*. https://venturebeat.com/2021/10/13/why-enterprises-are-massively-subcontracting-cybersecurity-work/

Marrone, M., & Kolbe, L. M. (2011). Impact of IT Service Management Frameworks on the IT Organization. *Business & Information Systems Engineering*, *3*(1), 5–18. doi:10.100712599-010-0141-5

Mathur, N., Mathur, H., & Pandya, T. (2015). Risk management in information system of organisation: A conceptual framework. *International Journal of Novel Research in Computer Science and Software Engineering*, *2*, 82–88.

Monica, R., Henry, Q., & Estela, M. (2020). Why Implement Continuity Plans in Organizations? Approach of a Prospective Study Based on ITIL. *2020 International Conference on Intelligent Systems and Computer Vision (ISCV)*, (pp. 1–5). IEEE. 10.1109/ISCV49265.2020.9204335

Müller, S. D., & de Lichtenberg, C. G. (2018). The Culture of ITIL: Values and Implementation Challenges. *Information Systems Management*, *35*(1), 49–61. doi:10.1080/10580530.2017.1416946

Nyre-Yu, M., Gutzwiller, R. S., & Caldwell, B. S. (2019). Observing Cyber Security Incident Response: Qualitative Themes From Field Research. *Proceedings of the Human Factors and Ergonomics Society Annual Meeting*, *63*(1), 437–441. doi:10.1177/1071181319631016

Oliveira, D. L., Paula, E. C., & Lovo, O. A. (2017). IT outsourcing in small business: A view of risk and mitigating actions. *Sistemas e Gestão*, *12*, 328–340. doi:10.20985/1980-5160.2017.v12n3.1078

Ormond, D., Warkentin, M., & Crossler, R. E. (2019). Integrating Cognition with an Affective Lens to Better Understand Information Security Policy Compliance. *Journal of the Association for Information Systems*, *20*, 1794–1843. doi:10.17705/1jais.00586

Paananen, H., Lapke, M., & Siponen, M. (2020). State of the Art in Information Security Policy Development. *Computers & Security*, *88*, 101608. doi:10.1016/j.cose.2019.101608

Percivall, G. (2010). The application of open standards to enhance the interoperability of geoscience information. *International Journal of Digital Earth*, *3*(sup1), 14–30. doi:10.1080/17538941003792751

Phillips-Wren, G., Daly, M., & Burstein, F. (2021). Reconciling business intelligence, analytics and decision support systems: More data, deeper insight. *Decision Support Systems*, *146*, 1–13. doi:10.1016/j.dss.2021.113560

Qadir, S., & Quadri, S. (2016). Information Availability: An Insight into the Most Important Attribute of Information Security. *Journal of Information Security*, *7*(03), 185–194. doi:10.4236/jis.2016.73014

Quader, F., & Janeja, V. P. (2021). Insights into Organizational Security Readiness: Lessons Learned from Cyber-Attack Case Studies. *Journal of Cybersecurity and Privacy*, *1*(4), 638–659. doi:10.3390/jcp1040032

Rantao, T., & Njenga, K. (2020). Predicting Communication Constructs towards Determining Information Security Policies Compliance. *South African Journal of Information Management*, *22*(1), 1–10. doi:10.4102ajim.v22i1.1211

Rashid, Y., Rashid, A., Warraich, M. A., Sabir, S. S., & Waseem, A. (2019). Case Study Method: A Step-by-Step Guide for Business Researchers. *International Journal of Qualitative Methods*, *18*, 1–13. doi:10.1177/1609406919862424

Reiter, M., & Miklošík, A. (2020). Digital Transformation of Organisations in the Context of ITIL® 4. *Mark. Ident.*, *1*, 522–536.

Rid, T., & Buchanan, B. (2014). Attributing cyber attacks. *The Journal of Strategic Studies*, *38*(1-2), 4–37. doi:10.1080/01402390.2014.977382

Rieke, R., Repp, J., Zhdanova, M., & Eichler, J. (2014). Monitoring Security Compliance of Critical Processes. *22nd Euromicro International Conference on Parallel, Distributed, and Network-Based Processing*, (pp. 552-560). https://doi.irg/10.1109/PDP.2014.106

Rios, O. K. L., Filho, J. G. A. T., & Rios, V. P. S. (2017). Melhores Práticas Do COBIT, ITIL e ISO/IEC 27002 Para Implantação de Política de Segurança da Informação em Instituições Federais do Ensino Superior. *Revista Gestão & Tecnologia*, *17*(1), 130–154. doi:10.20397/2177-6652/2017.v17i1.1084

Ross, R. (2018). *Risk Management Framework for Information Systems and Organizations: A System Life Cycle Approach for Security and Privacy.* National Institute of Standards and Technology. doi:10.6028/NIST.SP.800-37r2

Sarala, R., Zayaraz, G., & Aravindanne, S. (2015). Prediction of Insider Threats for Effective Information Security Risk Assessment. *International Journal of Applied Engineering, 10*, 19033–19036.

Sausalito, C. (2021). Cybercrime to Cost the World $10.5 Trillion Annually By 2025. *Cyber Security Ventures.* https://cybersecurityventures.com/cybercrime-damages-6-trillion-by-2021/

Schinagl, S., & Shahim, A. (2020). What do we know about information security governance? "From the basement to the boardroom": Towards digital security governance. *Information and Computer Security, 28*(2), 261–292. doi:10.1108/ICS-02-2019-0033

Serban, R. A. (2017). The impact of big data, sustainability, and digitalization on company performance. *Studies in Business and Economics, 12*(3), 181–189. doi:10.1515be-2017-0045

Shojaifar, A., & Jarvinen, H. (2021). Classifying SMEs for Approaching Cybersecurity Competence and Awareness. *The 16th International Conference on Availability, Reliability and Security*, (pp. 1-7). IEEE. 10.1145/3465481.3469200

Silva, T. S., Carvalho, H., & Torres, C. B. (2003). *Segurança dos Sistemas de Informação.* Famalicão: Centro Atlântico.

Sivaraman, V. (2019). Security Management at the National Institute of Management: To Outsource or Insource? Cases (A) and (B). *Vikalpa, 44*(2), 95–96. doi:10.1177/0256090919854813

Soomro, T. R., & Wahba, H. Y. (2011). Role of Information Technology Infrastructure Library in Data Warehouses. *American Journal of Applied Sciences, 8*(12), 1384–1387. doi:10.3844/ajassp.2011.1384.1387

Spasic, B., & Markovic, A. (2013). Information and Communication Technology Unit Service Management in a Non-Profit Organization Using ITIL Standards. *Management, 18*(66), 39–70. doi:10.7595/management.fon.2013.0005

Stepenko, V., Dreval, L., Chernov, S., & Shestak, V. (2022). EU Personal Data Protection Standards and Regulatory Framework. *J Journal of Applied Security Research, 17*(2), 190–207. doi:10.1080/19361610.2020.1868928

Van der Kleij, R., Kleinhuis, G., & Young, H. (2017). Computer Security Incident Response Team Effectiveness: A Needs Assessment. *Frontiers in Psychology, 8,* 1–8. doi:10.3389/fpsyg.2017.02179 PMID:29312051

Virani, R. (2022). *Small businesses are most vulnerable to growing cybersecurity threats. Help Net Security.* https://www.helpnetsecurity.com/2022/01/11/small-businesses-vulnerable/

Whitman, M. E., & Mattord, H. J. (2017). *Principles of Information Security.* Cengage Learning.

Whitten, D. (2008). The Chief Information Security Officer: An Analysis of the Skills Required for Success. *Journal of Computer Information Systems, 48,* 15–19.

Yamakawa, P., Noriega, C. O., Linares, A. N., & Ramírez, W. V. (2012). Improving ITIL compliance using change management practices: A finance sector case study. *Business Process Management Journal, 18*(6), 1020–1035. doi:10.1108/14637151211283393

Yee, C. K., & Zolkipli, M. F. (2021). Review on Confidentiality, Integrity and Availability in Information Security. *Journal of ICT in Education, 8*(2), 34–42. doi:10.37134/jictie.vol8.2.4.2021

Yin, R. K. (2017). *Case Study Research and Applications: Design and Methods.* SAGE Publications.

ADDITIONAL READINGS

Ali, R. F., Dominic, P. D. D., Ali, S. E. A., Rehman, M., & Sohail, A. (2021). Information security behavior and information security policy compliance: A systematic literature review for identifying the transformation process from noncompliance to compliance. *Applied Sciences (Basel, Switzerland), 11*(8), 3383. doi:10.3390/app11083383

Baiyere, A., Salmela, H., & Tapanainen, T. (2020). Digital transformation and the new logics of business process management. *European Journal of Information Systems, 29*(3), 238–259. doi:10.1080/0960085X.2020.1718007

Bokhari, S., & Manzoor, S. (2022). Impact of Information Security Management System on Firm Financial Performance: Perspective of Corporate Reputation and Branding. *American Journal of Industrial and Business Management, 12*(05), 934–954. doi:10.4236/ajibm.2022.125048

Diesch, R., Pfaff, M., & Krcmar, H. (2020). A comprehensive model of information security factors for decision-makers. *Computers & Security*, *92*, 101747. doi:10.1016/j.cose.2020.101747

Faruq, B. A. (2020). Integration of ITIL V3, ISO 20000 ISO 27001:2013 for IT Services and Security Management System. *International Journal of Advanced Trends in Computer Science and Engineering*, *9*(3), 3514–3531. doi:10.30534/ijatcse/2020/157932020

Figueira, P. T., Bravo, C. L., & López, J. L. R. (2020). Improving information security risk analysis by including threat-occurrence predictive models. *Computers & Security*, *88*, 101609. doi:10.1016/j.cose.2019.101609

Heidt, M., Gerlach, J. P., & Buxmann, P. (2019). Investigating the security divide between SME and large companies: How SME characteristics influence organizational IT security investments. *Information Systems Frontiers*, *21*(6), 1285–1305. doi:10.100710796-019-09959-1

Ključnikov, A., Mura, L., & Sklenár, D. (2019). Information security management in SMEs: Factors of success. *Entrepreneurship and Sustainability Issues*, *6*(4), 2081–2094. doi:10.9770/jesi.2019.6.4(37)

Malimage, K., Raddatz, N., Trinkle, B. S., Crossler, R. E., & Baaske, R. (2020). Impact of Deterrence and Inertia on Information Security Policy Changes. *Journal of Information Systems*, *34*(1), 123–134. doi:10.2308/isys-52400

Martinez, F. (2019). Process excellence the key for digitalization. *Business Process Management Journal*, *25*(7), 1716–1733. doi:10.1108/BPMJ-08-2018-0237

Mathenge, J., Stevens-Hall, J., & Raza, M. (2019). Service Desk in ITIL 4. *BMC Blogs*. https://www.bmc.com/blogs/itil-service-desk/

Pérez-González, D., Preciado, S. T., & Solana-Gonzalez, P. (2019). Organizational practices as antecedents of the information security management performance: An empirical investigation. *Information Technology & People*, *32*(5), 1262–1275. doi:10.1108/ITP-06-2018-0261

Qazi, A., Quigley, J., Dickson, A., & Ekici, Ş. Ö. (2017). Exploring dependency based probabilistic supply chain risk measures for prioritizing interdependent risks and strategies. *European Journal of Operational Research*, *259*(1), 189–204. doi:10.1016/j.ejor.2016.10.023

Rabii, A., Assoul, S., Touhami, K. O., & Roudies, O. (2020). *Information and cyber security maturity models: a systematic literature review*. Information & Computer Security.

Salehi, A., & Vazife, Z. (2019). The Effect of the Implementation of Information Security Management System (ISMS) and Information Technology Infrastructure Library (ITIL) on the Promotion of Information Systems and Information Technology Services Continues. *Public Management Researches*, *12*(43), 225–249. doi:10.22111/JMR.2019.4751

Somepalli, S. H., Tangella, S. K. R., & Yalamanchili, S. (2020). Information Security Management. *HOLISTICA–Journal of Business and Public Administration*, *11*(2), 1–16. doi:10.2478/hjbpa-2020-0015

Tewamba, H. N., Kamdjoug, J. R. K., Bitjoka, G. B., Wamba, S. F., & Bahanag, N. N. M. (2019). Effects of information security management systems on firm performance. *American Journal of Operations Management and Information Systems*, *4*(3), 99–108. doi:10.11648/j.ajomis.20190403.15

Topa, I., & Karyda, M. (2019). From theory to practice: Guidelines for enhancing information security management. *Information & Computer Security.*, *27*(3), 326–342. doi:10.1108/ICS-09-2018-0108

Tuptuk, N., & Hailes, S. (2018). Security of smart manufacturing systems. *Journal of Manufacturing Systems*, *47*, 93–106. doi:10.1016/j.jmsy.2018.04.007

KEY TERMS AND DEFINITIONS

Availability: A security purpose that ensures the ability of an IT service or other configuration item to perform its agreed function when required.

Confidentiality of Information: A security purpose that ensures information is not made available or disclosed to unauthorized entities.

Incident Management: Is the practice of minimizing the negative impact of incidents by restoring normal service operation as quickly as possible.

Incident: An unplanned interruption to a service or a reduction in the quality of a service.

Information Security Management: Is the practice of protecting an organization by understanding and managing risks to the confidentiality, integrity, and availability of information.

Information System: It involves a set of people, procedures, and resources (hardware, software, and data) in the collection, processing, and provision of information in the organizational context.

Integrity of Information: A security purpose that ensures information is only modified by authorized personnel and activities.

Process: Is a set of interrelated or interacting activities that transform inputs into outputs.

Recovery: Is the activity of returning a configuration item to normal operation after a failure.

Risk: A possible event that could cause harm or loss or make it more difficult to achieve objectives.

Service Continuity Management: Is the practice of ensuring that service availability and performance are maintained at a sufficient level in case of a disaster.

Chapter 2
Usability of Security Mechanisms of E-Health Applications:
Cases From Ethiopia

Lemma Lessa
https://orcid.org/0000-0002-2890-9721
Addis Ababa University, Ethiopia

Antonyo George Etoribussi
Addis Ababa University, Ethiopia

ABSTRACT

Extant literature supports that e-health applications are developed with a proper set of security mechanisms in place. However, the majority of the security mechanisms were not considered from the users' point of view. As a result, the security of health information is becoming an important and growing concern. The objective of this study is to evaluate the usability of security mechanisms of e-Health applications functional at health facilities operating under the Addis Ababa Health Bureau, and identify the strengths and weaknesses of the usability of the security features of the e-Health applications. This study uses a qualitative research methodology. The findings revealed that out of the thirteen criteria, learnability, aesthetics and minimalist design, and user language complied; on the contrary, revocability and user suitability were not in compliance with security features according to all the experts' review of all e-Health applications. Finally, recommendations were given for practice, and suggestions were forwarded for future research.

DOI: 10.4018/978-1-6684-6581-3.ch002

BACKGROUND

Information security (IS) has become a major concern of different stakeholders, users, governments, service providers, systems developers, and systems administrators (Jang-Jaccard & Nepal, 2014; Ksibi et al., 2022). These concerns are even growing more in health systems. Health systems play an important role in information processing in healthcare for the benefit of the patient as well as the hospital health professionals. Additionally, they have many benefits, such as quick and easy access, storage, and retrieval of Patient Health Information (PHI) data in a protected manner for authenticated and authorized users. An E-health application is a health information management system that supports healthcare providers to maintain a record of patient diagnosis and treatment for current use as well as future reference (Evans, 2016; Mehrtak, 2021). Due to the sensitivity of the PHI, a proper security measure must be in place to protect it from a data breach (Smith, 2019; Argaw et al., 2020). Many e-Health systems have been developed to meet the purposeful requirement and more with a proper set of protection mechanisms from the development point of view (Bourgeois, 2014). However, these security mechanisms were not considered from the users' point of view (Hof, 2012; Giansanti et al., 2021). In addition, it is a major concern that requires new approaches in systems design to balance the developers' view with the users' view of security mechanisms (Dalpiaz et al., 2016). Therefore, e-health applications need to provide effective, high-quality support for providing the best care for patients without compromising security.

Protection within the e-health device deals with securing private health-associated information from unauthorized access, use, disclosure, disruption, change, or destruction. Patients worry that their private medical data may influence their employers' decisions approximately promotions or downsizing or be made public in press reviews or civil court movements (Institute of Medicine, 2009). Also, privacy is the right of persons, agencies, or establishments to regulate private and sensitive information of dissemination to other parties with a proper and indicated use of that information (Holvast, 2009). Nowadays, many healthcare organizations are vulnerable to security attacks since they contain sensitive patient information (Chowdhury et al., 2018). Patients are required to share information with their physicians to facilitate accurate analysis and treatment, especially to avoid unfavorable drug interactions (Burton et al., 2004). Patients trust their health providers if their information is kept private and secure (Institute of Medicine, 2009) and this leads them to be more willing to discuss their symptoms, conditions, and past and present risk behaviors. However, patient data can be hacked, manipulated, or destroyed by internal or external users and result in improper modification of diagnosis results that can threaten patient health or even his/her life. Also, patient health information plays a major role in conducting medical research for improving healthcare quality.

However, the disclosure of health information for various reasons raises concerns about privacy (Institute of Medicine, 1994).

Ensuring the usability of security mechanisms of the e-health system is the key component to maintaining the balance of security and usability (Sittig et al., 2018) and making the e-Health application more secure and usable. But, developing a secure and usable e-Health application is a difficult task due to the higher complexities within the healthcare environment (Ross et al., 2016). Usability as per the ISO definition is the quantity to which a product may be used by designated users to acquire exact goals with effectiveness, efficiency, and delight in a specific context of use (ISO-9241/11, 2018). Nielsen (2012) also defines usability as a high-quality attribute that relies upon five additives: learnability, efficiency, memorability, errors, and pleasure. The usability of software program applications is one thing that reduces security and privacy at a significant level (Alshamari, 2016).

If security and usability have been taken into consideration throughout the design of a software program system, it would have helped to reduce the number of security cases, which might be affecting users. The outcome of any software device that implements the balance of each security and usable interface design, might be an outstanding gain, although little has been achieved to deal with those areas (Kainda et al., 2010). Most of the works that have been accomplished on the balance between usability and security seem to be aware extra on the authentication techniques, however, it has to move beyond simply this part of a system to think about the mixing into every part of the user interface layout (Nwokedi et al., 2016). Lampson (2009) stated that for usable security to be successful, we have to focus on the essential part rather than on the perfection of the systems. Moreover, we need simple models of security that users can understand (Bourgeois, 2014). To make systems truthful we want accountability; and to maintain freedom, we want separate green and red mechanisms that protect the information you care about from the public net (Lampson, 2009).

In developing nations, health data from Health Information Systems (HIS) turn out to be a vital factor in strengthening health structures (Braa et al., 2007). The use of health information is extended not only for patient care and administrative purpose but also for making plans and decisions for enhancing healthcare delivery (Institute of Medicine, 1994; Assa-Agyei et al., 2022). Therefore, this led to a shift from paper-based to computer-based processing of health information which increases the opportunities for handling patient data efficiently. However, many patient records are lost due to a lack of security or there is no well-documented privacy and security policy and procedures implemented in hospitals (Virtual Mentor, 2012). The technological complexity challenge in using advanced tools for processing health data also raises security and privacy issues (Abouelmehdi et al., 2018).

Highly sensitive personal and clinical information is recorded and shared in health systems (Institute of Medicine, 1994). An e-Health application, with its security mechanisms in place to protect this information using proper and usable security mechanisms, becomes very crucial (Sulaiman et al., 2008). Therefore, this study aims to evaluate the usability aspect of security mechanisms of e-Health applications by taking a few cases from Ethiopia.

OBJECTIVES

The general objective of this study is to evaluate the usability of security mechanisms of e-Health applications at health facilities under the administration of Addis Ababa Health Bureau and identify strengths and weaknesses of the usability of the security features of the e-Health applications. In line with the general objective, the research seeks to meet the following specific objectives:

- Identify/formulate evaluation criteria from literature to evaluate the usability aspect of security features in an application
- Analyzing the usability of current e-Health application security mechanisms.
- Propose a possible recommendation to address weaknesses in the current e-Health applications and future e-Health applications.

RELATED WORKS

How people interact with security policies and mechanisms is not limited to the point of interaction (Eysenbach, 2001). Usability research suggested that a system with a difficult user interface can harm its functionality, even though a well-designed, easy-to-use user interface could not have a positive impact if the system does not provide the required functionality (Sasse & Flechais, 2005). In addition, designers dedicate more effort to making a security mechanism as simple as possible, and users still fail to use it easily. The security mechanism which was designed well still needs more effort when they are in use, and users always are drawn to overpass them, especially when users are eager to complete their tasks (Cranor & Garfinkel, 2005). To make an effort for security, users must believe that their assets are at risk and that the security mechanism provides effective protection against that risk (Sasse, & Flechais, 2005). The deployment of e-Health systems using different platforms enables personal health information to be maintained in digital form and ready to be accessed and shared by the right people for the right reason using proper authentication and authorization (Fernández-Alemán et al., 2013).

The security of health information is an important concern for all those delivering healthcare by protecting these sensitive patient records from unauthorized people using security mechanisms (Institute of Medicine, 2009). These security mechanisms are in place to protect data, systems, and networks. Also, security experts can handle them to achieve a sufficient level of security for any given system. However, many information systems security mechanisms were not designed based on the consideration of novice users and usability aspects (Hof, 2012). The average end-user is often overwhelmed with understanding and using security mechanisms, which are simply annoying end-users (Hof, 2013). In general, the security feature of any information system is only as strong as the weakest link in the system, undesirable usability of IT security mechanisms may also result in making errors, resulting in an insecure system (Hof, 2015) which has an impact on the decisions of novice users' usage. Hence, software developers intend to deliver software without a security mechanism than one with difficulty or no usability. Security mechanisms' usability is the most undermined attribute of information systems and applications, and also, these attributes were often the afterthought of an afterthought (Hof, 2013).

Security in the systems is found to be one of the barriers to the adoption of ICT in healthcare (Anwar & Shamim, 2011; Kotzé et al., 2013). E-Health application has a security measure to protect PHI from unintended use (Kruse et al., 2017). Effective security is achieved with the increase of usable security to users and requires the developers to see over the user interface of security tools, where the majority of research and development effort is centered (Sasse, & Flechais, 2005). Furthermore, the ISO standards for the protection and security of personal information are important to all people, corporations, institutions, and governments. There are special requirements in the health sector that need to be met to protect the confidentiality, integrity, suitability, and availability of personal health information (ISO-27799, 2016). Health information integrity must be protected to ensure patient privacy, and continuity of protection is also auditable at all times (ISO 27799, 2008). Effective healthcare delivery is highly dependent on the availability of health information (National Academy of Engineering (US), and the Institute of Medicine, 2005). Health informatics systems security is intended to be operational in the case of disasters, failures, and service denial attacks while protecting the Confidentiality, Integrity, and Availability (CIA) of health information, therefore, it requires domain expertise for the health sector (ISO-27799, 2016).

In addition, the act of human error or failure is described as an entry of invalid data, accidental deletion, or modification of data by staff to be the second category of security threat (Whitman & Mattord, 2018). Health Insurance Portability and Accountability Act (HIPAA) security rule (2014) indicates the standards that can be applied to protect Electronic Protected Health Information (ePHI) when it is in storage as well as in transit. Also, there are three pillars to address the security protection measure, namely technical, physical, and administrative security in the HIPAA compliance checklist.

The protection of sensitive data is simply as strong as the weakest link, which often turns out to be the human user and not the firewall (Sasse et al., 2001). This makes the users' consciousness of the data created as well as the threat associated with a data breach critical, subsequently shifting from an understanding of complex security procedures to an understanding of organizational pressures. This implies that information security awareness is the key to mitigating security threats caused by human weaknesses (Metalidou et al., 2014). Besides, information security challenges related to employees, face daily must be understood and resolved. Therefore, employees should have a proper education, and awareness about the significance of information security ought to be a priority of the organization (Margit, 2018).

Usability as a success factor of security, a reliable evaluation of current security mechanisms and procedures in terms of their usability aspect has a great need for application-specific research (Kainda et al., 2010). Maintaining security in a digital-technology world has many challenges (Hiranandani, 2011). Risks can be high, varying from loss of information and privacy to loss of important assets (Stoneburner et al., 2002). This demands advanced security measures to be in place to secure and protect. Moreover, customers or users want the applications to be not only safe but also easy to use. Security measure is deemed to be a trade-off or unbalance between ease of use and ultimate security (Yee, 2004; Braz et al., 2007). Therefore, this research is aimed to identify the existence of unbalance issues within security and usability issues of selected e-Health applications in the Ethiopian context.

METHODS AND MATERIALS

This research employed a qualitative research approach with a case study method. Qualitative research mainly collects unstructured text-based data, which is in the form of interview transcripts, observation notes, and diary entries. In some cases, qualitative data can also include a pictorial display, audio or video clips, or other multimedia materials. Data analysis of qualitative research is more of a dynamic, intuitive, and creative process of inductive reasoning, thinking, and theorizing (Basit, 2003).

The e-Health applications OpenEMR, DHIS2, and SmartCare are installed on a laptop or desktop and configured without any clinical data, to protect data privacy, even though the evaluation was done only on the security mechanisms. On the other hand, DHIS2 has an online demo version available for evaluation. After all the necessary setup and configuration are made, the experts were contacted to introduce the overall evaluation process and research objective to create awareness among the experts. Purposive sampling method is employed for the selection of the applications as well as the participants. Open-ended questions and focus-group-discussion are used to collect the data. Thematic analysis, which is a common data analysis strategy for qualitative data, is concerned with the identification and analysis of patterns of meaning themes and constitutes a widely applicable, cost-effective, and flexible tool for exploratory research. Thematic analysis is particularly suitable for analyzing experiences, perceptions, and understandings. It is appropriate for the analysis of small, medium-sized, and even large data sets (Clarke, and Braun, 2013). Braun and Clarke (2006) indicated the six phases of thematic analysis processes this study adopted are: Familiarization with the data, Coding, Searching for themes, Reviewing themes, Defining and naming themes, and Writing up.

RESULTS AND DISCUSSION

Security Heuristics Compliance

All the three e-Health applications, according to the experts' evaluation, were found to comply with these three security heuristics; namely, Learnability, Aesthetics and Minimalist, and User Language.

Learnability

In using certain e-Health applications the authentication steps should be easy enough to learn and remember by users (Al-Sarayreh et al., 2015). The experts' evaluation of using the learnability criteria indicated that the three applications comply which implies that these e-Health applications were found to be easy to learn and remember for users. In supporting their judgment, the experts were making the following remarks, for example, Expert1 commented "These settings are either access denied or hidden from the users. DHIS2 allows for multiple users to access the system simultaneously, each User is a member of a defined set of Roles with defined permissions." Also, Expert 2 commented, "Similar actions are grouped and sequenced logically in tabs and with a brief explanation for each and the simple titles and the mapping of individual function keys for the simplest action possible action, promotes easy learning". Moreover, Expert 3 commented, "No vague language of the security word is clearly stated in low-level understanding". All of the experts agreed that the security operations were easy to learn and use, these imply that security operations use a simple title with clear language and descriptions for the users. Similar prior study indicated that ease-of-learning measures the ease of learning the use of security or privacy features and also ease in remembering features after not using them for a time. One of the applications scored very well, while the other one scored barely acceptable by using different research approaches (Yeratziotis et al., 2011).

Aesthetics and Minimalist

Only relevant information should be visible in the system security mechanisms, without overwhelming the user with information, the number of settings, and passwords to remember (Fierro & Zapata, 2016). The evaluation of aesthetics and minimalistic criteria indicated that compliance with the three applications, and relevant security actions were observed to inform users (Pierotti, 2005). Besides, Expert 2 commented, "If/When present, informative messages are displayed in a way that assists the user to make decisions on the action they are about to perform." Security-related information that would affect the decision of security action should be presented clearly to the users (Pierotti, 2005). Also, security labels should be visually and conceptually district icons with clear descriptions (Pierotti, 2005).

User Language

User language criterion states that the system should use language which is easy to understand for the users (Yeratziotis et al., 2012). In this regard, Expert 2 commented, "There are no jargons related to security". Also, Expert 3 stated, "the security actions and security objects are shown consistently across all prompts". Security should use language appropriate for users, simple, clear can be understood easily (Hausawi et al., 2014). Besides, the system should avoid any unnecessary technical jargon and confusing acronyms (Akash, & Janet, 2009).

The design of security action, object, and information should be consistent, accurate, complete, and in simple language across all. One study showed that terminology which measures the logical, natural order of information. It uses phrases and concepts familiar to users and avoids complicated security or privacy terms. In the study, both website applications scored very well and well. However, barely acceptable, and poor ratings also occurred (Yeratziotis et al., 2011). In this regard, OpenEMR and DHIS2 applications were found to comply with these three security heuristics - Errors, User Assistance, and Identity Signal.

Errors

Prior study shows that error messages should prevent users before the error occur and present or prompt the users for their confirmation (Nielsen, 1994). These messages should be polite, precise, humane readable, and constructive to reduce the work required to fix the problem and educate users along the way, for example, the "404 error message" web's most common error violates most of these guidelines and recommended for custom error message "page not found" (Nielsen, 1994). Experts' evaluation of the criteria of errors showed that OpenEMR and DHIS2 e-Health applications comply with this heuristic criterion. Expert 2 stated, "When error message was displayed, in a constrictive, descriptive and accurate way". Errors messages should inform their severity, their cause, and corrective actions for users to understand them well and act appropriately (Pierotti, 2005).

User Assistance

The system help should be able to assist users when there is a need arises and at the same time educate them along the way for security-related activities (Yeratziotis et al., 2012). The experts' evaluation of OpenEMR and DHIS2 on the criteria of user assistance indicated that they comply with this heuristic. Two of the three experts commented, "Online/offline User manual is availed and there is an online help/manual with explanations for security features". Security help for users should be able to assist users in such a way that security help information was visible, relevant, and educational (Akash, & Janet, 2009).

Identity Signal

Valid certificates and information about the certificate should be available for the users while using an application on the browser (Yeratziotis et al., 2012). Based on the experts' evaluation of the criteria of identity signal observed at OpenEMR and DHIS2, applications comply with this heuristic. Two of the three experts commented, "the identity signal includes readable information about the certificate subject which also includes the advises that the user will do". Information about the validity of certificates should be available for users who are using a secure way of communicating with the system they use (Yeratziotis et al., 2012).

Clarity

Good error messages should be designed carefully which prevents a problem from occurring in the first place. Either eliminate error-prone conditions or check for them and present users with a confirmation option before they commit to the action (Nielsen, and Mack, 1994). The experts' evaluation of clarity criteria revealed that OpenEMR and SmartCare applications comply with the standard. As stated by Expert 2 "all function keys were located on a similar location for all security actions of a user". Also, Expert 3 "such kinds of messages are displayed and highlighted to make it visible/accessible for the user". Clarity is a criterion aimed to increase users' understanding of the communication of security actions by informing users in advance about the consequences of any security action (Nielsen, 1994). Prompts, warnings, and notifications are e-System communication means to provide information to users, but this information should be simple and clear to be understood by novice users (Nielsen, 1994).

On the other hand, these e-Health applications have similar function keys for security and were grouped in a similar location, these make it clear for the users to easily locate and remember them (Nielsen, 1994). User action and its consequences should give proper warring feedback clearly (Capilla et al., 2014). One of the e-Health applications found to comply with one or two of the security heuristics criteria is discussed below respectively; OpenEMR compliance Visibility, DHIS2 compliance Satisfaction, and Security and Privacy.

Visibility

OpenEMR was found to comply with this criterion based on expert evaluation. An appropriate user security login provides security-related error messages that are displayed next to the field where the user committed an error (Nielsen, 1994; Nielsen, 2001). The e-Health application should provide a feedback message indicating that the subsequent collection of the task needs to be started (Nielsen, 1994). The expert also revealed in their evaluation that the application offers feedback for each security-related incident (Nielsen, 1994). A study shows that pop-up windows should display an error message with apologetic means significantly decrease users' frustration (Park et al., 2012).

Satisfaction

The overall system of user satisfaction was determined by the combination of the user satisfaction values of its components (Norman, 1983). Security settings should be a member of a family of security options and differentiated with consistent color throughout the system, ease of understanding for users' attention, and changes for security-related actions and information security settings were a member of a family of security (Pierotti, 2005).

Security and Privacy

Integrity, availability, confidentiality, and privacy should be considered for the criteria of security and privacy with security-related activities (Yeratziotis et al., 2012). Breach of sensitive e-health data would severely cause threats leading to tampering with health and personal-related information. So, preserving the privacy of patient information is an important feature in e-health systems (Sahama et al., 2013). Based on the experts' evaluation, DHIS2 complies with the security and privacy criteria. For example, two of the experts out of three commented, "protected areas are completely inaccessible, the backend/confidential areas of the system can be accessed with passwords, session lockout with specific time-bound, enforce the minimum requirement and complexity of the password, passwords are encrypted in storage, and users can modify only their information".

Security Heuristics Non-Compliance

In this section, two security heuristics criteria that all three e-Health applications do not comply with are discussed.

Revocability

Revocability was included in user control and freedom of Nielsen's ten heuristics; users often choose system functions by mistake and will need a marked "emergency exit" to leave the unwanted state without having to go through an extended dialogue (Nielsen, 1994). Based on the experts' evaluation of revocability, none of the three e-Health applications comply with this heuristic criteria, stated by the experts' "no Undo buttons to reverse security action means to terminate an act in the middle of an operation or in-progress". The method that enables users to de-selection of a security option gives users a chance to correct the security action, and notification of the correction is visually communicated to notify users that the error was reverted (Nelson, 1994). The user of the e-Health application can do a security action error unintentionally or intentionally, to take correction, reverting method should be available to facilitate the action (Nelson, 1994). Not all three applications have an "undo" button or means of termination of security action in progress. Undo function should help users to reverse their actions and clear, consistent message with GUI menus regarding the reversing action success (Pierotti, 2005). The experts revealed in their evaluation that the applications were not able to revoke any of the security-related actions by users (Nelson, 1994).

User Suitability

Users at different levels should use the system with their level of skills and experience in security (Yeratziotis et al., 2012). Also, the system should support customization to the level of user preference (Akash & Janet, 2009). All three e-Health applications do not comply with the criteria of user suitability. For instance, Expert1 and Expert

2 commented, "User is a member of a defined set of Roles with Security & Access Control Groups of permissions". Users with different levels of skill and experience in security should have options that are appropriate to their level of understanding of security-related actions (Yeratziotis et al., 2012). OpenEMR and SmartCare were found not to comply with the security heuristics of Convey Features/Expressiveness, Satisfaction, and Security and Privacy. This is discussed as follows.

Convey Features/Expressiveness

The system should convey relevant messages to guide users on security and freedom of expression (Yeratziotis et al., 2012). The user interface of the authentication screen should convey the available security feature clearly and appropriately (Mendoza-González et al., 2011). Based on the experts', evaluation of Convey Features/ Expressiveness indicated that there is no prompting for the next security action, no description of the security state, and users are not initiators of security actions. In line with this, Expert 2 indicated, "It is not observed on the system for a prompt or showing a message for next action expected from users and different security capabilities, most of them are not readily understandable by all users. Hence, a technical person can easily understand them but not in the case of non-technical". Besides, security capabilities were not easy for non-technical persons to understand well. Users should be able to view the security features and their capabilities and act if appropriate (Neilson, 1994). The e-Health system should be able to propose the next security action, security state, and clear information on security capabilities for the users (Pierotti, 2005). Accordingly, OpenEMR and SmartCare applications do not comply with the criteria.

Satisfaction

The overall system user satisfaction is determined by the combination of the user satisfaction values of the system components (Norman, 1983). One of the experts commented, "No hierarchical security relationship is available. No inheritance of security settings is also included in any of the security settings. No distinct coloring is implemented for security-related changes. There are no prompts that are related to security." Security settings should be a member of a family of security options and differentiated with consistent color throughout the system, ease of understanding for users' attention, and changes for security-related actions and information security settings were a member of a family of security (Pierotti, 2005). Based on the experts' evaluation of the satisfaction criteria OpenEMR and SmartCare do not comply.

Security and Privacy

Breach of sensitive e-Health data would severely cause threats leading to tampering with health and personal-related information. So, preserving the privacy of patient information is an important feature in e-health systems (Sahama et al., 2013). Based on the experts' evaluation, OpenEMR and SmartCare do not comply with the security and privacy criteria. All the experts commented, "Users are members of a predefined Security & Access Control Groups. There is no lifetime restriction on the passwords. The user can reuse the password without any limited time. No Password history maintenance with unlimited Attempt and the system will not lock with specific time-bound unless the user lockout it." Also, no consent is requested from users about the information they provide. Backups are available as an integral part of the system but there is no policy about how copies of such information will be utilized. Furthermore, no notification on the access privileges. On the other hand, DHIS2 and SmartCare applications were found not to comply with the Visibility criteria, which are discussed below.

Visibility

Experts' evaluation of visibility criteria revealed that no significant delay is observed in the three applications until the user is to perform the next security action, a brief delay for each failed attempt and a long delay for several failed login attempts were used as a security measure from brute force login attacks (Cobb et al., 2015). An appropriate user security login provides security-related error messages that will be displayed next to the field in which the user committed an error (Nielsen, 1994; Nielsen, 2001). Based on this, all three e-Health application does not comply with the specified criteria.

In e-Health applications, once the expert finalized a security action, the application should provide a feedback message indicating that the subsequent collection of the task needs to be started (Nielsen, 1994). However, DHIS2 and SmartCare do not have such a feedback feature for what to do next once a successful login is accomplished. The experts also revealed in their evaluation that the application offers feedback for each security-related incident (Nielsen, 1994). A study shows that pop-up windows should display an error message with apologetic means significantly decrease users' frustration (Park et al., 2012). But in this study, Expert 2 commented, "There are no pop-up windows for security-related issues or there was no security action completion feedback, it will not indicate specific fields but data entry boxes that resulted in the errors." Expert 3 also added "When you enter a correct username but wrong password though the system does not specify the error is username or password. If the username is correct, it shouldn't be requested again."

CONCLUSION

This study was aimed to evaluate the usability of security mechanisms of e-Health applications that are in use in Ethiopia. After a rigorous literature review, the researchers found a framework for evaluating usable security in the health domain. The framework uses three phases to identify the higher level of security heuristics for the purpose of evaluation. These higher levels of a heuristic checklist are adopted for this study. Moreover, based on the evaluation framework, the evaluation of the usability of the security mechanisms of the e-Health application in Ethiopia was done.

The health sector in Ethiopia was implementing e-Health applications throughout the health facilities to facilitate clinical data collection and dissemination electronically (JSI, 2019; USAID, 2019). DHIS2 and OpenEMR applications are recent and open-source. On the other hand, SmartCare is the earlier application still in use in government health facilities. Many of these e-Health applications were developed in-house or open-source and customized, furthermore, donor-funded projects. The study result shows that the three e-Health applications tend to comply with some criteria and not comply with other criteria of usable security. Accordingly, OpenEMR application comply with Learnability, Aesthetics and Minimalist Design, User Language, Errors, User Assistance, Identity signal, and Visibility criteria; and does not comply with Revocability, User Suitability, Revocability, and User Suitability criteria. Whereas DHIS2 application comply with Learnability, Aesthetics and Minimalist Design, User Language, Errors, User Assistance, Identity Signal, Satisfaction, Clarity, Visibility, Security and Privacy, criteria; and does not comply with Clarity and Visibility criteria. Finally, Smartcare application comply with Learnability, Aesthetics and Minimalist Design, and User Language; and does not comply with Revocability, User Suitability, Visibility, Errors, Identity Signal criteria.

RECOMMENDATIONS

The significance of security mechanisms for e-Health applications is undeniable. These mechanisms are in place to protect the privacy of personal and clinical data in the system without question. In doing so usability aspect of security mechanisms seems to be given less focus on the development of e-Health applications or in general any information system application. Therefore, for the security mechanism to be more secure, they should be usable too. Based on the study result, the researchers recommend giving due attention, especially for the usability aspect of security mechanisms in the development of e-Health application SDLC. Besides, system developers should give equal consideration for security and usability in the design phase to get a usable and secure application at the end. Security experts should also involve usability experts to come up with a win-win application with usable security for the end-users. To that end, the requirement gathering and analysis phase should incorporate the usability aspect of security mechanisms. Besides, an evaluation of usable security should be done before the implementation of any e-Health applications.

LIMITATIONS OF THE STUDY

This study was designed to follow a security heuristic checklist from one source as a data collection method for each e-Health application considered. The evaluation process was completed beyond the estimated time of six days, two days for each e-Health application was dedicated, and the third and the last data received took three weeks. Finally, two experts were not able to finalize the evaluation process due to personal reasons and they were omitted from the study.

FUTURE WORKS

To deal with the current advance in system security breaches, threats, and risks of e-Health applications, the usability aspect of a security mechanism is an emerging topic for future research. Future researchers can deal with the development of an easy tool for the identification of usability issues of security early in the development stage; identification of factors for the cause of usable security challenges; and also security mechanisms challenges in e-Health applications.

ACKNOWLEDGMENT

This research received no specific grant from any funding agency in the public, commercial, or not-for-profit sectors. The researchers would like to express their gratitude to the study participants for their participation in this research.

REFERENCES

Abouelmehdi, K., Beni-Hessane, A., & Khaloufi, H. (2018). Big healthcare data: Preserving security and privacy. *Journal of Big Data*, 5(1), 1. doi:10.118640537-017-0110-7

Alshamari, M. (2016). A Review of Gaps between Usability and Security/Privacy. *International Journal of Communications, Network and Systems Sciences*, *9*(10), 413–429. doi:10.4236/ijcns.2016.910034

Anwar, F., & Shamim, A. (2011). Barriers in Adoption of Health Information Technology in Developing Societies. Food Chemistry -. *Food Chemistry*, *2*(8). doi:10.14569/IJACSA.2011.020808

Argaw, S. T., Troncoso-Pastoriza, J. R., Lacey, D., Florin, M.-V., Calcavecchia, F., Anderson, D., Burleson, W., Vogel, J.-M., O'Leary, C., Eshaya-Chauvin, B., & Flahault, A. (2020). Cybersecurity of Hospitals: Discussing the challenges and working towards mitigating the risks. *BMC Medical Informatics and Decision Making*, *20*(146), 146. doi:10.118612911-020-01161-7 PMID:32620167

Assa-Agyei, K., Olajide, F., & Lotfi, A. (2022). Security and Privacy Issues in IoT Healthcare Application for Disabled Users in Developing Economies [JITST]. *Journal of Internet Technology and Secured Transactions*, *10*(1), 770–779. doi:10.20533/jitst.2046.3723.2022.0095

Bourgeois, D., & Bourgeois, D. T. (2014). *Information Systems Security*. Information Systems for Business and Beyond.

Braa, J., Hanseth, O., Heywood, A., Mohammed, W., & Shaw, V. (2007). Developing Health Information Systems in Developing Countries: The Flexible Standards Strategy. *Management Information Systems Quarterly*, *31*(2), 381–402. doi:10.2307/25148796

Braz, C., Seffah, A., & M'Raihi, D. (2007). Designing a Trade-Off Between Usability and Security: A Metrics Based-Model. *Lecture Notes in Computer Science Human-Computer Interaction – INTERACT 2007*, (pp. 114-126). Springer. doi:10.1007/978-3-540-74800-7_9

Burton, L. C., Anderson, G. F., & Kues, I. W. (2004). Using electronic health records to help coordinate care. *The Milbank Quarterly*, *82*(3), 457–481. doi:10.1111/j.0887-378X.2004.00318.x PMID:15330973

Chowdhury, M., Jahan, S., Islam, R., & Gao, J. (2018). Malware Detection for Healthcare Data Security. In R. Beyah, B. Chang, Y. Li, & S. Zhu (Eds.), *Security and Privacy in Communication Networks. SecureComm 2018. Lecture Notes of the Institute for Computer Sciences, Social Informatics and Telecommunications Engineering* (Vol. 255). Springer.

Cranor, L. F., & Garfinkel, S. (2005). In F. L. Cranor & S. Garfinkel (Eds.), *Security and usability: Designing secure systems that people can use* (p. 21). O'Reilly Media.

Dalpiaz, F., Paja, E., & Giorgini, P. (2016). *Security requirements engineering: Designing secure socio-technical systems*. The MIT Press.

Evans R. S. (2016). Electronic Health Records: Then, Now, and in the Future. *Yearbook of medical informatics, Suppl 1*(Suppl 1), S48–S61. doi:10.15265/IYS-2016-s006

Eysenbach, G. (2001). What is e-health? *Journal of Medical Internet Research, 3*(2), E20. doi:10.2196/jmir.3.2.e20 PMID:11720962

Fernández-Alemán, J. L., Señor, I. C., Lozoya, P. Á., & Toval, A. (2013). Security and privacy in electronic health records: A systematic literature review. *Journal of Biomedical Informatics, 46*(3), 541–562. doi:10.1016/j.jbi.2012.12.003 PMID:23305810

Giansanti, D. (2021). Cybersecurity and the Digital-Health: The Challenge of This Millennium. *Health Care, 9*(62), 62. doi:10.3390/healthcare9010062 PMID:33440612

Hiranandani, V. (2011). Privacy and security in the digital age: Contemporary challenges and future directions. *International Journal of Human Rights, 15*(7), 1091–1106. doi:10.1080/13642987.2010.493360

Hof, H. J. (2012). *User-Centric IT Security - How to Design Usable Security Mechanisms*. Cornell University.

Hof, Hans-Joachim. (2013). Towards Enhanced Usability of IT Security Mechanisms-How to Design Usable IT Security Mechanisms Using the Example of Email Encryption. *International Journal on Advances in Security. 6.*

Hof, H.-J. (2015). *User-Centric IT Security - How to Design Usable Security Mechanisms*. Cornell University. https://arxiv.org/abs/1506.07167

Holvast, J. (2009) History of Privacy. In Donaldson MS, Lohr KN, (eds.) *Health Data in the Information Age: Use, Disclosure, and Privacy*. National Academies Press. https://www.ncbi.nlm.nih.gov/books/NBK236546/

Institute of Medicine. (2009). Committee on Health Research and the Privacy of Health Information. In Nass SJ, Levit LA, Gostin LO, (eds.) *Beyond the HIPAA Privacy Rule: Enhancing Privacy, Improving Health Through Research*. National Academies Press. https://www.ncbi.nlm.nih.gov/books/NBK9579/

ISO-9241-11. (2018). Ergonomic of Human-system interaction - Part 11:Usabililty: Definitions and concepts. ISO 9241-11:2018.

Jagadeesh, G., Balakumar, P., & Inamdar, M. (2013). The Critical Steps for Successful Research: The Research Proposal and Scientific Writing. *Journal of Pharmacology & Pharmacotherapeutics*, *4*(2), 130. doi:10.4103/0976-500x.110895

Jang-Jaccard, J., & Nepal, S. (2014). A survey of emerging threats in cybersecurity. *Journal of Computer and System Sciences*, *80*(5), 973–993. doi:10.1016/j.jcss.2014.02.005

Kirlappos, I., & Sasse, M. A. (2014). What Usable Security Means: Trusting and Engaging Users. *Lecture Notes in Computer Science Human Aspects of Information Security, Privacy, and Trust,* (pp. 69-78). doi:10.1007/978-3-319-07620-1_7

Kotzé. (2013). *Paula & Adebesin, Funmi & Greunen, Darelle & Foster, Rosemary*. Barriers and Challenges to the Adoption of E-Health Standards in Africa.

Kruse, C. S., Smith, B., Vanderlinden, H., & Nealand, A. (2017). Security Techniques for the Electronic Health Records. *Journal of Medical Systems*, *41*(8), 127. https://doi.org/10.1007/s10916-017-0778-4

Ksibi, S., Jaidi, F., & Bouhoula, A. (2022). *A Comprehensive Study of Security and Cyber-Security Risk Management within e-Health Systems: Synthesis, Analysis and a Novel Quantified Approach; Mobile Networks and Applications*. Springer. doi:10.1007/s11036-022-02042-1

Kulkarni, R. (2018). *Mitigating Security Issues While Improving Usability* [Thesis or Dissertation, University of Ohio, USA]. https://etd.ohiolink.edu/

Kurtinaityte, L. (2007). E-Health – The Usage of ICT Developing Health Care System : Multiple-Case Study of European Countries Denmark and Lithuania [Dissertation, Högskolan i Halmstad/Sektionen för Ekonomi och Teknik (SET), Sweden]. http://urn.kb.se/resolve?urn=urn:nbn:se:hh:diva-779

Lampson, B. (2009). Privacy and Security, Usable security. *Communications of the ACM*, *52*(11), 25–27. doi:10.1145/1592761.1592773

Mairiza, D., Zowghi, D., & Nurmuliani, N. (2010). An investigation into the notion of non-functional requirements. *Proceedings of the ACM Symposium on Applied Computing* (pp. 311-317). ACM. doi:10.1145/1774088.1774153

Mehrtak, M. (2021). Security challenges and solutions using healthcare cloud computing. *Journal of Medicine and Life*, *14*(4).

Metalidou, E., Marinagi, C., Trivellas, P., Eberhagen, N., Skourlas, C., & Giannakopoulos, G. (2014). The Human Factor of Information Security: Unintentional Damage Perspective. *Procedia: Social and Behavioral Sciences*, *147*, 424–428. doi:10.1016/j.sbspro.2014.07.133

Nielsen, J. (1994). How to Conduct a Heuristic Evaluation. *Nielsen Norman Group.* https://nngroup.com/articles/ten-usability-heuristics/

Nwokedi, Ugochi, Amunga, Beverly, & Rad, Bashari, Babak. (2016). Usability and Security in User Interface Design: A Systematic Literature Review. *International Journal of Information Technology and Computer Science.*, *8*, 72–80. doi:10.5815/ijitcs.2016.05.08

Punchoojit, L., & Hongwarittorrn, N. (2017). Usability Studies on Mobile User Interface Design Patterns: A Systematic Literature Review. *Advances in Human-Computer Interaction*, *2017*, 1–22. doi:10.1155/2017/6787504

Ross, J., Stevenson, F., & Lau, R. (2016). Factors that influence the implementation of e-health: A systematic review of systematic reviews (an update). *Implementation Science; IS*, *11*, 146. https://doi.org/10.1186/s13012-016-0510-7

Sasse, M. A., Brostoff, S., & Weirich, D. (2001). *BT Technology Journal*, *19*(3), 122–131.

Sasse, M. A., & Flechais, I. (2005). Usable Security: Why Do We Need It? How Do We Get It? In L. F. Cranor & S. Garfinkel (Eds.), *Security and Usability: Designing secure systems that people can use. (13 - 30).* O'Reilly.

Sittig, D. F., Belmont, E., & Singh, H. (2018). Improving the safety of health information technology requires shared responsibility: It is time we all step up. *Health Care*, *6*(1), 7–12. doi:10.1016/j.hjdsi.2017.06.004

Smith, J. (2010). Web Page Design: Heuristic Evaluation vs. User Testing. *International Journal of Industrial Ergonomics.*

Smith, L. (2019). *Fordney's Medical Insurance - E-Book - Ch2 Privacy, Security.* And HIPPA.

Stoneburner, G., Goguen, A., & Feringa, A. (2002). *Risk management guide for information technology systems.* Springer. doi:10.1023/a:1011902718709

Sulaiman, R., Sharma, D., Ma, W., & Tran, D. (2008). A Security Architecture for e-Health Services. *International Conference on Advanced Communication Technology*, *ICACT. 2.* (pp. 999 – 1004). IEEE. doi:. doi:10.1109/ICACT.2008.4493935

Harman, L., Flite, C., & Bond, K. (2012).. *The Virtual Mentor*, *14*(9), 712–719. doi:10.1001/virtualmentor.2012.14.9.stas1-1209

Whitman, M. E., & Mattord, H. J. (2011). *Principles of Information Security* (4th ed.). Cengage Learning.

Yee, K.-P. (2004). Aligning security and usability. *Security & Privacy, IEEE.*, *2*, 48–55. doi:10.1109/MSP.2004.64

Chapter 3
Applications of Information Systems and Data Security in Marketing Management

Arshi Naim
https://orcid.org/0000-0003-1325-6964
King Khalid University, Saudi Arabia

Hamed Alqahtani
King Khalid University, Saudi Arabia

Anandhavalli Muniasamy
https://orcid.org/0000-0001-8940-3954
King Khalid University, Saudi Arabia

Syeda Meraj Bilfaqih
King Khalid University, Saudi Arabia

Ruheena Mahveen
King Khalid University, Saudi Arabia

Reshma Mahjabeen
King Khalid University, Saudi Arabia

ABSTRACT

This chapter is an extended research work showing the role of applications of Information Systems (IS) and importance of data security in Marketing Management. This research focuses on the application of Decision Support Systems (DSS) models of what-if analysis (WIA) for customer relationship management (CRM) at Analysis, Operational and Directional (AOD) level and also shows the dependence on the

DOI: 10.4018/978-1-6684-6581-3.ch003

Information Success model (ISM). The second part of the chapter shows the role of data security in the growth of marketing for the companies. Hypothetical data are analyzed for (AOD) by three types of (WIA) to attain CRM and profit maximization. The results show that the analytical method based on the concepts of DSS can be used by all customer-oriented firms as a general model for achieving CRM and data security is a key to success for all firms.

INTRODUCTION

Customer relationship management (CRM) (Raab et al., 2016) is the branch of management that gives the scope of operational demonstration of relationship marketing and explains the characteristics of a customer, criterion and features for developing relationship between customers and firms, achieving customer loyalty and way of customers' retention, firms, therefore, apply CRM to explore prospects for their products and services, understand customer's requirements and their expectation for quality (Raab et al., 2016) (Peppers & Rogers, 2004). CRM is particularly regarded as the firm's efforts to develop and retain customers through increased satisfaction and loyalty. DSS-based CRM systems have been applied in many business areas, and R&D is continuing to contribute to its expansion (Naim et al., 2021).

Marketing management is a process of controlling the marketing aspects, setting the goals of a company, organizing the plans step by step, taking decisions for the firm, and executing them to get the maximum turn over by meeting the consumers' demands.

There are four types of marketing mix also termed as four Ps of marketing. The four Ps are product, price, place, and promotion. They are an example of a "marketing mix," or the combined tools and methodologies used by marketers to achieve their marketing objectives (Chan & Ip, 2011).

Marketing management is especially important for smaller businesses because it gives them a level footing to compete with larger players in the field. Thorough customer research, creative campaigns and marketing strategies and positive branding can go a long way in providing a brand with an edge over its competition (Grover et al., 2018).

Marketing Management has the responsibility to perform many functions in the field of marketing such as planning, organizing, directing, motivating, coordinating and controlling. All these function aim to achieve the marketing goals.

IS application is a collection of interrelated elements that work collaboratively to convert data into information that is used to support various organizations activities including control, planning, forecasting, decision making, coordination, and operational activities (Grover et al., 2018) (Naim, 2022a) and DSS is one of its important application that helps in the above tasks and besides, DSS can help organization's employees and managers in visualizing complex subjects, create new products, and problems analysis. Nowadays IS applications in the business area can be categorized into different types such as support of business operations or support of managerial decision making (Naim, 2022a). Any ideal organization applies six major applications of IS such as Transaction Processing System (TPS), Office Automation System (OAS), Knowledge Work System (KWS), Management Information System (MIS), Executive Support System (ESS), Decision Support System (DSS) (Naim, 2021) (Filip, 2020) (Palmatier & Martin, 2019). Figure 1 shows the types and basic information about the IS applications.

This research is based on the application of (WIA) which is the DSS model-based analysis for three levels of (AOD) of CRM. DSS (WIA) is a computer-based application aiding in the decision making process for management related areas such as SCM, ERP, CRM, etc. (WIA) aids CRM in managing customers' inquiries and also in attracting, retaining, developing, and identifying customers and figure 2 gives a framework of DSS (WIA) for how decisions are supported for different management decisions (Palmatier & Martin, 2019) (Naim, 2022b).

Figure 1. Types of IS Applications (Palmatier & Martin, 2019)

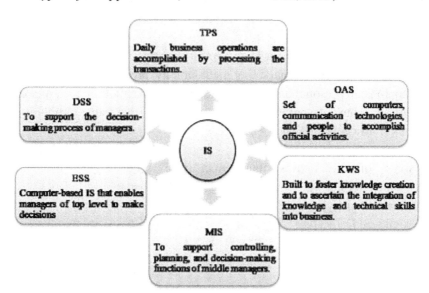

Figure 2. DSS(WIA) supporting the decisions (Putra et al., 2020)

What if Analysis (WIA)		
Phases	Tools	Management Disciplines
Intelligence	SBWIA/GSWIA/DBWIA	Expert Systems/CRM
Design	SBWIA/GSWIA/DBWIA	Expert Systems/CRM
Choose	SBWIA/GSWIA/DBWIA	Expert Systems/CRM
Implementation	SBWIA/GSWIA/DBWIA	CRM/SCM

Data security is the process of safeguarding digital information throughout its entire life cycle to protect it from corruption, theft, or unauthorized access. It covers everything—hardware, software, storage devices, and user devices; access and administrative controls; and organizations' policies and procedures (Martin & Murphy, 2017).

Marketers should care about Data Security for three reasons such as trust is a cornerstone of the inbound marketing methodology, prospects and customers trust marketers to keep personal data secure and proper protection of customer data.

There are many reasons for the leak in the data that cause problems to the marketers (Putra et al., 2020).

- Some of the causes that affect data security are given below: Accidental Sharing
- Overworked Cybersecurity Teams
- Employee Data Theft
- Ransomware
- Bad Password Hygiene
- Bribery

- Too Much Data Access
- Phishing Emails
- Fraud
- Denial

This research paper is segmented into six parts; the first part gives an introduction and the second part covers the historical aspects of concepts used in this paper and previous studies showing the contribution of DSS (WIA) in management in general and specifically in CRM. The third part gives the details on conceptual hypothesis and Research methodology, the fourth part covers the major explanation of the research procedure and implications in Discussion. In the fifth and sixth part results and findings are illustrated followed by a conclusion.

This research paper shows the application of DSS (WIA) in customer-oriented firms at three levels (AOD) for achieving profit and building relationships and eventually impacting CRM by the use of hypothetical data. Also this chapter covers the relevance of data security in marketing management.

LITERATURE REVIEW

Before the 1960s, the IS role was simple, basically, were used to achieve the goals of electronic data processing (EDP), such as accounting and transaction processing. EDP is defined as the use of a computer to perform various processes on data including summarizing, classifying, manipulating, and recording. EDP is also called transaction processing systems (TPS) (Esteve, 2017) (Appelbaum et al., 2017).

In the 1960s, other functions were added to IS which were for processing of data into useful informative reports, and MIS was therefore introduced. MIS gave new roles to the managers, they started to use IS for making decisions and developing business applications with the IS contribution (Naim, 2022b).

By the 1970s, the IS reports produced by MIS were not enough to satisfy the management decision-making needs that were when (DSS) emerged and it provided computer-based interaction and specialized support for managers and end-users to facilitate decision-making processes (Naim, 2022b). End users now could support their job requirements by using their own computing resources; they did not need to wait for a centralized corporate information services department to provide indirect support. In later years EIS and AI were techniques introduced with different advantages and scope. ES and KMS gave a new role to IS in the late 90s and 1990 ERP emerged for corporate resource planning and allocation (Naim, 2022b). In the same era, internet growth started that gave a new significance to all the IS applications and DSS applications became very popular in the decision making process in management systems particularly for CRM (Naim, 2022b) (Appelbaum et al., 2017) (Pavoine et al., 2009).

Past researches have shown how firm's use CRM for motivating their employees to essentially develop customer-focused thinking (Pavoine et al., 2009) and here IS has played an important role as a technology solution. In the past, researchers have focused on methods of IS affecting customer-oriented firms for CRM profitability and also formulated models such as the CRM profitability model from relationship marketing and system efficiency perspective (Naim, 2022b) (Pavoine et al., 2009) (Naim, 2021).

Previous studies have shown the importance of using software applications and technology for different types of management disciplines such as SCM, ERP, or CRM, but the expected results for CRM are not achieved because of its qualitative nature. However, CRM continued to apply IS applications for various purposes and identified different impact factors of IS applications for different levels of CRM but DSS is one application found to be most effective working for the achievement of CRM objectives (Naim, 2022b) (Pavoine et al., 2009) (Naim, 2021).

The Cybersecurity checking began in the 1970s when researcher Bob Thomas created a computer program called Creeper that could move across ARPANET's network. The true birth of cybersecurity occurred in the 1970s. This began with a project called The Advanced Research Projects Agency Network (ARPANET). This was the connectivity network developed prior to the internet itself.

Security relies on five major elements: confidentiality, integrity, availability, authenticity, and non-repudiation. The principles of security are Confidentiality, integrity, and availability (CIA) that define the basic building blocks of any good security program when defining the goals for network, asset, information, and/or information system security and are commonly referred to collectively as the CIA triad (Chatterjee et al., 2021).

The evolution of customer data protection started when Web cookies were invented in 1994 to enhance the user experience of the internet, but they quickly began to be used for marketing purposes as well. Furthermore, in 2012, Apple introduced its IDFA, a tool for the targeting and evaluation of advertising. These developments, however, have also enabled third-party actors to take advantage of personal data (Morse et al., 2011).

The past research suggests that only around 33 percent of Americans believe that companies are using their personal data responsibly. As a result of growing concern around data usage, government regulations have begun to limit the use of customer data; the European Union's GDPR was the first in 2018, but others—including the CCPA, the California Privacy Rights Act (CPRA), and the Delaware Online Privacy and Protection Act have followed.

European governments were coming under pressure to address data protection vulnerabilities and in 2016 launched the General Data Protection Regulation (GDPR), replacing the previous Data Protection Directive (Naim, 2022c).

This GDPR has important implications for digital marketers, because it outlines how to collect, store, and use any user or customer data that they collect. GDPR applies to companies operating in the EU. Other jurisdictions have different data protection guidelines, so be sure you understand your obligations if marketing in those areas. For example, if the company retains data on residents of California, firm must comply with the California Consumer Privacy Act (CCPA), which came into effect on January 1, 2020 (Shey et al., 2013).

Previous studies have shown the relationship of DSS for CRM but this research paper gives an analysis of the application of DSS (WIA) for showing the results for CRM at all three levels and suggests the same model for any customer-oriented firms for their applications (Naim, 2022d).

Research also presents the dependence of ISM with CRM for building brand image, increasing sales, strategic planning but this research paper also covers the aspects of ISM for CRM and how both can be considered for providing the research findings. Also this chapter will fill the gap from past to present studies while presenting discussions on relevance of data security in marketing management.

THEORETICAL PERSPECTIVES RESEARCH METHODOLOGY

CRM provides its services to firms at three levels; Analytical, Operational, and Directional levels (AOD), and each level benefits the firm in some way that eventually contributes to achieving CRM. (WIA) facilitates in building these levels and offers decision-making solutions to structured, semi-structured, and unstructured decisions for these levels. Figure 3 depicts the research framework used for this paper.

Three hypothetical examples are taken for showing the results, DSS decision-making models are applied to these three examples for all three CRM's levels and results are analyzed from (WIA) applications. The results are measured for three levels (AOD) by (WIA) and show its impact on CRM. To understand how the information from these three examples can be helpful for CRM, Delone, and McLean's perspective of ISM can be referred (O'Brien & Marakas, 2005). The ISM has been treated as a major issue of management research for any type of service for measuring satisfaction. DeLone and McLean have taken six major categories of measures of IS application like DSS success which are seen to form an integrated whole (Arnott, 2004). These measures are System Quality (SQ), Information Quality (IQ), Service Quality (SRQ), resulting to use and user satisfaction and finally to individual impact, and organizational impact and all these measures are a subpart of three levels (AOD) of CRM (Arnott, 2004). IQ, SQ, and SRQ measure A, SQ, and SRQ measure O, and SRQ measure D. Figure 5 depict how ISM is used in our study for preparing the criteria for measuring AOD. These criteria are used as inputs for decision-making processes by (WIA) based such as Scenario-based, Goal seeking, and Data-based for CRM. These criteria and information are extracted from the hypothetical data for three examples submitted for different services for three months (from March to May 2020) and show how the target of CRM can be achieved in the next month June 2020 for all three AOD levels using a classification of Information Success model.

Figure 3. Research Framework: Role of WIA in CRM

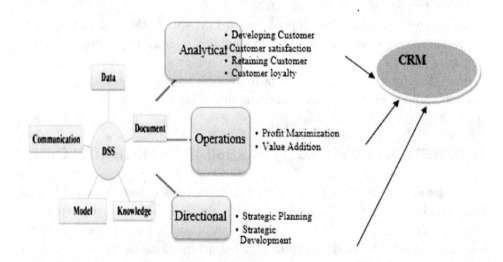

Figure 4. ISM by Delone and McLean (Kaiser et al., 2003)

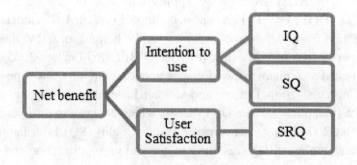

Figure 5. Criteria for ISM for (AOD)

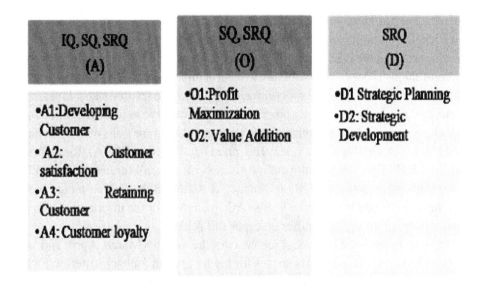

Figure 6. CRM scope (Watson, 2018)

RESEARCH PROCEDURE

General scenario: Three sets of criteria are developed for each level as mentioned in figure 5, referring to these criteria hypothetical data for three examples are created and categorized in the DSS framework to find out how DSS (WIA) can facilitate the decision-making process from structure to unstructured for each CRM. It is important to notice that (WIA) makes only recommendations not the results in absolute terms; it facilitates the decision-making process but does not force to implementation of a particular scenario. As mentioned above there are three types of (WIA); Scenario based (SBWIA), Goal Seeking (GSWIA), and Data-Based (DBWIA), for the three levels of CRM aligned with Information success models, all three types of (WIA) can be implemented for showing its impact on CRM. Below given tables below show the three Examples for three levels (AOD) aligned for the information success model, criteria used by three different types of (WIA).

Example-1 shows the analytical scenario for the month's March, April, and May for A1, A2, A3, A4, and the firm strives for higher growth for each criterion for the month of June in table 1. The firm can use SBWIA and while elaborating the target for each criterion and set a scenario to achieve that.

Table 1. Analytical by SBWIA

IQ,SQ,SRA (A) by SBWIA				
Criteria	Example-1			
	March	April	May	June [Target]
A1: Developing Customer	4000	5000	5500	8000
A2: Customer Satisfaction	4000	5000	6000	8000
A3: Retaining Customer	4000	5000	5500	8000
A4: Customer Loyalty	4000	5000	5500	8000

Table 2 depicts the profit for the example-2 for three months and by using DBWIA, the firm can predict O1 and O2 for the month of June and coming months. These figures are shown in sales and DBWIA helps in manipulating data for achieving the target sales. Example-2 also shows the variation as an increase and decrease in profit and value addition that usually occur in real situations so how DBWIA facilitated in predicting the Operational level CRM for all the criteria O1 and O2. It is important to mention that DBWIA at the operational level only provides values for prediction but possible decision-making analysis has to be conducted through SBWIA or GSWIA.

Table 2. Operation by DBWIA

SQ, SRQ (O) Analyzed by DBWIA			
Criteria	**Example 2**		
	March	**April**	**May**	**June [Target]**
O1: Profit Maximization	5000	6000	5500	8000
O2: Value Addition	5000	4500	6000	8000

Table 3. Directional by GBWIA

SRQ(D) Analyzed by GBWIA			
Criteria	**Example**		
	2010-13	**2013-16**	**2016-19**	**2020-23**
D1: Strategic Planning	4000	5000	5500	8000
D2: Strategic Development	4000	5000	6000	8000

Table 3 shows the directional level in CRM explains the strategic achievement for the products, services, and policies of the form in general. Usually, Directional level CRM focuses on short to long-term achievements, below given table shows two criteria such as D1 and D2 at Directional level CRM and measured by GSWIA. Goals are set for 2020-23 and analyzed from 2010-13 for criteria D1 and D2. Usually, data set for this level can be extracted from sales inferred through brand effectiveness or brand image.

Data collected from these examples are analyzed by (WIA) for decision making for achieving CRM for all these three levels and recommendations are made in the results section. (WIA) suggests which area is weak and the firm's need to concentrate on changing their strategies for meeting their goals. In above given three examples (WIA) stresses the prompt changes with minimum efforts and also provides assumptions for future improvements and meeting the target for the month of June for all three levels for CRM. (WIA) is applied at three levels and presents how targets can be met by supporting strongly the tools of decision-making processes. From the above given three examples in tables 2, 3, and 4 customer-oriented firms can refer (WIA) for AOD and can achieve the following benefits specified as criteria for AOD in CRM and ISM. Below given table 5 gives a comprehensive view and derived benefits from interrelationships between CRM, ISM, AOD, and (WIA) but details on findings from above mentioned hypothetical data in three examples are discussed in the results' part and table 4 explains all benefits in detail aligned criteria of AOD in the result section.

Table 4. Derived Benefits from (WIA) models for AOD

CRM level and ISM	DSS Model based What if Analysis	Benefits Achieved
IQ, SQ, SRQ (A)	[Analyzed by SBWIA]	
A1:Developing Customer		Customer Orientation (CO)
A2:Customer satisfaction		Information Quality Perception (IQP)
A3:Retaining Customer		Value addition in Services (VAS)
A4: Customer loyalty		Supporting customers and Grievance handing. (SCGH)
SQ, SRQ (O)	[Analyzed by DBWIA]	
O1:Profit Maximization		Achieving profit through sales (PS)
O2: Value Addition		Value addition in Services (VAS)
SRQ (D)	[Analyzed by GSWIA]	
D1: Strategic Planning		Enhancing brand value and increase systems efficiency (SE)
D2: Strategic Development		Performance based policies for long run and offer systems support (SSP)

DISCUSSION

Most of the service-oriented firms focus on achieving CRM by having customer interaction and creating an opportunity for increasing satisfaction level, improving retention, increasing revenue or profit, attain brand loyalty, strengthen brand value, etc. CRM helps service firms in particular and all other businesses, in general, to optimize customer relationships by integrating at the AOD level.

4.1 The CRM Advantages for customer-oriented firms: CRM reduces the time and cost to deploy integrated advantages with a comprehensive set of solutions based on the principles of services and types of levels. These benefits help inefficient business operations, receiving updated and accurate information, vision for successful business applications (Aronson et al., 2005). Figure 6 gives the scope of CRM for customer-oriented firms that cover five major areas as given above.

(WIA) provides computer-aided decision-making solutions to CRM for (AOD) and helps in getting the following key benefits. Below given table 5 give the key benefits that can be received by the CRM with an application of (WIA) and figure 7 explains the framework of WIA.

DSS (WIA) offers the advantages to CRM and that results in many benefits to the firm in general such as achieving competitive advantages, identifying business opportunities, receiving quick customers' responses, increasing sales, knowing demand value and customers' expectations. Figure 7 shows the framework of

DSS (WIA) that can be applied for user interfaces for receiving users' reviews and expectations by its three types (Sharkey & Acton, 2012).

4.2 Types of Decision-Support Systems: There are major two types of DSS, data-based, and model-based. (WIA) are a model-based DSS and below given figure 8 shows the basic types of DSS (Jia et al., 2017; Naim, Hussain, Naveed et al, 2019; Polkowski et al., 2012; Sigala, 2018). Figure 8 provides the list of DSS and figure 9 shows the process of decision making within the DSS.

Table 5. DSS (WIA) Solutions to CRM Key Benefits

DSS (WIA) offering solutions to CRM	Key Benefits Achieved
	Identifying Customers' preferences.
	Integrate all Management services
	Increase Productivity and Revenue by providing customer vision
	Achieving Customer satisfaction and Retention
	Strengthen Brand image and increasing Brand loyalty

Figure 7. WIA Framework for User Interface (Naim & Khan, 2021)

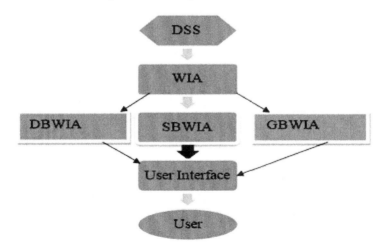

Figure 8. Types of DSS (Alt & Puschmann, 2004; Naim, 2021; Watanabe & Hobo, 2004)

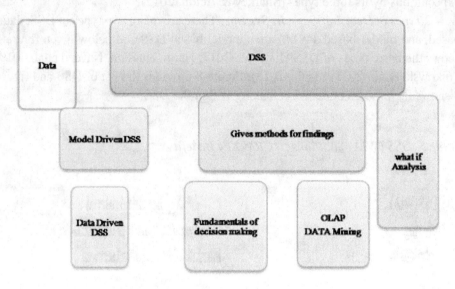

Figure 9. DSS Decision Making Process within (Naim, Khan, Hussain et al, 2019)

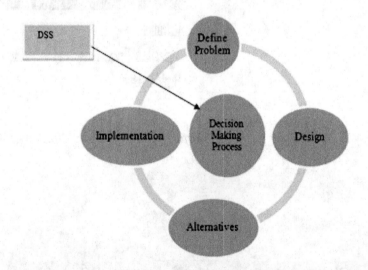

The philosophy is that DSS provides a strong and easy to use interface to the users based on (WIA) figure 9 shows the decision-making process that takes place within the DSS (Delone & McLean, 2003) that are accounted by (WIA) for processing decisions for external disciplines like CRM.

4.3 Data Privacy for Marketers: Data privacy has become a major concern for companies, especially now that firms have access to huge amounts of customer data. When companies fail to adequately protect the integrity and privacy of their customer data, it can lead to serious reputational damage, as well as legal and financial sanctions (Naim, 2022d).

Understandably, many companies have been concerned about their General Data Protection Regulation (GDPR) obligations in recent years. However, even if your company operates in markets where GDPR doesn't apply, firms still need to be aware of their obligations to protect customer data. Mining customer data offers great opportunities for marketers to develop highly personalized digital marketing campaigns, but marketers still need to apply best practices for data protection (Cuthbertson & Laine, 2003; Foss et al., 2008).

There can be 10 guidelines to explain the key principles of data privacy for the firms in marketing management. These ten guidelines are given below (Collins, 2001; Friday et al., 2018):

1. Use a Gold Standard data protection approach: See which areas in firm's digital strategy require the most stringent data protection policies, and use this approach as firm's "Gold Standard" in all areas.
2. Step through the personal data journey: Identify roles that are needed to ensure data protection at all stages. What can a firm do to protect the data subject at each stage of the journey?
3. Make the firm privacy policy a market differentiator: Demonstrate that companies are taking privacy concerns more seriously than competitors are. Show that data protection is a core value for the business.
4. Be clear with options and opting in: make sure people can clearly opt in and opt out and give those options for communications.
5. Revisit email lists: Check if the consumers need to be updated and work on the optimization strategies.
6. Keep up to date: Watch out for emerging privacy concerns (such as cookies or tracking pixels) and be ready to address them before have to.
7. Consider using data relationship management (DRM) programs. These programs can help the firms to better understand the different types of data and the relationships between them. This can also help firms to demonstrate data-protection accountability.
8. Stay up to date with technology advances: As new technologies (such as the metaverse, AI, and the Internet of Things, for example) emerge, new data privacy concerns arise.
9. Develop ethical awareness: Cultivate a culture where personal data is cherished and protected.

10. Be prepared for contextual advertising: The move away from cookies and from third-party to first-party data will see the emergence of contextual advertising, with corresponding data privacy concerns.

4.4 Principles of data protection & privacy: There are six general data protection principles which are given below (Eom, 2020; Friday et al., 2018; Naim & Alahmari, 2020):

1. Lawful, fair, and transparent processing
2. Purpose limitation
3. Data minimization
4. Data accuracy
5. Data retention
6. Data security, integrity, and confidentiality

4.5 *Responsibilities of Data privacy:* There are three major responsibilities of Data privacy in marketing management such as accountability, lawful basis and opportunity (Rupnik & Kukar, 2007).

RESULTS

The study covers the application of (WIA) for CRM for three levels of AOD using ISM. This study is based on a hypothetical data set that tried to explain how the DSS model-based can help in CRM for AOD. Table 5 shows the benefits of WIA for AOD.

The results show the high degree of relevance and dependence on (WIA) for three examples. Examples in Table 6 shows the role of SBWIA in successfully predicting the values for the month of June at an analytical level for four criteria which are developing customers, achieving satisfaction, retention, and loyalty.

Highlighted cells show the successful application of SBWIA for A1, A2, A3, and A4. Example-2 focuses on operational benefits of CRM that are expressed in sale and revenue therefore DBWIA is here and Table 7 shows the variation in target and how DBWIA can help firms to know the areas where they need to work to achieve the target value that will result in achieving level O of CRM. The results show the variation for each month against the target value required to be achieved in the month of June, therefore after applying DBWIA firms can get the variation at each level and needed values too for meeting the target as shown in table 8 for O1 and O2 criteria.

Table 6. Details on Benefits from (WIA) for AOD (Edwards et al., 2020)

4.3 CRM (CO)	CO refers to the commitment of the firm to identify and satisfy customer concerns and develop more customers through providing quality services. SBWIA gives the situation like quality for longer period of time and meet demand for new services about the quality and measures if more customers are developed for the particular services or not. SBWIA also explains how the given target can be met through elaborating the contingent approach. Results sections shows how A1 grows by using DSS model based SBWIA.
4.4 CRM (IQP)	SBWIA facilitates at A level of CRM to measure if customers are satisfied or not for that SBWIA creates a scenario for customers related to quality, reliability of information and after sales services as well then make a target for achieving it after implementation of this scenario. SBWIA takes the data from the previous month to show the variations to meet the target.
4.5 CRM (VAS)	Customer retention is the results of customer satisfaction which can be achieved through values added services, technology has played a great role in adding values and increasing retention rate. SBWIA creates a scenario for the past data for customer retention rate and based on that gives the variation from the expected retention target. Results provide clear understanding through scenario analysis for hypothetical data for example -1. CRM (VAS) is also a benefit for level O2 which measures the values addition in quantitative terms and it is measured by DBWIA. The results will show its impact in Exmaple-2.
4.6 CRM (SCGH)	To achieve customer loyalty, there are many factors to be considered by CRM; therefore scenario for A4 needs to refer many dimensions such as providing services of good quality on time, listening to the customer complaints, their reactions and eventually attaining customers' loyalty. There are some philosophies that give a direct relation between customer reactions to customer loyalty in relation to CRM performance for identifying the scenario for A4, SBWIA considers many few situations such as reaction to overall results of the customer's awareness, appraisal, and psychological feedback to the utilization experience with the product or service. As customer loyalty is commonly acknowledged as one of the most useful measurements of level A of CRM as it measures profitability, satisfaction and retention. Results for Example-1 shows for A4 achieve its target while comparing from past data to expected data for the scenario created.
4.7 CRM (PS)	At the operational level of CRM and from an ISM perspective, business process improvement that assures efficiency and excellence of enterprise operations is an important to be measured, therefore DBWIA is used to analyze previous months' sales and revenue and based on past trends predict the future sales and revenue for the firms. In this analysis CRM needs DSS model based approach for marketing, sales and earning maximum profits for the firm.
4.8 CRM (SE)	ISM and CRM work together at D level to build strategic planning for the firm where the major focus is brand loyalty, building brand image and strengthening the brand therefore GSWIA is the best DSS model to be implemented which sets the target and then make a plan for achieving it. GBWIA helps in decision making process and make possible recommendations for variations. Example-3 shows how data at D1 levels are aided by GSWIA for the successful of strategic planning. This process included many predetermined goals, parameters such as cost, time, function and efficiency in which they should be achieved. The assumption on which GSWIA works for D1 is that the relationships between CRM efficiency and customer reaction are managed by all CRM activities like customer reaction, perception, loyalty, retention and all contribute in strategic planning.
4.9 CRM (SSP)	D2 level of CRM is measured by GSWIA by measuring the performance of the firms based on what strategies were developed to attain that level. Also GSWIA studies the previous data for D2 and identifies that successful strategies bring more profits to the firm and contribute in customer satisfaction. Firms use GSWIA to measure of the D2 CRM for systems' performance and assume if the system has been implemented and adopted successfully all criteria such as resource utilization; reliability, response time, and ease of terminal use; data accuracy, reliability, completeness, system flexibility, and ease of use; consistency of the user interface, quality of documentation, and sometimes, quality and maintainability be able to reap its benefits.

Table 7. SBWIA for Level A of CRM

Changing Cells:	Current Values:	Developing customer	Customer satisfaction	Retaining customer	Customer loyalty
B4	4000	4000	4000	4000	4000
C4	5000	5000	5000	5000	5000
D4	5500	5500	5500	5500	5500
E4		8000			
B5	4000	4000	4000	4000	4000
C5	5000	5000	5000	5000	5000
D5	6000	6000	6000	6000	6000
E5			8000		
B6	4000	4000	4000	4000	4000
C6	5000	5000	5000	5000	5000
D6	5500	5500	5500	5500	5500
E6	8000	8000	8000	8000	8000

Table 8. DBWIA for Level O

	SQ, SRQ (O)[Analyzed by DBWIA]								
Criteria	**Example-2**					Variation to the target		Applied DBWIA	
	March	April	May	June[Target]		March	April	May	June 01	June 02
O1:Profit Maximization	5000	6000	5500	8000		3000	2000	2500	8000	
O2: Value Addition	5000	4500	6000	8000		3000	3500	2000		
										8000

Table 9. GSWIA for Level D

	SRQ (D) [Analyzed by GSWIA]					
Criteria	**Example-3**					
	2010-13	2013-16	2016-19	Average variation	Missing target to achieve	
D1: Strategic Planning	4000	5000	5500	4833.333		2020-2023
					-335544	8000
D2: Strategic Development	4000	5000	6000	5000		
					-335544	8000

The analysis of the measurement model indicates that the proposed (WIA) has a relatively high degree of validity and reliability. These measures can be used to evaluate what influences CRM profitability and strategies that can be a vision for the decision making process. Table 9 shows a successful application of GSWIA for the directional level of CRM. GSWIA is a backward assessment method that explains the missing value for the target value as given in the table for two criteria D1 and D2. It is important to notify that strategies do not work for months rather than be analyzed for a minimum of three years to five years therefore values for directional analysis are expressed in three years' timeline and GSWIA gives the results for 2020 to 2023 which means that target should be achieved in these three years. In this study, we identified the criteria that influence CRM and the use of

ISM for customer satisfaction and profitability measured by (WIA) which proved to be intuitively appealing and reliable.

Private companies are now following suit. In January 2020, Google announced that it planned to phase out support for third-party cookies in Chrome within two years. Chrome will be the third browser to make this restriction (Edwards et al., 2020). Apple has already done so, which means that more than 85 percent of the browser market will block third-party cookies starting next year. Apple has also begun to limit the sharing of digital identifiers with intelligent tracking prevention in Safari, and the IDFA has required users to opt in to let advertisers see their data since April 2021. Because customer protection is a key, these developments will have a significant impact on digital marketing and should therefore be welcomed. But companies that are no longer able to personalize their outreach to customers at scale may have to spend around 10 to 20 percent more on marketing and sales to achieve their current level of returns.

A New DRM Approach (Balmer & Burghausen, 2019)

Many large firms have already created a strategy to ensure compliance with current regulations, and some may even have started to devise a comprehensive first-party data strategy. However, current best practices for data management may not be sufficient in the new data ecosystem.

To be sustainable and effective, companies may consider rooting their approach to data in a stronger relationship with customers that is built on trust and a true exchange of value. This DRM approach has four key components: data invitation, a data security center, data dialogue, and a data value proposition (Naim, 2022e).

Data Invitation (Asemi et al., 2011)

Today's privacy communications typically take the form of jargon-filled notifications. These notifications feature a pronounced "accept," and customers may have little idea of what they are agreeing to. Until recently, the "accept" prompt on a website was the main interaction by which a customer opted into tracking. In today's data landscape, however, companies will need to take more responsibility (Naim et al., 2021). Apple's push for more overt language around granting data permissions, for example, may move customers away from blindly clicking "accept." These new standards are intended to make it easy for customers to comprehend, and thwart, tracking by advertisers.

A fully permission-based relationship should stand up to current and future regulations, as well as satisfy questions from skeptical customers. As citizens and customer-advocacy groups become more aware of and involved in issues around data privacy, building transparency based trust will likely require a comprehensive, documented permission process (Naim, 2022f; Paryasto et al., 2014; Xu et al., 2019).

Best Practices Around Data Invitation
Include the Following (Naim, 2022g)

- Leverage an omni-channel approach to ensure the data invitation is delivered
- Use pre-prompts. Explain the potential benefits of giving permission for data sharing before asking customers to make their decision.

A Data Security Center (Shao et al., 2021)

The second tenet of managing data relationships is the creation and promotion of a customer-facing data security center. This is not about changing or updating security protocols; it is about using transparent communication about existing data-protection measures to build trust and gain customer *consent. This security center should have the following three core elements:*

- *A granular list of data that are being collected with a description of how they are being used*
- *A preference center that enables customers to opt out of any future data collection or usage*
- *Rich, regularly updated content around data governance and protection*

In today's data ecosystem, every company is fast becoming a tech company. Data centers are therefore vital to demonstrate a commitment to creating and maintaining comprehensive data-protection protocols.

Data Dialogue (Popescul & Genete, 2016)

Much like customer relationship management, data relationship management requires an ongoing dialogue. In addition to increasing transparency, continued engagement acts as a reminder that the company both constantly strives to improve best practices for data security and uses customers' data to improve their overall experience of a product or service.

A large financial institution recently ran an email campaign that promoted its practices on data security. The email directed users to a robust data-security and preference center on the company's website. This campaign enabled users to set their preferences, but it also built trust, which made the campaign an important brand-building exercise.

Data Value Proposition (Naim, 2022h)

Customer value is at the core of the data relationship, and a data relationship with a clearly defined and articulated value proposition will help ensure that customers stay engaged. Our research indicates that around two-thirds of customers would be happy to share their data, or would consider sharing data, if they got something of value in return.

Improving the customer experience can be another way to create a compelling value proposition. Data can be used to improve customer experience by helping customers find what they are looking for more quickly, and by directing them to the new products and services that are likely to be most relevant to them. While collaborative filters might work without personally identifiable information, advanced modeling that uses these data can help bring surprise and delight to an otherwise flat customer experience.

Information about customer preferences around call times and communication channels can also be used to ensure that customers receive communications at the time and in the format that they prefer. Shopping preferences can also be used to tailor suggested services; loyal online shoppers could be offered video-call access to a style consultant (Balachandar & Chinnaiyan, 2019).

There is evidence that customers prefer a personalized customer experience and may, therefore, be willing be provide data in return (Leonard, 2014). Firms have seen a decrease of up to 60 percent in customer churn as a result of a data-driven approach to customer experience. To increase the potential likelihood of customers opting in, companies should consider regularly reinforcing the customer-experience value those customers is getting in exchange for their data (Leonard, 2014).

Delivering on the new data relationship requires the right people, processes, and technology. Changes in policy and overall approach may not be enough to fully implement the new data relationship. Instead, companies may benefit from ensuring that they have the right people, processes, and technology to shift mindsets and embed these changes throughout their operations (Leonard, 2014).

Incremental changes are unlikely to be enough. The DRM strategy and its implementation should be central to the company's marketing function, which will require a fundamental shift in team structure and ways of working.

CONCLUSION

CRM is one of the most important areas in management and DSS (WIA) is one of the relevant methods for the decision-making process. This research presents a general scenario for any customer-oriented firm for using (WIA) impacting CRM where this model facilitates in developing customer satisfaction, retention, loyalty and also to contribute in sales and revenue along with the measuring the effectiveness of strategic planning for future growth.

When consent has been given and the appropriate security protocols are in place, there are instances when companies may want to use customer data securely in external platforms such as advertising exchanges. In these cases, appropriate portions of the company's total data lake should be transferred to a data clean room to ensure that no identifiable data are shared with partners. In addition, companies could consider a technology-enabled data map of all customer data points, along with information about how the data were collected and what consent was given when the data were collected. A consent management platform can help to ensure that the necessary permissions are captured, stored, and managed at each step of the customer journey. Without a platform of this sort, companies can be at risk of both losing (or misusing) data and being the subject of legal proceedings.

REFERENCES

Alt, R., & Puschmann, T. (2004, January). Successful practices in customer relationship management. In 37th Annual Hawaii International Conference on System Sciences, 2004. Proceedings of the (pp. 9-pp). IEEE. 10.1109/HICSS.2004.1265415

Anandkumar, R., Dinesh, K., & Ahmed, J. (2022). Securing e-Health application of cloud computing using hyperchaotic image encryption framework. Computers and Electrical Engineering, 100. doi:10.1016/j.compeleceng.2022.107860

Appelbaum, D., Kogan, A., Vasarhelyi, M., & Yan, Z. (2017). Impact of business analytics and enterprise systems on managerial accounting. *International Journal of Accounting Information Systems*, *25*, 29–44. doi:10.1016/j.accinf.2017.03.003

Arnott, D. (2004). Decision support systems evolution: Framework, case study and research agenda. *European Journal of Information Systems*, *13*(4), 247–259. doi:10.1057/palgrave.ejis.3000509

Aronson, J. E., Liang, T. P., & MacCarthy, R. V. (2005). *Decision support systems and intelligent systems* (Vol. 4). Pearson Prentice-Hall.

Asemi, A., Safari, A., & Zavareh, A. A. (2011). The role of management information system (MIS) and Decision support system (DSS) for manager's decision making process. *International Journal of Business and Management*, *6*(7), 164–173. doi:10.5539/ijbm.v6n7p164

Balachandar, S., & Chinnaiyan, R. (2019). Centralized reliability and security management of data in internet of things (IoT) with rule builder. In *International Conference on Computer Networks and Communication Technologies* (pp. 193-201). Springer. 10.1007/978-981-10-8681-6_19

Balmer, J. M., & Burghausen, M. (2019). Marketing, the past and corporate heritage. *Marketing Theory*, *19*(2), 217–227. doi:10.1177/1470593118790636

Chan, S. L., & Ip, W. H. (2011). A dynamic decision support system to predict the value of customer for new product development. *Decision Support Systems*, *52*(1), 178–188. doi:10.1016/j.dss.2011.07.002

Chatterjee, S., Chaudhuri, R., & Vrontis, D. (2021). Examining the global retail apocalypse during the COVID-19 pandemic using strategic omnichannel management: A consumer' data privacy and data security perspective. *Journal of Strategic Marketing*, *29*(7), 617–632. doi:10.1080/0965254X.2021.1936132

Collins, K. (2001). *Analytical CRM: Driving Profitable Customer Relationships*. Strategic Planning.

Cuthbertson, R., & Laine, A. (2003). The role of CRM within retail loyalty marketing. Journal of Targeting. *Measurement and Analysis for Marketing*, *12*(3), 290–304. doi:10.1057/palgrave.jt.5740116

Delone, W. H., & McLean, E. R. (2003). The DeLone and McLean model of information systems success: A ten-year update. *Journal of Management Information Systems*, *19*(4), 9–30. doi:10.1080/07421222.2003.11045748

Edwards, C. J., Bendickson, J. S., Baker, B. L., & Solomon, S. J. (2020). Entrepreneurship within the history of marketing. *Journal of Business Research*, *108*, 259–267. doi:10.1016/j.jbusres.2019.10.040

Eom, S. (2020, May). DSS, BI, and Data Analytics Research: Current State and Emerging Trends (2015–2019). In *International Conference on Decision Support System Technology* (pp. 167-179). Springer. 10.1007/978-3-030-46224-6_13

Esteve, A. (2017). The business of personal data: Google, Facebook, and privacy issues in the EU and the USA. *International Data Privacy Law*, *7*(1), 36–47. doi:10.1093/idpl/ipw026

Filip, F. G. (2020). DSS—*A Class of Evolving Information Systems*. In *Data Science: New Issues, Challenges and Applications* (pp. 253–277). Springer. doi:10.1007/978-3-030-39250-5_14

Foss, B., Stone, M., & Ekinci, Y. (2008). What makes for CRM system success—Or failure? *Journal of Database Marketing & Customer Strategy Management, 15*(2), 68–78. doi:10.1057/dbm.2008.5

Friday, D., Ryan, S., Sridharan, R., & Collins, D. (2018). Collaborative risk management: A systematic literature review. *International Journal of Physical Distribution & Logistics Management, 48*(3), 231–253. doi:10.1108/IJPDLM-01-2017-0035

Grover, V., Chiang, R. H., Liang, T. P., & Zhang, D. (2018). Creating strategic business value from big data analytics: A research framework. *Journal of Management Information Systems, 35*(2), 388–423. doi:10.1080/07421222.2018.1451951

Jia, P., Cheng, X., Xue, H., & Wang, Y. (2017). Applications of geographic information systems (GIS) data and methods in obesity-related research. *Obesity Reviews, 18*(4), 400–411. doi:10.1111/obr.12495 PMID:28165656

Kaiser, R., Spiegel, P. B., Henderson, A. K., & Gerber, M. L. (2003). The application of geographic information systems and global positioning systems in humanitarian emergencies: Lessons learned, programme implications and future research. *Disasters, 27*(2), 127–140. doi:10.1111/1467-7717.00224 PMID:12825436

Leonard, P. (2014). Customer data analytics: Privacy settings for 'Big Data' business. *International Data Privacy Law, 4*(1), 53-68.

Martin, K. D., & Murphy, P. E. (2017). The role of data privacy in marketing. *Journal of the Academy of Marketing Science, 45*(2), 135–155. doi:10.100711747-016-0495-4

Morse, E. A., Raval, V., & Wingender Jr, J. R. (2011). Market price effects of data security breaches. *Information Security Journal: A Global Perspective, 20*(6), 263-273.

Naim, A. (2021). Applications of Marketing Framework in Business Practices. *Journal of Marketing and Emerging Economics, 1*(6), 55–70.

Naim, A. (2021). Green Business Process Management. *International Journal of Innovative Analyses and Emerging Technology, 1*(6), 125–134. https://openaccessjournals.eu/index.php/ijiaet/article/view/651

Naim, A. (2021). Applications of MIS in building Electronic Relationship with customers: A case-based study. Periodica Journal of Modern Philosophy. *Social Sciences and Humanities, 1*, 1–8.

Naim, A. (2022a). Measurement Consumer Mood and Emotions for Fast Moving Consumer Goods. *International Journal of Innovative Analyses and Emerging Technology, 2*(2), 83–86.

Naim, A. (2022b). Neuro-Marketing Techniques for Proposing Information Driven Framework for Decision Making. *International Journal of Innovative Analyses and Emerging Technology*, 2(2), 87–94.

Naim, A. (2022c). Mapping of Social Customer Relationship Management with Electronic Customer Relationship Management. *European Journal of Interdisciplinary Research and Development*, 2, 14–25. https://ejird.journalspark. org/index.php/ejird/article/view/10

Naim, A. (2022d). Understanding The Customer Centric Approach To Add Value To Social Ecrm (Secrm). *British Journal of Global Ecology and Sustainable Development*, 4, 1–17. https://journalzone.org/index.php/bjgesd/article/view/45

Naim, A. (2022e). Measurement of Electronic Commerce Effectiveness. Neo Science Peer Reviewed Journal, 1, 1–10. Retrieved from https://neojournals.com/index.php/ nsprj/article/view/6

Naim, A. (2022f). Factors of Consumer Behaviour of youth from middle-east when purchasing Organic Food. Global Scientific Review, 3, 1–7. Retrieved from http:// www.scienticreview.com/index.php/gsr/article/view/13

Naim, A. (2022g). Role of Artificial Intelligence in Business Risk Management. American Journal of Business Management. *Economics and Banking*, *1*, 55–66.

Naim, A. (2022h). Cost Trend: Meaning and Importance Of Cost Trend in Public Enterprises. *American Journal of Technology and Applied Sciences*, *1*, 37–46. https://americanjournal.org/index.php/ajtas/article/view/11

Naim & Malik. (2022). Competitive Trends and Technologies in Business Management. doi:10.52305/VIXO9830

Naim, A., & Alahmari, F. (2020). Reference model of e-learning and quality to establish interoperability in higher education systems. *International Journal of Emerging Technologies in Learning*, *15*(2), 15–28. doi:10.3991/ijet.v15i02.11605

Naim, A., Alahmari, F., & Rahim, A. (2021). Role of Artificial Intelligence in Market Development and Vehicular Communication. Smart Antennas. *Recent Trends in Design and Applications*, 2, 28–39. doi:10.2174/9781681088594121020006

Naim, A., Hussain, M. R., Naveed, Q. N., Ahmad, N., Qamar, S., Khan, N., & Hweij, T. A. (2019, April). Ensuring interoperability of e-learning and quality development in education. In *2019 IEEE Jordan International Joint Conference on Electrical Engineering and Information Technology (JEEIT)* (pp. 736-741). IEEE. 10.1109/ JEEIT.2019.8717431

Naim, A., & Kautish, S. K. (Eds.). (2022). *Building a Brand Image Through Electronic Customer Relationship Management*. IGI Global., doi:10.4018/978-1-6684-5386-5

Naim, A., & Khan, M. F. (2021). Measuring the Psychological Behavior of Consumers for Medical Services. Zien Journal of Social Sciences and Humanities, 2, 119–131. Retrieved from https://zienjournals.com/index.php/zjssh/article/view/316

Naim, A., Khan, M. F., Hussain, M. R., & Khan, N. (2019). "Virtual Doctor" Management Technique in the Diagnosis of ENT Diseases. *JOE, 15*(9), 88. doi:10.3991/ijoe.v15i09.10665

O'Brien, J. A., & Marakas, G. M. (2005). *Introduction to information systems* (Vol. 13). McGraw-Hill/Irwin.

Palmatier, R. W., & Martin, K. D. (2019). *The intelligent marketer's guide to data privacy: The impact of big data on customer trust*. Springer International Publishing. doi:10.1007/978-3-030-03724-6

Paryasto, M., Alamsyah, A., & Rahardjo, B. (2014, May). Big-data security management issues. In *2014 2nd International Conference on Information and Communication Technology (ICoICT)* (pp. 59-63). IEEE. 10.1109/ICoICT.2014.6914040

Pavoine, S., Vallet, J., Dufour, A. B., Gachet, S., & Daniel, H. (2009). On the challenge of treating various types of variables: Application for improving the measurement of functional diversity. *Oikos, 118*(3), 391–402. doi:10.1111/j.1600-0706.2008.16668.x

Peppers, D., & Rogers, M. (2004). *Managing customer relationships: A strategic framework*. John Wiley & Sons.

Polkowski, L., Tsumoto, S., & Lin, T. Y. (Eds.). (2012). *Rough set methods and applications: new developments in knowledge discovery in information systems* (Vol. 56). Physica.

Popescul, D., & Genete, L. D. (2016). Data security in smart cities: challenges and solutions. *Informatica Economică, 20*(1).

Putra, R. M., Maulida, M., & Rizki, M. R. (2020). The Moderating Role of Data Privacy and Protection Security on Service Quality, Brand Equity, and Tariff towards Firm Performance. In Conference Series (Vol. 3, No. 1, pp. 280-293).

Raab, G., Ajami, R. A., & Goddard, G. J. (2016). *Customer relationship management: A global perspective*. CRC Press. doi:10.4324/9781315575636

Rupnik, R., & Kukar, M. (2007). Decision support system to support decision processes with data mining. *Journal of Information and Organizational Sciences, 31*(1), 217–232.

Shao, X. F., Li, Y., Suseno, Y., Li, R. Y. M., Gouliamos, K., Yue, X. G., & Luo, Y. (2021). How does facial recognition as an urban safety technology affect firm performance? The moderating role of the home country's government subsidies. *Safety Science, 143*, 105434. doi:10.1016/j.ssci.2021.105434

Sharkey, U., & Acton, T. (2012). Innovations in information systems from transaction processing to expert systems.

Shey, H., Mak, K., Balaouras, S., & Luu, B. (2013). Understand the state of data security and privacy: 2013 to 2014. *Forrester Research Inc, 1*.

Sigala, M. (2018). Implementing social customer relationship management. *International Journal of Contemporary Hospitality Management, 30*(7), 2698–2726. doi:10.1108/IJCHM-10-2015-0536

Singh, D. K., Sobti, R., Jain, A., Malik, P. K., & Le, D.-N. (2022). LoRa based intelligent soil and Irrigation Using Machine Learning", Security and Communication Networks, vol. weather condition monitoring with internet of things for precision agriculture in smart cities. *IET Communications, 16*, 604–618. doi:10.1049/cmu2.12352

Singh, Sobti, Malik, Shrestha, Singh, & Ghafoor. (2022). IoT-Driven Model for Weather and Soil Conditions Based on Precision. doi:10.1155/2022/7283975

Watanabe, C., & Hobo, M. (2004). Co-evolution between internal motivation and external expectation as a source of firm self-propagating function creation. *Technovation, 24*(2), 109–120. doi:10.1016/S0166-4972(02)00043-3

Watson, H. J. (2018). Revisiting Ralph Sprague's framework for developing decision support systems. *Communications of the Association for Information Systems, 42*(1), 13. doi:10.17705/1CAIS.04213

Xu, H., Guo, S., Haislip, J. Z., & Pinsker, R. E. (2019). Earnings management in firms with data security breaches. *Journal of Information Systems, 33*(3), 267–284. doi:10.2308/isys-52480

Chapter 4
A Basic Process of Python Use for IOTAP, Data Science, and Rapid Machine Learning Model Development

Arun Kumar Singh

Papua New Guinea University of Technology, Lae, Papua New Guinea

ABSTRACT

Python is a more powerful high-level language created by Guido van Rossum (first appeared in 20 February 1991; 31 years ago), and its language constructs and object-oriented approach aim to help programmers write clear, logical code for small- and large-scale projects. Its design philosophy emphasizes code readability with the use of significant indentation. Python is an object oriented, scripted, and interpreted language for both learning and real-world programming. First in this paper, Python is introduced as a language, and a summary given about data science, machine learning, and IoT. Then, details are provided about the packages that are popular in the data science and machine learning communities, such as NumPy, SciPy, TensorFlow, Keras, and Matplotlib. After that, the authors will show the working criteria of Python for building IOT applications. The authors will use different code examples throughout. The learning experience, and executed examples, contained in this paper interactively used Jupyter notebook (notebook: 6.4.11) with Python (v3.10.4:9d38120e33, Mar 23 2022) on macOS Catalina-Version 10.15.7.

DOI: 10.4018/978-1-6684-6581-3.ch004

INTRODUCTION

Basic About Python

For general-purpose Python is high-level programming language which became popular in the recent times. With this concern Python allows programmer to write the code in fewer lines, just like simple mathematical equation, that is not possible with other languages. The main feature in Python programming is that it supports multiple programming prototypes. Python also provides a large set of extensive standard library. The main lineament of Python are unproblematic and easy to understand, freeware and open source, high level programming language, platform independent, portability, and dynamically typed. Both are procedure oriented and object oriented, interpreted, extensible, embedded, and have an extensive library.

What we want to include in our programs/projects, a Python library, is a reusable chunk of code. If you compare it to languages like C++ or C, Python libraries do not pertain to any specific context in Python. The Python library contains built-in modules (written in C) and it provide access to system functionality such as file I/O that would otherwise be inaccessible to Python programmers, as well as modules written in Python that provide standardized solutions for many problems that occur in everyday programming.

In this article we are trying to give some basic idea about Python in the field of Data science, IOT and Machine learning. Python is known to have a copiousness of libraries that aided with data analysis and scientific computing and informatics.

Basic About Data Science

Data science is a multi-disciplinary area that uses scientific methods, procedures, tools and systems to extract knowledge and get insights into structured and unstructured data. Data science is related to data analytics, data mining and big data. It understands the phenomenon of the data. It employs techniques and theories drawn from many fields within the context of mathematics, statistics, computer science, and information science and apply knowledge and actionable insights from data across a broad range of application domains.

The most important disciplines of Statistics to provide tools and methods to find structure, to give deeper insight into data, and the most important discipline to analyse and quantify uncertainty. Python provides various predefined modules to work on Data science projects.

Figure 1. An accompanying w3school repository is provided to aid the tutorial. It contains a number of notebooks of Python code for reference. It helps to go through number of examples related to different modules of Python
https://www.w3schools.com/Python/default.asp

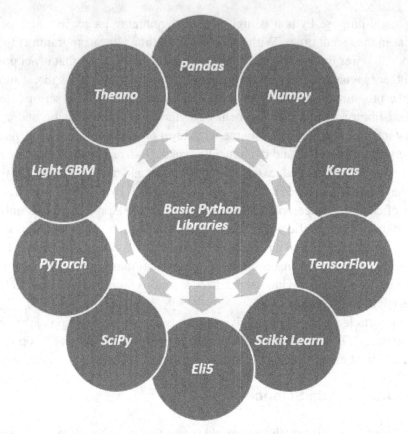

The figure given below representing the five stage of the data science life cycle:

- Capture, (data acquisition, data entry, signal reception, data extraction)
- Maintain (data warehousing, data cleansing, data staging, data processing, data architecture)
- Process (data mining, clustering/classification, data modeling, data summarization)
- Analyse (exploratory/confirmatory, predictive analysis, regression, text mining, qualitative analysis)
- Communicate (data reporting, data visualization, business intelligence, decision making).

Figure 2. Representing the five stages of the data science life cycle

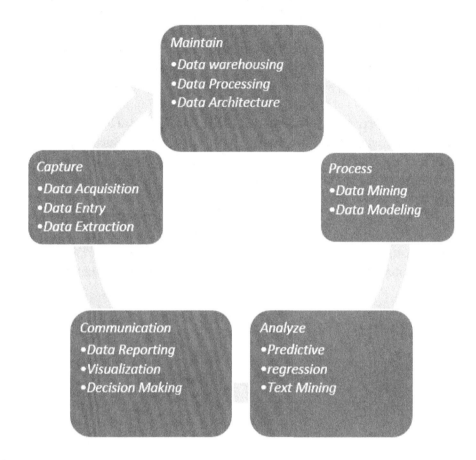

Intro About Machine Learning

Machine learning (ML) is a type of artificial intelligence (AI) which is the study of computer algorithms that can improve automatically through experience and by the use of data that allows software applications to become more accurate at predicting outcomes without being explicitly programmed to do so. ML algorithms are using historical data as input to predict new output values. ML also refers to the automated detection of meaningful patterns in data. In the past couple of years it is a common tool in almost any task that requires information extraction from collected data sets. Now a days we are surrounded by a machine learning based technology: search engines learn how to bring us the best results (while placing profitable ads), anti-spam software learns to filter our email messages, and credit card transactions are secured by software that learns how to detect frauds. Digital cameras learn to detect faces and intelligent personal assistance applications on smart-phones learn to recognize voice commands.

Morden level vehicles are equipped with accident prevention systems that are built using machine learning algorithms. ML is also widely used in scientific applications such as bioinformatics, medicine, and astronomy. One common fact of all of these applications is that, in contrast to more traditional uses of computers, in these cases, due to the complexity of the patterns that need to be detected, a human programmer cannot provide an explicit, fine-detailed specification of how such tasks should be executed. Taking example from intelligent beings, many of our skills are acquired or refined through learning from our number of programs with the ability to "learn "and adapt, Machine learning tools are main concern. Because machine learning is typically used to process large volumes of data, you may want to choose a powerful low-level language. However, if you're only just beginning to explore this field, it might be better to start with Python. Python for beginner-friendly, and can do the same thing that other coding languages can, but in fewer lines of coding.

Figure 3. machine learning algorithms

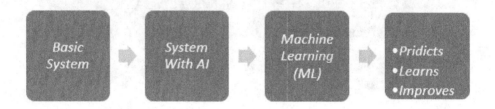

Basic of IOTAP

The Internet of Things Application and Protocol (IOTAP) is a scenario in which objects, animals or people are provided with single identifiers and the capability to automatically transfer and the capability to automatically transfer data more to a network without requiring human-to-human or human-To-computer communication. The Internet of things describes physical objects with sensors, processing ability, software, and other technologies that connect and exchange data with other devices and systems over the Internet or other communications networks.

IOTAP has evolved from the meeting of wireless Technologies, micro-electromechanical systems (MEMS) and the internet.

Figure 4. IOTAP map

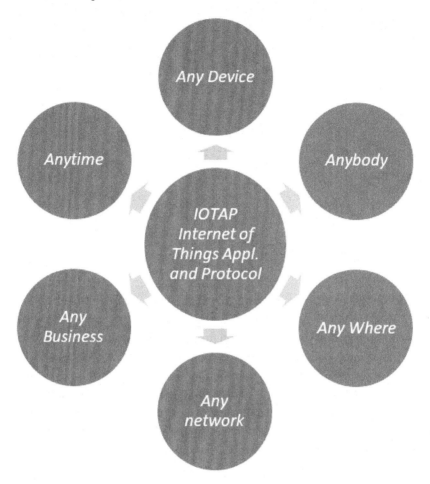

As per the TIOBE (The Importance Of Being Earnest)- TIOBE stands for The Importance of Being Earnest, the title of an 1895 comedy play by Oscar Wilde. The index is calculated from the number of search engine results for queries containing the name of the language. The index covers searches in Google, Google Blogs, MSN, Yahoo!, Baidu, Wikipedia and YouTube.

Index for Python:

- Highest Position (since 2001): #1 in Apr 2022
- Lowest Position (since 2001): #13 in Feb 2003
- Language of the Year: 2007, 2010, 2018, 2020, 2021

Figure 5. TIOBE index for Python

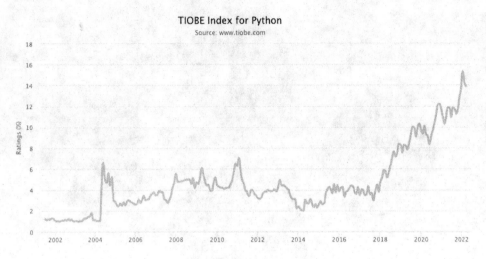

Python is mostly used for writing web applications, but it has gained popularity in the IOT system. It is an interpreted language that offers readability with syntax without compromising the size. This language has a large number of libraries; it can get more stuff done with fewer codes. Python's clean syntax is suitable for database arrangement. In case your app needs the data to be arranged in a database format or use tables. Python is the right choice available. Python is the right choice, for data analysis in IOT systems. The language is simple and can be easily deployed. Its large community helps in providing help and libraries as and when required. It is the ideal language for data-intensive applications.

OBJECTIVES OF STUDY

1. To gestate the features of Python
2. To follow up Python modules for Data Science like Numpy which is used for matrix and vector manipulation, Scipy and 2D plotting library Matplotlib etc
3. To concern on Python modules for Machine learning like Tensor flow numerical computations for machine learning, Keras for neural networks and deep learning

All points are discussed in this paper.

WORKS RELATED TO CONCERN TOPIC

Basic Working Features of Python

Python is a much more powerful high-level language created by Guido van Rossum (First appeared in 20 February 1991; 31 years ago) and Its language constructs and object-oriented approach aim to help programmers write clear, logical code for small- and large-scale projects. Its design philosophy emphasizes code readability with the use of significant indentation. Python is an object oriented, scripted and interpreted language for both learning and real world programming.

Why Python?

- Python works on different platforms (Windows, Mac, Linux, Raspberry Pi, etc).
- Python has a simple syntax similar to the English language.
- Python has syntax that allows developers to write programs with fewer lines than some other programming languages.
- Python runs on an interpreter system, meaning that code can be executed as soon as it is written. This means that prototyping can be very quick.
- Python can be treated in a procedural way, an object-oriented way or a functional way.

Basic Working Features of Python

- Python is Interpreted – Python is processed at runtime by the interpreter. You do not need to compile your program before executing it. This is similar to PERL and PHP. Python can be used to handle big data and perform complex mathematics.
- Python is Interactive – you can actually sit at a Python prompt and interact with the interpreter directly to write your programs. Python can connect to database systems. It can also read and modify files.
- Python is Object-Oriented – Python supports Object-Oriented style or technique of programming that encapsulates code within objects. Python can be used alongside software to create workflows. Python can be used for rapid prototyping, or for production-ready software development.
- Python is a Beginner's Language – Python is a great language for the beginner-level programmers and supports the development of a wide range of applications from simple text processing to WWW browsers to games. Python can be used on a server to create web applications.

Figure 6. Basic working features of Python

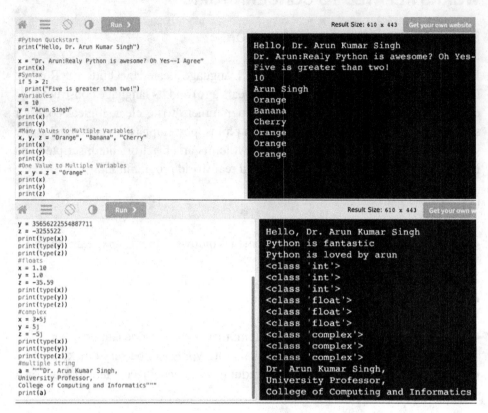

Python for Data Science

You have to know that there are the most essential Data Science libraries:

- Numpy
- Matplotlib
- Scipy

Numpy: Maybe it is difficult to do that directly, but since the concept is a crucial part of data science, many other libraries (well, almost all of them) are built on Numpy. Numpy will help us to manage multi-dimensional arrays very efficiently. Without Numpy it is difficult to use Pandas, Matplotlib, Scipy or Scikit-Learn.

Simple way we can say: NumPy is a Python library, NumPy is used for working with arrays and NumPy is short for "Numerical Python"

Figure 7. Numpy

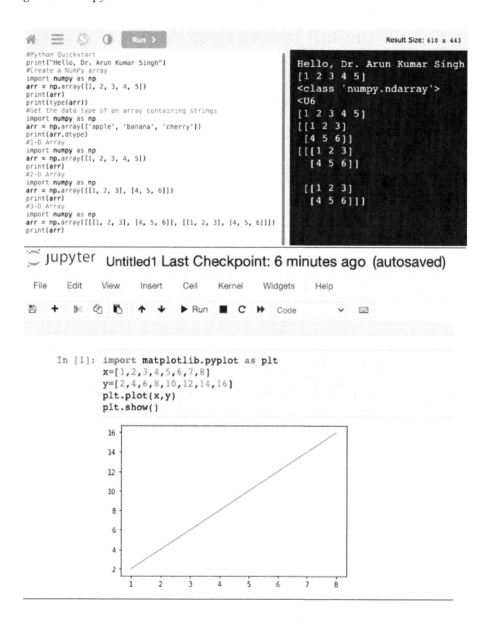

Figure 8. Numpy

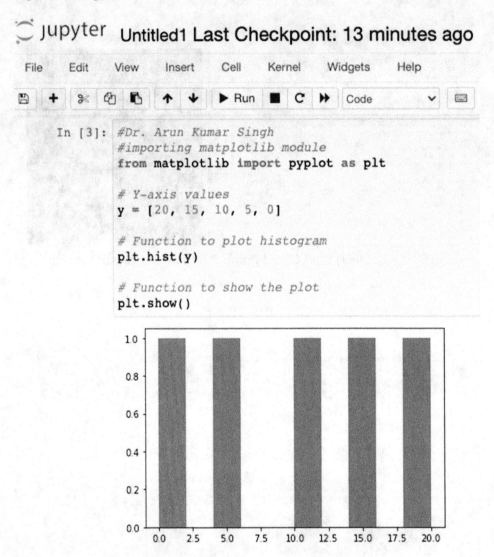

Dimensional Numpy Array

But on the other hand 3-dimensional Numpy array, it also has a few well-implemented methods. It's quite to use Numpy random function, which is found slightly better than the random module of the standard library. And when it comes to simple predictive analytics tasks like linear or polynomial regression, Numpy polyfit function will be favourite

Figure 9. matplotlib

```
In [1]: #Dr. Arun kumar Singh
        from matplotlib import pyplot as plt
        x = [1, 2, 3, 4, 5]
        y = [1, 4, 9, 16, 25]
        plt.show()
        plt.plot(x, y)
        # function to show the plot
        plt.show()
```

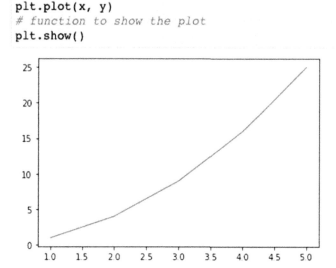

Matplotlib

For the Data lookout, Data visualization is very important and it's an easy process. Data visualization helps user to better understanding about the data, discover things that wouldn't discover in raw format and communicate findings more efficiently to others. The best and most well-known Python data visualization library is Matplotlib.

Scipy

SciPy is a scientific computation library that uses NumPy underneath. SciPy stands for Scientific Python, It provides more utility functions for optimization, stats and signal processing like NumPy, SciPy is open source so we can use it freely. SciPy was created by NumPy's creator Travis Olliphant. If SciPy uses NumPy underneath, why can we not just use NumPy? SciPy has optimized and added functions that are frequently used in NumPy and Data Science. Mathematics deals with a huge number of concepts that are very important but at the same time, complex and time-consuming. However, Python provides the full-fledged scipy library that resolves this issue for us. In this scipy, we will be learning how to make use of this library along with a few functions and their examples.

Before executing the program, user must install imageio and visvis as per your system.

Red colour text in the below program will give you the details about it and it will be easy to proceed.

```
''' imageio_vv_imageview101.py imageio can read many image file
formats
(also reads file objects, http, zipfiles and bytes) visvis can
display these images
get
imageio-0.5.1.tar.gz
from
https://pypi.Python.org/pypi/imageio
get
visvis-1.8.win-amd64.exe
from
https://pypi.Python.org/pypi/visvis/1.8
imageio and visvis come with
pyzo_distro-2014a.win64.exe
from
https://www.pyzo.org/downloads.html
(includes numpy, pyOpenGl and PySide)
imageio, visvis and pyzo_distro come in Linux and OSX flavors
too
see:
http://imageio.readthedocs.org/en/latest/formats.html
https://code.google.com/p/visvis/
tested with Python34-64bit by vegaseat  09nov2014'''
```

Figure 10. Open method

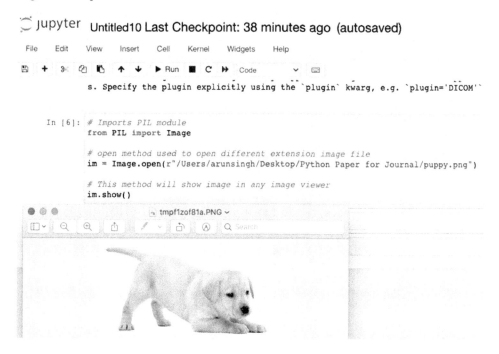

Python for Machine Learning

Tensor flow and keras libraries are general-purpose libraries for anything involving advanced data manipulation. This means they can all be used in implementing machine learning, and many of the higher level machine learning libraries makes use of some or all of these libraries. Getting acquainted with them is highly recommended if you plan on getting anywhere with scientific Python programming.

This list is by no means exhaustive; it is meant to be a starting point for you as you explore machine learning through Python! Already we discussed Numpy, Matplotlib and Scipy which are used for machine learning too. But we are showing the work phenomenon of Tensor flow and keras libraries in machine learning.

Tensor Flow

Tensor flow is the most well-known open source machine learning library available for Python. It was developed by Google, and is used in nearly every Google application that utilizes machine learning. If you've used Google Photos or voice search, then you've been using tensor flow. Tensor flow is extremely well documented and supported, and is optimized for speed. It is not easy to understand, however, because it is actually a Python front-end coded on top of C or C++, but as per your practice you can learn.

Figure 11. Return slope

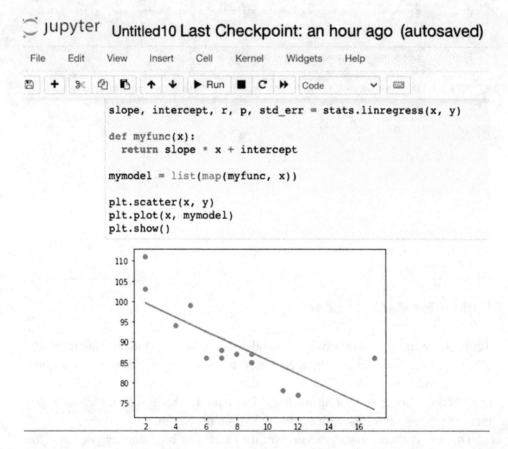

Keras

A high-level library for working with datasets and built on top of Theano and Tensor flow is Keras. Keras is best known for being one of the easiest machine learning libraries out there because it is coded entirely in Python, while using either Theano or Tensor flow as a back-end. It is easy and its beginner-friendly library for machine learning, includes functions for creating training datasets. Keras' neural networks API was developed for fast experimentation and is a good choice for any deep learning project that requires fast prototyping.

Figure 12. Keras

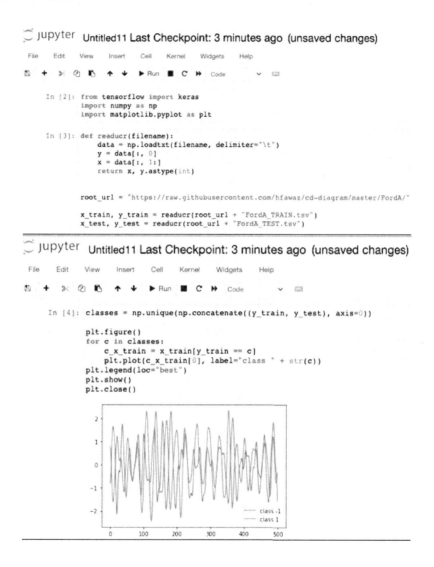

Python for IOTAP

Year back, Python was only used for web applications; no one thought it would apply in IOT development also. Now developer's are using Python programming language for developing the IOT Applications and Protocols. With efficient programming and easy syntax, most of us looking towards Python.

IoT applications function efficiently with the help of Python libraries/packages which include:

- Numpy.
- Sockets and MySQLdb.
- Matplotlib.
- Requests, Tkinter and Tensorflow.
- MQ Telemetry Transport (MQTT) sensor simulator.
- Azure IoT SDK in Python.
- Countly IoT Raspberry Pi SDK.

MQ TELEMETRY TRANSPORT (MQTT) SENSOR SIMULATOR

MQTT protocol for the IoT in Python enables high-speed data exchange with low payload communication between the devices. User-friendly requests of MQTT are made directly in Python. Data is collected in real-time and easily analysed in mathematical computation libraries like matplotlib. The diagram below shows the steps used for the data flow:

Figure 13. Steps used for data flow

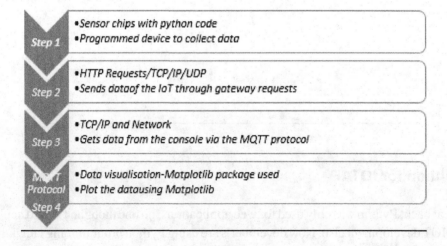

CONCLUSION

Basic points what we have presented in this paper usage of Python as a tool in various research areas like Data Science, Machine learning and IOTAP. Python design philosophy emphasizes code readability with the use of significant indentation. Python is an object oriented, scripted and interpreted language for both learning and real world programming.

Work in this paper first we introduce Python as a language, and give summary about Data science, Machine learning and IOT, and then details about the packages that are popular in the Data science and Machine learning communities, such as NumPy, SciPy, TensorFlow, Keras, Matplotlib etc. After that, we have shown the working criteria of Python for building IOT applications. We used different code examples throughout. Along with Python, there are many other languages are used for Data Science, Machine Learning and for developing IOT devices like Java, C++ etc. But right now most of the developers use Python scripting language than Java, C++. Because of its easy syntax, secure coding, and it's simplicity. When it comes to robust and performance, developers choose Python. IOTAP, when integrated with AI, will help developers to work with Python further.

With respect to the future work there is still huge space for this language to serve other upcoming research areas because of its features like simplicity, extensive library, Inbuilt and extensible modules. In future anyone can propose Python as a powerful tool which is using by many research communities.

REFERENCES

https://www.google.com/role-of-Python-in-iot-development

Anandkumar, R., Dinesh, K., & Ahmed, J. Obaid, P. M., Sharma, R., Dumka, A., Singh, S. K. (2022). Securing e-Health application of cloud computing using hyperchaotic image encryption framework. *Computers and Electrical Engineering, 100*. doi:10.1016/j.compeleceng.2022.107860

Engblom, S., & Lukarski, D. (2016). Fast MATLAB compatible sparse assembly on multicore computers. *Parallel Computing, 56*, 1–17. https://www.researchgate.net/publication/330513589_Internet_of_Things_IOT_Using_Raspberry_Pi. doi:10.1016/j.parco.2016.04.001

Fezari, M., & Dahoud, A A. (2019). *Internet of Things Using Raspberry Pi*. WSN Applications. https://www.researchgate.net/publication/330513589_Internet_of_Things_IOT_Using_Raspberry_Pi

Holzinger, A., Dehmer, M., & Jurisica, I. (2014). Knowledge discovery and interactive data mining in bioinformatics - state-of-the-art, future challenges and research direc-tions. *BMC Bioinformatics*, *15*(S6), I1. doi:10.1186/1471-2105-15-S6-I1 PMID:25078282

Jordan, M. I., & Mitchell, T. M. (2015). Machine learning: Trends, perspectives, and prospects. *Science*, *349*(6245), 255–260. doi:10.1126cience.aaa8415 PMID:26185243

Jupyter. (2022). *Introducing Functions*. NB Viewer. Https://nbviewer.jupyter.org/github/ehmatthes/intro_programming/blob/master/notebooks/introducing_functions.ipynb

Le Cun, Y., Bengio, Y., & Hinton, G. (2015). Deep learning. *Nature*, *521*(7553), 436–444. doi:10.1038/nature14539 PMID:26017442

Mester, T. (2018). Python Libraries and Packages for Data Scientists (the 5 Most Important Ones). *Data36*. Https://data36.com/Python-libraries-packages-data-scienTists/

Muiru, R. (2021). Python in IoT. *Top Coder*. https://www.topcoder.com/thrive/articles/Python-in-iot-internet-of-things

Naim, A. & Malik, P. K. (2022). *Competitive Trends and Technologies in Business Management*. Nova Science Publisher. doi:10.52305/VIXO9830

Naim, A., & Kautish, S. K. (Eds.). (2022). *Building a Brand Image Through Electronic Customer Relationship Management*. IGI Global. doi:10.4018/978-1-6684-5386-5

Scipy. (2022). *Image Manipulation and processing Using Numpy and Scipy*. Scipy Lectures. https://scipy-lectures.org/advanced/image_processing/

Singh, A. K. (2020). *IoT for Automation Clustering to Detect Power losses with Efficiency of Energy Consumption and survey of defense machinery against attacks*. CRC Press.https://www.routledge.com/Applied-Soft-Computing-and-Embedded-System-Applications-in-Solar-Energy/Pachauri-Pandey-Sharmu-Nautiyal-Ram/p/book/9780367625122

Singh, A. K. (2021). Machine Learning in OpenFlow Network: Comparative Analysis of DDoS Detection Techniques. *The International Arab Journal of Information Technology, 18*(2), 221-226.. https://iajit.org/PDF/Vol%2018,%20No.%202/19667.pdf doi:10.34028/iajit/18/2/11

Singh, A. K. (2020). Digital Era in the Kingdom of Saudi Arabia: Novel Strategies of the Telecom Service Providers Companies. *Webology, 17*(1), 227-245. http://www.webology.org/issue.php?volume=1&issue=1&page=2 doi:10.14704/WEB/V17I1/a219

Singh, A. K. (2019). High performance computing (HPC) data center for information as a service (IaaS) security checklist: cloud data supremacy. *Webology*, 16(2), 83-96., http://www.webology.org/issue.php?volume=2&issue=3 doi:10.14704/WEB/V16I2/a192

Singh, A. K. (2019). An Intelligent Reallocation of Load for Cluster Cloud Environment. *International Journal of Innovative Technology and Exploring Engineering (IJITEE), 8*(8). https://www.ijitee.org/download/volume-8-issue-8/

Singh, A. K. (2019). Texture-based Real-Time Character Extraction and Recognition in Natural Images. *International Journal of Innovative Technology and Exploring Engineering (IJITEE), 8*(8). https://www.ijitee.org/download/volume-8-issue-8/

Singh, A. K. (2019). A Wireless Networks Flexible Adoptive Modulation and Coding Technique in advanced 4G LTE. *International Journal of Information Technology, 11*(1), 55-66. doi:10.1007/s41870-018-0173-5 https://link.springer.com/article/10.1007/s41870-018-0173-5 doi:10.1007/s41870-018-0173-5

Singh, A. K. (2017). The Active Impact of Human Computer Interaction (HCI) on Economic, Cultural, and Social Life. *IIOAB Journal, 8*(2), 141-146. https://www.iioab.org/vol8n2

Singh, A. K. (2017). Security and Management in Network: Security of Network Management versus Management of Network Security (SNM Vs MNS). *International Journal of Computer Science and Network Security (IJCSNS), 17*(5), 166-173. http://search.ijcsns.org/07_book/2017_05.htm

Singh, A. K. (2017). Persona Of Social Networking In Computing And Informatics Era. *International Journal of Computer Science and Network Security (IJCSNS), 17*(4), 95-101. http://search.ijcsns.org/07_book/2017_04.h

Singh, D. K., Sobti, R., Malik, P. K., Shrestha, S., Singh, K., Ghafoor, K. Z. (2022). IoT-Driven Model for Weather and Soil Conditions Based on Precision 2022. *Hindawi.* doi:10.1155/2022/7283975

Singh, D. K., Sobti, R., Jain, A., Malik, P. K., & Le, D.-N. (2022). LoRa based intelligent soil and Irrigation Using Machine Learning", Security and Communication Networks, vol. weather condition monitoring with internet of things for precision agriculture in smart cities. *IET Communications*, *16*, 604–618. doi:10.1049/cmu2.12352

Tech A Team. (2017). *Top 6 Programing Languages for IoT Projects.* Tech Ahead Corp. https://www.techaheadcorp.com/blog/top-6-programming-languages-for-iot-projects/

W3Schools. (2022). *Machine Learning- Linear Regression.* W3Schools. https://www.w3schools.com/Python/Python_ml_linear_regression.asp

Wolfram, S. (1991). *Mathematica: A System for Doing Mathematics by Computer.* Addison Wesley Longman Publishing Co., Inc.

Chapter 5

A Study of Steganography Approach for Securing Data in a Confidential Communication Using Encryption

A. V. Senthil Kumar
Hindusthan College of Arts and Sciences, India

Rahul Ramaswamy G.
Hindusthan College of Arts and Science, India

Ismail Bin Musirin
Universiti Teknologi Mara, Malaysia

Indrarini Dyah Irawati
Telcom University, Indonesia

Abdelmalek Amine
ⓘD https://orcid.org/0000-0001-9327-7903
GeCoDe Laboratory, University of Saida Dr. Moulay Tahar, Algeria

Seddik Bri
Moulay Ismail University, Morocco

ABSTRACT

A steganography approach is a beneficial approach for hiding and encrypting messages in text, audio, video, and image formats. After the original text file is first encrypted, this encrypted file is embedded with an image file, and that image will be transferred to the recipient. The motive of this method is easy communication

DOI: 10.4018/978-1-6684-6581-3.ch005

and transferring of files to end users safely. The intruder is the only one who can view the unhidden message which is in text, audio, video, or image format. Thus, the message is encrypted successfully. Although there are many advantages for the steganography, which also has some limitations, these issues are mainly aimed in this paper. In this chapter, the challenges of steganography are rectified with the help of securing techniques. Finally, in the results section, findings in image size and the complexity of image quality at the sender side and receiver side in one-bit, two-bit, three-bit, and four-bit steganography images are stated. Thus, steganography methods are taking progressive steps to transform this capability into higher contributions.

INTRODUCTION

Steganography is the approach of hiding mystery records inside an ordinary document or message on the way to keep away from detection; the name of the game records is then extracted at its destination. The utilization of steganography may be mixed with encryption as an additional step for hiding or protective information. Steganography can be used to cover almost any form of digital content material, which includes textual content material, image, video, or audio content material; the information to be hidden can be hidden indoors almost each different form of digital content material. The content material to be hidden via steganography, known as hidden textual content, is regularly encrypted earlier than being integrated into the innocuous-seeming covers textual content document or records stream. If now no longer encrypted, the hidden textual content is typically processed in a few manners on the way to growth the issue of detecting the name of the game content material (Gunavathy & Meena, 2019).

In the previous days, the conversation became achieved head to head. But now the time has moved the technology develop wider and plenty of extra trends had been achieved. In vintage times, humans used to share the information with the useful resource of talking to each other, and with the useful resource of the usage of painting pictures, later it changed to letters and books. That became the time of gaining knowledge of new languages, human beings found out to jot down and study the paper materials. Then it have become a decade of letters and envelopes, human beings to begin with made use of pigeons to provide the letters to the predicted recipient. After that globe became on every other tempo to use postal addresses to ship the letters. It became the approach for an extended time (Qu et al., 2019).

Examples for steganography:

Steganography is practiced with the useful resource of the use of those wishing to convey an anonymous message or code. While there can be numerous valid makes use of for steganography, malware builders have furthermore been determined to apply steganography too difficult to apprehend the transmission of malicious code. Forms of steganography were used for hundreds of years and encompass nearly any approach for hiding a mystery message in an in any other case innocent container (Shi et al., 2019).

For example, the use of invisible ink to cover mystery messages in any other case inoffensive messages; hiding files recorded on microdot which may be as small as 1 millimeter in diameter on or interior valid-seeming correspondence; or even with the aid of using the use of multiplayer gaming environments to percentage information (H. Shi et al., 2019).

Techniques in Data Hiding

Data hiding is a software program application development method particularly applied in object-oriented programming to shield internal object particulars. Data hiding ensures tremendous data get proper access to best participants and defends object truthfulness via in the manner of approach of preventing unintentional or intended variations. When a message is performed, think that an exclusive file is being handed from person A to person B. If person A is sending that file as an easy phrase document, anybody with inside the community can carry out social engineering and view, manage or alternate the vacation spot and ship that document to anybody the intruder thinks (Al-Juaid & Gutub, 2019)

Figure 1. Data hiding techniques

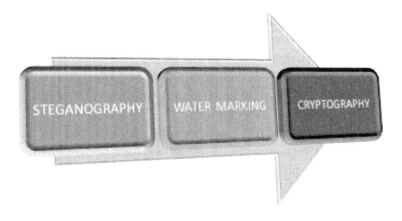

Technique 1 – Steganography: Playing an audio song backward to show a mystery message. Playing a video at a quicker body rate (FPS) to show a hidden image. Embedding a message withinside the red, green, or blue channel of an RGB image. Hiding facts inside a report header or metadata. These are some techniques used in steganography.

Technique 2 – Water Marking: Watermarking is a method combined to steganography. It has been around for hundreds of years and is generally utilized in cash and stamps to help in figuring out counterfeiting. The concept at the back of watermarking is to create a translucent photograph on the paper to offer authenticity. A watermark is a nevertheless photograph that overlaps a video. It can shield the complete size of the video, take a seat down with inside the middle of the video, or relaxation smartly in one of the corners. It may be opaque, for a maximum of the time it will likely be obvious as to now no longer intervene with the video itself (Pelosi et al., 2018).

Technique 3 – Cryptography: Cryptography is the study of stable communications strategies that permit the sender and recipient of a message to view its contents. Cryptographic strategies are used to make sure secrecy and integrity of facts with inside the presence of an opponent. Based on the safety wishes and the threats involved, diverse cryptographic strategies consisting of symmetric key cryptography or public-key cryptography may be used throughout transportation and storing of the facts (Saleh, 2016).

Types of Steganography

- *Audio Steganography*: Audio steganography is ready to hide the name of secret messages in the audio. It is a way used in the stable transmission of mystery records or disguise in their existence. Additionally also offer confidentiality to mystery message if the message is encrypted. In the number one diploma of security, the RSA set of policies is used to encrypt the message and, withinside the following diploma, the encrypted message is encoded into audio data (Gupta & Walia, 2014).

- *Video Steganography*: Video steganography is a department of records hiding isa way that embeds message into embed contents and is used in lots of fields consisting of scientific systems, regulation enforcement, copyright safety and get admission to control, etc.

- *Text Steganography*: Text steganography is a mechanism of hiding anonymous text messages inner to some other text as a protecting message or generating an embedded message related to the real anonymous message.

Figure 2. Types of steganography

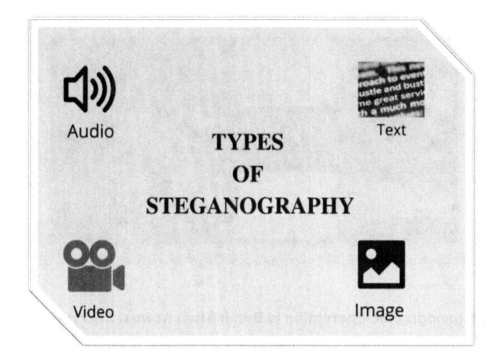

- ***Image Steganography***: Image Steganography refers back to the technique of hiding records inside a picture file. The picture decided on for this reason is referred to as the cover picture and the picture acquired after steganography is referred to as the stego image.

Process in Steganography

A message is embedded in a virtual photo via an embedding set of rules, with the help of a mystery key. The next stego image is transmitted over a channel to the receiver in which its miles processed with the resource of the usage of the extraction set of guidelines the use of the same key. During transmission of the stego image, it can be monitored with the resource of the usage of unauthenticated site visitors who will bestphrase the transmission of an image without discovering the existence of the hidden message (Pradhan et al., 2014).

In fig 3, the secret message is carried through the steganography encoder and it passes through the stego object into the communication channel. Finally, in the last stage, the steganography decoder is done using a stego object and passes to the secret message (Prabhjot & Kaur, 2017).

Figure 3. Process in Steganography

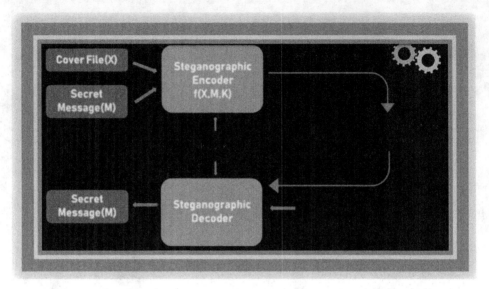

Steganographic Encryption Is Better Than Normal Encryption

Just protecting your files or data with app lock/password/pattern/pin is not enough. The intruder can easily hack your file by using this technique. To avoid such risks, the steganography approach is considered a better way to encrypt confidential data/files.

By using 4 types of steganography, one person's confidential files can be secured thoroughly. With the help of audio steganography, important data can be hidden using audio tracks. Thus the intruder thinks that it is some random tracks that are unnecessary for hacking. Next is with the help of video steganography, data is encrypted by hiding with a video. The intruder can only view that random video in the user selects. Similarly, with the usage of text steganography, the data can be protected by hiding it with a normal text file. Hackers think it will just be any normal text file. Finally, with the help of image steganography, the confidential file can be hidden with the random image file which is of jpg/jpeg/png or any image format extension file. The intruder can open only the random image file in which the user uploaded (Gayathri & Nagarajan, 2015).

So, in general, Steganography encryption is far better than just any normal encryption. The steganography method is not used commonly by normal people. It hasn't become a trend in today's world. If the steganography technique usage becomes higher in the future, non-ethical hackers will get in trouble for not getting to steal into others' confidential data. Encryption and decryption of files can be easily done with the help of a steganography approach for transferring files (Prabhjot & Kaur, 2017).

About Algorithm: Tiny Encryption Algorithm

Tiny Encryption algorithm has a very straightforward key schedule that mixes each key component consistently for each cycle. On the basis of the symmetry of the rounds, several multiples of a magic constant are utilized to defend against straightforward attacks. Tiny Encryption algorithm has added modifications to increase security. A "Cryptographic algorithm" designed to increase speed and decrease storage footprint is called the "Tiny Encryption Algorithm" (TEA). It uses operations from different (orthogonal) arithmetical collections and is referred to as a "Feistel type cypher." The "Tiny Encryption Algorithm" is little in size, as the name suggests. It can all be expressed and executed in a few lines of programming code. This is crucial since it implies that it can be included in almost any software package, even ones with deliberate space restrictions.

TEA appears to be very resistant to differential cryptanalysis and only achieves complete dispersion after six rounds. On a modern workstation or desktop computer, the time display is truly remarkable. The Tiny Encryption Algorithm corresponds to any additional encryption algorithm.

- *Why to Choose Tiny Encryption Algorithm?*

The Tiny Encryption Algorithm (TEA) has been spherical for genuinely round extra than ten years. It is probably the maximum "minimal" and ultimately relatively fastest—block cipher continually deliberates and however appears evidence in opposition to most outbreaks. Conventionally, whilst cryptography modified into the location of the fleet and, extra newly, of the lending communal, ciphers were commonly done in pc hardware. Every individual is familiar with the fantastically customary Enigma apparatuses used via the Germans in World War II, except a number of splendid tutelages on them have appeared in the one's portions of paper. Anybody who has laboured withinside the once more administrative center of a monetary group has seen the SWIFT stations used for inter-monetary group price range transfer. These are pc hardware devices and are not unusual place of the way in which cryptography modified into done from the maximum primary civilizations whole to the advent of the virtual laptop. Currently, nearly all cipher algorithms are compulsory in software program application for use with applications hitting on PCs. The cipher is notably stable and can (nearly) be involuntary from memory in any programming language or CPU education set for use in a huge style of safety applications which includes hashing, suppression and random wide variety generation. Contrasting numerous unique ciphers which includes IDEA or those from RSA Laboratories, TEA is not encumbered with the resource of the use of copyrights or each different business entitlement. It is absolutely network location and can be used freely. Its number one advantage can be very excessive speed, it is perfectly suited to fashionable applications which includes flow of real-time movie via the broadband Internet.

- *What are the benefits of the Tiny set of rules?*

This class of set of rules can alternative DES in software program package, and is satisfactorily short to inscribe into pretty much withinside the least software on rather all computers. Even though rapidity isn't always a strong goal with 32 cycles (sixty-four rounds), taking area on one operation it's far 3 instances as reckless as a decent software program operation of DES which has a be counted number of sixteen rounds. The procedures of utilization of DES are all appropriate. The cycle be counted number can willingly be wide-ranging, or maybe finished a part of the key. It is expected that protection may be boosted via way of means of cumulating the be counted number of iterations.

Figure 4. Applications of Steganography

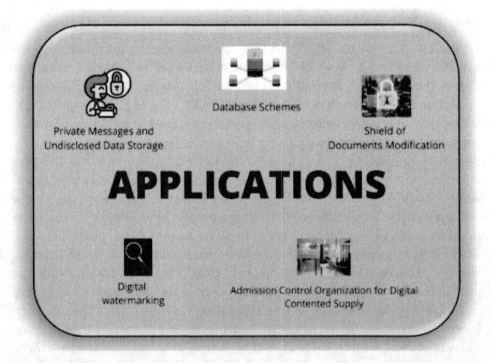

APPLICATIONS OF STEGANOGRAPHY

- *Private Messages and Undisclosed Data Storage:*

In this present day global each mystery message transmission is executed via the net. Most humans on this globe blindly believe that their messages dispatched via the net are secure and stable and it's our obligation to maintain their hope. We can stable our facts via way of means of overlaying statistics inside a few different files (audio, image).

- *Shield of Documents Modification:*

It is the procedure of editing statistics earlier than or after it's far entered into the system, producing a defective output. While processing huge quantities of statistics, criminals adjust enter or internally make this system that processes the data to failure. It shields the documents securely and modifies the system effectively.

- *Admission Control Organization for Digital Contented Supply:*

Electronics access to manipulate structures in virtual networks that manipulate get entry to safety portals. These devices connect with a get access to govern panel, which provides get right of entry to authorizations based totally completely upon comparing the credential furnished at the door closer to a database of criminal credentials. Digital distribution is the shipping or distribution of virtual media content material consisting of audio, video, e-books, video games, and different varieties of software (Pooja Rani & Apoorva Arora, 2015).

- *Database Schemes:*

Database Systems or DBMS is a software program that provides the gathering of digital and virtual facts to extract beneficial data and store the data is referred to as Database Systems/ Database Management Systems or DBMS. The motive of a popular database is to store and retrieve data. These data can be embedded and embedded using the concept of steganography.

- *Digital watermarking:*

Digital watermarking is the procedure of embedding a virtual code (watermark) right into a virtual content material like photo, audio, or video. The embedded information once in a while referred to as a watermark is depending on the safety requirements (Sahu & Swain, 2019).

Digital watermarking generation is being followed to make sure and facilitate information authentication, protection, and copyright safety of virtual media. It is taken into consideration because the maximum critical generation in the modern-day world, to save you unlawful copying of information.

Watermarking is a method with similarities to steganography. It has been around for hundreds of years and is generally utilized in cash and stamps to help in figuring out counterfeiting. The concept at the back of watermarking is to create a translucent photo on the paper to offer authenticity (Moniruzzaman et al., 2014).

Benefits of Steganography

- *Hiding OTPs in mobile devices:* Image steganography is used to hide OTPs received in the user's mobile phones or any other gadgets. This is mainly used for the self-communication purpose for your safety.
- *Least Significant Bit (LSB) Encoding:* The intruder cannot locate the photograph. The authentic photograph and the altered photograph are very much like the intruder's eye that is a gain to the users.
- *Short Frequency Encoding:* The range of the message is unknown to the intruder. That's an advantage because the encrypted file can be transferred to a long distance.
- *Mid Frequency Encoding:* The edited picture or file is almost similar to the original. Since its frequency is slightly larger than the shorter one, still mid-frequency encoding is a benefit to the users (Rajawat & Tomar, 2015).

CHALLENGES OF STEGANOGRAPHY

Every field has its challenges and limitations. Some of the challenges in this field include:

- **Security and privacy**
- **Time Delay**
- **Execution**
- **Accuracy**

- **Data Transfer Rate**

Another major challenge included is High-frequency encoding is discussed in section 3.1

Figure 5. Challenges of Steganography

- ***Security and privacy:*** The data can't be considered 100% safe security-wise. When steganography is utilized by itself, it is safety insignificant that can cause the name of the secret message to be revealed. If you need to cover a message from adversaries, however additionally defend it in the case discovered. It is great to mix steganography with cryptography. Some implementations of steganography that lack a shared mystery are kinds of safety insignificant and key-established steganography schemes (Malonia & Kumar, 2016).
- ***Time Delay:*** When transferring files there is a chance of getting a delay in the period. When the data is secured properly for better results it will get slight interruptions in the time phase. Normally while opening an unsecured

file, it opens in a quick phase but if the file is encrypted process gets slow in opening it.

- *Execution:* Another challenge includes the time in executing the whole process. There are two concepts of time required in this challenge. One is the execution time and the other is response time. For encryption and decryption of files, the execution time is always slow compared to opening unsecured files. The time taken to respond to the particular process is the response time.

- *Accuracy:* Another major challenge is the accuracy of the output produced. The receiver thinks that the file is safe to open, but the accurate information of this challenge is always unpredictable. The intruder is having the advantage in using this type of encryption process.

- *Data Transfer Rate:* Transfer rate is the amount of data taken to move from one place to another digitally. For processing this method, a numerous amount of data is being required. And also transfer rate is a major issue in this method. The size of the file is also considered when processing (Sanjay & Ambar, 2016).

Major Challenge: High-Frequency Encoding

The image is inaccurate. Communication is simply misplaced if the image focuses on compression such as JPEG. While compressing the picture file there is a possibility to get the image corrupted. There is a chance to get the audio file corrupted too. This is a major challenge faced in the steganography approach. If the size of the file is larger, the problem gets even bigger. So always choose low frequency-based files (Yanyan et al., 2014).

During the audio steganography approach, frequency plays a major role. The audio track should be kept at a minimal frequency. The source of audio along with the message is directly processed into the encoding stage. In this encoding stage, a stego audio file is generated. Here the audio file can be played and heard by the users. Finally, this stego audio file gets into the decoding stage which goes to its initial position and gets the required message to the receiver. The whole process is shown in fig 6.

Figure 6. Flow process of audio steganography

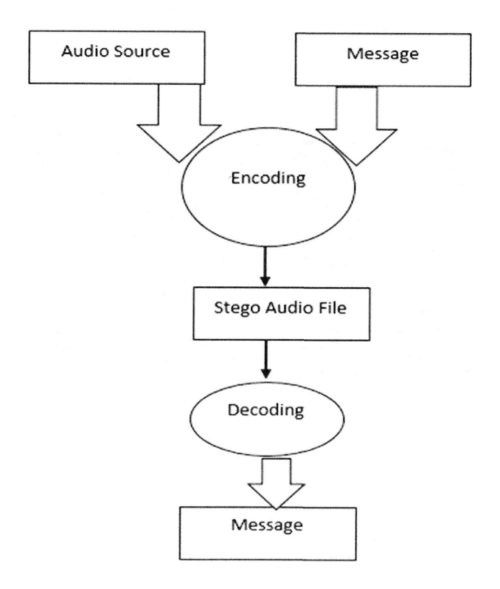

RESULTS AND DISCUSSIONS

One-Bit Steganography

Figure 7. Image size vs. Complexity of image quality at sender side in one-bit steganography

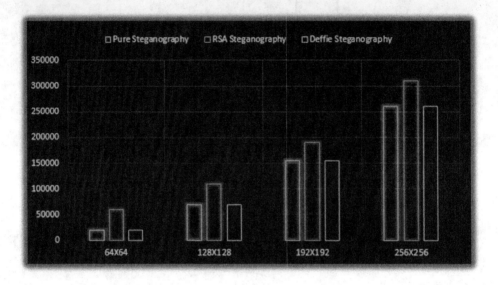

Findings from one-bit steganography:

- Technically, there is no change in the sender side and the receiver's side in picture quality for pure, Diffie Hellman, and RSA steganography techniques.
- The complexity of Diffie Hellman steganography is almost similar to that of pure steganography.
- As the number of pixels in image increases, the complexity at the sender and receiver sides rises (Ghosh et al., 2015).

Figure 8. Image size vs. Complexity of image quality at receiver side in one-bit steganography

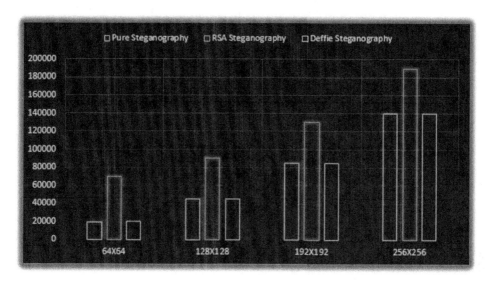

Two-Bit Steganography

Figure 9. Image size vs Complexity of image quality at sender side in two-bit steganography

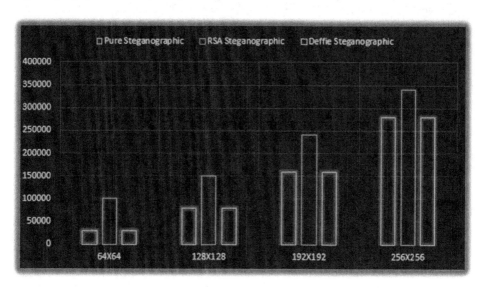

Findings from two-bit steganography:

- As you may see from the above graphs, the quantity of pixels withinside the picture will increase on the identical time, the complexity in addition to receiver additionally will increase.
- Compared to the one-bit steganography, approximately in the range of 10% and 70% rise of complexity in the case of pure steganography combined with RSA algorithm.
- Compared to the one-bit steganography, approximately in the range of 10% to 70% rise of complexity in the case of pure steganography combined with Diffie Hellman algorithm.
- Steganography combined with RSA algorithm complexity has higher complexity than pure with Diffie Hellman algorithm (Anusree & Binnu, 2014).

Figure 10. Image size vs Complexity of image quality at receiver's side in two-bit steganography

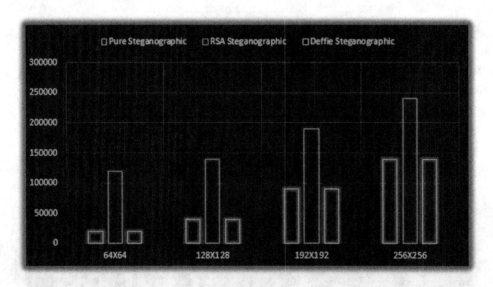

Three-Bit Steganography

Figure 11. Image size vs Complexity of image quality at sender side in three-bit steganography

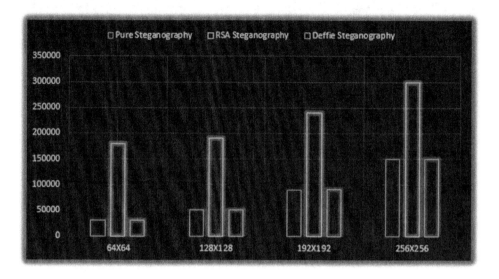

Findings from three-bit steganography:

- There is more alteration done in the three-bit steganography compared to one and two steganography.
- There is an increase in the range of 15 – 40% complexity in pure with RSA algorithm compared to two-bit steganography in pure with RSA.
- As the image size increases the complexity at both the sender and receiver sides increases.
- As the size of the image increases, the complexity of the sender and receiver's side also rises.
- Pure combined with the Diffie Hellman algorithm steganography's complexity is almost similar (Karakış et al., 2015).

Figure 12. Image size vs Complexity of image quality at receiver's side in three-bit steganography

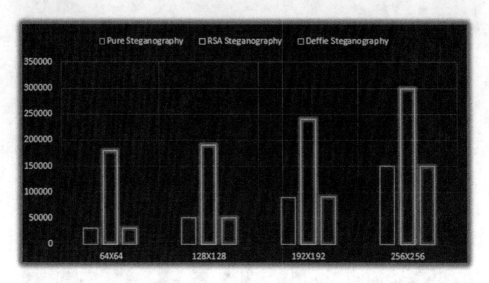

Four-Bit Steganography

Figure 13. Image size vs Complexity of image quality at sender side in four-bit steganography

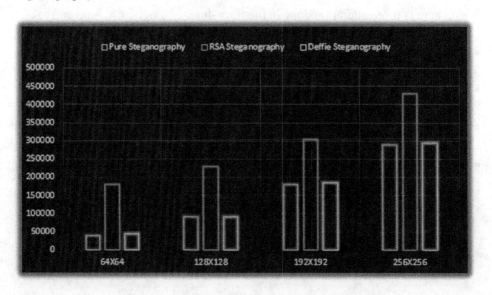

Findings from four-bit steganography:

- The complexity at the sender and receiver side gradually rises when the image's size rise.
- Compared to the Diffie Hellman algorithm, the RSA algorithm is more protected. Also, it has the top time complexity.
- Pure steganography may be used with each Diffie Hellman and RSA algorithms.
- The amount of embedded bits in the picture rises concerning the complexity of the time.

Figure 14. Image size vs Complexity of image quality at receiver's side in four-bit steganography

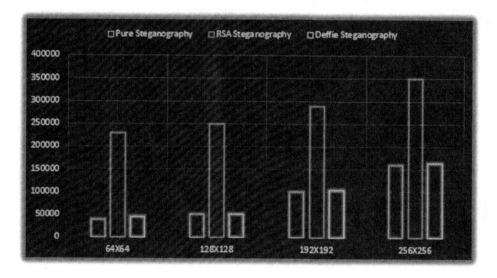

From the above all the four-bits steganographic approaches, we can conclude it by a graph given below which is the size of sample versus probability of embedding (in %) (K. Rabah, 2004).

The above graph is represented from the four-bit steganography approaches of images in which the x-axis is taken as the size of the sample images and the y-axis is taken as how much probability of embedding is done to the images. We can conclude from the above graph that the probability of embedding comes to 0% to the size of samples that are above 60%. This statement means that the probability of embedding does not take place after it comes to 60% size of sample images. The average probability of embedding is in the range of 75-100% (Sahu & Swain, 2015).

Figure 15. the size of sample vs probability of embedding of images in steganography approach

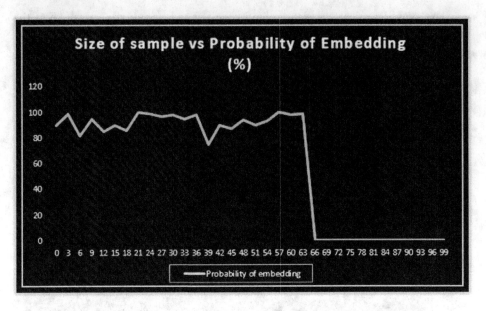

CONCLUSION

In conclusion, the Steganography approach is a beneficial approach for hiding and encrypting messages. These messages can be of text, images, audio, videos, etc. Steganography can be a difficult process but it is a possible approach. To detect the encrypted and normal messages, this approach is more suitable. The steganography approach can save your confidential data from getting hacked. Although there are numerous merits of the internet, it has additionally opened a brand new manner for invasion of our privateness and intelligent belongings via way of means of hackers and illegal users. One such technique to secure confidential data is the steganography method.

This paper ensures the encrypted file embeds in an audio, video, text, or image format. The challenges of steganography were discussed. The main challenge which is high-frequency encoding was also mentioned. The hiding techniques in data were also stated. Why choosing steganography encryption over normal encryption was also discussed. Finally, in the results section, findings in image size versus the complexity of image quality at sender side and receiver side in one-bit, two-bit, three-bit, and four-bit steganography images were also stated. Size of sample versus probability of embedding of images through steganography approach was also discussed (Jai Singh, 2015).

REFERENCES

Gunavathy, S., & Meena, C. (2019). A Survey: Data Security In Cloud Using Cryptography And Steganography. *International Research Journal of Engineering and Technology, 6*(5), 6792–6797.

Weng, X., Li, Y., Chi, L., & Mu, Y. (2019). Convolutional video steganography with temporal residual modeling. arXiv.

Al-Juaid, N., & Gutub, A. (2018). Combining rsa and audio steganography on personal computers for enhancing security. *SN Applied Sciences, 1*(8), 830.

Pradhan, A., Sahu, A. K., Swain, G., & Sekhar, K. R. (2016). Performance evaluation parameters of image steganography techniques. *2016 International Conference on Research Advances in Integrated Navigation Systems (RAINS)*, (pp. 1-8). IEEE. 10.1109/RAINS.2016.7764399

Saleh, M. E., Aly, A. A., & Omara, F. A. (2016). Data security using cryptography and steganography techniques. *International Journal of Advanced Computer Science and Applications, 7*(6), 390–397.

Pelosi, M., Poudel, N., Lamichhane, P., Lam, D., Kessler, G., & Mac-Monagle, J. (2018). *Positive identification of lsb image steganography using cover image comparisons*. ADFSL.

Mohammad, A., & Zeki, A. M., Chebil, J., & Gunawan, T. S. (2013). Properties of Digital Image Watermarking. IEEE 9th International Colloquium on Signal processing and its Applications, (pp. 8-10). IEEE.

Gayathri, R., & Nagarajan, V. (2015). Secure data hiding using Steganographic technique with Visual Cryptography and Watermarking Scheme. IEEE ICCSP conference, (pp. 0118-0123). IEEE. doi:10.1109/ICCSP.2015.7322691

Rajawat, M., & Tomar, D. S. (2015). A Secure Watermarking and Tampering detection technique on RGB Image using 2 Level DWT. *IEEE Fifth International Conference on Communication Systems and Network Technologies*, (pp. 638-642). IEEE. 10.1109/CSNT.2015.245

Moniruzzaman, Hawlader, A. K., & Hossain, F. (2014). Wavelet Based Watermarking Approach of Hiding Patient Information in Medical Image for Medical Image Authentication. *IEEE 17th International Conference on Computer and Information Technology (ICCIT)*, (pp. 374-378). IEEE.

Malonia, M. & Kumar, A. S. (2016). Digital Image Watermarking using Discrete Wavelet Transform and Arithmetic Progression. *IEEE Students's Conference on Electrical*. IEEE.

Sanjay, K., & Ambar, D. (2016). A Novel Spatial Domain Technique for Digital Image Watermarking Using Block Entropy. *IEEE Fifth International Conference on Recent Trends in Information Technology*. IEEE.

Ghosh, S., De Sayandip, S. P. M., & Rahaman, H. (2015). A Novel Dual Purpose Spatial Domain Algorithm for Digital Image Watermarking and Cryptography Using Extended Hamming Code. *IEEE Proceedings of International Conference on Electrical Information and Communication Technology (EICT 2015)*, (pp. 167-172). IEEE.

Han, Y., He, W., Shuai, J., & Qing, L. (2014). A Digital Watermarking Algorithm of Colour Image based on Visual Cryptography and Discrete Cosine Transform. *IEEE Ninth International Conference on P2P*, (pp. 527-530). IEEE.

Anusree, K., & Binnu, G. S. (2014). *Biometric Privacy using Visual Cryptography Halftoning and Watermarking for Multiple Secrets*. IEEE. doi:10.1109/NCCSN.2014.7001156

Karakış, R., Güler, İ., Çapraz, İ., & Bilir, E. (2015, December). A novel fuzzy logic-based image steganography method to ensure medical data security. *Computers in Biology and Medicine*, *67*, 172–183. doi:10.1016/j.compbiomed.2015.10.011 PMID:26555746

Rabah, K. (2004, March). Steganography—The art of hiding data. *Information Technology Journal*, *3*(3), 245–269. doi:10.3923/itj.2004.245.269

Sahu, A. K., & Swain, G. (2019, September). an optimal information hiding approach based on pixel value differencing and modulus function. *Wireless Personal Communications*, *108*(1), 159–174. doi:10.100711277-019-06393-z

Sahu, A. K., & Swain, G. (2019). A novel n-Rightmost bit replacement image steganography technique. *3D Res. 10*(1), 2.

Singh, J., Hasan K., & and Kumar, R. (2015). Enhance security for image encryption and decryption by applying hybrid techniques using MATLAB. *IJIRCCE*, *3*(7).

Rani, P. & Arora, A. (2015). Image security system using encryption and steganography. *IJIRSET, 4*(6).

Prabhjot, N. S., & Kaur, H. (2017). A Review of Information Security using Cryptography Technique. *International Journal of Advanced Research in Computer Science, 8*, pp. 323-326, 2017

Gupta, A., & Walia, N. K. (2014). Cryptography Algorithms: A Review. *International Journal Of Engineering Development And Research*, 2(2), 1667–1672.

Shi, H., Zhang, X.-Y., Wang, S., Fu, G., & Tang, J. (2019). Synchronized detection and recovery of steganographic messages with adversarial learning. *Proc. Int. Conf. Comput. Sci*, (pp. 31-43). 10.1007/978-3-030-22741-8_3

Qu, Z., Cheng, Z., Liu, W., & Wang, X. (2019, April). A novel quantum image steganography algorithm based on exploiting modification direction. *Multimedia Tools and Applications*, 78(7), 7981–8001. doi:10.100711042-018-6476-5

Chapter 6
Deception Preclusion, Discretion, and Data Safety for Contemporary Business

Srinivasa Rao Gundu
Department of Computer Science and Applications, Government Degree College Sitaphalmandi, Hyderabad, India

Panem Charanarur
Department of Cyber Security and Digital Forensics, National Forensic Sciences University, India

J.Vijaylaxmi
PVKK Degree and PG College, Anantapur, India

ABSTRACT

Talking about 'big data' refers to datasets that are either extraordinarily large or have a complex structure. These traits may sometimes be accompanied by more difficult data storage, processing, and application of following activities, or the extraction of discoveries. The practice of doing analytics on massive, complex datasets, sometimes known as 'big data,' is a method that may be utilized to discover links and patterns in these datasets that were previously undiscovered. However, attempts to protect the privacy and security of big data are undermined by its rapid spread.

DOI: 10.4018/978-1-6684-6581-3.ch006

INTRODUCTION

Big data, as defined here, refers to datasets that are too large or complicated to be analyzed using traditional techniques. This could go either way. The volume of data, both organized and unstructured, that a firm creates on a daily basis is the most difficult aspect of running a corporation. Thanks to technological advancements, the daily data output of the internet, social media sites, sensor networks, healthcare applications, and many other types of enterprises are growing exponentially. This is a natural result of technological development. Massive volumes of data in several forms are being generated at an ever-increasing pace; this phenomenon has been dubbed "big data". Big data is the term for the new mass of information that has been available. This new kind of information is known as "big data" which comes from its initials. The goal of big data systems is to "economically extract value from exceptionally large volumes of a wide spectrum of data" by facilitating quick data gathering, processing, and analysis. The term for this process is "economically isolating value from extraordinarily huge amounts of data". Data volume, data velocity, and data variety are often cited as the defining characteristics of big data (Zhang et al., 2021).

These three characteristics, it is said, are what set big data apart. After further investigation, it became clear that the 3Vs concept couldn't properly account for the enormous datasets we currently have at our disposal. Trustworthiness, validity, value, variety, context, vocabulary, and opacity were therefore constructed to facilitate a deeper comprehension of extensive datasets. Large data sets are often characterized by their heterogeneity. For instance, large data sets may include not just text but also various media forms like audio and visual recordings. The term "diversity" is used to describe when there is a large variety of features present in the data. Several methods for hiding the existence of enormous datasets have been developed in recent years. The many steps in the big data life cycle, including data gathering, storage, and analysis, provide a suitable framework for classifying the various technologies involved in managing and analyzing this data. Information gathering, data processing, and information storage are all instances of this. Confidentiality is maintained all the way through the data-generation process by means of access restriction and data falsification.

Most security professionals agree that using encryption techniques is the best way to protect individuals' private data while it is being stored. Identity-based encryption (IBE), attribute-based encryption (ABE), and storage-path encryption are three further categories of encryption-based methods. Identity-based encryption (IBE) is shorthand for attribute-based encryption (ABE), while identity-based encryption (IBE) is shorthand for both. To further strengthen cloud computing's security, private cloud storage is used to store sensitive data inside hybrid cloud systems. The phase of the process known as "data processing" contains two subsidiary phases: the first is known as "Privacy - Preserving Data Publishing", or PPDP, and the second is referred to as "Knowledge Extraction". The protection of sensitive information is achieved through the utilization of privacy-preserving data processing (PPDP), which employs anonymization strategies such as generalization and suppression.

This allows for the information to be processed without compromising the individual's right to privacy. Cluster analysis, classification trees, and association rule mining are some of the subcategories that may be further subdivided into when these approaches are further dissected and analyzed. Methods that are based on association rule mining can unearth important links and patterns hidden within the input data, while methods like clustering and classification divide the data into several distinct categories. It is essential to design frameworks that are both efficient and effective in their ability to analyze enormous volumes of data that are rapidly arriving from a variety of sources. This is because big data can take on a variety of forms and dimensions, and it is important to keep this in mind when designing frameworks. The life cycle of big data should be divided up into numerous distinct stages.

In 2012, it was predicted that every day, 2.5 quintillion bytes of new data will be created. The data production rate is skyrocketing, and the data and information landscape is becoming worldwide. Research into the use of lightweight incremental algorithms is required because of their ability to offer robustness, precision, and speed with little pre-processing. Lightweight feature selection algorithms like swarm search and accelerated PSO might replace labor-intensive conventional classification methods in the mining sector, saving significant time and effort. There will be an unprecedented explosion in the volume of data generated in the coming years as the internet of things (IoT) links together all the things that people care about throughout the globe. This growth rate is predicted to skyrocket in the future. The proliferation of IoT devices is unquestionably a major driving force behind the rise of big data analytics.

In the modern day, when "big data" collect massive quantities of information, it's conceivable that researching these databases may uncover new solutions to solve fundamental problems, like healthcare inequities, that plague modern civilization. Since big data collects so much information all at once, this makes sense. In many ways, the challenges and difficulties of big data analytics for smart energy are similar to those of big data analytics in general. Since data intelligence may significantly impact the secure operation of systems in real-time, physical processes are of paramount importance to the field of big data for smart energy (Liang et al., 2020).

Consider the following usage: Marketing agencies and other forms of business may gain from this as well. Since the database likely contains sensitive information, it is not recommended that its contents be made easily accessible to analysts and researchers. Undermining the privacy of others in this manner is unethical behavior, especially given the potential for legal repercussions and the fact that it is illegal. All expenses should be eliminated to prevent this behavior. The findings of this article are generalizable to a wide range of historical epochs. As can be seen from the cited works, the research spans the years 1998-2016. The number of articles found in the search results and any preexisting citations based on the keywords may both be double-checked. The user may choose one of these two alternatives.

The sections under "Privacy and security problems" and "Privacy obligations in big data" discuss the potential risks to individuals' privacy when dealing with such a massive volume of data. What follows are explanations of how these flaws manifest themselves. One may divide the concept of privacy in regard to big data into three parts: privacy during the creation phase, privacy during the storage phase, and privacy-preserving big data during the processing phase. In the article titled "Privacy-Preserving Methods in Big Data," we go through the many options available for safeguarding private information during the processing of massive data sets. The approaches are explained in depth. In the next part, headed "Recent Strategies of Privacy Preserving in Big Data," we describe some of the more recent ways that have been utilized to safeguard the privacy of people inside large datasets, and we also offer a comparison of the aforementioned methodologies.

AIM OF THESTUDY

This study provides an overview of the methods that are utilized to protect the privacy of persons inside massive databases. In addition to this, it explores cutting-edge methods, such as data hiding, for concealing the identity of individuals who are included inside massive databases. The expansion of large amounts of data works directly against attempts to protect its integrity and secrecy.

MOTIVATION FOR THE STUDY

When dealing with vast volumes of data, it is essential to give careful consideration to the principles of privacy and security. Data is continually in danger of being easily corrupted if there is not sufficient data protection in place to prevent it. When it comes to the possibility that their private information may be seen by other parties when it is sent over the internet, users have a responsibility to exercise the utmost care (Yang, 2018).

Concerns over the privacy and safety of huge volumes of data are warranted for a number of important reasons. Because it is not recommended to utilize this security paradigm when dealing with complex systems, the massive data security paradigm is disabled by default. This is due to the fact that it is not possible to properly implement such a paradigm. However, in its absence, there is a persistent and ever-present danger that the data may be readily damaged. Therefore, we will be devoting a great deal of effort to addressing concerns related to data privacy and security. Privacy Information privacy, often known as data privacy, refers to an individual's right to limit the collection and use of personal information. The most significant aspect of information privacy is the capacity to restrict the sharing of sensitive data to a smaller subset of the population than that for whom it was originally intended. Users are obligated to use extreme caution while sending personal information over the internet if there is any chance that the recipient might monitor the transmission. Security The term "data and information security" refers to the steps taken to ensure that private data, networks, devices, and other assets are protected against unwanted access, disruption, manipulation, examination, recording, and deletion. Information security and data security are related concepts.

The difference between individual liberty and collective security in the context of data privacy, the collection, distribution, and use of sensitive information about consumers is subject to certain safeguards. An email account that requires a password to access is a good illustration of this principle. Security measures are necessary for data safety, but not enough on their own to guarantee privacy. The main goal of data security is to shield sensitive information from malicious assaults and stop stolen data from being used for profit.

DATA AND BIG DATA THEIR ROLES IN BUSINESS

With the assistance of capabilities for protecting individuals' privacy, it is possible to develop the foundational components and expansion strategies of a framework that enables the following:

1. The creation of effective monitoring systems for the policies at issue;
2. The design of privacy regulations that control access to data that is maintained in the planned big data platforms; and
3. The integration of the produced metrics into the intended analytic frameworks. It would seem that the techniques of enforcement that were developed for conventional DBMSs do not apply to many of the old techniques for data management are insufficient because of the stringent execution requirements posed by the big data environment, the diversity of the data, and the pressing nature of the analysis that must be performed on the data.

There has been the creation of significant data sets as well as the ongoing collection of information by a broad range of governmental and private entities. More recently, there has been a trend toward appreciating more comprehensive data sets, and it is probable that this will continue. Develop chances and paths that lead to a better knowledge of the processing of such data across a wide variety of disciplines by doing so.

The privacy of individuals is often invaded. Compliance with privacy rules and legislation is challenging in today's big data analytics and mining operations. Developers must be able to ensure that their apps comply with privacy agreements and that sensitive information is kept private regardless of whether the governing privacy laws or applications change (Liu, 2018).

Before trying to solve these issues, we should determine whether new contributions are needed in formal techniques and testing processes. This has to be done before trying to resolve the problems at hand. First and foremost, this paper shows that Hadoop's preprocessing is operational by providing extensive descriptions of each of the four phases that make up the Extract, Transform, and Load process. This stage serves as an example of the data loading procedure. The currently applicable privacy standards specify the many types of personally identifiable information that must be protected. Similar restrictions based on the need to protect individual's privacy may be applied to the choice of which data points may be stored and for how long. Additional restrictions based on the schema may be put in place immediately if they are deemed essential.

The validation of the map-reduce process comes in second. This method modifies vast data resources in order to better accommodate the requirements of a user. It's possible that data sharing across processes will be restricted, and that privacy regulations would dictate that just a specific number of records that have been returned will need to be accounted for in order to cover individual values.

Thirdly, validating the ETL procedure. To ensure compliance with privacy regulations, we must verify that the data will be stored for a legitimate business need. To some extent, this tactic may be compared to the procedure's second stage. Any personally identifiable information should be deleted from the data warehouse or aggregated before it is stored there. Test reports are a different sort of inquiry, but they are ones that are likely to be more advertised and, as a result, reach a larger audience. It is essential to utilize privacy phrases that specify 'purpose' in order to avoid the disclosure of sensitive information that goes beyond the bounds of what is legally allowed to be done with it.

SECRECY FOR BIG DATA DURING THE COLLECTION PHASE

User-involved and user-independent data production are two separate but equal types of data creation. The term "passive data production" is meant to convey the idea that the data are produced by the data owner's online behaviors like surfing without the data owner's knowledge that the data are being captured by a third party. We may potentially minimize the probability of having our privacy exposed by hiding or inventing information throughout the data-collecting process.

Constructing Entrance Bans

It is quite likely that the data owner will refuse to furnish the information at issue if the owner has cause to think that the data in question may reveal secret information that must not be exposed to the general public. Script or ad blockers, as well as encryption software, may help ensure a user's privacy while supplying information passively. Substituting bogus information in certain circumstances, may not be possible to prohibit unauthorized access to sensitive information due to practical considerations. It is possible that the data will be modified using the aforementioned technologies before it is received by a third party. The skewed representation of the data makes it harder to ascertain the truth. The following strategies are used by the originator of the data in order to manipulate it:

A tool Users are able to disguise their identities over the internet by using the Socket puppet service, which relies on deception. Through the use of a large number of Socket puppets, it is possible for the information of a single user to be connected with several distinct identities. In the event that this transpires, the data collector won't have sufficient information to connect together the several socket puppets that belong to the same individual.

It is feasible, for instance, to conceal one's genuine identity by making use of a security solution such as Mask Me. When making purchases online, where the data owner must often provide credit card information, this is beneficial in the context of such transactions (Liu et al 2020).

CONFIDENTIALITY OF BIG DATA DURING DATA ARCHIVING

Recent advancements in data storage technologies, such as the rise in popularity of cloud computing, have made the storage of massive amounts of data much less of a problem. These advancements solve the problem altogether. If the large data storage system is breached in any manner, it might cause a lot of harm since people's personal information could be made public. An application running in a decentralized setting may need access to data stored in many data centers. This makes it more challenging to ensure user privacy in such a context. Standard security measures in place to secure data may be broken down into four distinct groups. File-level, database-level, media-level, and application-level strategies for protecting information are all examples. To effectively respond to these three characteristics of big data analytics, the underlying storage infrastructure must be flexible and scalable.

It should be dynamically configurable to provide optimal performance across a broad variety of applications. Cloud computing's new storage virtualization paradigm is one promising solution for achieving these goals. Through a technique known as storage virtualization, many storage devices may be combined via a network to act as if they were a single, unified storage system. Storage pooling is the mechanism that allows this to happen. SecCloud refers to a method for protecting data in the cloud. The auditing of computations and concerns about the safety of cloud storage are taken into account in this method. As a result, there has been surprisingly little focus on protecting sensitive information throughout cloud computing's rise to prominence.

Recent advancements in data storage technologies, such as the rise in popularity of cloud computing, have made the storage of massive amounts of data much less of a problem. These advancements solve the problem altogether. If the large data storage system is breached in any manner, it might cause a lot of harm since people's personal information could be made public. An application running in a decentralized setting may need access to data stored in many data centers. This makes it more challenging to ensure user privacy in such a context. Standard security measures in place to secure data may be broken down into four distinct groups. File-level, database-level, media-level, and application-level strategies for protecting information are all examples. To effectively respond to these three characteristics of big data analytics, the underlying storage infrastructure must be flexible and scalable.

It should be dynamically configurable to provide optimal performance across a broad variety of applications. Cloud computing's new storage virtualization paradigm is one promising solution for achieving these goals. Through a technique known as storage virtualization, many storage devices may be combined via a network to act as if they were a single, unified storage system. Storage pooling is the mechanism that allows this to happen. SecCloud refers to a method for protecting data in the cloud. The auditing of computations and concerns about the safety of cloud storage are taken into account in this method. As a result, there has been surprisingly little focus on protecting sensitive information throughout cloud computing's rise to prominence (Wang et al., 2021).

METHODOLOGY

Strategies for protecting users' information in the cloud Keeping data safe on the cloud in terms of privacy, security, and accessibility is of the utmost importance. The first two are more directly relevant to preserving data privacy, since a breach in any of these areas may have serious consequences for a user's safety and privacy. When we say that information has been "made available," we imply that it has been provided to the right people. Having the Information Available Whenever Necessary. The major goal of the system is to protect users' privacy, which is crucial for the long-term storage of big databases. Several precedents have been set for doing this.

With the aim of satisfying such requirements. Data sent by a sender, for instance, may be encrypted with the recipient's knowledge of the sender's public key. encryption (PKE) so that the information may be read only by the designated recipient. The following are some steps that may be performed to safeguard the personal information of cloud storage users subsequently,

An Attribute-Based Encryption Technique A user's identity is crucial to the operation of the access control system has complete freedom of choice over all available tools. Homo morphism decipherment It's updatable in both IBE and ABE setups and ready for deployment. A text message receiver with encryption capabilities is possible.

- Storage-path encryption guarantees the security of cloud storage for massive datasets.

Deployment of cross-cloud solutions to describe a certain kind of cloud computing infrastructure, the phrase "hybrid cloud" is used. Hybrid cloud computing, which makes use of both externally-provided public cloud services and in-house private cloud services, is being used by a growing number of businesses in coordinate between the two aforementioned mediums.

BIG DATA AND ITS SOFTWARE TOOLS AND THEIR SUPPORT

When a business relies on cloud computing to keep vast volumes of data, that business will no longer have access to the data it has stored. Any information that is transferred to a cloud server runs the risk of having its integrity compromised since the security of such servers can never be guaranteed. According to the service level agreement (SLA), a data owner has to have unwavering confidence that the information they store in the cloud is secure. Implementing a system via which the owner of the data may check in to ensure that his information is safe and secure is one method for protecting the personal information of cloud users. The safety and security of the cloud have not been jeopardized in any way. The Reed-Solomon code, checksums, "trapdoor" hash functions, and cryptographic protocols such as message authentication codes (MACs), digital signatures, and so on are all examples of the multitude of methods that are utilized by conventional systems in order to validate the integrity of the data storage. Having this capability is typical of systems like this. Because of this, keeping the data honest is crucial. It is impossible to stress the significance of having sufficient checks and balances in place. It compares and contrasts the various methods used to ensure the reliability of the data. talked about Data saved in the cloud can be checked for accuracy rapidly.

The objective is to bring everything down from the cloud as quickly as possible. Testing for data integrity is carried out in order to prevent the need of retrieving information from cloud storage. The cloud serves as a verification method for the integrity of the system. Only when all of the data are kept in a single place will a server be able to provide solid confirmation that data integrity has been maintained. It is suggested very highly that integrity checks be carried out on a regular basis. to provide the highest level of protection against unauthorized access to user data. Processing of data in this era of big data while maintaining confidentiality is essential.

Batch, stream, graph, and interactive BI systems are the four main types of processing environments employed in the big data paradigm. Technology based on the principles of machine learning. To safeguard private information at each level of data collection and processing and prevent its disclosure to third parties. The procedure might be divided into two parts if necessary. The protection of sensitive information is the first concern. Privacy, given that the information acquired may contain personal particulars that need to be shielded from disclosure that is not authorized by the individual. data owner's contact information in the second stage, we will concentrate on deriving actionable insights from the data that we have gathered. Data without breaching the privacy of any of the individuals involved in the process (Wang et al., 2018).

This study provides a short discussion of some of the most typical techniques to maintaining privacy in huge datasets. Security measures for large datasets are also covered in this page. Traditional methods, such as these, do safeguard the anonymity of users to some degree; nonetheless, the presence of some drawbacks encouraged the creation of more effective tactics. De-identification is done when it comes to data mining; de-identification is a tried-and-true strategy for preserving individual privacy. This process involves first-stage generalization being utilized to clean data in order to shield individual privacy. Replacing quasi-identifiers with values that are generic but semantically identical prior to releasing the data for data mining and suppression not disclosing certain numbers at all. By using k-anonymity, we may lessen the likelihood of being reidentified. Both l-diversity and t-closeness have been used to improve data mining without jeopardizing consumers' privacy.

De-identification is essential for protecting sensitive data, and it may one day be handed off to big data analytics that factor in consumers' desire for privacy protection.

Indeed, in my experience as an, an attacker could have access to extra external information in order to do de-identification. We must keep in mind that the use of big data comes with a larger risk of re-identification, despite the fact that it may provide us with certain benefits. De-identification is not, however, a failsafe strategy for concealing personally identifiable information in huge datasets.

Either the flexibility and efficiency requirements of privacy-safe big data analytics, or the avoidance of de-identification dangers, are very challenging to meet. As de-identification methods continue to progress, it will become more feasible to do big data analytics while protecting users' privacy. algorithms that protect privacy and are both quick and effective in lowering the possibility of re-identification becoming feasible. De-identification may be accomplished using one of these three methods, which can each be used to safeguard an individual's right to anonymity: On the right, we have closeness, and on the left we have k-anonymity and diversity. When addressing issues pertaining to privacy, some terms that are often used include the following techniques:

Facts that may be used to immediately and clearly identify a person include their name, driver's license number, and social security number. Attributes that are used as identifiers include these details. The terms "gender," "age," and "date of birth" are all examples of "quasi-identifier characteristics," which are groups of information that may be used to birthplace, postal code, and the like. For the purposes of this article, the terms "gender," "age," and "date of birth" are examples of "quasi-identifier characteristics." This identity may be used with other pieces of information in order to track down the persons who were the original owners of the property. Identities of people and other private information are two examples of things that might be considered sensitive. Illness is one example of this, along with wealth, etc. Those qualities are said to be insensitive which are either general or are not harmful in any other way. Groups of data points are referred to be equivalence classes when each of their fields has the same value.

The k-anonymity property is said to be present in data releases if no more than k-1 people can infer any information about any individual in the release from the information included in the release. A database is a table with n rows and m columns, where each row represents a record that refers to a specific person in a population, and where the contents of the various rows are not required to be unique to one another for k-anonymization purposes. Attribute values associated with individuals in the population are listed in the various columns.

Safeguarding the privacy of individuals included inside data sets, group-based anonymization does so by reducing the granularity of the data's representation. This method, which is connected to L-diversity, is implemented to safeguard people's personal information. This decrease is the outcome of a trade-off in which the revenues gained through data management or mining techniques are sacrificed in exchange for somewhat greater personal privacy. Because each given record may be related to at least k other records in the dataset, the k-anonymity model can be generalized into the l-diversity model Distinct, Entropy, Recursive. To get there, we apply generalization and suppression methods to coarsen the data representation. Safeguarding identities at the k-individual level in the k-anonymity model is distinct from protecting the equivalent sensitive values after they have been generalized or omitted. This holds truer when there is uniformity among the sensitive values that make up the group. Some of the problems with the k-anonymity model are remedied by the l-diversity model. While dealing with delicate issues, the l-diversity paradigm encourages organizations to reflect that variety within themselves.

This helps further the process of anonymization enabled by the paradigm in question. This approach has the drawback of being very sensitive to all possible attribute values. If L-diverse data is still desired but there are not enough values for a sensitive characteristic, it may be necessary to insert phony information. While using this generated data would increase security, it might provide new challenges when doing analyses. Unfortunately, the L-diversity method cannot effectively avoid attribute disclosure since it may be attacked through skewness and similarity.

When it comes to privacy and safety in the cloud, HybrEx recommends the usage of the hybrid execution paradigm. A firm's private cloud stores and processes all of its data, whereas public clouds are only used to store and process data that has been designated as public by the company. It makes use of a company's own cloud and avoids using public clouds except for the safest operations. As a result, it only handles and saves data on the cloud that has been designated as such by the business. The amount of privacy at stake in the work at hand is taken into account while deciding whether or not to accept the assignment. It is a reliable choice that offers several practical benefits. HybrEx MapReduce may be used to create innovative applications in the following four domains, all of which can make use of both public and private cloud computing resources (Lei et al 2021).

In the First Place, We Have a Hybrid Map In the mapping stage, both the public cloud and a private cloud may be utilized, but in the reduction stage, only one can be used. Public data is used as input for map and reduce processes that are executed in the cloud, with intermediate data being exchanged between mappers and reducers and the final output likewise being stored in the cloud. The only real difference between private cloud computing and public cloud computing is how private data is handled. There are certain steps to take for each kind of work. Organized into horizontally-spaced sections in contrast to the mapping phase, which can only be performed on a public cloud, the reduction phase is handled by a private cloud.

Models will be shown that can do both thorough and quick integrity checks. However, when produced at both public and private clouds, the map phase presents a significant challenge that is not addressed by HybridEx since it just views the cloud as an opponent.

Homomorphism encryption is the foundation of privacy-preserving aggregation and is often used for collecting data for event statistics. Homomorphism public key encryption allows for the encoding of data from many sources with the same public key. Combining these cypher messages and deciphering the final text using the private key corresponding to each cypher is possible. However, aggregation is used for a more specific function. Using privacy-preserving aggregation, the processes of collecting and storing massive volumes of data may be carried out without compromising the confidentiality of the individuals involved. The rigidity of the system's design precludes sophisticated data mining that would allow it to take use of newly uncovered information. This suggests that research into massive datasets cannot rely on aggregation methods that do not compromise users' right to privacy.

Alterations to previously encoded data, in order to safeguard individuals' privacy, it is feasible to conduct operations on encrypted data during big data analytics. Processing encrypted data may be difficult and time-consuming, which might make it seem wasteful in the context of big data analytics. However, "big data" requires us to find fresh insights in a fair length of time from a massive quantity of data (Lee et al 2020).

Using Differential Privacy, researchers and database analysts may safely access and analyze sensitive personal data stored in databases without compromising the privacy of the persons whose information is being accessed. It is thus one of the most modern and one of the most successful approaches for safeguarding privacy in large data. Thus, the database system provides results with as few false positives as possible. This amount of background noise is just right; it serves to obscure sensitive information from prying eyes while still providing plenty material for analysts. Attempts to maintain secrecy using certain means in the past have ultimately been ineffective.

Group Insurance Commission (GIC) of the Commonwealth of Massachusetts started granting researchers access to subscribers' protected health information in the middle of the 1990s. In an effort to respect its clients' right to anonymity, GIC conceals some information about them, such as their full names and physical addresses. At the time, Latanya Sweeney was a PhD student at MIT. She used publicly accessible voter data and the GIC database to successfully identify the health record. That's why it's not a good idea to try to hide our true identity by keeping certain details about ourselves under wraps.

Differential Privacy is a mechanism designed to address this issue (DP). Analysts in DP are not given complete access to a database where sensitive information is stored. In order to protect the confidentiality of the data, an extra layer of software is added between the database and the analyst. The term "privacy guard" may be used to refer to this additional layer of software.

The analyst will first run a database query utilizing the temporary privacy guard. As a second step, the privacy guard receives the analyst's query and compares it to all the others to determine the level of privacy risk associated with each. after thinking about the potential violations of privacy that may occur.

As a third step, the privacy guard checks the database to determine the best next steps. Modify it based on the level of privacy risk identified in Step 4, and then provide it to the analyst.

Data that would normally be clean will be contaminated with extra noise if there is a serious privacy risk. If the risk to privacy is low, the amount of distortion created won't be enough to dramatically compromise the correctness of the response, but it will be enough to keep the data secret. Once a serious privacy risk has been identified, however, more distortion is imposed.

Disguising one's true identity by using false documents or other means, It was attempted to employ anonymization, privacy protection, and big data approaches all at once for the goal of analyzing use data without disclosing any user identities. Unfortunately, this caused a lot of problems. Intel's Human Factors Engineering team aimed to improve the usability of the company's wildly popular internal web portal by analyzing user behavior based on the pages that are often visited. Intel workers' privacy requires a change to the repository for the portal's usage logs so that PII may be stripped without hindering the use of big data technologies for analysis or the ability to re-identify a log entry for the purpose of investigating possibly criminal behavior. As a result of its novel and appealing basic notion, cloud computing has quickly become a dominating force in the world of information and communications technology during the last several years. The phrase "cloud computing" is used to describe a computer model with similarities to distributed computing on a massive scale. It offers the chance to enhance the administration of IT systems while altering how computers and other electronic gadgets are seen, acquired, and used. There are several advantages of storing data using a cloud storage service, some of which include, but are not limited to:

The four main benefits of cloud computing are (1) lessening the load of storage management and equipment maintenance for cloud users, (2) avoiding costly investments in hardware and software, (3) making data accessible regardless of one's physical location, and (4) providing access to data at any time and from any location. To achieve these goals, Intel developed an open architecture for anonymization (Shao et al 2021).

Many different anonymization and re-identification technologies that leverage information gleaned from web server logs may make use of this framework. During the design phase, it became clear that corporate data had properties that set it apart from the typical examples seen in the literature when discussing anonymization. Some examples of these traits are: Incorporating big data techniques into a commercial setting was validated here, even when dealing with anonymized data. Intel also discovered that obfuscating data, such as IP addresses and users, did not make the data more secure against correlation attacks. Again, Intel made this finding.

They analyzed the benefits and drawbacks of closing these security loopholes and determined that information about the user's browser and operating system the "User Agent" provides unmistakable proof of the user's identity. This case study illustrates how anonymization may be used to protect sensitive company data during big data analysis without sacrificing speed or thoroughness. It also details the challenges encountered on the road to full anonymization. In this study, k-anonymity criteria were employed to evaluate the success of the anonymization procedure. Intel's usage of Hadoop to analyze the de-identified data aided the Human Factors specialists in making better use of the data. While this is helpful, we have learned that it is not sufficient to just hide information or draw generalizations about it; rather, anonymized datasets need rigorous analysis for security risks.

Individuals' privacy is a top concern; thus, the MapReduce design has a number of safeguards to keep it that way. Existing privacy-preserving association rule algorithms include noise into their search processes, which modifies the original transaction data and makes it more difficult to find the proverbial needle in the haystack. Since the goal of this inquiry is to preserve as much of the original transaction's value as possible while simultaneously avoiding privacy breaches, the original transaction was left unmodified inside the noised transaction. Because of this, there is still a chance that a dishonest cloud service provider may distort the true frequency of item collection and contaminate the approach.

The notion of "hiding a needle in a haystack" is at the heart of this privacy-protection technique, therefore enough privacy protection must be provided despite the likelihood of association rule leaking.

Finding the right information in a large database may be like trying to locate a needle in a haystack. Due to the need to carefully examine a variety of aspects, the presently existing solutions are unable to randomly produce noise.

An analysis of the privacy threats posed by online shopping. Since noise must be generated to create the "haystack" that will hide the "needle," the overall computational cost of this strategy is higher than that of the alternatives. Therefore, it is crucial to assess the level of challenge associated with addressing each issue using the Hadoop framework while it is hosted on the cloud. Figure 5 shows the association rule after being "noised," with empty circles, and the original association rule, shown by dark diamond points. Considering the plethora of noised association rules already in place, the service provider may insert a dummy item into the first transaction to facilitate the exposure of the true rules. Since there are already a lot of noisy association regulations, this is what is done.

The data was compiled by the data supplier. Next, each object, authentic or not, is given a unique identification number. An external cloud platform will extract a set of frequently occurring items, and then the service provider will save the necessary encoding information to identify and remove the fake item. Information is sent from the service provider's private cloud to a public cloud, where an a priori algorithm is implemented. The external cloud platform feeds back on the most commonly used items and the value of assistance. The provider filters the collection of often occurring items that is affected by the erroneous item using a code to make determining the correct association rule easier. Since the extraction of the association rule does not need a large amount of mathematical work, the service provider is not unduly burdened in any way.

Distribution of voluminous data while protecting consumers' privacy. More and more public resources, including social media and mobile phones, provide the opportunity to collect data. Over time, this has led to a rise in the volume of related data, which is now a crucial part of many industries and fields of study, including medicine. Input privacy and output privacy are the two main buckets into which privacy-protecting models may be sorted. The publication of data that has been anonymized using methods like k-anonymity and l-diversity has significant implications for input privacy. Privacy-preserving issues that arise while manipulating or auditing the output of different data mining algorithms are of special relevance in the field of output privacy. Association rule hiding and query auditing are two common methods of addressing these issues in the interest of privacy (Ramirez-Asis et al 2022).

A lot of work has been done to improve both the quality of privacy protection by the quantification of vulnerabilities and the worth of publicly available data. To address this issue, it is necessary to first segment the data into smaller pieces, sometimes called fragments, and then anonymize each fragment separately. While k-anonymity is successful at preventing identity attacks, it is vulnerable to attribute disclosure assaults due to a lack of diversity in the sensitive characteristic inside the equivalence class. This is due to their being just one instance of the sensitive attribute inside the equivalence class. Each equivalence class has to have a minimum of l well-represented sensitive values for the l-diversity model to work. Distributed systems like the MapReduce framework are often utilized for this purpose. This is done so that a resource-intensive task may be distributed over several nodes, greatly boosting overall performance. To counteract these inefficiencies, new methods of privacy protection have been developed, each boasting higher standards of security.

Assessing the reliability of an individual or group is crucial to effective trust management. The output of a technological method for defining trust in digital processing is a trust value. Evidence-based trust assessments include a variety of contextual criteria before arriving at a final score, which may be continuous or discrete. In order to keep trust evaluations private, it offers two distinct methods. It has been proposed to use two servers so that requesters with different needs for privacy may share and discuss evaluation results.

Just pretend that two separate service providers, each motivated by their own financial concerns, have decided against working together. To protect the privacy of the firms under scrutiny, it is feasible to use an authorized proxy (AP) to oversee the safekeeping and transmission of all relevant evidence. An evaluation party, or EP, processes the data collected from several trusted-evidence suppliers which may be supplied by a cloud service provider. The EP encrypts the collected data before delivering a secret trust score for first assessment. When AP is asked for a pre-evaluation, EP will verify the requestor's eligibility. If the check produces a good result, the AP re-encrypts the pre-evaluation result that can be decrypted by the requester. This prevents the AP from acquiring the plain pre-evaluation result while still enabling the requester to decode the pre-evaluation result. The simple pre-evaluation result cannot be obtained by the AP without the EP's involvement in an extra stage.

Two privacy models, k-anonymity and l-diversity, have been identified as having room for improvement. Anonymization with the MapReduce architecture Applying the MapReduce framework is highly recommended for achieving optimal data processing efficiency. Large, MapReduce-like distributed frameworks are used to manage enormous data sets. In order to handle the data, a mapper must first divide it in half. It will be broken down into smaller pieces that the mappers will then analyze, leading to the creation of pairings. When the architecture is set up in this way, all of the keyed pairs are delivered to a single reducer. The sets obtained after the reduction are then used to get the ultimate outcome.

Privacy in a MapReduce Environment with K-Anonymity Since the data is separated automatically by the MapReduce architecture, the k-anonymization strategy cannot be picky about how the information is distributed among the mappers. Our MapReduce-based method is very similar to the Mondrian algorithm. In each cycle, the number of equivalence classes is increased by one, up to a maximum of q. The result is a greater degree of generality and, more significantly, fewer iterations overall.

Multiplicity using MapReduce for L-Diversity It is crucial to include private information into the mapper's output keys or values in order to broaden the privacy model from k-anonymity to l-diversity. Because of this, it is crucial to tweak the combinations that the mappers and combiners generate. The mapper takes both the sensitive characteristic and the quasi-identifiers into account when dealing with l-diversity, but simply the sensitive characteristic when dealing with k-anonymity (Xiaochun et al., 2021).

Oftentimes, the header information of a big data stream will include a timestamp. Sensor data, call center records, website analytics, patient records, and social media posts are just a few examples of the types of data that may be collected in large amounts. Quality of service (QoS) characteristics including latency, precision, and timeliness are just a few examples of factors that might limit the ability to analyze huge data streams. Before being used in highly confidential sectors like healthcare, big data mining must be carried out in a manner that safeguards the privacy of its users. To protect the confidentiality of stored data, k-anonymity is often used. Unfortunately, this method cannot be used to anonymize massive data streams. The following are a few of the reasons why:

Existing k-anonymity approaches are demonstrated to be NP-hard to implement, and real-time processing of data streams is required as opposed to the information that is generally maintained. As it stands, scanning the data many times during the anonymization process is necessary when using the currently known techniques for static k-anonymization. Data streams cannot be processed at the same rate as traditional data. The third reason anonymization is important is the dramatic increase in the volume of data being collected. Existing anonymization techniques are stymied by the ever-increasing number of data flows. The FADS algorithm was selected as the answer to the first and second problems described. If we need to hide our true identity inside a data stream, this is the method to use.

Since the FADS method handles tuples individually, it is unsuitable for processing a large data stream in real time. That's one of the problems with the FADS approach. Second, certain tuples may be kept in the system for an extraordinarily long time before being deleted when a particular threshold has been achieved. Three new pieces of information were uncovered as a result of this inquiry. First, parallelism is used to increase FADS's efficacy and make the method suitable for anonymizing massive data streams. For this purpose, FADS processing is parallelized using several threads. Second, we give a simple proactive heuristic estimated round-time that prevents a tuple from being published after its expiration date has passed. Finally, the experimental findings are used to prove that FAST is superior than FADS and other current algorithms in terms of efficiency and effectiveness, while also significantly cutting down on the amount of information lost and the cost metric during the anonymization process.

FADS considers a new parameter that reflects the greatest delay an application may sustain. Maximum delay that an application may withstand is represented by this setting. The name given to this setting is "expiration-time." A simple heuristic estimated-round-time has been built to ensure that a tuple is never made public after its expiration time has elapsed. A tuple's FADS residency status is not checked until there is a change in the couple's circumstances. This results in the publication of tuples that should have been deleted at a later time. This problem significantly inflates the costs of running a real-time application processing data stream and diminishes the utility of such an application (Ved et al., 2019).

When discussing measures to ensure one's own confidentiality and safety, when it comes to healthcare, big data has proven to be a game-changer. The current shift toward digitalizing medical data has had a significant impact on the medical care industry. As a result, healthcare providers must navigate data that is more sophisticated, multifaceted, and current than ever before. Big data is a collection of data sets that are so large and complex that they defy traditional techniques of analysis, storage, and dissemination. In general, it is not possible to manage this sort of data collection using current techniques. Many different initiatives provide the healthcare industry the push it needs to fully use big data. What we have seen is what happens when scientists combine genetic study with massive data mining.

It may be simpler for physicians to choose the optimal therapy for their patients if they have quick access to their patients' medical records. Insurers will have to entirely rework their prediction models as a direct result of big data. By using embedded sensors (which are attached to patients), medical professionals may be able to monitor patients' vital signs in real time and get immediate notifications if anything about the patient's state seems out of the ordinary. Electronic Health Records (EHRs) are crucial for the future of healthcare IT, which will place a premium on digitization and integrated analytics.

Healthcare organizations largely grasped the value proposition of electronic health records when HER incentive programs were established, namely, that they would increase access to comprehensive, accurate, and shareable healthcare data, eventually leading to better patient care. As a result of the ever-evolving risk environment and the emergence of new hazards and opportunities, it is predicted that the frequency of security breaches would increase in the years to come. Big data provided an in-depth analysis of the various methods and data sets used by ubiquitous healthcare, illuminating their conclusions with examples derived from a broad variety of diseases. Problems that may be quickly diagnosed and treated with the use of technology were discussed. These included falls (both deadly and nonfatal), Parkinson's disease, cardiovascular diseases, stress, and more. In order to deal with these illnesses and a wide variety of other permanent handicaps, such as blindness, mobility challenges, paralysis, and a host of others, we have explored a number of healthcare treatments that are comprehensive in nature.

A further advantage that can't be disregarded is the abundance of easily accessible healthcare items on the market nowadays. It talks about how many illnesses are linked to the lack of healthcare for the general population. Concerns about patient privacy and data security have been raised as the use of big data expands in the healthcare sector. Information on patients is first kept in data centers with varied degrees of security. Modern businesses, in especially those dealing with a huge number of naturally diverse data sets, have needs that are inherently incompatible with the security practices of the past (Kaplunovich et al., 2021).

Most notably, this is true for huge corporations. With the surge in popularity of healthcare cloud services has come an increase in the challenge of protecting large, widely dispersed SaaS systems. Escalating because more information comes in from more places and in more forms. Therefore, big data governance is necessary before analytics can be performed on the data. Overwhelming businesses could benefit from big data analysis if it helps them get insights that lead to better choices and more strategic actions. Despite this, data is seldom analyzed in its entirety. We begin our exploration of the privacy issues highlighted by big data with One crucial step is defining the specific privacy protections that must be in place for large data sets, and then double-checking to make sure that these measures are sufficient for processing massive amounts of data. The different methods available for protecting privacy in the context of big data applications, as well as the issues that occur with privacy at each step of the big data life cycle.

This study also analyses both conventional and state-of-the-art methods for protecting individuals' anonymity in huge databases. To illustrate how challenging it may be to maintain anonymity while doing association rule mining, the "needle in a haystack" analogy is sometimes used. This is because it is so challenging to discover the one useful piece of information among all the noise. Anonymity-focused theoretical frameworks, differential privacy studies, and an examination of the many cutting-edge technologies now in use may all contribute to solving privacy problems associated with big data. This study presents scalable methods of anonymization. context where MapReduce is used. Adding more nodes, such as mappers and reducers, is a simple way to make it bigger. Adopting fresh perspectives on privacy and security in the age of big data calls for effective solutions to the problem of scalability, which is our ultimate goal. Data, especially when it comes to the challenge of balancing private data security with public access models in the map-reduce architecture.

DATA SAFETY FOR CONTEMPORARY BUSINESS THE LATEST TRENDS

The rapid expansion of technology over the last several years has accelerated the rate at which development and innovation are taking place. Because of the COVID-19 outbreak that occurred in this year, IT professionals have been compelled to realize that their place in the contactless world is shifting. This is not the only item that is undergoing transformation at this time, however.

As a consequence of advancements made in natural language processing and machine learning, it is anticipated that the use of artificial intelligence will become more widespread by the year 2023. Using this strategy, AI is able to develop its comprehension of human beings and engage in activities that are progressively more complicated. In the not-too-distant future, it is anticipated that 5G would significantly enhance both the working and residential environments that we now occupy.

The dominance of computing power has already been established in this era of digital technology, with practically every appliance and item being transformed into a computerized version. And it's not going away any time soon, since data scientists' estimates imply that the computer infrastructure we're now developing will only become better over time. We are now living in the era of 5G, but very soon we will have 6G and much more power at our disposal and in every device that we use. The expansion of computer capability has led to an increase in the number of technology-related jobs available in the private sector. However, in order for people to be successful in these roles, they will need to acquire new skills. In the not-too-distant future, the jobs that are available in fields such as data science, robotics, and IT management will form the backbone of the global economy. The more complex the computer in our devices becomes, the more work there is for technicians, information technology departments, relationship managers, and the customer service industry as a whole.

It makes sense for us to investigate robotic process automation as part of a wider examination of computers.

The contributions of artificial intelligence have been essential to the intelligent and successful development that has been made in our world. It is not enough to just imitate what other people do; we must also go the additional mile to make our everyday tasks easier. Data scientists are working on developing artificial intelligence (AI) home robots, appliances, work gadgets, wearables, and much more, all of which will be available far beyond 2023. In almost every sector of the economy in the modern day, we depend on complex computer programs. As more companies move into digital industries, there has been an increase in the need for more sophisticated information technology equipment (Tong et al., 2020).

The process of automating every aspect of human life via the use of digital technology is referred to as "datafication," which is also a phrase. To express it in the simplest terms possible, datafication is the process by which operations that have historically been handled by people are automated via the use of data-driven technology. Data can be found in every corner of the internet, and it is not going away any time soon. This includes the software on our computers, the manufacturing gear we use, our phones, and even the artificial intelligence-powered devices we use. This indicates that there is a significant need for the capacity to guarantee that our data is preserved in an acceptable, secure, and safe manner.

Despite the fact that artificial intelligence (AI) has received a lot of attention over the last decade, it is still one of the developing technology trends. This is due to the fact that its ramifications for how we live, work, and play are still in their infancy. AI has demonstrated to be incredibly successful in a variety of sectors, including image and speech recognition, personal assistants on smartphones, navigation programs, and ride-sharing apps, to name just a few of them.

Additionally, AI will be used to analyze interactions in order to determine underlying connections and insights, to help predict demand for services such as hospitals, which will enable authorities to make better decisions regarding the utilization of resources, and to detect shifting patterns of customer behavior by analyzing data in near real-time, which will result in increased revenues and enhanced personalized experiences.

This overarching phrase refers to any and all types of "reality duplication" technology, including "virtual reality," "augmented reality," "mixed reality," and "extended reality." The creation of this technology is essential given that everyone in today's society has a burning desire to break free from the claimed physical restrictions of the planet. This technology is used in a wide range of sectors because to its capacity to provide a believable atmosphere without the need for actual presence. Some examples of these industries include modelling, gaming, medical, and retail.

The gaming industry is an important area for well-liked occupations that do not need a significant amount of schooling but rather a desire for online gaming, which is discussed while talking about virtual reality.

The use of 3D printing for the purpose of prototyping constitutes both a significant technological achievement and a developing trend in the field of technology. The biomedical and industrial industries have reaped significant benefits from the use of this method. We never anticipated that we would be able to print anything out and have it delivered to our front door. As a result, three-dimensional printing is another innovation that is expected to be relevant for the foreseeable future. Companies in the data and healthcare industries that rely largely on 3D printing for their products provide a broad range of well-paying opportunities all around the globe. These companies are located in almost every country.

Even though blockchain technology is most often linked with Bitcoin and other cryptocurrencies, it delivers security that is essential in a number of situations. This is the case despite the fact that blockchain technology is most commonly connected with cryptocurrencies. After being recorded, information that is saved in a blockchain cannot be altered in any way. Our network of linked computers that stores and transmits information is referred to as a "chain" after we came up with the term to describe it. Because it is not possible to modify blocks that have already been constructed, it is incredibly safe. Due to the fact that blockchains are driven by consensus, it is impossible for a single entity to assert control over the data. In a blockchain network, there is no need for a centralized authority or an independent verifier to exist.

Even though it has been around for quite some time, the field of cyber security is still very much in the development stage, just like any other field. This is due, in part, to the fact that the threats posed by contemporary technology are continually evolving. There will always be individuals in the world with bad intentions who want to get into computer systems in order to steal sensitive information, and these people will always discover new methods to get beyond even the most stringent security mechanisms. The use of cutting-edge security measures is another factor that adds to this phenomenon. As long as there are people who commit crimes online, cybersecurity will be a hot subject (Uskenbayeva et al., 2021).

CONFIDENTIALITY OF BIG DATA DURING DATA ARCHIVING

Practical Aspects

However, despite the fact that the phrases are often used synonymously, there is a substantial distinction between data protection and data privacy. Both data protection and data privacy restrict the manner in which information may be accessed, as well as the parties that have permission to do so. Compliance regulations help assure that businesses are safeguarding the personal information of their consumers, which is the responsibility of the businesses themselves.

The majority of the time, rules that are intended to protect sensitive information are also relevant to private data, such as medical records and other information that may be used to identify a person (PII). It is essential for the development and financing of any company, as well as the seamless operation of the firm itself. If a company takes the necessary procedures to protect the information it maintains, it reduces its risk of experiencing a data breach, suffering damage to its reputation, and failing to comply with applicable regulations. The current components of data protection systems include data loss prevention (DLP), encrypted storage, firewalls, and endpoint security.

Implementing certain data protection measures is necessary in order to guarantee the confidentiality, integrity, and accessibility of our data. This idea is also referred to as data security in certain circles. Every company that collects, processes, or stores personally identifiable information need to have a data protection policy in place. This is true whether the information is being collected, processed, or stored. Utilizing an appropriate strategy in the event of a breach in data security or a natural disaster may help prevent the loss of data, the theft of data, or the corruption of data, or at least lessen the impact of these events.

Where can we get information on the best practices for securing sensitive data, and what are those best practices?

The fundamentals of data protection ensure that information is both secure and readily available under any and all circumstances. The backup of operational data, business continuity and disaster recovery (often abbreviated as BCDR), data management, and data deployment are all components of data availability.

The following are examples of important concerns with data management that need to be addressed in order to guarantee the safety of data:

The process of making data available to users so that it may be accessed and used by those users even after the data has been deleted or destroyed is referred to as data availability. We may effortlessly move our most critical files to both local storage and storage in the cloud with the assistance of data lifecycle management. This process does not need any manual labor on our part.

In the context of information lifecycle management, valuing information assets, classifying them, and protecting them against a wide variety of threats, such as failures and interruptions at the facility, mistakes made by applications and users, failed equipment, and attacks by malicious software and viruses, are all components of this process.

Every company that gathers or retains information that is critical or sensitive makes the security of private information a top priority in their operations. There are numerous different manifestations of sensitive information, the most common of which being personally identifiable information and protected health information (PII). The information that is made public includes particulars about bank accounts, medical histories, identification numbers, dates of birth, and telephone numbers (Ananda et al., 2021).

Concerns with data privacy apply to every piece of personally identifiable information (PII) that a business either holds or processes. These details are often necessary for the sustained prosperity, expansion, and financial stability of a company.

Data privacy guarantees that only those users who are specifically authorized to do so are able to access any personally identifiable information. Data thieves are deterred from utilizing stolen information for malevolent purposes, and organizations are assisted in completing their regulatory requirements as a result.

In order to maintain compliance with the legislation governing the protection of personal data, some pieces of information cannot be collected, transmitted, or utilized. Names, photographs, electronic mail addresses, financial information, IP addresses, and biometric data are all forms of personal data.

Regulations regarding privacy and the protection of personal information might be quite different depending on where we are. Data privacy law was implemented in China on June 1, 2017, and the General Data Protection Regulation was passed by the European Union (EU) in 2018. (GDPR). If we fail to comply with the requirements of the many different laws and regulatory agencies, we might suffer damage to our reputation in addition to financial consequences.

If we obey one set of rules, it does not always mean we will follow another. In addition, any and all rules are subject to modification, and the requirements of various laws may be applied differently depending on the particular circumstances. Due to the complexity of the situation, it is difficult to apply compliance procedures in a way that is both consistent and acceptable.

BIG DATA AND ITS SOFTWARE TOOLS AND THEIR SUPPORT

Practical Aspects

Integrate.io focuses on the integration of data as well as the processing of that data and the preparation of that data for analytics in the cloud. It will bring together all of the various data that we utilize. With the help of its user-friendly graphical interface, we are able to construct an ETL, ELT, or replication solution. Integrate.io gives developers a choice between a no-code and a low-code alternative when it comes to constructing data pipelines. Included are choices pertaining to business, service, advertising, and overall growth. By using Integrate.io, we are able to get the most out of our data without having to make costly investments in new gear, software, or staff. Customers have the ability to get in touch with the Integrate.io support staff through a variety of mediums, including e-mail, live chat, the phone, and video conferencing.

Adverity is a versatile end-to-end marketing analytics platform that enables marketers to track the effectiveness of their marketing efforts from a variety of perspectives and find new insights in real time. Adverity assists marketers in analyzing the effectiveness of their marketing from a unified perspective and quickly locating insights that can be put into action in real time. This is accomplished by combining data from over 600 sources, utilizing stunning data visualizations, and applying AI-powered predictive analytics. It is possible to monitor results, which enables businesses to make choices that are better informed and ultimately leads to improved growth.

Dataddo is a web-based ETL solution that eliminates the need for us to write any form of code by giving us the freedom to choose our own metrics and characteristics. The task of establishing data pipelines that are trustworthy is made much easier with Dataddo. To support Dataddo, we did not need to make any changes to our fundamental processes, nor did we need to add any new components to our architecture. Instead, it operated without any issues with the data stack that we already had. We are able to concentrate on integrating our data thanks to Dataddo's basic setup and user-friendly interface, which frees us from the need to learn how to utilize yet another platform.

The Apache Hadoop software architecture can easily handle large data volumes and file systems that are spread across several nodes. In order to manage enormous amounts of data, the programming approach known as MapReduce is used. Hadoop is a framework that is open-source, adaptable, and written in Java. It is compatible with a wide variety of operating systems. This is the most powerful device for dealing with large amounts of data that we can discover. Hadoop is used by more than 50 percent of the Fortune 50 organizations currently in operation. Big Names include companies such as Amazon Web Services, Hortonworks, IBM, Intel, Microsoft, and many more besides. Other examples include Facebook.

Cloudera has initiated the Cloudera Distribution for Hadoop (CDH) project with the intention of bringing this breakthrough to the masses. It's a free version of the platform that comes with open-source technologies like Hadoop, Spark, and Impala already installed. It provides the way for an infinite amount of information to be accumulated, managed, organized, discovered, modelled, and disseminated (Vij et al., 2020).

The Apache Cassandra database management system (DBMS) is a free and open-source distributed NoSQL database management system that can handle enormous amounts of data across numerous commodity machines. CQL may be used in order to access the database (Cassandra Query Language). Cassandra is put to use by a wide variety of major organizations, some of which include Accenture, American Express, Facebook, General Electric, Honeywell, and Yahoo, amongst many more.

DATA AND BIG DATA THEIR ROLES IN BUSINESS PRACTICAL ASPECTS

1. Increased likelihood of making a good first impression: Many contemporary organizations may explore a diverse variety of data sources in an effort to improve their understanding of a certain market segment or consumer base. Purchases and calls to customer service are the most common types of information that are collected directly from consumers. The most common types of information that are collected from third parties include credit reports and financial transactions, activity on social media, survey data, and cookies. Understanding how consumers traverse a company's numerous web pages and menus to get what they're searching for is essential in today's increasingly digital economy. Clickstream analysis of e-commerce activity is a strong tool that may help businesses accomplish this goal. By keeping a record of the items that consumers add to their virtual shopping carts before deciding to delete them or leave them there without purchasing them, companies may get insight into

the kind of things that customers were considering buying but eventually decided against. In addition, conventional retailers may be able to get information about their consumers that is of benefit to them. Watching films of people traversing a physical area and contrasting it to the way they would navigate a website is a frequent way to accomplish this goal. Another technique is to ask people directly (Li et al., 2020).

2. Advantage is increased visibility in the market: It is probable that by analyzing vast volumes of client data, we will be able to get a more comprehensive grasp of the dynamics of the market and a better understanding of the intricacies of the purchasing habits of consumers. It is normal practice to use social media as a resource for determining how the market is responding to a wide variety of items, ranging from breakfast cereal to vacation package deals. Opinions, ideas, and even photos taken by individuals are important commodities in almost every kind of business transaction. Even the breakfasts they provide in the morning. These viewpoints on collaboration are very necessary for those who operate businesses. If, for instance, it is possible to rank the various requirements of customers in descending order of importance, big data could be valuable in product creation and market research. The majority of business intelligence in the e-commerce and internet industries is propelled by the use of big data as the primary motivating factor. This is due to the fact that business intelligence is just one of the numerous applications that may make use of big data.

3. Chains of supply that are flexible: Be aware that contemporary supply networks are very vulnerable to calamities such as shipwrecks in the Suez Canal, shortages of toilet paper and other necessities caused by pandemics, and trade disruptions caused by Brexit. As a culture, we have a tendency to ignore our supply networks until there is a huge disruption, which is why this new phenomenon is so shocking. Thanks to big data, which allows near-real-time predictive analytics, we are able to maintain an effective worldwide network of demand, production, and distribution. This is made possible by the globalization of our operations. Big data systems have the potential to give previously unimaginable levels of insight by merging data on customer behaviors obtained from e-commerce websites and retail apps with data on product suppliers, current pricing, and even shipping and weather conditions. These are considerations that need to be given by any form of business. With the use of consumer data and real-time pricing, even the smallest e-commerce enterprises would be able to improve their decision-making in areas such as stock management, risk reduction, and the hiring of temporary or seasonal employees (Yang et al 2018).

4. Increased accuracy in audience segmentation and the use of recommendation systems: Customers who, like me, make frequent use of recommendation engines may not be aware of how much farther they have progressed since the advent of big data since we are so used to using them. In the past, association rules that determined which products were bought on a regular basis were used to give predictive analysis for

recommendation engines. It is possible that soon, online sellers will have the capacity to demonstrate to us that customers who purchased widgets also purchased related items, such as fidget spinners. We just finished talking about a large customer data collection that makes contemporary recommendation algorithms far more advanced than that by making them more responsive to consumer behavior and demographics. In addition, the uses of these technologies extend far beyond than the sphere of internet-based retailing. There is a possibility that a waiter's recommendations are based on data collected by the point-of-sale system. This data may take into account a variety of factors, including the current supply of ingredients, the level of popularity of particular menu items, the level of profitability of particular products, and even the most recent trends on social media. We may provide another piece of data for big data engines to process simply by snapping a photo of our food and sharing it online. This will allow them to better understand our eating habits. The providers of streaming content utilize technologies that are far more advanced. It's possible that consumers won't even be questioned about the shows they often watch when they make a purchase. The following option is presented to the viewer before the currently playing movie, program, or song has completed playing. This deters viewers from leaving in the middle of the content being viewed by combining their preferences with a large quantity of big data research obtained from other users and social media.

5. Creativity driven by empirical evidence: Although motivation is required, it is not sufficient on its own to trigger innovative thought. To generate fresh ideas that are interesting enough to warrant further investigation requires an investment of both time and effort. Research and development, which usually culminates in the production of brand-new goods and services, may be supported by a range of big data technologies and approaches. There are times when data that has been prepared for transmission (that is, cleaned, organized, and controlled) could be regarded a product in and of itself. This is the case when the data is ready to be sent. As an example, the London Stock Exchange is able to generate far more revenue from the sale of data and research than it does from trading stocks. Data, even when integrated with the most cutting-edge big data technologies, is not sufficient on its own to provide novel insights. Data scientists, business intelligence analysts, and other analytics specialists are still needed because of the creativity and innovation they bring to the table. The amount and diversity of big data may be daunting in an environment where it is stored in separate silos; but, when it is stored in a Hadoop cluster or a cloud data lake, it may provide teams a fresh perspective on patterns that would otherwise be concealed.

6. Multiple uses for data sets: In the course of my professional experience, I have come across instances in which the data that was carefully modelled and generated for one business objective turned out to be wholly inappropriate for another. A customer's history of using many credit cards is likely to pique the interest of the

marketing department of a credit card firm, for example. Unhappily, the inquiry was complicated by the large number of unsuccessful swipes and cancelled transactions, which were caused by either connection issues with the payment terminal or flaws in the magnetic stripes of the cards. These problems may have been caused by a combination of both. As a direct consequence of this, the botched financial dealings were painstakingly removed from the system. The information that was acquired as a direct result was beneficial to the marketing campaign that was planned. Because reviewing declined transactions that would have left card fraud signals prevented the fraud prevention team from making use of it, the team was unable to use it. The fact that the data had been stored on cassettes indicated that it had been lost forever and could not be retrieved. It is now feasible, because to the development of big data, to store raw data in a data lake without first processing it and then just modelling it whenever it is required for analysis. After that, ad hoc queries or data pipelines that are specifically designed for each use case may be utilized to feed the analytics methods. Because of this, the potential depth and breadth of applications that may use the same data pool has been significantly expanded (Mei et al., 2020).

SECRECY FOR BIG DATA DURING THE COLLECTION PHASE

Practical Aspects

Privacy and security in terms of big data is an important issue. A big data security model is not suggested in the event of complex applications due to which it gets disabled by default. However, in its absence, data can always be compromised easily. As such, this section focuses on privacy and security issues. Privacy Information privacy is the privilege to have some control over how personal information is collected and used. Information privacy is the capacity of an individual or group to stop information about themselves from becoming known to people other than those they give the information. One serious user privacy issue is the identification of personal information during transmission over the Internet. Security is the practice of defending information and information assets through the use of technology, processes and training from Unauthorized access, Disclosure, Disruption, Modification, Inspection, Recording, and Destruction. Privacy vs. security Data privacy is focused on the use and governance of individual data—things like setting up policies in place to ensure that consumers' personal information is being collected, shared and utilized in appropriate ways. Security concentrates more on protecting data from malicious attacks and the misuse of stolen data for profit. While security is fundamental for protecting data, it's not sufficient for addressing privacy (Liu et al., 2021).

DATA SAFETY FOR CONTEMPORARY BUSINESS THE LATEST TRENDS

The security team is tasked with maintaining vigilance on the enemy in order to detect any indications of abnormal behavior or upcoming assaults. When an opponent has established a foothold in a market and is contemplating the best course of action to take, it is possible for a corporation to exploit the opportunity.

Companies have a duty to educate themselves on the many privacy rules and regulations that are now in effect. As a consequence of this, workers will have a higher propensity to conduct themselves in an organized way, and any possible violations of data privacy will go undiscovered.

When it comes to operating a successful company, honesty and openness are vital qualities. Customers will have a better understanding of the value of their data as well as the safeguards that are accessible to them. As a result of consumers' shifting beliefs around privacy, businesses will become more vigilant and attentive.

It's possible that enhanced data security may be achieved by implementing risk management and risk assessment strategies, as well as mandating compliance from business partners, suppliers, and vendors. When it comes to safeguarding themselves against damage, companies need to increase the amount of work they put out, especially in cases when the threat originates from external sources (Riasetiawan et al., 2021).

Education and Awareness of All Relevant Concerns for Employees Because there are so few individuals educated in cybersecurity and data privacy, companies have a responsibility to educate their employees and raise awareness of all pertinent issues in order to avoid the leak of sensitive data.

When we have more tools for cyber defense, each individual instrument will have less of an impact on the overall defense. Utilizing a multitude of technologies, many of which perform duties that are comparable to one another, results in time wasted and may throw a terrible light on the administration of our company. Because of this, it is quite important to make the most of the tools at our disposal and to do in-depth analyses of how well they are working.

Hackers are prevented from accessing private networks and the data they contain by firewall software. A set of interoperating computer programs is what makes up a firewall. Firewalls should be installed and maintained in order to prevent unauthorized users from the outside world from accessing our private network. If our employees will be telecommuting, it is essential to have firewalls in place to protect the network.

The standard operating procedures may be improved with security orchestration, automation, and response solutions by incorporating a broad range of technologies into simplified processes. It is necessary for security managers to find a means to automate mundane processes in order to release a significant amount of analysts' time and raise productivity. This, in turn, would increase the company's capacity to earn a return on investment. For a successful strategy to budget for cybersecurity, it is vital to concentrate on the primary advantages that the money may provide. Pay close attention to the return on investment (ROI) of the money by considering the demands of our firm, putting into practice cost-effective practices, and demonstrating to the security executives that we have done all in our power to acquire a better ROI.

The use of big data analysis is becoming more popular in many other fields, not only cyber security. Mobile devices and online social networking sites are by far the most prevalent means to get such information in today's modern world. The quick pace at which this data is being created poses a number of security problems since it is very crucial to safeguard the confidentiality of this data because it includes personal and critical information such as credit card and bank account details. Additionally, technical advancements in big data analytics have made it easy to gather and use this data, which, in turn, has made it simpler for individuals' privacy to be violated. Because of this, it is essential that we include safeguards against misuse as we progress the technology behind big data.

Data is often the most alluring target for cyberattacks; however, businesses have the ability to turn the tables by applying data analytics tools such as machine learning (ML), artificial intelligence (AI), statistics visualization, and other similar methods to launch their own attacks. The analysis of attack data from both the present and the past may help businesses become more prepared for future attacks. By analyzing data from the period right before an attack, big data analytics provides firms with the ability to detect potential threats and the tactics used to carry them out.

CONCLUSION

There is a pressing need for the development of more reliable strategies for protecting privacy. One of them is the concept of differentiated privacy. This has a great deal of unrealized potential that is just waiting to be realized. In addition to this rapid growth, challenges emerge when the Internet of Things and big data clash owing to the sheer amount of data sources, as well as the fact that the data itself is varied and of low quality. Having a broad range of representations and classifications, as well as depending on the setting, the data may be organized, semi-structured, or fully unstructured. Having a wide variety of representations and classifications, raises further concerns and problems for the researchers who are worried about protecting their privacy. As a result, several different methods are being taken toward the development and implementation of privacy-preserving mining in the future. Given that this is the case, there is a significant window of opportunity for new discoveries to be made in the subject of protecting the privacy of large amounts of data.

ACKNOWLEDGMENT

We, the writers of this book chapter, would like to extend our gratitude to the late Mr. Panem Nadipi Chennaih for his assistance in the creation of this book chapter as well as the support he provided during its growth. This book chapter is dedicated to him.

REFERENCES

Ananda, D., Taqiyyuddin, T. A., Faqih, I. N., Badrahadipura, R., & Pravitasari, A. A. (2021, October). Application of Bidirectional Gated Recurrent Unit (BiGRU) in Sentiment Analysis of Tokopedia Application Users. In *2021 International Conference on Artificial Intelligence and Big Data Analytics* (pp. 1-4). IEEE.

Kaplunovich, A. (2021, December). COVID-19 Multi-Modal Data Analysis with Alexa Voice and Conversational AI Applications: Voice First System Tracking Novel Coronavirus. In *2021 IEEE International Conference on Big Data (Big Data)* (pp. 4514-4517). IEEE.

Lee, R., Jang, R. Y., Park, M., Jeon, G. Y., Kim, J. K., & Lee, S. H. (2020, February). Making IoT data ready for smart city applications. In *2020 IEEE International Conference on Big Data and Smart Computing (BigComp)* (pp. 605-608). IEEE.

Lei, J., & Huang, G. (2021, June). Smart Management System of Employment in Universities Based on Big Data Collection and Intelligent Analysis. In *2021 5th International Conference on Trends in Electronics and Informatics (ICOEI)* (pp. 1110-1113). IEEE.

Li, D., Gong, Y., Tang, G., & Huang, Q. (2020, May). Research and design of mineral resource management system based on big data and GIS technology. In *2020 5th IEEE International Conference on Big Data Analytics (ICBDA)* (pp. 52-56). IEEE.

Liang, T. (2020, October). Design and Implementation of Big Data Visual Statistical Analysis Platform. In *2020 2nd International Conference on Machine Learning, Big Data and Business Intelligence (MLBDBI)* (pp. 287-291). IEEE.

Liu, L., Liu, P., Luo, J., & Zhao, S. (2021, July). Big Data-Based Dynamic Decision-Making Algorithm for Power Enterprise Operation Risk Management. *In 2021 International Conference on Big Data and Intelligent Decision Making (BDIDM)* (pp. 70-74). IEEE.

Liu, S. (2018, January). Business management system and information analysis platform for economic innovation projects. In *2018 International Conference on Intelligent Transportation, Big Data & Smart City (ICITBS)* (pp. 408-411). IEEE.

Liu, X., & Liu, C. (2020, August). An Empirical Analysis of Applied Statistics and Probability Statistics based on Computer Software. In *2020 International Conference on Big Data and Social Sciences (ICBDSS)* (pp. 69-71). IEEE.

Mei, J., Chen, Y., Ye, T., Huang, C., & Ye, H. (2020, June). Research on User Behavior Analysis Model of Financial Industry in Big Data Environment. In *2020 IEEE International Conference on Artificial Intelligence and Computer Applications (ICAICA)* (pp. 1237-1240). IEEE.

Ramirez-Asis, H., Silva-Zapata, M., Ramirez-Asis, E., Sharma, T., Durga, S., & Pant, B. (2022, April). A Conceptual Analysis on the Impact of Big Data Analytics Toward on Digital Marketing Transformation. In *2022 2nd International Conference on Advance Computing and Innovative Technologies in Engineering (ICACITE)* (pp. 1651-1655). IEEE.

Riasetiawan, M., Ashari, A., & Prastowo, B. N. (2021, November). 360Degree Data Analysis and Visualization for COVID-19 Mitigation in Indonesia. In *2021 International Conference on Data Science, Artificial Intelligence, and Business Analytics (DATABIA)* (pp. 7-12). IEEE.

Riasetiawan, M., Ashari, A., & Prastowo, B. N. (2021, November). 360Degree Data Analysis and Visualization for COVID-19 Mitigation in Indonesia. In *2021 International Conference on Data Science, Artificial Intelligence, and Business Analytics (DATABIA)* (pp. 7-12). IEEE.

Shao, P., & Yao, L. (2021, October). Empirical analysis on textile industry big data using computer mathematical statistics and double difference method. In *2021 IEEE International Conference on Data Science and Computer Application (ICDSCA)* (pp. 224-227). IEEE.

Tong, S., Liu, Q., Huang, W., Hunag, Z., Chen, E., Liu, C., & Wang, S. (2020, November). Structure-based knowledge tracing: an influence propagation view. In *2020 IEEE International Conference on Data Mining (ICDM)* (pp. 541-550). IEEE.

Uskenbayeva, R. K., Kuandykov, A. A., Kuatbayeva, A. A., Kassymova, A. B., Kuatbayeva, G. K., & Zhussipbek, B. K. (2021, September). Burn disease data analysis model in SAS UE. In *2021 IEEE 23rd Conference on Business Informatics (CBI)* (*Vol. 2*, pp. 197-201). IEEE.

Ved, M., & Rizwanahmed, B. (2019, July). Big data analytics in telecommunication using state-of-the-art big data framework in a distributed computing environment: a case study. In *2019 IEEE 43rd Annual Computer Software and Applications Conference (COMPSAC)* (*Vol. 1*, pp. 411-416). IEEE.

Vij, A., Saini, S., & Bathla, R. (2020, June). Big Data in Healthcare: Technologies, Need, Advantages, and Disadvantages. In *2020 8th International Conference on Reliability, Infocom Technologies and Optimization (Trends and Future Directions) (ICRITO)* (pp. 1301-1305). IEEE.

Wang, X. (2021, June). Application of Big Data Technology in Economic Statistics. In *2021 International Wireless Communications and Mobile Computing (IWCMC)* (pp. 861-864). IEEE.

Wang, Z., Bin, W. U., Demeng, B. A. I., & Jiafeng, Q. I. N. (2018, December). Distributed big data mining platform for smart grid. In *2018 IEEE International Conference on Big Data (Big Data)* (pp. 2345-2354). IEEE.

Xiaochun, D., & Bing, W. (2018, June). Design and Application of Website Data Analysis Software in the Era of Big Data. In *2018 International Conference on Smart Grid and Electrical Automation (ICSGEA)* (pp. 334-337). IEEE.

Yang, G. (2018, August). Design of Performance Evaluation Model for Accurate Poverty Alleviation Projects Based on Big Data Analysis. In *2018 International Conference on Virtual Reality and Intelligent Systems (ICVRIS)* (pp. 102-105). IEEE.

Yang, M., & Wang, Q. (2018, May). Research on product development mode of network menswear brand based on big data statistics. In *2018 33rd Youth Academic Annual Conference of Chinese Association of Automation (YAC)* (pp. 694-700). IEEE.

Zhang, H., Zhang, J., Tian, M., & Qiao, B. (2021, December). Design of Offline Analysis System for Remote Sensing Data Service Based on Hive. In *2021 International Conference on Digital Society and Intelligent Systems (DSInS)* (pp. 300-303). IEEE. 10.1109/DSInS54396.2021.9670605

Chapter 7
Evaluation of Usability of E–Commerce Websites in Pakistan Using System Usability Scale and Heuristics Methods

Awais Ashraf
Bahria University, Pakistan

Sehrish Aqeel
Universiti Malaysia Sarawak, Malaysia

Abdul Hafeez Muhammad
Bahria University, Pakistan

ABSTRACT

Online shopping platforms "Draz.pk," "Homesopping.pk," and "Telemart.pk," were the most often used online stores in Pakistan. E-commerce platforms have not achieved their complete objectives, because they are faced with many usability issues. It is recommended that an evaluation of the usability of e-commerce platforms should be explored through different usability scales. This research study evaluates the usability of e-commerce platforms in Pakistan. In this research study, three e-commerce platforms were selected for usability evaluation. For this purpose total of 15 users were selected and performed the System Usability Scale method of assessing the usability. The result of the System Usability Scale method indicated usability of the "Homesopping.pk" and "Telemart.pk" was less than below 70%, which indicated that these websites need to improve the user interface. Five expert evaluators were also selected for Heuristic evaluation to perform on "Homesopping.pk" to find out the usability issues.

DOI: 10.4018/978-1-6684-6581-3.ch007

INTRODUCTION

E-Shopping is a global phenomenon in which retailers sell out products on the internet. Due to new enhancement in information technology and economic globalization, e-shopping between different countries has become a new growth point of business development of foreign trade and local trade. E-commerce business growth rates increased day by day (Aljifri et al., 2003). Website is compulsory for every organization because the organization delivers its data on the website for end-users. The main aim of making any website is that it satisfies customer needs. The importance of usability in websites described by various authors in your research studies. Nielsen is called the father of usability (Tsai, 1996). Nielsen describes the five usability attributes. There are five metrics defined by Nielsen's are:

- **Learnability:** How easily users learn product task when it's used the first time to perform a task.
- **Memorability:** How difficult for users to again perform the task after a period of leave the system.
- **Efficiency:** How quickly a user can perform tasks using the system.
- **Error Rate:** What is the error rate ratio of the product? What is the error condition?
- **Satisfaction:** How much user Pleasant when it used design?

ISO is one of the top international organizations that defined usability as: "The extent to which a product can be used by specific users to achieved specific goals with efficiency, effectiveness, and satisfaction in a specific context. ISO is still working on usability standards and metrics. **ISO** gives three usability attributes for usability (Standard, 1998).

- **Efficiency:** How quickly a user can perform your task using the product.
- **Effectiveness:** How quickly the user completes your tasks with less error action.
- **Satisfaction:** How much users enjoy/ pleasant with the product when it is used.

Calculating the usability of any website is often difficult because it depends on many usability metrics. These metrics are introduced by many authors of your research studies. The usability of any website is highly subjective. There are lots of methods to measure usability in terms of qualitatively and quantitatively and various methods have been adopted to ensure the authenticity of required goals with respect to quality (Aqeel, 2017; Tabassam & Al-Qahtane, 2019; Tabassam, Hassan, Al-Qahtnae et al, 2019). System Usability Scale is one way to measure usability in terms quantitatively. SUS calculated satisfaction with websites through 10 pre-built questions. Ten years previously research studies indicated that SUS is a quick and easy method to measured usability in terms of quantitatively (Bangor et al., 2008).

LITERATURE REVIEW

This section explores various aspects of the usability of e-commerce websites using Heuristics and SUS methods and a literature review related to these usability concepts.

In their research study, Astani and Elhindi used the heuristic method to evaluate the usability of the top 50 colleges and universities' websites. These two experts organized this study and used five attributes to measured the usability of websites. Another study in has revealed the detailed steps to perform comprehensive study (Aqeel et al., 2021) on various social media platforms to calculate its effect individually either on personality (Malik et al., n.d.; Tabassam, Shah, Alghamdi et al, 2019) or quering (Tabassam, Al-Saeed, Almughram et al, 2019) to find out results on the desired designed system (Aqeel, 2017). Requirements play a vital role in this regard and through structured requirement engineering techniques (Tabassam & Al-Qahtane, 2019), usability could be find out in an organized way. Following are the five attributes used by authors in their study are information content, usability, customization, navigation and security, and download speed. The researchers detected that some usability problems with old content and layout in websites (Astani & Elhindi, 2008).

In their research study, Kostaras and Xenos also used the heuristic method to identified usability problems in Hellenic Open University by using the 10 guidelines of Nielsen. Research of this study identified the 38 usability problems in university websites. These usability problems are lack of navigational support links, inconsistency problems, inappropriate design of menu, and font size problems (Kostaras et al., 2007).

In their research study, the authors indicated that the usability of the system increased end-users satisfaction level, productivity, trust, and cost-saving. The industry thinking out that evaluates the usability of the system is a costly and time-saving process. There is no need to spend time and money to improve the usability of the system. In their research study, the authors concluded that heuristic evaluation is more effective and better than user testing (Sheikh et al., 2015).

In their research studies, Ebba Thora Hvannberg finds out that four different methods were used to identify usability problems in websites. The heuristic evaluation method is one of those which identified the largest number of problems (28). User testing is the second method which identified the second largest number of problems (18). Guidelines are the third method which identifies the third-largest number of problems and lastly is a cognitive walkthrough that identified the usability problems.

Researchers of this study suggest that user testing and heuristic are the best methods for identifying the major usability problems. (Hvannberg et al., 2007).

This research study evaluated the usability of e-commerce websites in Pakistan by using the System Usability Scale (SUS) and Heuristic methods. In this study, the usability of e-commerce platforms measured both ways respectively qualitatively and quantitatively. HE is a qualitative assessment method to identify usability problems in the system interface. Heuristic evaluation is also used to identify usability problems during the iterative design process. HE method involve four to five usability experts to identified usability problem in the user interface using checklists (Nielsen, 1994). Both System Usability Scale (SUS) and Heuristic evaluation are well famous and widely used research methods to evaluate the usability of the human-machine system, software products, and online websites. More than 1200 research articles have been cited as the SUS method to measured satisfaction with software products (Peres et al., 2013). These studies have clearly shown the behavioiur of the user towards the ebsities as was expected through deep learning models designated for interaction of human traits (Aqeel et al., 2021; Muniasamy et al.,). As these are the expected behavior of the application software and that too through proper heuruistics to capture best possible response of the user involving numerous cloud computing services to make the system successful with full recovery and back up mechanisms (Rajab et al., n.d.; Jenni, 2013) .

To conduct this usability study, three e-commerce platforms "Draz.pk", "Homeshopping.pk" and "Telemart.pk" were selected to checkout the end-users satisfaction by using SUS and identified usability issues using the heuristic method.

METHODOLOGY

Usability Scale (**SUS**) is a well famous and widely used research method to evaluate the usability of e-commerce platforms. For this purpose, three e-commerce websites which are Draz.pk, Homesopping.pk and Telemart.pk had been selected to study the usability. Usability inspection method uses Nielsen's Heuristic Guidelines. HE is an inspection method in which four to five expert evaluators used checklists to identified problems in the system interface. These checklists are made up of different guidelines and principles.

System Usability System Evaluation

Participants

Fifteen participants were selected to conduct the SUS method of calculating the satisfaction level of these e-commerce platforms. All fifteen participants were over 21 years old and thirteen males and two females were out of the total number.

Material and Equipment

For SUS evaluation, the experiment session was running simultaneously in a selected participant computer machine at web browser: **Google Chrome**.

Usability Questionnaire

To conduct this research study, A System Usability Scale (SUS) is used to the measured satisfaction level of these websites. SUS questionnaire survey form consists of ten question items. This survey form is provided to participants and collects the participant's response using the five Likert scale method. On this Likert scale, 5 means strongly agree and 1 means strongly disagree.

Procedures

To conduct this research study, A System Usability Scale (SUS) is used to the measured satisfaction level of these websites. SUS questionnaire survey forms consist of ten question items. Firstly, Participants filled up Demographic Information form and

Figure 1. Experimental procedure

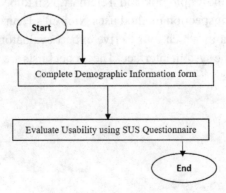

next SUS survey form provided to participants and collect the participant's response using five Likert scale method. In this Likert scale, 5 means strongly agree and 1 means strongly disagree. A complete experiment flow procedure is shown in figure 1.

Heuristic Evaluation of Homeshopping.pk

Participants

Five Experts were recruited for Heuristic Evaluation. The selected five participants were over 21 years old and belong to the male gender.

Table 1. Represent experts profile information

Number of Experts	Education	Experience
1	MSCS	1year Websites Design Development
2	MBA	Online Marketing
3	MSCS	3-year work Experience in Software Quality Department
4	MSCS	5-year e-shopping Experience
5	MSCS	1-year Website Designing

Evaluation Procedures

One E-commerce website was selected for heuristic evaluation. The evaluation for each e-shopping interface was completed before moving on to the next one. To conduct the heuristic evaluation, used two heuristic evaluation approaches: one is Task phase Analysis and the second is Free-Flow.

Tasks Based Approach

The Determined tasks were as follows:

1. Browse the websites and buy shoes for winter.
2. Revisit the old order status: Find related pages
3. You want to learn the procedure of how to return the order
4. Find help and contact information.
5. Checking out the payment process.

Free-Flow Approach

In this approach, each website's interface was inspected several times using a heuristic checklist provided by Jacob Nielsen. Each expert evaluates the user interface of Homesopping.pk and finds out usability issues. Each expert is a free hand to evaluate every part of the website and find out issues in it.

Heuristic Checklists for Evaluation Interface

To find out usability problems in Homeshopping.pk, Jacob Nielsen Heuristics with checklists provided to experts.

Figure 2 illustrates the Jacob Nielsen Ten Heuristics with Explanation.

Figure 2. Jacob nielsen ten heuristic with explanation

Heuristics	Explanation	Heuristics	Explanation
H1: Visibility of system status	The system should always keep user informed about what is going on by providing appropriate feedback within reasonable time.	H6: Recognition rather than recall	Make objects, actions, and options visible. The users should not have to remember information from one part of the dialogue to another. Instructions for use of the system should be visible or easily retrievable
H2: Match between system and the real world	The system should speak the user's language, with words, phrases and concepts familiar to the user, rather than system-oriented terms. Follow real-world conventions, making information appear in a natural and logical order	H7: Flexibility and efficiency of use	Allow users to tailor frequent actions. Provide alternative means of access and operation for users who differ from the "average" user (e.g., physical or cognitive ability, culture, language, etc.)
H3: User control and freedom	Users should be free to develop their own strategies, select and sequence tasks, and undo and redo activities that they have done, rather than having the system do these for them	H8: Aesthetic and minimalist design	Dialogues should not contain information that is irrelevant or rarely needed. Every extra unit of information in a dialogue competes with the relevant units of information and diminishes their relative visibility.
H4: Consistency and standard	Users should not have to wonder whether different words, situations, or actions mean the same thing and the system should follow platform conventions	H9: Help users recognise, diagnose and recover from errors	Error messages should precisely indicate the problem and constructively suggest a solution. They should be expressed in plain language.
H5: Error prevention	Even better than good error messages is a careful design, which prevents a problem from occurring in the first place	H10: Help and documentation	Even though it is better if the system can be used without documentation, it may be necessary to provide help and documentation.

Rating Scale for Severity of Usability Problems

During the evaluation process, experts find out problems using Jacob Nielsen guidelines in Homeshopping.pk. After this, Experts have given a rating of the severity of these problems. Table 2 shows the Rating Scale with all details.

Table 2. Rating scale for usability problems

Problems	Severity	Meaning
No Problem	0	It means "No Usability problem".
Cosmetic	1	Problem But, No need to fix it.
Minor	2	Minor Usability Problem with low Severity.
Major	3	Fixed it with High Priority.
Catastrophe	4	Solved it before releasing the Product.

RESULT

Characteristics of Users for SUS Evaluation

Table 3 provides the Demographic information frequencies for each selected participant for SUS Evaluation.

Table 3. Demographic information for Users

Number of Factors	Category	Frequency	Percentage
Gender	Male	13	80%
	Female	2	20%
Age	20-22	5	33%
	23-25	8	53%
	Above 25	2	13%
Education	Bachelor	2	66%
	Master	13	87%
Internet Frequency of use	1 to 3 times per day	4	32%
	More than 3 times per day	11	68%
Online Shopping Access (Weekly)	1 to 3 times per weekly	14	97.8%
	More than 3 times per weekly	1	2.2%

Mean SUS Scores Rating

All selected participants filled out the SUS Google survey form after evaluated each website's interface. We used the method for calculating the average score of each website SUS that is suggested in (Cowley, 2006). The average SUS score for each website is present in Figure 3.

Figure 3. Average SUS score for each E-commerce Platforms

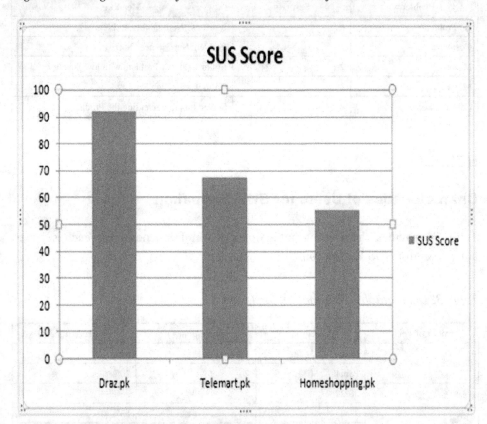

Result of Heuristic Evaluation

During conducting heuristic evaluation, each evaluator carefully visits the website's interface according to Jacob Nielsen's heuristics and finds out the violation of heuristic rules. After this evaluation, all evaluators discussed the severity of usability problems and given rating.

Table 4 Illustrates all usability problems find out during heuristics evaluation.

Table 4. Quantitative Result of HE in Homeshopping.pk

Heuristics	Severity Rating					
	0	**1**	**2**	**3**	**4**	**Total**
H1	0	0	0	3	0	3
H2	0	0	1	0	0	1
H3	0	0	0	0	0	0
H4	0	0	1	0	0	1
H5	0	1	0	0	0	1
H6	0	0	1	0	0	1
H7	0	1	0	0	0	1
H8	0	0	0	4	0	4
H9	0	0	1	0	0	1
H10	0	0	0	1	0	1
Total	**0**	**2**	**4**	**8**	**0**	**14**

RECOMMENDATION

Table 5 Provides the Recommendations for Homeshopping.pk to improved usability for their interface.

Table 5. Recommendations for Homeshopping.pk

Sr	Issues/Recommendations	ScreenShot
1	**Visibility of System Status** **Issue:** There is no Welcome Notification on the home screen and Gmail id notification after sign up for websites for new users. **Recommendation:** Websites should give proper welcome notifications to new users.	
2	**Visibility of System Status** **Issue:** There are no show header contents when navigating the website's pages. **Recommendation:** The website should display a Header at each website page whenever Users scroll down navigation.	

continues on following page

Table 5. Continued

Sr	Issues/Recommendations	ScreenShot
3	**Visibility of System Status** **Issue:** There is a clear button to delete items from add to the card. **Recommendation:** The website should display a Properly clear delete button icon on the Shopping cart page.	
4	**Match Between System and Real World** **Issue:** Confusion Terminology used in mobile categories for new novice users. **Recommendation:** The website should easy meaningful words instead of confusing Terminology.	
5	**Consistency and Standards** **Issue:** There is no present consistency in the footer menu. **Recommendation:** The website should provide consistency in size and font all over the websites especially in footer contents.	
6	**Error Prevention** **Issue:** The user adds an item to the shopping cart without login. The system does not restrict the user to do this. **Recommendation:** The website should provide an Error Warning.	
7	**Flexibility and Efficiency of Use** **Issue:** There are no keywords available for quick search. **Recommendation:** There should add some keywords for quick search.	
8	**Minimalist Design** **Issue:** There are lots of unnecessary advertisements present on all website pages. This thinks to create unnecessary confusion about decision making. **Recommendation:** The website should display only the essential information.	
9	**Help users recognize, diagnose and recover from errors** **Issue:** Some options are not working correctly not given any suggestions to users. **Recommendation:** For those options which are not working properly, the user should be given a popup about some kind of suggestions.	

continues on following page

Table 5. Continued

Sr	Issues/Recommendations	ScreenShot
10	**Help and Documentation** **Issue:** These are not FAQ available for user's common problems. **Recommendation:** There should be an FAQ section where user can search out there common problem's solution.	

CONCLUSION

This research study measures the SUS score of each e-commerce platform in Pakistan. The result of the SUS evaluation method showed that Draz.pk has more than 70% SUS Score. The SUS Score of Telemart.pk and Homeghopping.pk platforms are less than 70%. The finding of this research study indicated that these two e-commerce platforms are in the marginal range. There is a need to improve the usability of these platforms. The heuristic evaluation also highlights usability issues in homeshppoing.pk.

REFERENCES

Malik, H. A. M., Abdulhafeez, M., Aqeel, S., & Amin, A. (n.d.). The Impact of Social Media on the Personality Trait of Under-graduates students: A Descriptive Analytical Approach.

Rajab, Aqeel, Al Reshan, Ashraf, Almakdi, & Rajab. (n.d.). Cryptography based Techniques of Encryption for Security of Data in Cloud Computing Paradigm. International Journal of Engineering Trends and Technology, 69(10), 1-6.

Aljifri, H. A., Pons, A., & Collins, D. (2003). Global e-commerce: A framework for understanding and overcoming the trust barrier. *Information Management & Computer Security*, *11*(2–3), 130–138. doi:10.1108/09685220310480417

Aqeel, S. (2017). *Study on Enhancement on Software Quality by Scheduling Techniques of Real Time Systems. European Journal of Advances in Engineering and Technology*, *4*(3), 201–208.

Aqeel, S., Khan, A. S., Ahmad, Z., & Abdullah, J. (2021). *A comprehensive study on DNA based Security scheme Using Deep Learning in Healthcare*. EDPACS. doi:10.1080/07366981.2021.1958742

Astani, M., & Elhindi, M. A. (2008). an Empirical Study of University Websites. *Issues in Information Systems*, *9*(2), 460–465.

Bangor, A., Kortum, P. T., & Miller, J. T. (2008). An empirical evaluation of the system usability scale. *International Journal of Human-Computer Interaction*, *24*(6), 574–594. doi:10.1080/10447310802205776

Cowley, A. W. (2006). IUPS—a retrospective. *The Physiologist*, *49*(3), 171–173. PMID:16805368

Hvannberg, E. T., Law, E. L. C., & Lárusdóttir, M. K. (2007). Heuristic evaluation: Comparing ways of finding and reporting usability problems. *Interacting with Computers*, *19*(2), 225–240. doi:10.1016/j.intcom.2006.10.001

Jenni, K. (2013). *Improve the Performance of Clustering Using Combination of Multiple Clustering Algorithms. International Journal of Data Mining Techniques and Applications*.

Kostaras, N., Kostaras, N., Xenos, M., & Xenos, M. (2007). Assessing Educational Web-site Usability using Heuristic Evaluation Rules. *Evaluation*, (May), 543–550.

Muniasamy, A., Tabassam, S., Hussain, M. A., Sultana, H., Muniasamy, V., Bhatnagar, R., & 2019). Deep Learning for Predictive Analytics in Healthcare. In *The International Conference on Advanced Machine Learning Tech-nologies and Applications (AMLTA2019)*. Springer International Publishing.

Nielsen, J. (1994). *Human Factors Computing Systems: Enhancing the Explanatory Power of Usability Heuristics*. Hum. Factors Comput. Syst.

Peres, S. C., Pham, T., & Phillips, R. (2013). Validation of the system usability scale (sus): Sus in the wild. *Proc. Hum. Factors Ergon. Soc*, *57*(1), 192–196. doi:10.1177/1541931213571043

Sheikh, J. A., Abbas, A., & Mehmood, Z. (2015). Design Consideration of Online Shopping Website to Reach Women in Pakistan. Procedia Manuf., 3, 6298–6304. doi:10.1016/j.promfg.2015.07.942

Standard, I. (1998). *Iso 9241-11*.

Tabassam, S., & Al-Qahtane, E. (2019). Comparative Analysis on Requirement Engineering Modelling Techniques Case Study of Personal Al-Haj E-Guide. 2019 2nd International Conference on Computer Applications & Information Security (ICCAIS), 1-8. 10.1109/CAIS.2019.8769549

Tabassam, S., Al-Saeed, W., Almughram, O., Alghamdi, K. (2019). Scalable Data Analysis and Query Processing. *International Journal on Engineering Applications, 7*(3), 81-87. doi:10.15866/irea.v7i3.17012

Tabassam, S., Hassan, O., Al-Qahtnae, E., & Al-Ahmary, N. (2019). Goal Question Metrics and Its Application to Process Man-agement and Improvement. International Journal on Engineering Applications (IREA), 7(2), 52-58. doi:10.15866/irea. v7i2.17013

Tabassam, S., Shah, H., Alghamdi, K., & Badshah, A. (2019). *"Social Networks and Digital Security," 2019 International Con-ference on Electrical, Communication, and Computer Engineering*. ICECCE. doi:10.1109/ICECCE47252.2019.8940808

Tsai, P. (1996). A Survey of Empirical Usability Evaluation Methods. A Surv. Empir. usability Eval. Methods.

Chapter 8
Privacy and Security Under Blockchain Technology:
Challenges and Solutions

Amir Manzoor

(iD) https://orcid.org/0000-0002-3094-768X

Karachi School of Business and Leadership, Karachi, Pakistan

ABSTRACT

Blockchain technology enables online sharing of digital information. A blockchain acts as public ledger that everyone has access to but is not controlled by a central authority. It is a technology that empowers people and organizations to collaborate and transact in an online environment that is trusted and transparent. The blockchain technology provides many benefits, including increased transparency and traceability of transactions. However, the security and privacy issues of blockchain can outweigh its benefits. This literature-review based study explores the privacy and security challenges of blockchain technology and their solutions.

INTRODUCTION

Blockchain technology is defined as a decentralized, shared ledger of all transactions across a peer-to-peer network. Blockchain is the architecture on which the popular cryptocurrency Bitcoin runs. Blockchain and Bitcoin are not the same terms. Blockchain is the technology that secures Bitcoin. Blockchain technology has been deployed by many businesses to improve their operations and to ensure the anonymity and security of the users. The blockchain-based solutions provide recording of information in a chronological and decentralized manner (Patil, 2021). A blockchain

DOI: 10.4018/978-1-6684-6581-3.ch008

consists of an array of blocks in which each block is connected individually and keeps several transactions. A blockchain thus is a distributed, incontrovertible data store that can be used in a broad range of applications (Yli-Huumo et al., 2016). Being an enabling technology, blockchain provides maximum benefits when integrated with technologies (such as internet of things) (Deloitte, 2022). As an enabling technology, blockchain is at the driving seat for the next IT revolution. Blockchain technology has been implemented for a variety of applications in different areas of business.

In online business transactions, security, privacy, and safety of information have become very important (Farhadi et al., 2012). Blockchain technology has revolutionized the traditional trade. Its distributed ledger secures all recorded transactions using encryption techniques (Fanning & Centers, 2016; Gad et al., 2022). Blockchain is an emerging technology that has many applications for business. Blockchain consists of a chain of blocks that register and transfer information in a safe and auditable way, open to anyone. A system built on Blockchain does not have an institution or organization as an intermediary such as a bank; the transactions occur directly peer-to-peer.

Blockchain technology can be used to manage global payment systems and digital assets since the technology enables the creation and sharing of a distributed digital account book amongst computers within a network (Dinçer & Yüksel, 2019). This account book will be accessible by all network participants but no central authority would be involved (Dinçer & Yüksel, 2019). It is possible for organizations to use Blockchain technology within their organization to watch all the transactions that occur and detect suspicious activities within their online systems.

Blockchain technology is also critical in revolutionizing IoT security and performance. Blockchain-based IoT applications have increased. The use of blockchain in these applications help verify and trace multistep transactions. Blockchain can also help secure the business transactions, reduce compliance costs, speed up data transfer processing, contract management and audit the origin of a product, and document suspicious transactions. Blockchain can use its distributed voting systems to prevent DDOS attacks against IoT devices (Techtarget.com, 2021; Karame & Capkun, 2018).

It is important to explore blockchain technology because it promotes trust between peer-to-peer networks. The blockchain technology acts as a ledger that tracks of all bitcoin transactions. However, this ledger is public, and everyone can see the details of transactions. As such, privacy concerns arise. The major issues related to modern electronic technologies are privacy, security, and trust. There are three major dimensions of concerns related to information privacy: collection, control, and awareness. Collection refers to concern about how much personal data is held by other parties and the benefits received by the individual. Control refers to individual's concern about the possible use and modification/deletion of their data by others. Awareness refers to individual's concern about how much he/she knows about the privacy practices of organizations collecting the data (Fortes & Rita, 2016).

The security issues of Internet have generated a strong debate revolving around security, privacy, and trust dimensions of online transactions. Privacy, security, and trust are key issues for online technologies (Gupta & Dubey, 2016). One of the major reasons for existence of banks is that they are considered a reliable and trustworthy third-party for conducting financial transactions. Without such intermediary, transactions through peer-to-peer networks would always face the issue of trust. Blockchain is a promising technology to address this trust issue.

Blockchain is a potential, cheap, and faster alternative to existing cross-border payment systems for e-commerce. Blockchain can provide an alternative model to proof-of-existence. A blockchain user can store his/her signature and timestamp with a legal document. Later on, the user can always use blockchain to validate this document (Crosby et al., 2015). Blockchain technology provides its users an alternative and trusted solution to facilitate their online transactions. Therefore, this study seeks to explore issues related with security and privacy of blockchain technology and their solutions. The findings could be very helpful for individuals and organizations considering a trusted solution for their online transactions.

Blockchain is not only an emerging technology but also the most disruptive technology in decades. Blockchain has enormous potential to enable innovations in the financial and commercial area and revolutionize the way we interact with each other. The three fundamental pillars of blockchain technology are data tracking and storage, trust, and peer-to-peer transactions. The blockchain is a decentralized and distributed system across an extensive network of computers. This system provides secure data storage and tracking. Users can trust blockchain because blockchain enables its users to interact directly with their data in real-time. Every change in transaction record is verified by all the users on the network. Blockchain involves no intermediaries and data is shared directly with all users of blockchain. This system provides a new way of conducting and verifying transactions (Pereira et al., 2018). Researchers argue that blockchain technology has the potential to create an "unhackable messaging system" (Shackelford & Myers, 2017).

The use of internet is increasing day by day due to a variety of reasons. The internet has reduced the distance between the people and countries by providing new ways of communication (Arai & Bhatia, 2019). Due to its ability to store data across its network, blockchain can help eliminate the risks of data stored in a central database. The Internet has many security challenges that blockchain technology can address (Yang et al., 2018). Blockchain is a very useful emerging technology that needs further exploration while it is still in its early stages of development (Abdel-Aziz et al., 2016). Blockchain technology has provided an opportunity to regain safety in the online environment. This study seeks to explore blockchain technology in terms of privacy concerns, security challenges and solutions.

BENEFITS OF BLOCKCHAIN TECHNOLOGY

Blockchain technology provides substantial benefits in several industries. Some of the notable benefits include enhancement of transparency, security, traceability, efficiency and swiftness of transactions as well as minimization of transaction costs (Hooper, 2018).

Increased Transparency

Blockchain technology guarantees transparent, tamper-proof and secure systems that can facilitate innovative business solutions (Andoni et al., 2019; Yiannas, 2018). The use of cryptography makes blockchain networks resilient and secure to withstand attacks. Each user on a blockchain-based network can check the validity of any transaction. Any transaction can be recorded only after collective consent, implying that each of the players must agree on the decision to be made. To alter record of any transaction, one would need to change all subsequent records. This increases the transparency and trust in the system. Increased transparency makes it easier to provide real-time respond to unexpected occurrences. For example, blockchain-based supply chain management systems can assist in minimizing the level of fraud and errors, reduces shipping costs, reduce waste, and improve inventory management (Treiblmaier, 2018). Blockchain technology increases transparency and security. Transactions on a blockchain are permanent and can't be altered making it much more difficult for hackers to hack into the system. (Yoo, Parameswaran, & Kishore, 2015).

Improved Security

Security is one of the major benefits of blockchain-based applications. The unchangeable record of transactions with end-to-end encryption ensures no fraud or unauthorized activity can happen. The data stored on blockchain network is nearly impossible to hack. Blockchain can also address privacy concerns more than the traditional computer systems by un-attributing the data and acquiring permissions to limit access (Yuan & Wang, 2018; Cai et al., 2018). In blockchain-based systems, a transaction must be decided before it is recorded. Then it is encrypted and connected with previous transactions. This procedure, along with the fact that blockchain transactions are stored in a decentralized system, makes it near impossible for third parties to interfere with the transaction data (Park et al., 2017; Karame & Capkun, 2018).

Better Traceability

In blockchain-based solutions, important traceability records can be immutable. Once a piece of information is entered into the shared blockchain-based system, nobody can change it. Blockchain ensures end-to-end transparency of the ownership of the asset across blockchain. Blockchain also provides more accurate asset tracking. The applications of blockchain can contribute to better efficiency and auditable tracking of assets.

Blockchain networks are tamperproof and transparent, and they can help improve traceability of transactions better than other systems (Bodó et al, 2018; Gordon & Catalini, 2018). This traceability of transactions can be really important in some cases such as in supply chain management. In a complex supply chain, it can be really tough to trace an item back to its source. A blockchain-based system can always provide an audit trail that displays the whole journey of the item through the supply chain. This chronological transaction data can assist in the verification of the authenticity of assets and reduce incidences of fraud (Gordon & Catalini, 2018).

Improved Efficiency

By design, blockchain is based on a shared network infrastructure. As such, blockchain-based system provides improve communication and collaboration for all parties in the blockchain. The complete visibility of asset information across blockchain results in lower transaction processing times, uncertainty, and risk (Higgins, 2021). The blockchain technology can improve efficiency and speed of operations of an organization. The blockchain's ability to track transactions can really help improve operations speed and efficiency. Removal of third parties can significantly reduce transaction costs. Restructuring and automation of transactions through blockchain technology the transactions can be accomplished more quickly and efficiently. Since blockchain technology uses a distributed ledger, there is no need to reconcile multiple ledgers (Yaeger et al., 2019; Augustine & Giberson, 2017; Drescher & Kirk, 2017)

Minimized Costs

For several businesses, minimizing costs is a main concern. Blockchain-based systems do not require intermediaries to provide guarantees for various transactions (Gupta & Dubey, 2016; (Longenecker et al., 2017). The blockchain can cut costs for the organization, increase efficiency of processing transactions, and reduce manual tasks.

In long run, blockchain can cut the costs by eliminating the middlemen, vendors, and third-party providers.

LIMITATIONS OF BLOCKCHAIN TECHNOLOGY

Complexity

Blockchain technology uses a jargon that is new to many people (Smith, 2018). Blockchain technology requires the use of a brand-new lexicon. Blockchain technology is highly specialized, and it is not everybody's cup of tea (Srivastava, 2022). The blockchain network is inherently complex. With increased number of participants, the applicability of blockchain increases. Many of existing implementations of blockchain are being done in phases. Instead of implementing a fully centralized or decentralized solution, companies have taken a hybrid approach which has further increased complexity. In addition, organizations must involve dedicated blockchain experts, even for small scale implementations of blockchain (Smith, 2018; Bashir, 2017).

Lack of Privacy and High Costs

Each node of blockchain-based system stores complete history of transaction data. This increased transparency can be beneficial in some cases. In cases where privacy of transactions is an important concern, this feature can be a limitation of blockchain-based systems. The blockchain processes requires considerable computational resources. This feature of blockchain has security benefit but it can become a limitation if the size of the blockchain network is large. In order to manage blockchain, organizations need to hire programmers and other professionals well-versed in blockchain technology. Organizations also incur costs of licensing and maintaining blockchain-based solutions. This could be a limitation for organizations with limited financial resources.

Security Architecture

Blockchain use public-key encryption for transaction authentication and execution (Stallings, 2011). This process uses a public and a private key. In case, the private key is revealed due to any reason, there is no additional mechanism to ensure the safety of transactions.

Flexibility Limitations

In blockchain-based solutions, important traceability records can be immutable. Once a piece of information is entered into the shared blockchain-based system, nobody can change it. This characteristic of blockchain ensures the integrity of transactions but it can be a limitation in cases where changes in the transactions are required.

Latency

The blockchain-based solutions provide recording of information in a chronological and decentralized manner. All blockchain nodes keep complete record of all transaction in various information blocks. This ensures the network security. However, you would incur increase computational cost if you want to add new blocks and subsequent transaction records.

Governance

A blockchain is a distributed data store that can be used in a variety of applications The distributed architecture of blockchain can be very beneficial in some specific use cases, but it also makes overall control and governance very limited. This could be an issue for organizations that require intensive oversight of the transaction network (Sabbagh et al., 2021).

Policy and Regulatory Framework

A proper policy and regulatory framework for blockchain still doesn't exist. Policies that govern that govern the use of blockchain are still developing. In the past several years, various regulatory changes have been implemented globally to regulate blockchain-based applications especially those involving cross-border transactions and Anti Money Laundering compliance.

Data Protection and Privacy

Data protection and privacy is a major issue for blockchain technology. This is because data stored in blockchain network is immutable. European Union (EU) has implemented "Right to be Forgotten" under the General Data Protection Regulation. Under this regulation, once written, blockchain data cannot be removed. Implementation of this regulation has created many privacy issues. The participants of blockchain network cannot remove their trace from the blockchain network even if they want to. Another major concern for governments is that one can keep his/her identity unknown in blockchain-based system. This raises a serious security issue when it comes to comply with anti-money laundering regulations.

Lack of Maturity of the Technology

The blockchain technology is still in its nascent stages of development. This lack of technology maturity makes many businesses reluctant to adopt it. The true benefits of blockchain technology can be realized once a critical mass of participants is reached. That would require a large number of participants from a wide array of sectors to adopt blockchain technology.

Lack of Interoperability

Another issue of blockchain is its interoperability with other platforms and systems. The different systems and platforms can use a variety of interfaces and algorithms that may or may not be compatible with blockchain. This is because different types of blockchain networks operate differently (CBI, 2022).

Blockchain Privacy and Security

This section presents a general review of various studies conducted on the security and privacy issues of blockchain.

Using blockchain technology, users can record transactions in a way that no transaction can be altered once completed. Blockchain users send individual transactions to the blockchain network using the block software that include desktop apps, mobile apps, among others (Yaga et al., 2018; Gordon & Catalini, 2018). The key concept to warrant data integrity and validity in blockchain technology is a computational method known as mining. The technology allows users to append a new block of data to the current blockchain by solving a compute-intensive proof-of-work that generates a hash value for connecting previous block to the existing block. After solving the proof-of-work, the outcome is transmitting to other miners in the networks for authentication as the new block is effectively added in case most of the miners come to an understanding or reach an agreement (Xiong et al., 2017).

Researchers argue that blockchain technology has significantly improved to become very secure. Each participant of blockchain receives a unique ID linked to his/her account. This ensures that only account owner is able to operate his/her transactions. An increasing trend of digital transformation of businesses has resulted in increased use of blockchain as a promising technology for digital transformation (Khalaf et al., 2021; Kashinath et al., 2021; Zhou et al., 2021). Blockchain technology can help grow businesses because it enables digital innovation (Gausdal et al., 2018).

Over the years, Blockchain technology has received increased attention from researchers and practitioners. Blockchain has been considered an important breakthrough for independent innovation of core technologies (Blockchain Technology, Cryptocurrency: Entropy-Based Perspective). Recently, new trends have emerged for use of blockchain: Central Bank Digital Currencies and Decentralized Finance. Experiments were held to complement or replace traditional physical money with digital equivalents issued by the central banks. These new digital currencies will retain the advantages of crypto currencies while providing traditional fiat money security (Sebastião et al., 2021). The Decentralized Finance is kind of finance that is independent of traditional institutions and rely on blockchain (Cunha et al., 2021).

The blockchain technology is in its early development stages but has become one of the most interesting technology topics (Joshi et al., 2018). Blockchain technology continues to impact ordinary people and businesses alike. Due to its nature, blockchain technology would continue to be involved in the provision of more and more dependable and beneficial services in various sectors such as healthcare, finance, logistics etc. (Joshi et al., 2018). Therefore, it is important to explore the privacy and security challenges of blockchain technology.

There are several privacy and security challenges associated with Blockchain technology. In an assessment of the major regulatory challenges impacting blockchain-based solution, Yeoh (2017) found that the smart regulatory hands-off approach adopted in the EU and the USA provided a promising regulatory approach for blockchain-related innovations in the financial services and related sectors. Any participant can see the data but cannot corrupt it. Blockchain technology does not involve a central authority to conduct financial transactions (Deblao et al., 2018). The decentralized nature of blockchain means an individual can verify and undertake financial transactions in real- time.

Over the recent past several Blockchain applications have been invented. Bitcoin is one of the most popular real-world applications of blockchain. Fundamentally, Bitcoin is data with assigned ownership. This ownership can be transferred when transactions are made. The Bitcoin depends on blockchain technology. Blockchain technology helps verify whether the spender actually owns the Bitcoins he/she intends to spend (Bodó, Gervais, & Quintais, 2018). However, Bitcoin has many privacy and security issues. For example, once an individual's public key is linked with his/her personal identity, it is possible to browse and examine all the transactions linked to that public key. The main challenge here striking the balance privacy, security, and accountability of an individual. The decentralized nature of blockchain means all participating devices must be connected to a network to participate in any transaction. This constant connectivity to the network leaves these devices vulnerable to many security risks (Faroze, 2018).

Transaction propagation in blockchain networks have many privacy and security issues. Transaction payloads can be encrypted. Blockchain technology ensures authenticity of senders and receivers and the integrity of data payloads. Permission less networks can be vulnerable to techniques that bind IP addresses to blockchain accounts. If hackers get access to considerable amount of transaction traffic, they can discover the link between IP addresses and blockchain account addresses (Romano & Schmid, 2021). The IoT is a collection of physical objects equipped with sensors, processing power, software etc. The IoT devices are capable of connecting and exchanging data with other devices and systems. Blockchain technology can be combined with IoT to enable machine-to-machine transactions (Fernández-Caramés & Fraga-Lamas, 2018).

The concept of Bitcoin is centered on the concept of privacy enabled by the combination of cryptography and a decentralized network (Henry et al., 2018). However, despite an increasing interest in Bitcoin, it appears that Bitcoin has many privacy issues inherent in its design. Anyone can download the transaction history and analyze it at will. The Bitcoin addresses, transaction amounts and timestamps saved to the ledger can be used to follow a transaction (Dapp & Lyons, 2021). These privacy loopholes highlight the importance of studying privacy issues of blockchain technology and solution to assure protection of users' privacy. To ensure privacy protection, some researchers suggest that businesses should use anonymous communications systems (such as Tor). However, some other researchers have challenged this approach. These researchers have suggested that businesses should use non-anonymous users to publish business transactions that cannot be connected to their network addresses during communication procedures. That would enable the users to collect details of transactions without revealing specific transactions they pursue (Henry et al., 2018).

Security and privacy form the basis of the blockchain technology (Karame & Capkun, 2018). These aspects can either make or break blockchain technology. In IoT, a central server ensures information interchange and data authentication. That results in security and privacy issues. The security and privacy in the centralized system can be managed through the adoption of blockchain technology (Kumar & Mallick, 2018). The distributed ledger based blockchain technology plays a significant role in the success of the interaction among devices in an IoT-based environment (Jesus et al., 2018). Blockchain has been widely applied in IoT-based smart homes thereby minimizing the time needed for user authentication and authorization (Vermesan & Bacquet, 2018).

Blockchain is a distributed data structure that works through the integration of security, dependability, and centralization of system resources (Cai et al., 2018). Researchers have suggested to use a local peer network to resolve the challenges of resource constrains in blockchain-based applications. This local peer network would use a scalable local ledger to limit the number of transactions that go into the global blockchain system (Biswas et al., 2018; Cai et al., 2018). The market for security-centered blockchain technology is expected to increase to approximately $20 billion by 2020 and its uses are projected to increase in the future of the technology applications. Blockchain technology can also be combined with cloud computing to provide secure business solutions (Park et al., 2017).

Most of the security concerns related to blockchain revolve around the idea of applying data security on principles of blockchain technology. As a result, an emerging approach to counteract the growing number and complexity of cyber threats is to harness cybersecurity blockchain principles aimed at reinforcing security. Blockchain could be a main advancement in cybersecurity technology for securing sensitive information, particularly in extremely regulated industries such as the finance sector, government agencies among others (Cresitello-Dittmar, 2016; de Leon et al., 2017). Given the global cyber security landscape, new regulatory approaches are needed directed towards reducing short-term security practices. Researchers argue that the trust in blockchain transactions is maintained through a proof of work challenge (Cresitello-Dittmar, 2016). One of the vulnerabilities encountered in the workplace include user malpractices, which is the biggest threat to an organization's cybersecurity status. Despite adopting and implementing state of the art systems and security measures that can safeguard against attacks by hackers, user bad practices can substantially lead to a reasonable compromise (Mowbray & Shimonski, 2014; Mowbray & Shimonski, 2014; Yli-Huumo et al., 2016).

BLOCKCHAIN PRIVACY AND SECURITY CHALLENGES

51% Attacks

To validate a blockchain transaction, miners are very important. In a 51% attack, a malicious blockchain user gets control of mining capability of blockchain. In the next step, this user obtains control of more than 50% of mining capacity. With that capacity, this user is able to mine faster than any other blockchain user. A 51% attack leaves the hackers in control of more than half of the hash rate and control of the entire system, which can be disastrous. Hackers can modify the order of transactions and prevent them from being confirmed. They can even reverse previously completed transactions, resulting in double-spending. If a blockchain is compromised, transactions can be reversed. In the past, three renowned cryptocurrency platforms (Ethereum Classic, ZenCash, and Verge) suffered from 51% attack. The 51% attacks have caused enterprises an annual loss of $20 million. These attacks generally occur in the initial stages of the blockchain. These attacks do apply to enterprise or private blockchains. To avoid 51% attacks, one measure organizations can take is to beef up monitoring of mining pools. The organizations also need to ensure to use a higher hash rate and avoid using Proof-of-Work consensus.

Endpoint Vulnerabilities

Another challenge is security of endpoints for blockchain transactions. The blockchain network's endpoint is where users interact with the blockchain e.g., mobile phone or laptop computer. Attackers can observe user behavior and target user devices to steal their key. For example, a transaction may involve large monetary value that could be stored in a virtual wallet. It is important to note here that you can ensure safety of actual blockchain blocks against hackers, but you cannot do the same for virtual wallet. In addition, many third parties (e.g., payment processors) play an important role to facilitate blockchain transactions. Any weaknesses in the apps and websites of these third-parties can make the whole system vulnerable.

Routing Attacks

A blockchain network and its applications are heavily dependent on the real-time movement of very large amounts of data. An attacker can use routing attacks to partition the blockchain network. The new partition contains two (or more) disjoint components. Here, nodes within a component cannot communicate with nodes outside of it. As a result, the hacker creates parallel blockchains. The most dangerous aspect of routing attacks is their anonymity. Everything appears normal and blockchain users notice no suspicious activity. Routing attacks can be very dangerous as considerable damage could occur before attack could be detected.

Phishing Attacks

A phishing attack is basically an attempt to fraudulently obtain the credentials of a user. A phishing attack is a targeted attack on a particular group e.g., crypto wallet users. With access to the credentials of a user, hackers are in a position to launch follow-up attacks against both the users and the blockchain. Phishing attacks on blockchain networks are increasing. In many cases, it has been noticed that attackers target individuals or corporate sector workers.

Transaction Privacy Leakage

On a blockchain network, user behaviors can be traced. As such, security of user transaction privacy is very important. Users must assign a private key for every transaction. This is important so that attackers are unable to determine the identity of the user conducting different transactions. However, privacy protection in blockchain is still an unfinished work. According to an estimate, 66% of samples Bitcoin transactions were vulnerable to hacker attacks (Joshi et. al., 2018).

SOLUTIONS TO PRIVACY AND SECURITY CONCERNS

51% Attacks

There are several ways to mitigate the danger of a 51% attack. In order to prevent 51% attacks, it is important to improve the monitoring of mining pool. It is also important that hash rate is kept higher, and proof-of-work consensus procedures should be avoided. The blockchain system must also use appropriate consensus algorithms and monitor behavior of other nodes.

Phishing Attacks

To prevent phishing attacks, the first step you take is to improve browser security. This can be done by installing a verified add-on. This add-on notifies if the website is unsafe to surf. Secondly, you should improve device security. To do so, install the malicious link detection software and antivirus software. Third, you should always confirm with the sender if he/she sent you the email. Fourth, you should avoid clicking the link without thorough review. As a precaution, you should always enter the web address into your browser rather than clicking on the link. Fifth, you should avoid open Wi-Fi networks for conducting any blockchain transaction. Sixth, you should ensure that your system and software are always up to date.

Routing Attacks

Secure routing protocols with certificates are a good first line of defense against routing attacks. The second step is the use of data encryption. Users should always be encouraged to use strong passwords and change the passwords regularly. Organizations should also educate their blockchain users about the risks associated with information security.

Endpoint Vulnerabilities

To prevent endpoint vulnerabilities, first the users must not save blockchain keys on their devices as text files. Users must also download and install antivirus software for their devices. Users must also review the system regularly and keep track of the time, location, and device access.

Transaction Privacy Leakage

To stop this leakage, a most popular technique is mixing service (cryptocurrency tumbler) that that allows users to reestablish their privacy in Blockchain network. In this arrangement, several users make transactions simultaneously with multiple inputs and outputs. As a result, it is not possible to link the transaction inputs with corresponding outputs (pixelplex.io, 2022).

CONCLUSION

Blockchain is an emerging technology that it still in its early development stages. The blockchain technology offers multiple benefits as well as limitations such as complexity, human error, scalability, security, and sustainability. However, these limitations have not hindered the success level and increased penetration of blockchain technology in the industry. This study has identified various privacy and security challenges of Blockchain technology and suggested solutions to overcome those challenges. An in-depth understanding of the security and privacy challenges of blockchain is crucial to enhance the level of trust that blockchain may potentially provide and in developing innovative defense and countermeasure solutions. Developing these security and privacy solutions would be driving force behind future development of blockchain and its applications.

REFERENCES

Abdel-Aziz, A. A., Abdel-Salam, H., & El-Sayad, Z. (2016). The role of ICTs in creating the new social public place of the digital era. *Alexandria Engineering Journal*, 55(1), 487–493. doi:10.1016/j.aej.2015.12.019

Andoni, M., Robu, V., Flynn, D., Abram, S., Geach, D., Jenkins, D., McCallum, P., & Peacock, A. (2019). Blockchain technology in the energy sector: A systematic review of challenges and opportunities. *Renewable & Sustainable Energy Reviews*, 100, 143–174. doi:10.1016/j.rser.2018.10.014

Biswas, S., Sharif, K., Li, F., Nour, B., & Wang, Y. (2018). A scalable blockchain framework for secure transactions in IoT. *IEEE Internet of Things Journal*, 6(3), 4650–4659. doi:10.1109/JIOT.2018.2874095

Bodó, B., Gervais, D., & Quintais, J. P. (2018). Blockchain and smart contracts: The missing link in copyright licensing? *International Journal of Law and Information Technology*, *26*(4), 311–336. doi:10.1093/ijlit/eay014

Cai, Z., Du, C., Gan, Y., Zhang, J., & Huang, W. (2018). Research and development of blockchain security. *International Journal of Performability Engineering*, *14*(9), 2040.

CBI. (2022). *Blockchain technology for agricultural ingredients*. CBI. https://www.cbi.eu/market-information/natural-ingredients-health-products/blockchain-technology-agricultural#limitations-of-blockchain

Cresitello-Dittmar, B. (2016). *Application of the blockchain for authentication and verification of identity*. Tufts University. http://www.cs.tufts.edu/comp/116/archive/fall2016/bcresitellodittmar.pdf

Crosby, M. Nachiappan, P. P., Verma, S., & Kalyanaraman, V. (2015, October 16). *Blockchain: Beyond Bitcoin—UC Berkeley Sutardja Center*. Berkeley College. https://scet.berkeley.edu/reports/blockchain/

da Cunha, P. R., Soja, P., & Themistocleous, M. (2021). Blockchain for development: A guiding framework. [).]. Taylor & Francis.]. *Information Technology for Development*, *27*(3), 417–438. doi:10.1080/02681102.2021.1935453

Dapp, M., & Lyons, T. (2021, December 14). Privacy in the era of cryptocurrencies. *Bitcoin Suisse*. https://www.bitcoinsuisse.com/research/theme/privacy-in-the-era-of-cryptocurrencies

de Leon, D. C., Stalick, A. Q., Jillepalli, A. A., Haney, M. A., & Sheldon, F. T. (2017). *Blockchain: Properties and misconceptions*. Asia Pacific Journal of Innovation and Entrepreneurship.

Deloitte. (2022, May 19). *When Two Chains Combine Supply Chain Meets Blockchain*. Deloitte Turkey. https://www2.deloitte.com/tr/en/pages/technology/articles/when-two-chains-combine.html

Dinçer, H., & Yüksel, S. (2018). *Handbook of research on managerial thinking in global business economics*. IGI Global.

Dresch, A., Lacerda, D. P., & Antunes, J. A. V. (2015). Design science research. In *Design science research* (pp. 67–102). Springer. doi:10.1007/978-3-319-07374-3_4

Drescher, D. (2017). *Blockchain basics: A non-technical introduction in 25 steps*. Apress, Frankfurt-am-Mein. doi:10.1007/978-1-4842-2604-9

Fanning, K., & Centers, D. P. (2016). Blockchain and its coming impact on financial services. *Journal of Corporate Accounting & Finance*, 27(5), 53–57. doi:10.1002/jcaf.22179

Farhadi, M., Ismail, R., & Fooladi, M. (2012). Information and communication technology use and economic growth. *PLoS One*, 7(11), e48903. doi:10.1371/journal.pone.0048903 PMID:23152817

Faroze, D. S. (2018). Block chain & internet of things: Security, challenges, research issues. *International Journal of Computer Science Trends and Technology*, 6(5), 35–38.

Fernández-Caramés, T. M., & Fraga-Lamas, P. (2018). A Review on the Use of Blockchain for the Internet of Things. *IEEE Access: Practical Innovations, Open Solutions*, 6, 32979–33001. doi:10.1109/ACCESS.2018.2842685

Fortes, N., & Rita, P. (2016). Privacy concerns and online purchasing behaviour: Towards an integrated model. *European Research on Management and Business Economics*, 22(3), 167–176. doi:10.1016/j.iedeen.2016.04.002

Gad, A. G., Mosa, D. T., Abualigah, L., & Abohany, A. A. (2022). Emerging Trends in Blockchain Technology and Applications: A Review and Outlook. *Journal of King Saud University-Computer and Information Sciences*.

Gausdal, A. H., Czachorowski, K. V., & Solesvik, M. Z. (2018). Applying blockchain technology: Evidence from Norwegian companies. *Sustainability*, 10(6), 1985. doi:10.3390u10061985

Gordon, W. J., & Catalini, C. (2018). Blockchain technology for healthcare: Facilitating the transition to patient-driven interoperability. *Computational and Structural Biotechnology Journal*, 16, 224–230. doi:10.1016/j.csbj.2018.06.003 PMID:30069284

Guin, U., Cui, P., & Skjellum, A. (2018). Ensuring proof-of-authenticity of IoT edge devices using blockchain technology. *2018 IEEE International Conference on Internet of Things (IThings) and IEEE Green Computing and Communications (GreenCom) and IEEE Cyber, Physical and Social Computing (CPSCom) and IEEE Smart Data (SmartData)*, (pp. 1042–1049). IEEE. 10.1109/Cybermatics_2018.2018.00193

Gupta, M. P., & Dubey, A. (2016). E-commerce-study of privacy, trust and security from consumer's perspective. *Transactions*, 37, 38.

Henry, R., Herzberg, A., & Kate, A. (2018). Blockchain access privacy: Challenges and directions. *IEEE Security and Privacy*, 16(4), 38–45. doi:10.1109/MSP.2018.3111245

Higgins, M. (2021, November 8). Blockchain In Supply Chain. *Forbes*. https://www.forbes.com/sites/forbestechcouncil/2021/11/08/blockchain-in-supply-chain/?sh=183f62404e1a

Hooper, M. (2018, February 22). Top five blockchain benefits transforming your industry. *IBM Supply Chain and Blockchain Blog*. https://www.ibm.com/blogs/blockchain/2018/02/top-five-blockchain-benefits-transforming-your-industry/

Jesus, E. F., Chicarino, V. R., De Albuquerque, C. V., & Rocha, A. A. de A. (2018). A survey of how to use blockchain to secure internet of things and the stalker attack. *Security and Communication Networks*, *2018*, 2018. doi:10.1155/2018/9675050

Karame, G., & Capkun, S. (2018). Blockchain security and privacy. *IEEE Security and Privacy*, *16*(04), 11–12. doi:10.1109/MSP.2018.3111241

Kashinath, S. A., Mostafa, S. A., Mustapha, A., Mahdin, H., Lim, D., Mahmoud, M. A., Mohammed, M. A., Al-Rimy, B. A. S., Fudzee, M. F. M., & Yang, T. J. (2021). Review of data fusion methods for real-time and multi-sensor traffic flow analysis. *IEEE Access: Practical Innovations, Open Solutions*, *9*, 51258–51276. doi:10.1109/ACCESS.2021.3069770

Khalaf, B. A., Mostafa, S. A., Mustapha, A., Mohammed, M. A., Mahmoud, M. A., Al-Rimy, B. A. S., Abd Razak, S., Elhoseny, M., & Marks, A. (2021). An adaptive protection of flooding attacks model for complex network environments. *Security and Communication Networks*. doi:10.1155/2021/5542919

Kumar, N. M., & Mallick, P. K. (2018). Blockchain technology for security issues and challenges in IoT. *Procedia Computer Science*, *132*, 1815–1823. doi:10.1016/j.procs.2018.05.140

Lau, F., & Kuziemsky, C. (2016). Handbook of eHealth evaluation: An evidence-based approach. University of Victoria.

Longnecker, J. G., Petty, W. J., Palich, L. E., & Moore, C. W. (2010). *Small business management: Launching & growing entrepreneurial ventures*. South-Western Cengage Learning.

Mallett, R., Hagen-Zanker, J., Slater, R., & Duvendack, M. (2012). The benefits and challenges of using systematic reviews in international development research. *Journal of Development Effectiveness*, *4*(3), 445–455. doi:10.1080/19439342.2012.711342

Mowbray, T. J. (2013). *Cybersecurity: Managing systems, conducting testing, and investigating intrusions*. John Wiley & Sons.

Park, J. H., & Park, J. H. (2017). Blockchain security in cloud computing: Use cases, challenges, and solutions. *Symmetry*, *9*(8), 164. doi:10.3390ym9080164

Patil, D. D. Y. (2021, December 31). *Blockchain Technology*. DPU. https://engg. dypvp.edu.in/blogs/blockchain-technology

Pereira, G. V., Virkar, S., & Vignoli, M. (2018). Exploring the political, social and cultural challenges and possibilities associated with trading data: The case of data market Austria (DMA). *Proceedings of the 19th Annual International Conference on Digital Government Research: Governance in the Data Age*, (pp. 1–2).

pixelplex.io. (2022, September 14). *Blockchain Security: Everything You Need to Know*. PixelPlex. https://pixelplex.io/blog/everything-you-need-to-know-about-blockchain-security/

Purtill, C. (2018, September 9). Equifax data breach: A year later, no punishment for the company. *Quartz*. https://qz.com/1383810/equifax-data-breach-one-year-later-no-punishment-for-the-company/

Rahmadika, S., & Rhee, K.-H. (2018). Blockchain technology for providing an architecture model of decentralized personal health information. *International Journal of Engineering Business Management*, *10*, 1847979018790589. doi:10.1177/1847979018790589

Rao, A. (2018, May 29). How to Secure your Personal Data using blockchain? *Coinmonks*. https://medium.com/coinmonks/guarantee-your-patients-privacy-today-securing-sensitive-data-with-blockchain-fcb179f1302c

Reyna, A., Martín, C., Chen, J., Soler, E., & Díaz, M. (2018). On blockchain and its integration with IoT. Challenges and opportunities. *Future Generation Computer Systems*, *88*, 173–190. doi:10.1016/j.future.2018.05.046

Romano, D., & Schmid, G. (2021). Beyond Bitcoin: Recent Trends and Perspectives in Distributed Ledger Technology. *Cryptography*, *5*(4), 36. doi:10.3390/cryptography5040036

Sabbagh, P., Pourmohamad, R., Elveny, M., Beheshti, M., Davarpanah, A., Metwally, A. S. M., Ali, S., & Mohammed, A. S. (2021). Evaluation and Classification Risks of Implementing Blockchain in the Drug Supply Chain with a New Hybrid Sorting Method. *Sustainability*, *13*(20), 11466. doi:10.3390u132011466

Shackelford, S. J., & Myers, S. (2017). Block-by-block: Leveraging the power of blockchain technology to build trust and promote cyber peace. *Yale JL & Tech.*, *19*, 334.

Smith, T. L. (2018a, March 23). The 6 Limitations of Blockchain Technology. *Everything Blockchain*. https://medium.com/everything-blockchain/the-6-limitations-of-blockchain-technology-2d1b686c0293

Srivastava, V. (2022, January 23). *Limitations of Blockchain Technology*. Include Help. https://www.includehelp.com/blockchain/limitations-of-blockchain-technology.aspx

Techtarget.com. (2021, September 9). *Using blockchain to improve security for IoT devices*. IoT Agenda. https://www.techtarget.com/iotagenda/post/Using-blockchain-to-improve-security-for-IoT-devices

Treiblmaier, H. (2018). The impact of the blockchain on the supply chain: A theory-based research framework and a call for action. *Supply Chain Management*, *23*(6), 545–559. doi:10.1108/SCM-01-2018-0029

Vermesan, O., & Bacquet, J. (2019). *Next generation Internet of Things: Distributed intelligence at the edge and human machine-to-machine cooperation*. River Publishers.

William, S. (2011). *Network Security Essentials: Applications and Standards (For VTU)*. Pearson Education India.

Woodside, J. M., Augustine, F. K. Jr, & Giberson, W. (2017). Blockchain technology adoption status and strategies. *Journal of International Technology and Information Management*, *26*(2), 65–93.

Xiong, Z., Zhang, Y., Niyato, D., Wang, P., & Han, Z. (2018). When mobile blockchain meets edge computing. *IEEE Communications Magazine*, *56*(8), 33–39. doi:10.1109/MCOM.2018.1701095

Yaeger, K., Martini, M., Rasouli, J., & Costa, A. (2019). Emerging blockchain technology solutions for modern healthcare infrastructure. *Journal of Scientific Innovation in Medicine*, *2*(1), 1. doi:10.29024/jsim.7

Yaga, D., Mell, P., Roby, N., & Scarfone, K. (2018). *Blockchain Technology Overview*. NIST. https://nvlpubs.nist.gov/nistpubs/ir/2018/NIST.IR.8202.pdf

Yang, Y., Wu, L., Yin, G., Li, L., & Zhao, H. (2017). A survey on security and privacy issues in Internet-of-Things. *IEEE Internet of Things Journal*, *4*(5), 1250–1258. doi:10.1109/JIOT.2017.2694844

Yeoh, P. (2017). Regulatory issues in blockchain technology. *Journal of Financial Regulation and Compliance*.

Yiannas, F. (2018). A new era of food transparency powered by blockchain. *Innovations: Technology, Governance, Globalization, 12*(1–2), 46–56. doi:10.1162/inov_a_00266

Yli-Huumo, J., Ko, D., Choi, S., Park, S., & Smolander, K. (2016). Where is current research on blockchain technology? A systematic review. *PLoS One, 11*(10), e0163477. doi:10.1371/journal.pone.0163477 PMID:27695049

Yuan, Y., & Wang, F.-Y. (2018). Blockchain and cryptocurrencies: Model, techniques, and applications. *IEEE Transactions on Systems, Man, and Cybernetics. Systems, 48*(9), 1421–1428. doi:10.1109/TSMC.2018.2854904

Zhou, X., Ma, Y., Zhang, Q., Mohammed, M. A., & Damaševičius, R. (2021). A reversible watermarking system for medical color images: Balancing capacity, imperceptibility, and robustness. *Electronics (Basel), 10*(9), 1024. doi:10.3390/electronics10091024

Chapter 9
Protection of Personal Data and Internet of Things Security

Panem Charanarur
Department of Cyber Security and Digital Forensics, National Forensic Sciences University, India

Srinivasa Rao Gundu
Government Degree College Sitaphalamandi, Hyderabad, India

J. Vijaylaxmi
PVKK Degree and PG College, Anantapur, India

ABSTRACT

Every aspect of our life, from travel and healthcare to entertainment and governmental interactions, stands to benefit greatly from the advent of the internet of things. Despite this enormous potential, however, a number of significant obstacles must first be overcome. The race to create laws, rules, and governance that will lead this progress without strangling innovation has become more difficult because of the exponential expansion in the number of connected devices. Discover the origins of the IoT, its many definitions, and some of its most important uses in this in-depth read. Future fears and difficulties relating to security and privacy are taken into account, both generally and in the more specific context of individual applications.

INTRODUCTION

The advent of the internet of things, or IoT, has been hailed as a game-changing innovation with the potential to greatly improve the quality of our lives. Manufacturing, healthcare, transportation, and logistics are just some of the sectors that stand to

DOI: 10.4018/978-1-6684-6581-3.ch009

benefit from this. Thanks to its cyber-physical features, the internet of things will serve as a catalyst for the development of new market niches, leading to the creation of unique, cross-disciplinary software and services that will aid in the optimization of processes via the use of cutting-edge data analysis (Almeida et al., 2015).

INTERNET OF THINGS

Connecting disparate physical objects via the Internet was a well-established concept long before the phrase "internet of things" was used. A group of 1980s Carnegie Mellon University students connected the soda machine's photo sensors to the web and installed them inside the machine. This allowed them to track how many cans were being distributed at any one time. Thus, anybody with access to the internet may observe how many alcoholic and nonalcoholic beverages were served. Afterward, after that, how many were there? In the 1990s, John Romkey and Simon Hackett developed the first web-connected toaster. There was no such thing as the Internet at this point. Romkey gave a talk at the 1990 Interop Conference, which was shown on an online-capable Sunbeam Deluxe Automatic.

Romkey, President of Interop, and Dan Lynch, CEO of Interop, had a chat the prior year that led to the creation of the Radiant Control toaster. Lynch's assurance to Romkey that, should he do well, he would be the focus of everyone's attention. The TCP/IP-enabled toaster, which has an SNMP MIB controller for managing base network management protocols, only activates and deactivates the power supply. Conventional wisdom is that it was Ashton Kutcher who initially coined the phrase "internet of things" and introduced the idea (Ashton, 2009). It was the name of a presentation given in 1999 at Procter & Gamble.

The number of devices that can establish an internet connection has skyrocketed as a direct result of the widespread adoption of IoT. Many experts in the field, including Cisco's Dave Evans and Ericsson's Hans Vestburg, have estimated that by 2020, there would be 50 billion internet-connected devices in use. Due to the inherent uncertainty in these computations, both parties have just recently revised their initial projections downward. At the time of writing (2021), Evans, who is now employed at Stringify, projected that the platform will have 30 million users, whereas Ericcson predicted that there would be 28 billion. As of right now, reliable data on the total number of internet-enabled gadgets is not available, making it difficult to establish reliable growth estimates.

The problem of different understandings of how the internet of things functions contributes to the fact that estimates might vary substantially even when using the same terminology. The GSMA's analysis of M2M, which "focuses on cellular M2M connectivity and excludes computing devices in consumer electronics such as smartphones, e- readers, tablets, and other types of M2M connection technologies that support the wider universe of the internet of things," is one set of numbers that makes the distinction between internet of things devices and M2M devices clear. Predictions given by Machine Research in 2015 indicate that the number of connections between M2M devices will increase from 5 billion in 2014 to 27 billion in 2024. As of the 2015 Macintosh, the. In 2016, Gartner forecasted 6.4 billion devices, IDC predicted 9 billion with the same exclusions as Gartner, while IHS estimated 17.6 billion, as reported by Nordrum (2016). Smartphones, tablets, and desktop computers were not included in any of these forecasts including smartphones, tablets, and computers. According to their findings, Juniper Research has determined that there are now 16 billion unique kinds of devices in use (Fabiano, 2017).

There may not be precise estimates of the total number of IoT-connected devices, but it is clear that there are a lot of them, and their numbers are only expected to keep growing quickly. Ashton said that "the internet of things" (IoT) "is still commonly misunderstood" in the article he wrote about the first time he used the phrase "internet of things." When talking about the internet of things, he made this comment. The term "internet of things," or "IoT" for short, has been used to refer to this network of interconnected devices in many different contexts (Atzori, Iera, and Morabito 2010; Bandyopadhyay and Sen 2011; Malina et al. 2016). Although it should not come as a surprise that laypeople and researchers with just a passing interest in the problem would have various interpretations, it is intriguing that individuals who are regarded to be specialists in the area may have such varied points of view on what something means. The IEEE defines the internet of things as "a network of devices, each equipped with sensors, that are linked to the Internet" in their paper titled "The Internet of Things". According to the Internet Engineering Task Force, another highly regarded expert organization, "in the vision of the internet of things, "things" are very varied, including computers, sensors, people, actuators, refrigerators, TVs, vehicles, mobile phones, clothes, food, medicines, books, and so on."

The European Commission's Directorate-General for Information Society and Media and the European Technology Platform on Smart Systems Integration define a "thing" as "an item not completely recognized". After reviewing several IoT initiatives, the European Cluster established its Strategic Research Agenda. The Consortium for Internet-of-Things Related Research Projects has its own, distinct definition of the internet of things. It has also been criticized for including elements that were previously only discussed in the context of other concepts, such as pervasive or ubiquitous computing. This was shown to be the case by three researchers.

Because of this, distinguishing between the two proved difficult. Multiple technologies, perspectives of view, and research domains may be connected to and inspired by the IoT. IoT, mobile computing, ubiquitous computing, wireless sensor networks, and cyber-physical systems have commonalities and are converging, as described by Stankovic. According to the definition provided by Atzori, Iera, and Morabito, the internet of things is the result of the combination of the following three technological advances.

There are three crucial perspectives: one focused on the Internet such as IP for smart devices, one on "things" such as RFID, NFC, and Wireless Sensor Actuators, and one on "semantics" for example reasoning over data. Since the IoT links so many different but equally important domains, defining what it is and how its growth should be interpreted is challenging. Still, it can't be denied that the IoT connects many essential sectors. So, in light of the foregoing.

It is not surprising that the internet of things confronts difficulties in the areas of security, privacy, and regulation given the interconnected nature of the IoT with other aims and advancements and the lack of a common understanding of the IoT's meaning and scope or even of what 'things' are. The IETF's definition of "things" will serve as the basis for our analysis here (Lu et al., 2014).

Regarding M2M and the IoT, the concept of "machine-to-machine communication" has been around for some time but is now enjoying a surge in popularity due to the Fourth Industrial Revolution and the Industrial internet of things. For some time now, M2M connections have served as the backbone of standard SCADA (supervisory control and data acquisition) systems.

The term "machine-to-machine" (or "M2M") refers to a kind of communication in which no human beings take part. This interaction might happen through a wired or wireless connection, and there is a vast and ever-expanding selection of communication methods, norms, and protocols. Both wired and wireless connections may be used for this kind of communication. Cellular networks, among others, are widely used for this purpose. Point-to-point no requirement for a base station, intermediate, or access point and cellular networks offer different attack vectors. Rising technologies include wireless local area networks, radio frequency identification, and dedicated short-range communication. Near field communication, ZigBee, and short-range communication are a few more examples like DSRC. These technologies operate at a wide range of frequencies. The distance, the range, and other characteristics are all governed by a variety of factors, and they may vary considerably. Newly developed standards, such as the Meter-Bus standard, allow utility companies to use application-specific meters for gas and electricity that can be read remotely such as EN 13757-x. ISO/IEC has established guidelines for the development of "smart home" technology. EN 50090-x and ISO/IEC 14543-3 were both created by the European Committee for Electrotechnical Standardization. In-House and Commercial Electronics, it's important to remember that "the internet of X" might refer to a variety of different things depending on the context. According to studies using the ABI 2017, IoT is seen as a natural development that supplements existing internets like the Internet of People and the internet of things. In their research,

Buxmann and his colleagues examine how the Internet of Services has evolved over time. While other firms have been concentrating on establishing the internet of things, ABB has been working on goods and services for the service sector and individuals Buxmann, Hess, and Ruggaber in 2011. We are now in the midst of a concerted endeavor to usher in the Fourth Industrial Revolution. The Internet of Vehicles is evolving from the connected vehicle agenda with the assistance of the Industrial IoT. Advancements like the Internet of Animal Health Things that get less media coverage. Cisco and Qualcomm are now in the forefront of spreading the phrase "internet of things" to the general public (IoE). While Cisco's marketing department may have been responsible for the creation of the phrase "the cloud," there is still value in establishing a framework that takes into account more than just cloud computing. most common IoT applications, particularly now that the technology has matured beyond M2M usage. If you classify M2M communication as belonging to the IoT, then IoE, or the industrial internet of things, is a larger category.

Interdependencies across humans, systems, things, and information are central to the IoE framework. Things in this context are tangible objects like sensors, gadgets, actuators, and the like that may create data independently or collect data from external sources. Human-made and interconnected systems, such as social networks and apps for health, wellbeing, and fitness, can be more important than humans themselves. Data analysis and processing provides insights that may be used to make informed decisions and manage regulatory regimes. Understanding the internet of things as a system that incorporates both machines and humans is now feasible thanks to the notion of the internet of everything (IoE), which also integrates the data and knowledge that emerges from analyzing various services, contexts, and settings. This idea of the IoE may not be as great of a leap as originally thought when placed within the framework of the IETF's definition of the IoT. In conclusion, the emergence of the internet of things may be traced back to the implementation of many foundational technologies from various perspectives (Jha et al., 2022).

Its current form is the result of input from a wide variety of organizations, some of whom are not formally affiliated with one another but who have certain overlapping but unique sets of views. Similar innovations have also been applied to a variety of other domains, frequently using vendor- and domain-specific standards. The dispersed character of growth makes it hard to implement effective management and create standards because of the lack of harmony and common vision. As a result, establishing criteria becomes more problematic. Many existing security and privacy flaws in the IoT may be traced back to this lack of standardization and regulation. It has also stripped technicians and end users of the authority they need to maintain, update, and fix devices and services when issues emerge, leaving them vulnerable to disruption. Analyzing, assessing risks, and putting preventative measures in place become far more challenging tasks than they would be if the growth path were more deliberate and planned. This increase is swift and large, and it demands prompt effort to find a solution to the problems it presents.

Interdependencies across humans, systems, things, and information are central to the IoE framework. Things in this context are tangible objects like sensors, gadgets, actuators, and the like that may create data independently or collect data from external sources. Human-made and interconnected systems, such as social networks and apps for health, wellbeing, and fitness, can be more important than humans themselves. Data analysis and processing provides insights that may be used to make informed decisions and manage regulatory regimes. According to this interpretation.

The internet of everything (IoE) not only enables the study of the IoT as a system including machines and humans, but it also unifies the data and knowledge that emerges from researching those services, contexts, and settings. This is only one of the numerous advantages provided by the IoE. surgical procedure. This idea of the IoE may not be as great of a leap as originally thought when placed within the framework of the IETF's definition of the IoT. In conclusion, the emergence of the internet of things may be traced back to the implementation of many foundational technologies from various perspectives. Its current form is the result of input from a wide variety of organizations, some of whom are not formally affiliated with one another but have certain overlapping but unique sets of views. Similar innovations have also been applied to a variety of other domains, frequently using vendor- and domain-specific standards.

The dispersed character of growth makes it hard to implement effective management and create standards because of the lack of harmony and a common vision. As a result, establishing criteria becomes more problematic. Many existing security and privacy flaws in the IoT may be traced back to this lack of standardization and regulation. Not only that, but it has also left professionals and users without the authorization and means to maintain, update, and fix devices and services when issues emerge. Without proper oversight, direction, education, and uniformity, the security infrastructure is vulnerable. Analyzing, assessing risks, and putting preventative measures in place become far more challenging tasks than they would be if the growth path were more deliberate and planned. This increase is swift and large, and it demands prompt effort to find a solution to the problems it presents.

Concerning IoT Use Cases Many scholars have studied IoT to learn more about its potential uses and impacts in many industries. The researchers have developed their taxonomy to categorize the wide variety of IoT application spaces. The advantages and disadvantages of various internet of things taxonomies depend not only on the goal being sought but also on the definition and the context in which the IoT is being analyzed. Table 2 lists works that should be consulted by anybody with an interest in the topic. Numerous potential uses for the technology have been identified by both the private sector and the academic community. As an example, the Libelium

Industry brochure from 2015 features 61 IoT applications from a broad range of industries and sensor board types (Varadi et al., 2018).

Academics Atzori, Iera, and Morabito classify possible applications across four interconnected domains: transportation and logistics; healthcare; smart environment; home, office, plant; personal; and a more distant and futuristic subcategory, the social transportation and logistics; healthcare; smart environment; home, office, plant; personal. Some of the six categories used are revised, but the focus on healthcare remains the same. Despite this, they focus mostly on the domains of protection and surveillance, rather than the commercial and public sectors, which are, perhaps, the most important. The need for a new labeling system arose from the realization of the game-changing potential of the internet of things and the rejection of a futuristic, time-based strategy for reorganizing the transportation and logistics industries, as well as the smart environment sectors and their roles in supply chains and logistics. In addition, a new umbrella term, "smart infrastructure," has emerged.

In this research, it is focused on the three most important applications of the internet of things: business, the environment, and society. However, the study concluded that it is impossible to isolate applications and services at the intra- and inter-domain levels. Programs that allow for domains to existing and services that meet a specific need or skill set inside and across domains are what we should be focusing on instead. Therefore, businesses need to evaluate their current state of cyber security. In spite of how obvious it may seem, focusing just on the domain level for assessing security risk is a dangerous mistake. Taking into consideration several perspectives across a wide range of application and domain types makes our current risk assessment technique inefficient, as should be readily apparent.

While threat modelling and risk assessment may have certain similarities depending on the situation, both processes are usually quite different from one another. Different types of danger exist. The internet of things applications should be prioritized above cyber security at the domain level. Focusing on a subset of apps that pose a substantial cyber security risk because of the consequences of an attack is the goal of this section. Self-driving cars are connected to the internet and do not need human drivers. usage of sensors in automobiles is one of the fastest-growing markets. The engine, different systems, pollution controls, and braking systems of a car all rely largely on the precision and dependability of its sensors to function as intended. A few examples of accessible monitoring gadgets include those that track things like crank position, cam position, manifold absolute pressure, throttle position, and tire pressure through a Bluetooth connection (Rivera et al., 2019).

The United Kingdom has made considerable expenditures in this subject through programs like Highways England's Smart Motorways, and sensors that are incorporated into transportation networks to the point where they are an integral component of such networks. In order to reach this objective, communication infrastructure must be developed along more than 40 kilometres of urban roads, dual-carriageways, and motorways. By sharing information between moving vehicles and fixed structures, we can make streets and highways more efficient for everyone. Vehicle-to-vehicle (V2V) communication occurs when two or more cars are in close proximity to one another. Technologies like Dedicated Short-Range Communications, Long-Term Evolution for Vehicles, and Visible Light Communications are making platooning possible in an effort to decrease fuel consumption and improve road safety. inform people in advance about upcoming events.

It is possible that deploying such ITSs using edge and cloud computing can improve accident management. Location-specific traffic and weather alerts are offered as a service to help drivers. prioritizing one's health, happiness, and free time Sensing devices are playing a bigger part in today's high-tech healthcare systems. Medical services and applications might potentially benefit from the use of internet of things technology. Attracting a significant share of the healthcare industry's overall revenue, ambient assisted living is one of the most promising developments.

Some of the technologies being incorporated into mobile technologies include the Internet of Mobile Health which makes use of medical sensors, Smart Home Technology which makes use of smart houses to enable for patient monitoring and treatment in autonomous contexts, semantic medical access using semantics, IoT healthcare apps may make use of medical rule engines to analyze vast volumes of sensor data, and ADRs drug-related adverse reactions such allergies and medication interactions may be anticipated by careful labelling and research of medical databases avoided.

Examples of healthcare applications that have been developed or are in the planning phases include the monitoring of blood pressure and glucose levels, the tracking of body temperature, and the diagnosis of abnormal heart rhythms. Wheelchair upkeep, oxygen saturation testing, and patient tracking are all part of keeping tabs on the rehabilitation process. One of the many worldwide effects that the internet of things will have on Industry 4.0 is the introduction of new technologies. During this Fourth Industrial Revolution, the internet of things will be employed across the whole of the manufacturing process. An upgrade to clever automated systems is essential. Synergistic integration of hyperphysical systems, robotic automation, big data analytics, and cloud computing (Fedorov) is becoming commonplace in manufacturing (Rivera et al., 2019).

The internet of things enables a better manufacturing process, which is offered by intelligent logistics when smart, connected equipment with proactive maintenance is used throughout the development lifetime. This allows for the lean manufacturing process to be used as well as rapid product iteration. Smart grid technologies, improved decision-making, and creative planning will allow for substantial gains in the plant energy efficiency of things technology may dynamically improve logistics in the face of rising volumes of shipments and stockpiles by allowing the service provider to simultaneously increase operational efficiency, automation, and reduce the need for human activities.

It was Buckelew and Chung 2015 that first proposed the term of things implementation in logistics may have a noticeable effect on intelligent inventory management, damage detection, real-time visibility, precise inventory control, optimal asset utilization, predictive maintenance, and freight management. This was shown to be the case by three researchers. This request is being sent When used to supply chain management, RFID technology allows firms to foresee data, forecast trends, assess risk, and implement corrective measures sooner. This has the potential to improve firms' responsiveness to market fluctuations and supply chain risk management. In the age of the smart grid, The United Kingdom has recently taken the lead in the European deployment of a broad variety of potential smart grid systems thanks to the country's increased investment in smart grid research and development in recent years.

The term "Smart Grid" refers to an intelligent electrical system that integrates data and communication into the preexisting power grid. Sensors, digital meters, and controllers with analytical tools make it feasible to monitor and enhance grid performance, forestall power outages, and restore service. Several intelligent systems, including community energy management systems (CEMS) and building energy management systems (BEMS), will be built throughout the creation of a Smart Grid to meet the needs of smart cities. One potential use for IoT sensors is to identify grid-connected appliances and relay that data in real time to the user.

Included are both private residences and commercial establishments. From 2010 to 2016, IHS Markit (IHS 2016) found that 161 businesses together supplied over a million smart home devices; shipments increased by 64% from 2015 to 2016. Since its introduction in 2010, smart home technology has skyrocketed in popularity, resulting in over a million units shipped by 161 different firms. Expenditures on HVAC systems, home security systems including smart locks like August's, and digital home assistants like Amazon's Echo, Bosch's Mykie, and Google Home also contributed to this growth. The addition of purchases of Nest and other smart energy management systems to this increase is also significant (Neisse et al., 2014).

With more people using smart technologies at home, there has been a corresponding rise in demand for smart tools in the office. Recent research on Academy by British Land and Worktech found that 88% of those polled wanted a bigger voice in the choices that affected them. Of those surveyed, roughly a third were leaders. The work environment for the better. The results show that implementing a smart workplace would have far-reaching effects on how a company functions and on the local ecosystem. Increased efficiency of over 40% is predicted, along with a 37% increase in the production of well-being and happiness, a 38% increase in the loyalty of customers, and a 38% increase in the satisfaction of customers. Increasing demand for internet of things installations in homes, businesses, and public areas is a factor that will help "smart cities" take new shape. As sensor technology advances, the internet of things will be able to let companies and their consumers engage in more satisfying ways.

Oversight and management of the process's businesses will flourish as a consequence of enhanced data quality and streamlined machinery. enhancement via real-time monitoring of existing data. Accurate projections of the possibility of future issues may be made using data accumulated over time from the input of sensors. Utilizing business analytics and large amounts of data helps speed up the process of adaptation. Reactive and proactive supply, which assists reduce waste of resources and future advancements, needs an understanding of customer wishes and requirements, as revealed by contemporary market research. There'd be no way to succeed in business without this knowledge. When more people start using the internet of things, retailers can more easily satisfy demand and stock up on goods that may better fit their consumers' needs (Ziegler et al., 2015).

For instance, a client may purchase particular devices, but in addition to or as an alternative to the current level of interoperability, battery life, or anything else, there may be other items that give exactly the necessary number. This inference might be the result of sensor data and function similarly to when we update our mobile phone or internet plans based on recommendations from our service providers for the service that is best suited to meet our demands. High levels of customer satisfaction may be aided by a company's ability to accurately identify its customers and adapt to changing circumstances.

In terms of farming, it's no secret that the agriculture industry is hard at work creating its cutting-edge technologies. In the past, field data has been collected using reporting systems that rely on human input, which might introduce mistakes. If we're talking numbers, of course. Using the internet of things sensors and technology to systematically optimize and simplify agricultural product manufacturing raises output and reduces the need for human intervention. contribute more significantly and scientifically to agricultural crop production. By monitoring atmospheric conditions using wireless sensors such as pressure, humidity, and temperature, this is achievable. Beneficial effects on agriculture may be shown via the adaptation of agricultural needs.

In addition, during the whole manufacturing and distribution processes, food safety must be monitored to guarantee that it is fit for human consumption. This applies across the board throughout the supply chain. approaches that may gain from sensor data and pervasive computing.

Imaginative work, media, and the arts, the entertainment and media industries stand to gain from developments in this area as well. In addition to the internet of things, studies are currently being undertaken on services for exchanging audiovisual content. Through the many home-based IoT private networks. Because of this, customizing your experience and the material is a breeze, and you can easily share media with others. Personalized advertising might be used to the benefit of certain neighborhoods and their residents. The entertainment sector might be affected by filters that limit user access to content based on their age. Other forms of mobile apps, such as on-the-go location-based news collecting, are also possible. To say the video game industry is important would be an understatement. One area where the IoT may have a significant impact is the entertainment business. The unprecedented success of Pokémon Go has made it clear to us that IoT and AR technologies may have far-reaching implications for the development of future video games (Visoottiviseth et al., 2021).

There are worries about the internet of things security. As the IoT grows and becomes a more fundamental part of our daily lives and the backbone of our nation's infrastructure, it is crucial that its systems be protected. You can increase the safety of your system by adhering to information security principles like the CIA triad privacy, anonymity, and authenticity; access, the four pillars of information assurance vulnerability, confidentiality, integrity, and availability, the Parkerian hexad confidentiality, integrity, and non-repudiation; access, authenticity of ownership, and usability, and so on. There is a wide variety of guiding principles employed by IoT systems, and academic papers are important for the security of cyber-physical systems as opposed to information systems.

In 2007, additional concepts such as "robustness," "reliability," and "scalability" were added in addition to these older ones. high levels of toughness, longevity, efficiency, and resilience to the effects of time and use. There is no denying that each and every one of these safety measures, particularly those that are part of the internet of things, is an advanced cyber-physical system.

However, for the sake of this research, we will be using the three basic classifications used by the CIA, with the caveat that a breach may include assets in any of these categories, not only information. Here, we'll talk about some of the biggest obstacles and point out the values that are under jeopardy. There are, however, additional risks that must be ignored. We cannot stress the importance of this enough. Because of its physical construction, electrical and telegraphic transmission have certain limits.

Regardless of their main purpose, many IoT devices are designed to use very little energy and take up very little space. While "the Internet Protocol could and should be deployed even to the most basic devices," there is still some skepticism. Things that can be linked to the Internet are subject to tight regulations. hardware processing speeds may be limited due to energy consumption restrictions CPU, RAM, and so on. That's why it's crucial to have reliable and robust security measures in place. The two goals of high performance and minimal resource use are mutually exclusive.

The scope, impact, and dependability of IoT systems all play a role in determining the parameters within which information may be kept secret. Take into account that the IEEE 802.15.4 standard which forms the foundation for other protocols like Zigbee and 6LoWPAN limits the size of physical layer packets to 127 bytes. The MAC layer allows frames up to 102 bytes in length, which includes a maximum of 25 bytes for frame overhead. Preserving Confidentiality Link-layer security even decreases the maximum frame size that may be used, so although encryption is useful, it is important to keep that in mind.

This is not something to be overlooked. Using the 128-bit Advanced Encryption Standard-Cipher Block Chaining Mode-128, which has its special mode of operation called "CCM mode" for authentication and secrecy, would use up the whole 128 bits. There are just 81 available bytes after 21 have been taken up by allocations. For AES-CCM-32, though, you'll need just 9 of those 93 bytes. Data is frequently carried across "lossy" and channels with a low data rate, making it challenging to design in necessary levels of safety and strength.

To ensure the safety of digital signatures, a public key infrastructure is necessary. Most Internet-of-Things-enabled gadgets can't function without meeting this need. Thankfully, with the help of PKI, both of these threats may be avoided. It's a breach of both integrity and privacy. In addition to that, encrypting using Insufficient memory and processing power limit the usefulness of many wireless devices when dealing with the public key. In situations where frequent data transmission from sensor systems is required, as is frequently the case.

Current fears regarding the stability of the internet. Article authors Roman, Najera, and Lopez point out that heterogeneity has "huge influence on the mandatory protocol and network security services" used in the internet of things in their 2011 publication. Security systems must be able to verify and authorize a wide variety of devices, including those connected to the internet of things. Due to the many different parts that make up the IoT, it is unrealistic to assume that every item will provide a complete protocol stack (IoT) (Alarabi et al., 2018).

The security of IoT devices is jeopardized due to the wide range of services that might be given and implemented, as well as the fact that service management will need to deal with different types of resources. The widespread adoption of inadequate private solutions in lieu of open standards is a major roadblock. Integrating with "black boxes" is crucial for a comprehensive security setup.

There is a risk of "security by obscurity" when businesses rely on their own internally designed procedures to protect sensitive data. The approach outlined in is widely acknowledged to be inappropriate for usage in the field. in terms of being risk-free. Users who are "transient and untrustworthy" add another layer of complexity to security concerns. Permanent, sporadic, and frequent failures are possible; these events make systems vulnerable to assault.

The internet of things is inherently ad hoc, meaning that standard operating procedures will need to be adapted to suit a wide variety of use cases. The increasing prevalence of networked gadgets is an undeniable phenomenon.

Concerns regarding people' safety and privacy online have been exacerbated by the expanding number of internet users. The internet of things allows for several domains to be accessed from any mobile device. Examples of these fields include logistics and supply chain management and the healthcare industry. Because of this, it is more difficult to verify the efficiency of current security protocols. Behave appropriately in a mobile setting by connecting with various parts and systems, each of which may provide a unique set of options, procedures, and regulations. Fluidity is a defining feature of mobile settings.

Management and authentication of identities In contrast to managed identities, which focus on providing and confirming unique IDs for things, authentication verifies the claimed identity of a person or group of users. To "create, converge, and interoperability of technologies for identity and authentication that can function at a global scale," the CERP report calls for further study. The availability, privacy, and security of IoT devices are all at risk without proper authentication. This is because there is a danger to the data's confidentiality, integrity, and availability if an adversary who has successfully impersonated a genuine user may view all of that user's data.

Issues with user authentication and identity persist with the internet of things. Password-username combinations are the standard for securing access to computers and networks. This is true despite the potential rise in popularity of alternative forms of identity and authentication in the near future, such as shared keys, digital certificates, or biometric credentials. Eventually, the physical interaction interfaces that are now utilized to convey credentials will become obsolete because of the internet of things' grand ambition to become omnipresent.

For typical online settings, single sign-on (SSO) procedures may be advantageous since they only need users to authenticate once before granting them access to several services. Authentication procedures are shortened as a result. While there have been efforts to make improvements to OAuth2, it is still not able to provide ubiquitous SSO in IoT deployments. Not only that, but IoT systems have specific needs that technologies like Shibboleth OpenID and OAuth2 were not designed to meet. Individuals may find it difficult to choose their preferred identity provider in the IoT setting given the present standards (Alarabi et al., 2018).

More investigation and study into questions of mobility, privacy, and anonymity is also urgently required. Users of IoT systems that deliver mobile services will need to learn their way around many designs and infrastructures, each of which will be maintained by a separate service provider.

It may be difficult to maintain track of users' identities across the many contexts they use in a world as mobile, diverse, and privately owned as the present one.

Anonymity in the IoT has its own unique set of issues, particularly in settings where mobile devices are present, and this is a topic that will be addressed in the next section, where the subject of privacy in the IoT will be considered. While some clients need privacy, they have exacting criteria for the service they get. In most cases, knowing "whom" the service is meant for is essential to achieving these goals. Finally, if dependable service provision is essential, then openness and ownership are highly valued qualities. It's hardly surprising that assigning blame would be difficult in a society where no one's identity can be confirmed. Pseudonymity is a middle ground for people who value anonymity and transparency equally. Pseudonymous systems avoid the requirement to attribute behavior to a specific individual by instead associating it with a randomly generated identifier. To ensure full delivery of a service from start to finish, a pseudonym may be used as a permanent identifier. Pseudonyms still have the difficulty of performing in a standardized fashion across many different domains, which must be overcome for them to be useful in IoT systems.

User authentication and identity verification are just two parts of the puzzle. The identification and verification of services and devices are also required for IoT infrastructure. Depending on "the nature of the device or the environment in which it is being used," authenticating Internet-of-Things devices might be difficult. No means exists to confirm that the data came from the intended device or that the intended device received the data from the intended device if proper authentication procedures are not performed. Even if the gadgets are legitimate, the service must also be verified, since only authorized services should have access to sensitive information.

The need for permission and other access controls It is well-established that "implemented at the edge of the network in the device or, at the very least, a local access controller for the device" is necessary for effective access control in the internet of things. When a user is identified and authenticated, the next step is to check their permissions to make sure they may utilize the requested resources. Since individuals affect the system via the software entities they govern, access control necessitates communication between entities, which is often limited to software entities rather than humans, to seek and give access. Discretionary access control (DAC), role-based access control (RBAC), and attribute-based access control are the three most used techniques for regulating who has access to what (ABAC). Each of these models relies on rules that take into account the specifics of the requesting user, the requested resource, and the surrounding context in order to decide whether or not to give access.

Access control in an internet of things context may be difficult to set up. Although a discretion-free access control architecture is preferable, deploying RBAC and ABAC on low-powered internet of things devices may be difficult. In addition, RBAC necessitates the creation of specific activities. The complexity of managing an ever-expanding set of roles must be accounted for if fine-grained access control is to be deployed widely throughout the IoT. When it comes to software upgrades, this is crucial. Similar difficulties arise with ABAC, particularly in decentralized structures. For this reason, neither antecedent-based nor retrospective-based "lack the scalability to "effectively satisfies the dynamicity and scaling requirements of IoT settings" and the "controllability to "provide scalable, effective, and efficient processes. This is due to the fact that neither ABAC nor RBAC "provides scalable, controlled, effective, and efficient methods ".

Capability-based techniques provide yet another alternative to the traditional access control list (ACL) paradigms like RBAC, ABAC, and DAC. The user must have some kind of reference or capability that grants them access to the desired service before they may use these strategies. This calls for the usage of a reference that can be shared across a group of individuals like a key to a safety deposit box but cannot be copied. Although these techniques are an improvement over traditional ACL models, they still lack the ability to "tailor access depending on particular qualities or constraints". One example of a capability-based approach is identity-authentication with capability-based access control. Another is capability-based access control, or CapBAC. Capabilities-based access control, or CapBAC, for short.

The value of installing and upgrading is often discussed, but is often disregarded. There has to be a balance between the ease and low cost of implementing security measures. It's possible that IoT networks may span a wide range of locations. Protracted, requiring both sensors and actuators, and occurring under dangerous conditions. The integrity of the computerized system can only be maintained if all security holes are patched. as soon as it is made clear to them that gaining remote access to the system is required in order to implement these Changes is crucial to reaching their aim (Brumfitt et al., 2015).

Cloud-based frameworks allow for the automated loading of the most current program updates and the management of the process. This progress does not exclude the possibility of creating a secure technique. Constantly shifting installations might be difficult to maintain. Furthermore, users should be aware that updating a device's firmware might affect its functionality and that the ensuing modifications might not meet their specific needs. Because of this, everyone who has the means to do so should upgrade as soon as possible.

Can opt out of the update if it's assessed that doing so would likely have unfavorable consequences. influence on the worth of the item. The 2016 Dyn assault showed the far reaching effects of a botnet that includes devices including unpatched printers, IP cameras, and routers. It also showed how easily infants, security cameras, and even house gateways may contribute to a DoS assault. The implications for the internet of things accountability, insurance, and responsibility are also substantial. The devices, communication channels, infrastructure, and services that make up the internet of things are all the responsibility of different companies. Thus, concerns about accountability and duty persist. While it's possible that a single company could be found legally accountable for the issue, it's also possible that numerous firms will share the obligation. Even a seemingly tiny assault on a single component may have devastating effects. The unforgivable evil done to someone If a consumer complains about a service that was compromised due to malfunctioning equipment or third-party infrastructure, the maker of the gadget or the architect of the building would be immune to any repercussions.

In contrast to the actual service provider. Some parties may choose to be more vigilant in light of the possibility of such events happening. mistakes by not being as careful as they should be in safeguarding their digital and physical possessions. Nothing good can come from this for either side. The already difficult scenario is made much more so by the intricate structure of the assault surface. It is possible for an easily exploitable flaw in a device or service to be used in conjunction with other, less obvious flaws in other parts of the system, under the control of other entities, or with information obtained from a third party. This might lead to an assault that does more harm than the flaw itself. It is not often apparent who is responsible for what aspect of this massive agreement, if any, and it is also not always clear what, if anything, comes next. This makes the argument for investing in supplementary security measures more difficult to establish. Unmanned and connected cars raise a variety of security concerns. It's fair to say there's a lot going on in the world of CAVs connected and autonomous vehicles.

The phrase encompasses elements like as sensors, actuators, networks, protocols, and applications. There is a spectrum in the provision of support services, from the really basic and dependent on a small number of components to the globally performed and significantly impacting key areas of national infrastructure. Due to this, the project cannot account for all possible assaults on the system or its implementation. However, the deadliest assaults may be emphasized here. Almost every part of a modern car relies on hydraulics in some way, from the engine management and transmission to the suspension and brakes. It's estimated that there are between 70 and 100 ECUs of electronic control units in a contemporary car. Sensors of many kinds provide information to electronic control units, and one example is tyre pressure monitoring systems (SK et al., 2021).

The infotainment system is equipped with a camera, LIDAR, and RADAR, among other sensors including those for the engine and the brakes. The system also has a radar component. Communication ECUs may be accessed by a variety of network protocols, including CAN (Controller Area Network), Ethernet (Internet Protocol), FlexRay (Media Oriented System Transport), and LIN Network (Local Interconnect Networks). Modern automobiles use many networks, each optimized for specific purposes by the respective manufacturer. include a wide range of network architectures.

While developing these guidelines, however, safety and security took a back seat to ensuring the maximum possible effectiveness and protection. Similar findings were made using a physical endpoint, who found that they could attack a wide variety of both on-board and off-board vehicle vulnerabilities by other researchers.

On-Board Diagnostic (OBD) devices and other external connections, such Bluetooth and USB, are available for use in the diagnostic process. Synergy between DSRC and Bluetooth technology. Miller and Vallesek's 2015 Nature publication received more coverage. exploited through remote execution a vulnerability and a bug, Mansfield-Devine in 2016 Jeep Cherokees using Sprint's UConnect® remote access device. Even though the automobile was moving, they were able to keep it under control. While it's true that cyber-attacks against linked vehicles are currently unlikely, the growing importance of these vehicles, along with the rise of tools like ransomware, and other forms of cybercrime, pose a serious new threat to the security and dependability of the world's interconnected and self-driving car technology. However, there is little doubt that terrorist organizations, national governments, and hacktivists are all attempting to breach these networks for various purposes, including financial gain.

The mobility of both humans and machines is required in a variety of scenarios that may be addressed by CAVs. data that may be used to determine the identity of the sender that is sent to an outside party. The privacy of these details may be safeguarded. among other forms of privacy infringement, sniffing is prevalent at many stations. Since there are no physical obstacles to overcome, man-in-the-middle attacks may also happen with wireless communications. getting entry to a vehicle and so jeopardizing data privacy. Miller and his partner used a man-in-the-middle assault, also known as a man in the middle attack, to take control of a Jeep remotely. Valasek. Because of the critical role that infrastructure like roads, bridges, and parking lots play in facilitating interactions between linked cars and their reliance on them, the prevalence of cloud and edge-cloud computing will increase the risk of attacks on system availability as well as the effects of such attacks.

Unease over the state of safety in the medical, recreational, and amusement sectors There has been a rise in the number of incidents where victims required hospitalization over the course of the previous several years. How many real and prospective assaults there are on connected people is mind-boggling. technology, some examples of which are insulin pumps, electronic health implants, medication delivery system pumps, and heart-rate monitors. It was only in recent years, however, that reports of sexual assault began to emerge. Due to their immense size and unusual composition, no one has ever seen anything like them before. Considering MEDJACK as an option in 2015, Trend Micro was the first business to uncover the ransomware attack known as Storm 2015. The device was aimed towards digital blood gas analyzers. medical imaging devices such as X-ray, MRI, and CT scanners the protocols that regulate communication have also been the target of attacks. Ten times implanted cardiac defibrillators (ICDs) use ten different communication protocols. All three pillars of the CIA's security network are obviously compromised by such healthcare systems. Not only are there obvious issues, but Leaks of sensitive information add to the already significant challenges of availability and integrity compromises.

Identity theft, fraud, and the discovery of drug prescriptions that allow hackers to buy medicines online are all facilitated by hackers gaining access to sensitive medical information. Hackers may use system hacking as an alternative to keeping data for ransom. additional blackmailing of people who have ailments they would not be made public. Health data obtained through the internet of things face similar threats to its privacy, accessibility, and integrity. Fitness trackers offer another option, despite the fact that the fitness tracker's availability and integrity are less likely to be compromised in the event of a security attack. There may have an effect on availability. In terms of data privacy, this is not the case (Squillace et al., 2022).

The degree of safety in the industry 4.0 space has been called into question. Many people consider Industry 4.0 as a potentially transformative innovation because of the way it integrates information and communication technology. Autonomy, and maybe even a quicker advent of the Fourth Industrial Revolution. But despite this, there are exceptions Cyber-physical systems face a growing number of possible catastrophic dangers. Large-scale cyber-physical assaults have been rumored for some time, and there have also been Considering how many assaults are likely to go undetected because they aren't reported, it's clear that this is a major problem. In particular, the assault on Australia's Maroochy Water Services in the year 2000 stands notable. A string of misfortunes led to the sirens being turned off and the sewage pumps failing to stop running at the appropriate times. The already tenuous position became even more so as a result of a failure in the communication between the main computer and the numerous pumping units. Stuxnet, another kind of attack, had a similarly dramatic and rapid effect on Iran's nuclear program.

Recent examples of strikes include interruptions to the Ukrainian electrical grid and an assault on a German steel factory in 2014. Another kind of privacy invasion occurs when someone utilizes your ideas without your permission. Decrease a company's competitive edge in the market. Moreover, it would open the door for rivals to impede the development of forthcoming breakthroughs. Transportation and storage security concerns, when applied to logistics, the internet of things seems to have great promise for boosting productivity and opening up new markets. Many applications increase the attack surface. One kind of attack that has been identified in the past involves the manipulation of embedded data (Li et al., 2018).

In this case tags may be modified by adding or removing data. Despite logistics' common association with road infrastructure, it's important to emphasize that air and sea shipping are also pieces of that jigsaw. The risk arises from the potential exposure of sensitive data about the ship, including its location, final destination, cargo, speed, country of registration, and name. Beyond the current MMSI (Mobile Maritime Service Identity) configuration. An attack's degree of violence might be greatly amplified by the fabrication of phoney boats that seem and act in every other way like genuine ones.

It's not out of the question to improve upon an existing ship by capitalizing on its enviable qualities. An Iranian ship, for example, was seen in international waters near the United States shore, and it was believed to be transporting nuclear materials. In this way, the information has lost both its trustworthiness and its confidentiality. Linked to how the system works, Issues with the Reliability of Smart Grids as reported, China has been planning attacks on critical American infrastructure, including the electric grid. If successful, such attacks might have far-reaching effects., and Russian influence over the USA.

Attacks on Ukraine have received a lot of attention in recent white papers and scholarly publications, or the more conventional kinds of media. Most of these assaults have a sexual overtone. Although this might be considered a system in and of itself, efforts to interrupt the availability of cyber physical systems are being studied. Despite this, there have been other assaults inside Smart Grid in addition to the ones that have previously been published technologies. It's not only the national level that's vulnerable; any level of infrastructure might be attacked. Architecture-related terms. Less centralized than traditional management systems, Community Embedded Management Systems (CEMS) are used to strike a regional equilibrium.

Power requirements, including determining the number and sizes of generators needed. allow peak demand to be supplied by the temporary usage of transmission lines. CEMS, which stands for "conventional measurement and evaluation system," has been in use for quite some time. Accessibility and reliability are compromised since the system may be easily hacked and communications can be falsified. The use of "intelligent" technology at the lowest possible levels of design has increased dramatically. Meters. More than 500,000 people in the UK were living with mental health issues in September 2016, according to data released by the government. In the UK, there may be a huge number of smart metres. Nonetheless, there is evidence to suggest that the lack of encryption and digital signatures in smart metres has been shown to be a security risk.

Disquiet over the general security of a wide range of places, from homes to public spaces to workplaces. There is a wide selection of products available for the "smart home," each of which claims to increase productivity by making better use of resources already present in the house. Using both close-range and remote methods of management. While these resources undoubtedly help the economy and make products more useful, there is a risk that they might also compromise national security. Key Dangers believe these tools contribute to one's capacity for secrecy and privacy. We should be worried about a few things, one of which is how Evidence suggests that a person's energy use might reveal important details about their identity (Stuurman et al., 2016).

Another emerging pattern is the increasing use of Internet-enabled home appliances and the part they played in the assault on Dyn. A wide variety of electrical gadgets have been hacked before, including cameras, printers, and even doorbells. In the UK, home routers have become more common in recent years, and digital scales are just another example. Although the availability of such technology could be improved, the prospects they provide are promising. The effects of a botnet, which consists of many interconnected computers and other electronic devices, might have far-reaching consequences. Cybercriminals aren't only eyeing the smart gadgets in people's homes and workplaces; they're also looking at other, more valuable targets.

Multiple control and monitoring systems are installed in buildings. Among the most essential tactics ever used This hack aimed to get access to Target's internet-connected building control systems. The heating, ventilation, and air-conditioning (HVAC) system was the first service provider to assault Target. In doing so, it will have successfully used Target's existing infrastructure. Facilitating remote monitoring and servicing; this provides an entry point into the system from which an attacker may escalate access and reveal private data.

Data on forty million individual customers. Unauthorized entry into a person's home or place of business obviously poses a greater threat to not just their privacy, but also their availability and the security of their system. The internet of things raises Privacy Concerns, A lack of privacy is commonly cited as one of the most serious threats faced by the internet of things.

Through the IoT, we now have access to a plethora of data that may or may not contain the following: Not just to consumers, as the Internet does, but also to members of diverse, cooperative, and formal groups. As a result, we'll be able to zero down on the specifics of our research interests.

About where we're going, what we want to accomplish, and where we're from. However, we should consider how much we value our privacy in light of the exciting possibilities for enhanced service that this may bring about. Customer participation in the market is crucial. Assurance that the service providers they use will treat their information with respect and discretion. Trust's importance cannot be emphasized, since it is crucial to the establishment of any relationship and is needed for the adoption of novel behaviors.

When new technologies are complicated and difficult to use, consumers are less likely to have faith that their personal data will be kept secure. This is especially true in the area of artificial intelligence. The IoT, or internet of things, is a highly developed network system. the actual lives of the locals the collected data will be analyzed in aggregate, compared to one another, integrated with other data sets, and mined for insights that can power smart and pervasive services. Knowing when and with whom it's okay to divulge a secret is a crucial part of feeling secure in oneself. disseminated or made accessible to the general audience.

In 2010, Facebook's creator Mark Zuckerberg bravely took the stage to introduce many new functions for the popular social networking site. to the point that the whole idea of "personal privacy" is seen as unusual in contemporary society. This topic has been discussed at length among a small number of experts in the area of education. A dilemma about personal privacy rights was put forward in 2006. Unlike their more privacy-conscious elders, young people are more open to sharing personal details (Torre et al., 2016).

Since it contains references totaling over 900 and shows that the contradiction is evident in real-world applications, this fundamental argument has gained considerable scholarly attention. But things have changed at the Oxford Internet Institute, and a new privacy dilemma has been laid out in a report. For example: Young people "are significantly more inclined than older folks," according to the studies of Blank and Bolsover. Social networking services (RNSs) do not give clients with necessary security for personal information, and this is the basis for the new paradoxical notion that "social life is increasingly conducted online." Young people "are significantly more disposed than older folks to get involved in political and social causes," as observed by Blank and Bolsover.

The tools that would provide individuals effective command over their data and privacy, and would work best for them specifically. An overwhelming majority of internet users (86%) have taken measures to hide their digital footprints according to research from the Pew Research Center. Some of the methods used included changing their IP address to one from a virtual private network, encrypting their communications to hide their IP address, and deleting cookies without removing the true identity. Maintaining consumers' trust in decentralized systems relies in large part on increasing the amount of control people have over their own data. The P3P (Platform for Privacy Preferences) and related initiatives are in the hands of Internet browser users. The World Wide Web Consortium initiated the P3P project (W3C). In 2002, the World Wide Web Consortium (W3C) made it possible for websites to determine who they were aiming their content.

Data is collected from a wide range of browsers on the web and used in a variety of ways. Its foundational principle was the concept of translation. to make the web more accessible, the process of transforming privacy laws used on websites into a form that computers can read. In addition to offering a wider variety of options to buyers in that niche. Due to the untimely cancellation of the project, relatively few actual deployments of the software have taken place. The reasons why P3P failed are many, and many have speculated on them, but according to one source, firms and consumers' lack of enthusiasm was the main factor. Organizational hesitation browser reluctance, and user reluctance, which may result from regional and national cultural variations as well as a worldwide audience, fail to register strongly enough with a significant number of PET technology's prospective users. Websites haven't begun utilizing it yet, which is an issue (Du et al., 2016).

Several distinct privacy-protecting technologies are now available. VPNs, Transport Layer Security, Domain Name System Security Extensions, Onion Routing, and a slew of other similar technologies Recovering Lost Data and Redirecting Its Flow. The P3P initiative that we've been talking about is one subset of PET and a language used in privacy rules. Individuals with PPLs that are PETs. Internal with support for enforcement PPLs and external with no such internal norms PPLs are two types of PPLs declarative without support for enforcement. P3P is an example of a PPL that is used just inside the organization. SAML, which stands for "Security Assertion Markup Language," is another kind of PPL. Access Control Markup Language (XACML) is an OASIS standard that has many implementations, including PPL, A-PPL, and XACML. Some examples of these extensions include XPref, P2U, EPAL, P-RBAC, FlexDDPL, Jeeves, PSLang, ConSpec, and SLAng for extending XACML; GeoXACML for extending XACL; SecPAL for extending XACL to process personally identifiable information; SecPAL4P for extending SecPAL to account for RDF; and Accountability in RDF (AIR) for extending XML access control. There is no one PPL that has won out as the de facto standard in the business, and none of them have been widely adopted. Since PPLs are still very uncommon, this is the case persists in being difficult (Li et al., 2016).

As was previously said, success requires both personalized and optimal service. together with the need of having one's own isolated space. To balance these opposing goals, it is important to get the customer's permission before collecting, storing, or revealing any personal information. There are several methods for achieving this goal. Nonetheless, this raises a wide range of issues that must be addressed. Historically, permission has been granted via an open and honest procedure. This implies that service providers must explain in clearly what data they collect and why they need it. There's no doubt that a lot of individuals have wondered whether it's obvious, especially at the time, that a client has to be given 70 pages of information. being looked into by the proper authorities at this time The General Data Protection Regulation necessitates revisions to the European Union's Data Protection Directive (GDPR) The Information Commissioner's Office (ICO) of the United Kingdom has released a Consent Guidance Document (ICO 2017), a clear intention on the part of the data subject to allow the processing of his personal data. "Any freely granted, particular, informed permission to the processing of personal data relating to him," Article 4(11) of the General Data Protection Regulation (GDPR). Data Subject's affirmative statement of purpose, by which he consents to the processing of his personal information, although Article 6 of the Data Protection Directive stipulates that "any freely granted explicit and informed consent," (Kang et al., 2020).

A clear and unmistakable manifestation of the data subject's consent to the processing, such as the marking of a checkbox or the pressing of a button. a hint to data that may be utilized to pin out who they are. This means that in the future, if the internet of things becomes widespread, we will be communicating with systems that do not have a standard graphical user interface (GUI). Just so we're clear and this is important to emphasize, it is tough to offer consumers with access to information about their personal data and privacy while at the same time acquiring their permission to anything. Furthermore, more complex permissions are required due to the General Data Protection Regulation that went into force in 2016.

In addition, getting your hands on that cash is a breeze. It will be far more difficult to overcome these obstacles if suitable interfaces do not exist. to provide permission or withdraw already granted approval. There will also be in-home trials of internet of things-related devices in addition to testing in public spaces. The findings from the Pressure sensors, infrared sensors, and radio frequency identification devices are all an opponent needs to keep watch over a target. in addition to having a solid grasp of typical human domestic behavior. Some examples of such data include It is possible that the user's physical and mental health will be impacted by the data collected by the smart refrigerator. possession of a policy or contract for life insurance. Combining data from a wide variety of sensors with AI Toy manufacturing has also increased in recent years. a child's perspective, analysis, and engagement, toys with artificial intelligence may recognize faces, sounds, and other noises. The majority of these playthings have Bluetooth connectivity printed on their outside. and wireless network connectivity, which leaves endpoints vulnerable to assault from malicious entities. There is a risk that children's personal data may be leaked if they used these gadgets.

The situation is worrying. worrying parents by allowing criminals to track their children's whereabouts through mobile devices leaves them open to attack. Furthermore, it is feasible for these toys to perform surveillance-related services. As a result, manufacturers have a substantial problem in establishing baseline safety standards for connected toys at the outset of the design phase. As Nelson puts it by giving their kid an electronic device, parents either consent to the collection, processing, and storage of personal data on their child, or they perpetuate the practice of doing so.

Concerns regarding privacy in the age of the internet of things shouldn't be limited to individual customers. possible repercussions on the business and manufacturing sectors. When compared to more conventional forms of information and communication technology, the internet of things' complexity in the industrial setting is staggering. As a result of the vastness of the intended area and the abundance of potential access points, Waidner (2015). Defining the necessary levels of privacy protection is critical. Loss of intellectual property presents risks beyond the obvious, such as the exposure of confidential employee or customer information or particulars, and provides opportunities for rivals to learn as much as they can about the affected organization in order to reproduce its successes. This might eventually lead to a decline in a company's competitive edge.

Although it is well understood that corporate spies may be located either within or outside an organization, theft of intellectual property can still arise from an assault, and loss of sensitive data can occur if privacy is breached. In reference to the relevant data, A rival may gain an advantage by anticipating the manufacturing supply of not just what we need now, but also what we'll need tomorrow and cutting-edge technologies that are presently being developed, if only industrial orders are kept secret. Potential threats to data privacy include Companies may affect the cost of insurance or access to credit for an industry by disclosing their financial performance, procedures, and business intelligence (BI) for that industry. Yet, there is a dearth of research on this topic. In this article, we traced the development of the IoT and explained why an increase in the number of connected devices is a bad thing. towards agreement and a common goal.

Challenges have emerged as a direct result of this. safety and confidence all across the IoT. Getting others to take action is not just a difficult task, but also one of the most crucial ones. Standardization and cooperation are crucial for the IoT. There are a lot of challenges that come with having to cope with this situation. None of these questions have simple solutions. technological, operational, and even political factors. Although they may have divergent opinions, it is essential to take into consideration the perspectives of all important stakeholders when discussing the internet of things. The P3P experiment showed that there are many obstacles to building confidence and coming to an agreement amongst groups whose goals and objectives are diametrically opposed. Despite being an admirable goal, the P3P movement encountered several obstacles. Similarly, it would be great for IoT, but it's crucial to ensure that everyone's needs are met and that everyone is happy with the results. New communication protocols should aim to be P3P compliant.

By means to make informed decisions and retain ownership of their data, education is a need. ways through which individuals may direct and manage the collection, organization, transmission, storage, and display of personal information the lessons picked up from working on the P3P project Working on any standard requires a good grasp of the political situation to assure its eventual acceptance. Advocates for people's right to privacy could find this troubling. The P3P protocol—which has been called "industrial espionage" by some critics—should not let firms to offer users the impression of anonymity while really tracking their online movements and accumulating private data. Data. Realizing that any one criterion is unlikely to provide more than a partial solution, it is possible that just adopting the standard will not be sufficient to guarantee safety. This is because it is very unlikely that any one criterion would provide anything more than a partial solution.

Therefore, the standard is intended to be used in tandem with a suite of additional privacy-focused Tools. It is important to remember that compliance with existing rules and regulations should be a primary goal of any standard development process. compliance. The business case for implementing the protocol will fail if there is no need to comply with legal requirements or expenses associated with doing so.

Data management is still a major issue for places with little resources, such as those that lack adequate means of storing or sharing information. Because many current approaches to ensure the security of IoT devices rely on firmware with significant energy costs, this presents a problem for many IoT devices (Healy, Newe, and Lewis 2009). This is according to (Healy, Newe, and Lewis, 2009). IoT system security and privacy relies largely on authentication and identification procedures (Blanchard et al., 2018).

The most apparent solution is the use of biometric id systems, maybe in combination with a token. may be advantageous over present systems, but care must be taken to prevent the system from being clogged and slowing down. We've come a long way in our quest to ensure devices' validity. media streaming and internet of things services. Now that PUFs (Physical Unclonable Functions) exist, we can't just copy our way to success. PUFs have a famously convoluted and unpredictable but repeatable input-output mapping scheme. Trustworthy authentication relies on The function has to be readily repeatable for both security and assessment purposes. In a perfect world, it would be difficult to predict. Some defects, such as age-related decrease, which may result in incorrect PUF answers, and newer, more secure methods based on greater challenge-response are now being developed. In 2012, Maiti, Kim, and Schaumburg published a study that found. The SIM card is being linked with the PUF. Embedded SIM (eSIM) technology for secure authentication and access management. If turned on, the eSIM might deal with issues including scalability, interoperability, and security protocol compliance.

Altering existing SSO methods or developing new ones to fit the internet of things is another critical concern. Despite the fact that this is dealt with by a number of approaches, we offer a hybrid design that incorporates all mechanisms by means of innovative artistically built middleware, and this is an area that needs further research. A standardized communication platform and architecture is also necessary, as are unified security considerations for ICT transport systems, with a focus on security at all levels. Invasion is shown to be feasible.

From the bottom up, communication may be moved from the network layer (CAN, LIN, etc.) to the facilities layer, allowing for anything from physical layer via Bluetooth or DSRC communications all the way up to just making tweaks to the ECUs. affected equipment includes the windshield wipers and the door locks. Several attacks on the IoT in industry have shown SCADA vulnerabilities such as slow reaction times. Fix, and authentication holes that might be exploited to gain unauthorized access to the network. Therefore, a dependable and secure design that can protect an in industrial IoT, the network and endpoint devices work together to regulate a specific industry.

The IoT has the potential to significantly impact our way of life. However, many major hurdles must be cleared before its full potential may be realized. avoid complete failure as a result. Various norms and suggestions exist for protections for personal data privacy on the internet of things are readily available. The United States Department of Homeland Security provides an overview of the challenges associated with securing the internet of things and offers possible solutions to these problems. criteria for the design, implementation, and maintenance of hardware and software. Having a quick and easy way to connect to the internet The Broad Institute's Technical Advisory Group has published a report analyzing and emphasizing the difficulties associated with ordinary people installing internet of things devices, such as data breaches and privacy misuse. Particular internet security precautions are required.

The GSMA has put up a comprehensive guide to the cellular world. analysis of the IoT's accessibility, id, privacy, and security problems, suggestions for a mobile solution, and examples of its use. As reported by the GSMA Association, 2016 was a landmark year for the industry. This overview study provides context for the more in-depth Service Ecosystem and Endpoint Ecosystem Reports. The best practice report for network security rounds of the collection. Concerns about privacy and the services provided by mobile network operators, as analyzed by the GSMA Association (2016d). Despite this data, there are still design obstacles to be resolved. as well as management of IoT systems. Although significant progress has been achieved, protecting the IoT remains a challenge.

CONCLUSION

The success of any strategy for consent management depends on its ability to win over both businesses and consumers. Irrespective of how you feel about the internet of things generally, it is crucial that: These rules, based on shared values, help to prevent mission creep and guarantee achievement. We know what we want to accomplish; we know how we'll get there; we know what it'll cost; we know how it'll affect our current operations; we got input from industry groups gatherings of representatives from end users and suppliers of services and infrastructure; and we made sure to follow all relevant laws and regulations in doing so. Whether or whether you have anybody else on board, carrying out the process is still important business. This case doesn't follow the protocol's guidelines; hence it can't work. Another time-sensitive issue that only requires a little amount of energy and space is one that has just come to light. elements of the structured internet of things. It's difficult to build secure systems with limited means that can nonetheless detect, diagnose, and bounce back from threats. Since it is difficult to provide strong security at a cheap cost, the IETF 6LoWPAN group has created standards for encapsulation and protocols. techniques for shrinking IPv6 packet headers to enable their transmission and reception across mobile LANs at low data rates. There are two secure modes that network nodes may engage in on IEEE 802.15.4-based systems: Prevention of Collisions Through Artificial Intelligence There are numerous modes to choose from, including system mode (which only enables trusted nodes to access the network), sequential mode, secure mode (which protects users' privacy, messages, and access), and freshness mode. Host Internet Protocol and other protocols were developed with this kind of problem in mind. The Secure Datagram Transport Layer (SDT) uses Hypertext Transfer Protocol (HTTP). This is because the former is more high-performing, while the latter has more restrictions due to the fact that limited adoption of the HIP causes significant constraints.

ACKNOWLEDGMENT

We, the writers of this book chapter, would like to extend our gratitude to the late Mr. Panem Nadipi Chennaih for his assistance in the creation of this book chapter as well as the support he provided during its growth. This book chapter is dedicated to him.

REFERENCES

Alarabi, S., Almuzeri, S., Alaradi, S., & Innab, N. (2018, April). Two Level Based Privacy Protection Approach for internet of things Users in Cloud Computing. In *2018 21st Saudi Computer Society National Computer Conference (NCC)* (pp. 1-6). IEEE.

Almeida, V. A., Doneda, D., & Monteiro, M. (2015). Governance challenges for the internet of things. *IEEE Internet Computing*, *19*(4), 56–59. doi:10.1109/MIC.2015.86

Blanchard, A., Kosmatov, N., & Loulergue, F. (2018). Tutorial: Secure Your Things: Secure Development of IoT Software with Frama-C. *2018 IEEE Cybersecurity Development (SecDev)*, 126-127.

Brumfitt, H. A., Askwith, B., & Zhou, B. (2015, October). Protecting Future Personal Computing: Challenging Traditional Network Security Models. In *2015 IEEE International Conference on Computer and Information Technology; Ubiquitous Computing and Communications; Dependable, Autonomic and Secure Computing; Pervasive Intelligence and Computing* (pp. 1772-1779). IEEE.

Du, W., Li, A., Zhou, P., Xu, Z., Wang, X., Jiang, H., & Wu, D. (2020). Approximate to be great: Communication efficient and privacy-preserving large-scale distributed deep learning in internet of things. *IEEE internet of things Journal, 7*(12), 11678-11692.

Fabiano, N. (2017, June) of things and blockchain: Legal issues and privacy. The challenge for a privacy standard. In *2017 IEEE International Conference on internet of things (iThings) and IEEE Green Computing and Communications (GreenCom) and IEEE Cyber, Physical and Social Computing (CPSCom) and IEEE Smart Data (SmartData)* (pp. 727-734). IEEE.

Jha, P., Baranwal, R., & Tiwari, N. K. (2022, February). Protection of User's Data in IOT. In *2022 Second International Conference on Artificial Intelligence and Smart Energy (ICAIS)* (pp. 1292-1297). IEEE. 10.1109/ICAIS53314.2022.9742970

Kang, J. J., Dibaei, M., Luo, G., Yang, W., & Zheng, X. (2020, December). A privacy-preserving data inference framework for internet of health things networks. In *2020 IEEE 19th International Conference on Trust, Security and Privacy in Computing and Communications (TrustCom)* (pp. 1209-1214). IEEE.

Li, C., & Palanisamy, B. (2018). Privacy in internet of things: From principles to technologies. *IEEE internet of things Journal, 6*(1), 488-505.

Li, Y., Nakasone, T., Ohta, K., & Sakiyama, K. (2014, January). Privacy-mode switching: Toward flexible privacy protection for RFID tags in internet of things. In *2014 IEEE 11th Consumer Communications and Networking Conference (CCNC)* (pp. 519-520). IEEE.

Lu, X., Li, Q., Qu, Z., & Hui, P. (2014, October). Privacy information security classification study in internet of things. In *2014 International Conference on Identification, Information and Knowledge in the internet of things* (pp. 162-165). IEEE. 10.1109/IIKI.2014.40

Neisse, R., Steri, G., & Baldini, G. (2014, October). Enforcement of security policy rules for the internet of things. In *2014 IEEE 10th international conference on wireless and mobile computing, networking and communications (WiMob)* (pp. 165-172). IEEE.

Rivera, D., García, A., Martín-Ruiz, M. L., Alarcos, B., Velasco, J. R., & Oliva, A. G. (2019). Secure communications and protected data for a internet of things smart toy platform. *IEEE internet of things Journal, 6*(2), 3785–3795. doi:10.1109/JIOT.2019.2891103

SK., W. H., Singh, S. P., & Johri, P. (2021, August). A Comprehensive Review on Securities and Privacy Preservation in IOT Healthcare Application for Diabetics. In *2021 Second International Conference on Electronics and Sustainable Communication Systems (ICESC)* (pp. 706-711). IEEE.

Squillace, J., & Bantan, M. (2022, June). A Taxonomy of Privacy, Trust, and Security Breach Incidents of Internet-of-Things Linked to F (M). AANG Corporations. In *2022 IEEE World AI IoT Congress (AIIoT)* (pp. 591-596). IEEE.

Stuurman, K., & Kamara, I. (2016, August). IoT Standardization-The Approach in the Field of Data Protection as a Model for Ensuring Compliance of IoT Applications? In *2016 IEEE 4th International Conference on Future internet of things and Cloud Workshops (FiCloudW)* (pp. 336-341). IEEE.

Torre, I., Koceva, F., Sanchez, O. R., & Adorni, G. (2016, December). A framework for personal data protection in the IoT. In *2016 11th international conference for internet technology and secured transactions (ICITST)* (pp. 384-391). IEEE.

Varadi, S., Varkonyi, G. G., & Kertész, A. (2018, April). Law and iot: How to see things clearly in the fog. In *2018 Third International Conference on Fog and Mobile Edge Computing (FMEC)* (pp. 233-238). IEEE. 10.1109/FMEC.2018.8364070

Visoottiviseth, V., Khengthong, T., Kesorn, K., & Patcharadechathorn, J. (2021, November). ASPAHI: Application for Security and Privacy Awareness Education for Home IoT Devices. In *2021 25th International Computer Science and Engineering Conference (ICSEC)* (pp. 388-393). IEEE.

Ziegler, S., & Chochliouros, I. (2015, December). Privacy Flag-collective privacy protection scheme based on structured distributed risk assessment. In *2015 IEEE 2nd World Forum on internet of things (WF-IoT)* (pp. 430-434). IEEE.

Chapter 10
Social Engineering and Data Privacy

Mumtaz Hussain
NEDUET, Pakistan

Samrina Siddiqui
NEDUET, Pakistan

Noman Islam
KIET, Pakistan

ABSTRACT

This paper presents the concept of social engineering. The internet has completely changed the mode of operations of modern-day systems. There are billions of internet users and this number is rising every day. Hence, ensuring the security is very important for any cyber physical systems. This paper focuses on one of the very important aspects of cyber security, i.e., social engineering. It is defined as a set of techniques of human manipulation by exploitation of the basic emotions of human beings. Different institutions deploy state-of-the-art systems to protect the data housed in their datacenter. However, it is also essential that an individual must secure their personal information from the social engineers. Hence, this paper discusses the data privacy issues and various relevant techniques under the umbrella of social engineering. It discusses various social engineering techniques and summarizes those techniques, thus concluding the paper.

DOI: 10.4018/978-1-6684-6581-3.ch010

INTRODUCTION

One of greatest invention in the history of humankind that single handedly changed the way of doing things is Internet. Internet does not only change the ways of communication, business but also how individuals interact with each other. Long gone are the days when an individual has to wait for hearing back from a person, he wrote a letter to. Now even business and individual get their payments instantly and even keep track of their fleets and cargo and all thanks goes to the internet for making our life easy. Researchers argues that all the Social Media platforms controls user's behavior to some extent by notifies them about different occasion and users' response to it as per Social Media platform's expectations. For instance, Facebook notifies about friends' birthdays and LinkedIn offers alters regarding work anniversary of connections (Haenschen, Frischmann, & Ellenbogen, 2021). According to internetlivestats.com the global internet users are more than 5 billion as of November 2021 and it keeps growing (internetlivestats, 2021). Merely the active internet users as of January 2021 are 4.3 billion as per the numbers of Statista as shown in the Figure 1 (Statista, 2021).The researcher (Li, Yu, Susilo, Hong, & Guizani, 2021) argues that the number of devices connected with the 5G cellular network only will be 50 billion by the year 2025. Let alone 5G mobile subscriptions worldwide are expected to rise from 0.6 from billion in 2021 to 3.4 billion in the year 2026 as per Statista (Statista, 2021). More user and more devices connected to the internet means creation of more data and more potential incidents of data breach and data theft.

Every technology has two sides just like a coin, one side can be used in positive way but other one is destructive. According to the official website of Nobel Peace Prize, Alfred Bernhard Nobel, who is the men behind Nobel prize, has a total of 355 patents to his credit and one of his greatest inventions was Dynamite. Royal Swedish Academy of Sciences gave an honorary award to Alfred Nobel for his invention of dynamite and called it a vital invention for the humankind (www.nobelpeaceprize.org). Dynamite has it industrial use but at the same time is can use to harm humankind and the invention of internet is no exception. Internet has enormous use for the prosperity and the well being of humans but at the same time some greedy people use it for their own gain and harm people. The recent advancement in the field of both hard and software technologies enabled companies to process data and get insights with the help of machine learning and it encourage them to collect more and more data. Companies do earn huge profits from there data collection, but number of high-profile data breaches are raising in recent times (Aridor, Che, & Salz, 2020). The data privacy at the corporate level is different from the individual level. The data privacy from a corporate point of view is the capacity to regulator the location of personal identifiers of users (Baik, 2020). However, from the individual's perspective, securing personal information is just data protection. Social Engineering is a collation of techniques of human manipulation by exploitation the basic emotions of human beings such as greediness, distress, & naiveness in order to obtain the required information. In simple words Social Engineering is method of persuading a potential victim to perform a particular action i.e., share particular personal information (Leonov, Vorobyev, Ezhova, Kotelyanets, Zavalishina, & Morozov, 2021).Another researcher describes Social Engineering as a physiological manipulation of victim in order to acquire required information (Soomro & Hussain, 2019). Comprising a system by identifying its vulnerabilities, writing code to exploit system's vulnerabilities and executing code on a target system requires a high level of understanding of target system and rate of it success is decreasing with advance security tools deployed by corporations (Leonov, Vorobyev, Ezhova, Kotelyanets, Zavalishina, & Morozov, 2021). Organizations deploy the state of art hardware and software technologies to safeguard the data they have in their datacenter but how can individual can secure his personal information from the Social Engineers and their persuading techniques is what this paper is going to discuss. This paper is comprised of three sections as follows: Section 2 explores Social Engineering techniques used by criminal to gain access to user data; Section 3 discusses preventive measures; Section 4 provides a brief summary of research findings, and finally conclusions and the future research areas are discussed.

Figure 1. Global digital population as of January 2021 (Source (Statista, 2021))

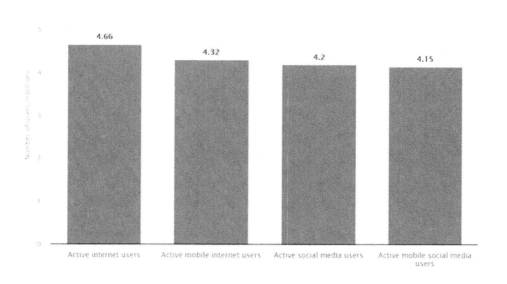

SOCIAL ENGINEERING AND DATA PRIVACY

With the growing use of internet privacy of user data is being breached from time to time. Data breach is not only a huge concerned by business and individual but it also comes with a great cost in terms of loss and fine to business (Aridor, Che, & Salz, 2020). In recent years the world has witnessed many incidents of data and privacy breaches (Norrman, Näslund, & Dubrova, 2016). In the year 2018, a British consulting firm named Cambridge Analytics, got access to more than 87 million Facebook users' data and their friends' data without their user's consent (Isaak & Hanna, 2018) (Schneble, Elger, & Shaw, 2018) (Baik, 2020). According to the BBC article, Facebook was fined 500,000/- pound by the UK's data protection watchdog, in October 2018 (Criddle, 2020).In the following year i.e., 2019, Disney+ a streaming service, was attached and thousands of its accounts were compromised .The Washington post reported that hackers took control of compromised accounts, changed their login credentials and start selling them for as low as 3$ per account on dark web (Telford, 2019).In the year 2020, researchers unearth 235 million user profiles of Instagram, TikTok and YouTube available online (BISCHOFF, 2020). The year 2021 is not completed yet and the IdentityForce, a U.S identity protection firm, reported more than 40 data breeches in various multinational companies around the globe (Bekker, 2021). IBM published a white paper on Cost of a Data Breach Report 2021 that offers insights from 537 real incidents of the data breaches and help us understand the future of security and privacy of data in the age of ever evolving modern technology. The report says the average cost of a data breach is $161 million US Dollars. Figure 2 shows the average cost of a data breach from the year 2015 to 2021 (IBM, 2021).

Figure 2. Average Cost of Data Breach (Source (IBM, 2021))

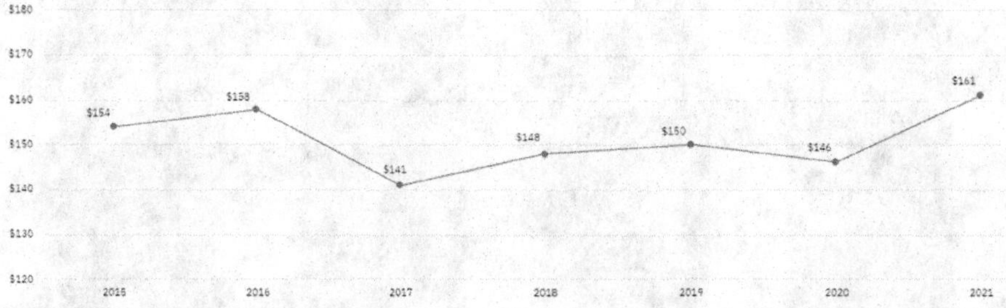

Average per record cost of a data breach
Measured in US$

The above-mentioned data breaches are at the corporate level on which an individual does not have any control but the incident of data theft using Social Engineering techniques are also on rise and these are the incident that can be prevented by the individuals. According to Internet Crime Report 2020 of Federal Bureau of Investigation, the Bureau received a total 5,679,259 complaints as of May 2020 which accounts to a total loss of $13.3 billion (FBI, 2020). To put the numbers in perspective, the loss is a light over to the Gross Domestic Product (GDP) of Madagascar for the year 2018 (worldpopulationreview, 2021).The Federal Trade Commission of United States released its report of Consumer Sentinel Network Data Book for the year 2020. The Federal Trade Commission received a total 4.7 million complaints in the year 2020.2.2 million reports are of Fraud which is 46% of all the complaints and Identity theft complaints is accounted for 1.4 million reports with 29% of weightage among total number of reports (Commission, 2021). Following are some of the most popular social engineering tactics which scammers are using actively now a days globally.

1) Covid-19 Scam Email
2) Reverse Social Engineering
3) Technical Support Scam
4) Romance Scam
5) Non-Deliver Scam
6) Recruitment Scam
7) Game Hack Scam
8) Phishing
9) Vishing
10) Smishing
11) Whaling

Covid-19 Scam Email

The way the world which was considered normal was ended in March 2020 and work from home emerged as a new normal. Schools, offices, workplaces, and even restaurants were shut down and humankind were forced adapt the new normal and restricted to remain in their home and maintain social distancing. The surge in the IT product was normal, demand for laptops, tablet Zoom enjoyed evolutionary growth within a couple of months and as the same time scammer saw this in an opportunity to deprive people from their hard-earned money through scamming emails in the name of Covid-19pandemic.Sophos is a British company that deals with both security of software and hardware as well. According to Sophos 2021 threat report, scam email of Covid-19 surged among the spam email within the couple of couple of days in March 2020 as per Figure 3 (SophosLabs, 2021).

Figure 3. Covid-19 and Coronavirus Email Scams on the Rise (Source (SophosLabs, 2021))

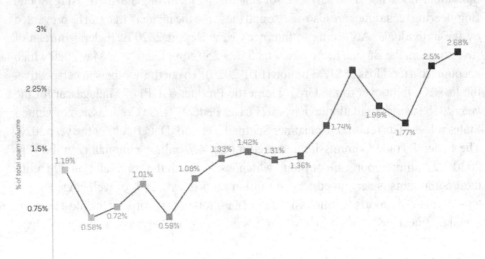

World witness many companies laying off their employees during Covid-19 Pandemic and it opened the door of opportunity for Social Engineers and they got an excellent opportunity to engaged their victim into action (SophosLabs, 2021). As the Covid-19 pandemic become a global hot topic, Social Engendering Scammers used this opportunity for their own personal gains. According to researchers, US Citizens reports Covid-19 scams more than 25 thousand complaints in every single month from the January to June of the year 2021. The month of march was at top with a huge number of 57,348 complaints (Chaganti, Bhushan, & Nayyar, 2021). The financial loss due to Covid-19 Scam email is accounted for a total of $545 million US dollar as of October 2021 and is merely within US only. These statistics reflect the latest modus operand of the Social Engineering Scammers which they keep changing in accordance with the global affairs (Chaganti, Bhushan, & Nayyar, 2021). According to article of Strategic Finance Magazine article, Covid-19 has offered a completely new field for scammers. Only in the month of March 2020, more than 60,000 phishing websites were reported and 18 million covid-19 related scam emails per day was reported by Google Threat Analysis Group (CASTELLUCCIO, 2021).

Reverse Social Engineering

Reverse Social Engineering (RSE) is a form of Social Engineering techniques in which the victim approaches to the scammer and provide him personal information.

Such kind of situation appears to be very unlikely, but it happens and the victim gets trapped in it. For instance, and phasing email impersonating as email from bank asking to contact bank's technical support on a provided number is classical example of the reverse social engineering (Thapar). Another type of RSE is gift or lottery scam where the victim received an email/SMS from the scammers impersonating as bank, financial institutes or an e-commerce website and offer him huge sum of money or gift. Here the scammers exploit the very basic emotion of human being i.e. greed and for the purpose of the outreach of the scam, fraudsters take help of Google ads and even host fake phishing websites as well (Chaganti, Bhushan, & Nayyar, 2021). In the case of gift card scam, criminals make their victim believe that they are legitimate organization and offer them huge money against gift cards from different e-commerce websites. Once the criminals get enough amounts of gift cards they stop communicating with their victims and sale those gift cards to get cash. According to the Consumer Sentinel Network Data Book 2020, gift card is the 5th highest mode fraud with a total 43,242 complaints accounted for 11.57% to total complaints reported with payment methodas per Figure 4 (Commission, 2021).

Figure 4. Fraud Reports by Payment Method (Source (Commission, 2021))

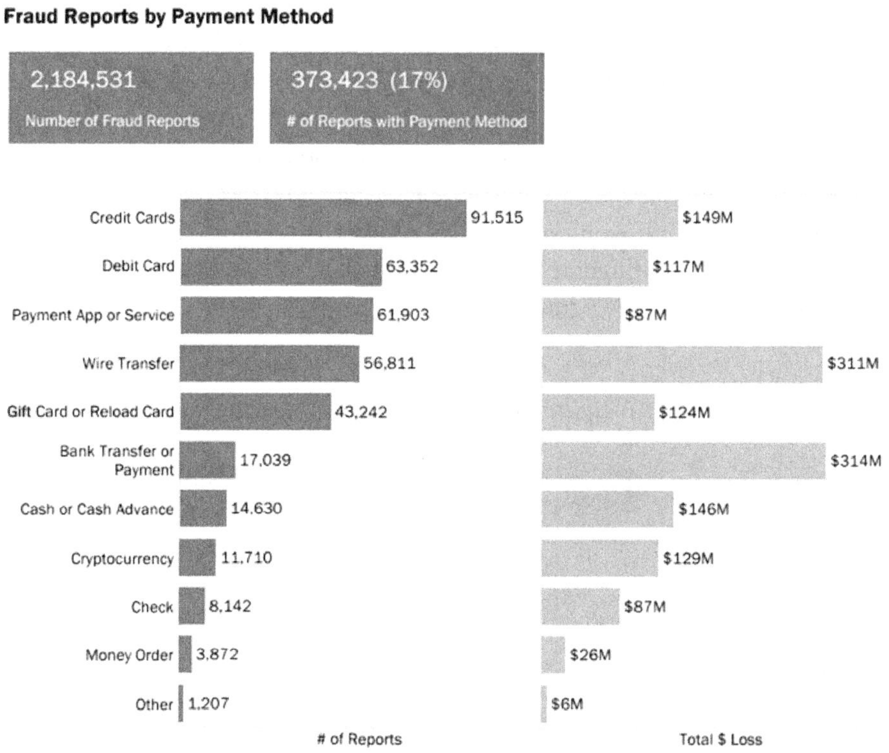

Fraud Reports by Payment Method

Technical Support Scam

People with less awareness of the digital world and the technologies involved in our daily life are usually most common victim of Technical Support Scam (TSS). Scammers either contact their victims directly or the victims contact the fraudsters as a result of phishing email using RSE techniques in a fearful situation that the victim might loss all its data due to a new virus or latest variant of a ransomware (Chaganti, Bhushan, & Nayyar, 2021). TSS is a not a new technique but a decades old modus operandi of the Social Engineering Scammers which force victims to pay hundreds of dollars for a fraudulent technical support. The researchers unearth over 9,000 domains and 3,365 phone numbers connected with TSS. The scammers use named of tech giants in their communication with victim to earn their trust such as Microsoft and give remote access of his computer to the scammers (Srinivasan, et al., 2018) (Faizal, Yahya, & Adham, 2019). The researchers argue that increase in the cybercrime is due the Covid-19 pandemic that forces work all around the globe to work from home which resulted in work in isolation with co-workers and inhouse tech support. People within in the age group of 50-80were most common victims of Technical Support Scam (Payne, 2020). Another researcher analyzed 5 million domains with the help of ROBOVIC tool and found 22 thousand URLs to be fraudulent which were offering Technical Support. Researchers argue that TTS is on rise and thousands of various unique are being registered every week (Miramirkhani, Starov, & Nikiforakis, 2016).According to the article published on Microsoft blogs, Microsoft received 6,500 average monthly complaints regarding Tech Support Fraud as of June 2021 and that is lower monthly average as compared to 13,000 monthly complaints in previous years (Schrade, 2021). According to the US Federal Trade Commission report, older adults have 5 times more chances of getting scammed by Tech Support Fraudsters (Fletcher, 2019). The Figure 5 shows the top fraud faced by people agreed over 60 years.

Figure 5. Fraud Reports by Adults Aged Over 60 Years (Source (Fletcher, 2019))

Tech Support Scams	25K
Shop-at-Home\Catalog Sales	22K
Business Imposters	13K
Government Imposters	11K
Prizes\Sweepstakes\Lotteries	10K

Romance Scams

Romance Scam (RS) is one of Social Engineering Techniques which criminals used to deprive victims from their hard-earned money. Scammers often make fake social media profile and communicate with their victim very frequently and once the scammers win the trust of their victim; they ask for money to be transferred. Middle aged youth including women are the common target of Romance Scammers. Victims of Romance Scam often suffers from tension, hopelessness, nervousness, post-traumatic disorder (PTSD) and even suicidal thoughts as well (Chuang, 2021). The researcher claims that many reports suggestion the RS often impersonate as US military personal in order to impress their victims and military impersonation is so common that US Army has to put warnings on its official website. Scammers not only impersonate military but all branches of the Army, peacekeeping forces and other law enforcement agencies to some extent. The researchers acquired 4,354 RS reports from Australian Consumer and Competition Commission and over served that majority of the victims were middle-aged adults (Cross & Holt, The Use of Military Profiles in Romance Fraud Schemes, 2021).Romance fraud not only accounts for $475 million dollar loss only in the United States as per the Internet Crime Complaint Center (IC3) report 2020 but also shocks lives of thousands of people globally every year (FBI, 2020) (Cross & Layt, *"I Suspect That the Pictures Are Stolen": Romance Fraud, Identity Crime, and Responding to Suspicions of Inauthentic Identities,* 2021). The Australian Consumer and Competition Commission reported $80 million Australian dollar loss in the year 2020 whereas Britain estimates a loss of £50 million pound in the year 2018. The complex natures of Social Media Platforms make it hard to verify the authenticity of Romance Scammer and in most cases not only the target but the person being impersonated is also become the victim of Romance Scammers (Cross & Layt, *"I Suspect That the Pictures Are Stolen": Romance Fraud, Identity Crime, and Responding to Suspicions of Inauthentic Identities,* 2021). According to Consumer Sentinel Network Data Book 2020, 52,593 complaints were regarding Romance Scam which account to 1.11% all the complaints as shown in the Figure 6.

Figure 6. Romance Scam Reported by Consumer Sentinel Network Data Book 2020 (Source (Commission, 2021))

Imposter Scams						
	Business Imposters	104,700	3.36%	106,718	3.29%	154,904	3.28%
	Family & Friend Imposters	21,655	0.70%	20,137	0.62%	25,106	0.53%
	Government Imposters	255,323	8.20%	388,566	11.97%	178,845	3.79%
	Romance Scams	22,264	0.71%	25,113	0.77%	52,593	1.11%
	Tech Support Scams	148,538	4.77%	108,103	3.33%	97,765	2.07%

Non-Delivery Scam

As the name suggests, a non-delivery scam is simply when scammers received the payment but do not send the good or provided the service as per agreement (FBI, 2020). According to the Europol report, a global crisis like Covid-19 pandemic could not hinder the speed of criminal and their illicit activities. Criminals has proved their ability to find opportunities in the most historic disaster and on contrary they have adapted the pandemic situation and expatiated their scams. Scammers have targeted the personal protective equipment and goods in high demand such as mask and hand sanitizers for non-delivery scam (Schotte & Abdalla, 2021).Consumers around the global are always concerned about damage to the goods during transport, delivery of goods to an incorrect address and delay but non-delivery scam is always the foremost point of concern. Non-delivery of a product is the biggest concern of consumer using e-commerce platform (Vishwakarma, Chaturvedi, & Yadav, 2021). Often the criminals enjoy the ease of his bedrooms, countries or continent away from their victim which hinders the prosecution by the law enforcement agencies. Police is now adapting fraud awareness strategy to proactively reduced the non-delivery scams from being happening at first place (Mehmedov, 2021). According to the Internet Crime Complaint Center (IC3) 14,534 victims of aged over 60 years reported non delivery scam, as shown in the Figure 7, which accounts for $40 million dollar loss in US only (FBI, 2020).

Recruitment Scam

Internet has changed the way in which organizations conduct their routine business and with the help of online hiring the job human resource department is become easier and organized. They can advertise opening on social media platforms or on their organization own personal recruitment portal and conduct online interviews. Scammers have overserved potential of fraud in the recruitment sector as well. Recruitment scammers public fake job vacancywith handsome salary package on internet and attract many job seekers. Once the victim goes through all the phases of hiring, scammers ask for fee in the name of application processing, administrative charges, security fees, and etc., and most time steal personal data of job seeker instead of offering any job (Mehboob & Malik, 2020) (Habiba, Islam, & Tasnim, 2021).A survey in UK shows that job seeker at the risk of landing on a fake bogus job opening is 67%. In United Kingdom along approximately 0.7 million job seekers registered their complaint to loss 0.5 million pound to Recruitment Scams. The students and specially the fresh graduates are the most common victims of fake recruitment driver started by job scammers (Habiba, Islam, & Tasnim, 2021).The average loss to Recruitment Scam in United States as reported by Consumer Sentinel Network

Data Book 2020 is $1,950 US Dollars. It is among the top 10 fraud categories with total 58,263 complaints and accumulated loss of $175 million US Dollars as shown in the Figure 8 (Commission, 2021).

Figure 7. Non-Delivery Scams Complaints (Source (Commission, 2021))

Over 60 Victim Count

Crime Type	Victims
Extortion	23,100
Non-Payment/Non-Delivery	14,534
Tech Support	9,429
Identity Theft	7,581
Phishing/Vishing/Smishing/Pharming	7,353
Spoofing	7,279
Confidence Fraud/Romance	6,817
Personal Data Breach	6,121
Misrepresentation	4,735
Government Impersonation	4,159
Lottery/Sweepstakes/Inheritance	3,774
BEC/EAC *	3,530
Other	3,259
Credit Card Fraud	3,195
Advanced Fee	3,008
Overpayment	2,196
Real Estate/Rental	1,882

Figure 8. Loss in US Dollar Due to Recruitment Scam (Source (Commission, 2021))

Top 10 Fraud Categories

Rank	Category	# of Reports	% Reporting $ Loss	Total $ Loss	Median $ Loss
1	Imposter Scams	498,278	22%	$1,190M	$850
2	Online Shopping and Negative Reviews	352,805	70%	$246M	$100
3	Internet Services	123,749	39%	$170M	$210
4	Prizes, Sweepstakes and Lotteries	116,205	10%	$166M	$1,000
5	Telephone and Mobile Services	81,221	22%	$32M	$225
6	Travel, Vacations and Timeshare Plans	73,388	53%	$175M	$1,100
7	Business and Job Opportunities	58,263	38%	$168M	$1,950
8	Health Care	49,821	39%	$21M	$134
9	Foreign Money Offers and Fake Check Scams	38,420	23%	$46M	$1,980
10	Investment Related	24,647	78%	$387M	$1,566

Game Hack Scam

The video game is billion-dollar industry which is estimated of having total market value of 131.3 billion US Dollar globally as of 2020 with a 2.725 billion gamers around the globe. Many games run ads inside game and offer in-game purchases to its users for generating profits. In order to progress in game some users pay the real money to buy in-game resources but other search for cracks and hacks to get the in-game resources. The popularity of games attracts the scammers to offer game hack and innocent gummers become victim of Game Hack Scam (GS). The obviously victims of the GHS are young adult and even underage children who are unaware about the consequences of share credit card details with scammers (Badawi, Jourdan, Bochmann, Onut, & Flood, 2019). Game Hack Scam is one of the most popular Social Engineering techniques used by scammers to fraud victims and get huge money easily. Here scammers make their victim believe that they will receive free of cost and unlimited in-game resources for their favorite game. In reality, the scammers are the one who will benefit from the victim who keep filling endless surveys, subscribe to some online services, install malicious spyware software and fill other type of research questionnaires (Badawi, Automatic Detection and Analysis of the "Game Hack" Scam, 2020). According to the researchers, the highest numbers of click to these GHS links is form US with 22.67% followed by India and Indonesia with 10.37% and 6.7% respectively as shown in the Figure 9.

Figure 9. Number of Clicks to Game Hack Scam Links (Source (Badawi, Jourdan, Bochmann, Onut, & Flood, 2019))

Rank	Top countries		Top referrals	
	Countries	% Clicks	Referrer	% Clicks
1	US	22.67	direct	77.17
2	India	10.37	jeuxvideo.com	5.18
3	Indonesia	6.7	piktochart.com	3.36
4	Philippines	5.82	kabam.com	1.51
5	UK	4.58	google.com	1.13
6	Brazil	3.78	flasygames.com	1.12
7	France	2.66	change.org	1.02

Phishing

The Phishing attacks simply exploit the human behavior and the victim falls in trap by providing his personal details. Scammers create a website that replicates a legitimate bank or a Social Media Platform and once the victim tries to login with his own login credential the scammer receives it the compromise the user account (Basit, Zafar, Liu, Javed, Jalil, & Kifayat, 2021). The researchers deployed CrawalPhish for 14 months and collected data from more than 11.2 million websites for analysis and that is a huge number of websites to host. Clearly there is reasonable profit in scamming which enable scammer to host that number of websites (Zhang, et al., 2021). Phishing is one of the most hazardous Social Engineering technique that put business network and intellectual property at risk (Nguyen, Jensen, Durcikova, & Wright, 2021). Another researcher considers Phishing as serious cybersecurity challenge and has very disturbing effect on netzines (Balogun, et al., 2021). Target with the technology awareness may easily distinguish between legitimate website and Phishing website but case is not the case when the potential target is not very well-versed with latest trends and technologies. The phishing websites are growing at rapid speed that was never seen before. According to researcher, phishing attacks have raised so much that 2020 witness high number of attacks in last three year. These attacks were mainly Covid-19-themed. Phishing is so powerful that the Verizon's Data Breach Report confirms that malware penetrated their system through Phishing email. 51,401 Phishing websites were reported by Anti-phishing websites and RSA, a cybersecurity solution provider, reported estimated loss of $9 billion US dollars in global phishing attacks. (Nguyen, Jensen, Durcikova, & Wright, 2021). According to Internet Crime Complaint Center (IC3) report 2020, Phishing was the top reported crime with 241,342 complaints as shown in the Figure 10 (FBI, 2020).

Figure 10. Phishing Complaints (Source (FBI, 2020))

By Victim Count

Crime Type	Victims
Phishing/Vishing/Smishing/Pharming	241,342
Non-Payment/Non-Delivery	108,869
Extortion	76,741
Personal Data Breach	45,330
Identity Theft	43,330
Spoofing	28,218
Misrepresentation	24,276

Baiting

As the name suggests, the Baiting attacks lure it victim to click on a provided link in order to get free stuff or a subscription of a service. The Baiting attacks persuade its victim to exchange personal information for getting free service or product. Once the user clicks the phishing link, the scammers either install some malware to expose the victim's computer or steal victim's personal information without the victim being aware of it (Salahdine & Kaabouch, 2019). The baiting attack is one of most successful attack as it not only exploits its victim psychologically but also emotionally (Manocha & Sharma, 202). The common source of Baiting attacks are SMS, Phone and email and such emails may offer a free iPhone and required credit card details for getting free iPhone (Syed, 2021) (ODEH, ELEYAN, & ELEYAN, 2021). Victim fall in trap by providing their banking details and losses their hard-earned money (Syed, 2021). Researcher finds publishing online advertisement is another medium through which scammers attracts their victim to get free product (ODEH, ELEYAN, & ELEYAN, 2021). The Batting attack is so powerful that it not only victimizes general public but also the military institutes as well. A malware named "agent.btz" penetrated the US military network through Baitting attack and to clean the network Pentagon launch an operation BuckSHot Yankee that took 14 months to clean the US Army Network (Shahrom, et al., 2021).

Healthcare Frauds

There are increasing concerns about frauds in healthcare domains (Coventry & Branley, 2018). Currently, healthcare organizations pay little concern for cybersecurity. Emphasis has been more on patient care though the internetworking technology provides more sophisticated ways to provide healthcare. The tremendous advancement in technology such as availability of inexpensive computing gadgets, the emergence of networking technologies such as WiFi and 5G communication has lead to explosive growth in healthcare technologies. The introduction of electronic health record (HER) is expected to reduce healthcare cost and deliver quality service. However, the integration of healthcare with technology is expected to increase security breaches. The compromise of patients' privacy and breach of their healthcare data is highly probable. One of the possible attacks is the distributed denial of service (DDOS) attack which not only costs financial loss but also leads to the unavailability of service and might lead to loss of lives at the time of the attack.

(Bhuyan, et al., 2020) discussed various types of attacks on health-care systems. Another type of attack is the privilege escalation where the hacker gains unauthorized elevated access to for instance change patients' personal record and communication, thus compromising the safety of the patient. Several types of man-in-the-middle attack has also been reported in the literature. Structure Query Language (SQL) injections have been reported in several healthcare systems in the past. The hackers can also introduce malicious software such as virus, worms, Trojans and spyware to harm the healthcare system. Medical Device Hijack (Medjack) is a type of attack in which a malicious user injects malicious software code in to medical devices to move across the hospital network. Insecure medical devices provide an entry point to the hospital network and other mission-critical equipments such as magnetic resonance imaging (MRI) machines, infusion pumps and life supporting equipments (ventilators).

Most of the healthcare systems are found to be using legacy technologies leading to by-passing detection techniques and attacks such as Wannacry attack. The possible motivation for attacks on healthcare technologies may be financial or political. The attacker may use the credentials for false claim or sell drugs on dark web. This will not only lead to compromising privacy but also the reputation of the healthcare organization. The healthcare insurance can be a useful approach to get quality service in case of a security breach.

Holiday Scam

Holiday scams occur in holiday seasons where people become victim of deals that seem too good to be true (Holiday Scams, FBI). Similarly, there are scams related to non-payment or non-delivery of items to consumers. These scams cost around $337 million according to various studies. Some of the related scams are as follows:

- **Charity Scams:** Most of the charities in US are done in December most of them from fake websites and pushy telemarketers.
- **Delivery Scams:** Items not delivered when payment has been made by victim
- **Travel Scams:** This has been based on travel deals that looks too good to be true (spoof booking sites and email offers)
- **Letter From Santa Scams:** Scammer scavenge to get personal information of victim via fake letter from Santa

To avoid these scams, maintain a good cybersecurity hygiene. Don't open any potentially dangerous link or attachments in your email. Limit the sharing of your personal information to your known ones. Make sure you that you know who you are buying or selling from. Check each website uniform resource locator (URL).

Scams with Adults

In United States (US), scams with adults have been an increasing concern for the past few years. The special committee in US in 2014 issued a warning to adults about targeted scams. This has been because of the decline in mental and physical abilities of adult. According to various studies, the scam correlates with the age of an adult. A special term geriatric syndrome is used to identify the common conditions experienced by adults. These include problems such as mental or physical health, cognitive impairments, neurological and psychological problems, social issues, loneliness, lack of family support etc. Other issues such as disability, anxiety and depression are also prevalent. In addition, lack of awareness in adults is also a common factor. Adults take less defensive actions against cybersecurity attacks and willing to trust people. There are dating and romance scams associated with adults, selling illegal medicines and inviting to donate to false charities. The older adults have twice the risk of becoming victim to phishing attacks. Other types of attacks include behavioral attacks, consumer fraud and identity theft.

FUTURE RESEARCH DIRECTIONS

Cybersecurity is one of the biggest challenges for future networks. A great deal of research is underway on providing counter measures as discussed in this study. The paper only discussed the work on social engineering and data privacy. This work can be extended to discuss other challenges related to security such as attack on data availability, integrity, non-repudiation and security threats such as denial of service (DoS) attacks, distributed denial of service (DDoS) attacks, Byzantine failures can be discussed in detail. The security challenges require a comprehensive and multi-layered solution embracing all the layers of protocol stack. The future work can be pursued in this direction. It is to be noted that only technological solution is not sufficient to resolve these challenges. Hence, all inclusive solution involving both technology and human collaboration must be developed.

CONCLUSION

Cyber-attacks on companies and massive data breeches are the incidents over which an individual has no control but on the other Social Engineering is the type of attack where an individual is targeted directly and using some tips and trick an individual can save from a great loss. Human Cognitive Bias are the basic flaws in the thought process of the human mind. Social Engineering Scammers exploits the Human Cognitive Bias and expect the misjudgment by the victim in a particular situation such as an impersonating call to technical support staff for password change. Cyber criminals often cover majority of their tracks but sometimes forget to cover some of their footsteps. Law enforcement agencies uses a technique called Behavioral Reverse Engineering (BRE)to think like a criminal. BRE is science and art as well to fathom the thought process of the fraudsters. BRE comprise of social engineering attack in chunks to back track the crime to reach the perpetrator. An investigator may first think of sources of publicly available information about victim such as social media platforms (Lekati, 2018). Just like an investigator working in a law enforcement agency, an individual can also benefit from the Behavioral Reverse Engineering techniques and think like a criminal in order to save him from any potential scam. Individuals can think of their publicly available information on social media platforms and make that information to confidential to the user himself. The following table 1 summaries the all the major social engineering techniques discussed in this paper and their prevention measures in a nutshell.

Table 1. Social engineering techniques & their prevention measures

S. No	Social Engineering Technique	Prevention Measure
		Social Engineering Technique& Their Prevention Measures
1	Covid-19 Scam Email	• Verify the source of the email. • Do not share personal banking credentials
2	Reverse Social Engineering	• Do not replay to emails that offers too good to be true. • There are little to none schemes that offers expensive product or services for free.
3	Technical Support Scam	• Do not provide remote access to any one claiming to be representative of big tech gain company. • Save the number or email through which you were contacted and called the helpline mentioned on the official website of the company and verify the legitimacy of those numbers and email.
4	Romance Scams	• Do not blindly trust a person in cyberspace. • Meet the person you like in person. • Do not fall in to sad soties and request for financial assistance.
5	Non-Delivery Scam	• Check the product and seller reviews before placing the order. • Keep an eye bad review, low rating, and fake reviews. • It is always better to buy from a well know e-commerce website instead of trying a new one.
6	Recruitment Scam	• Verify the source of the email.
7	Game Hack Scam	• Check the reviews of the website that offers free game resources. • Search for previously satisfied customer of that website. • Always remember these websites may have fake reviews.
8	Phishing	• Do not instant reply to emails having suspicious links. • Learn about new technologies to deal with such type of attacks. • Ensure the website you are visiting is legitimate by double checking it from google of any other search engine.
9	Baiting	• Never click any link send from an unknown source. • Do not provide personal and banking details to any free product or service offer. • Check reviews of new software products before downloading and installing it.

REFERENCES

Aridor, G., Che, Y.-K., & Salz, T. (2020). The Economic Consequences of Data Privacy Regulation: Empirical Evidence from GDPR. SSRN *Electronic Journal*. doi:10.2139/ssrn.3522845

Badawi, E., Jourdan, G.-V., Bochmann, G., & Onut, I.-V. (2020). Automatic Detection and Analysis of the "Game Hack" Scam. [JWE]. *Journal of Web Engineering*, *18*(8), 729–760. doi:10.13052/jwe1540-9589.1881

Badawi, E., Jourdan, G.-V., Bochmann, G., Onut, I.-V., & Flood, J. (2019). The "Game Hack" Scam. *International Conference on Web Engineering*. Daejeon, Korea.

Baik, J. S. (2020). Data privacy against innovation or against discrimination?: The case of the California Consumer Privacy Act (CCPA). *Telematics and Informatics*, *52*, 52. doi:10.1016/j.tele.2020.101431

Balogun, A. O., Adewole, K. S., Raheem, M. O., Akande, O. N., Usman-Hamza, F. E., Mabayoje, M. A., Akintola, A. G., Asaju-Gbolagade, A. W., Jimoh, M. K., Jimoh, R. G., & Adeyemo, V. E. (2021). Improving the phishing website detection using empirical analysis of Function Tree and its variants. *Heliyon*, *7*(7), e07437. doi:10.1016/j.heliyon.2021.e07437 PMID:34278030

Basit, A., Zafar, M., Liu, X., Javed, A. R., Jalil, Z., & Kifayat, K. (2021). A comprehensive survey of AI-enabled phishing attacks detection techniques. *Telecommunication Systems*, *76*(1), 139–154. doi:10.100711235-020-00733-2 PMID:33110340

Bekker, E. (2021). *2021 Data Breaches*. IdentityForce.

Bischoff, P. (2020). *Social media data broker exposes nearly 235 million profiles scraped from Instagram, TikTok, and Youtube*. CompariTech.

Castelluccio, M. (2021). *Phishing During Covid*. sfmagazine.com.

Chaganti, R., Bhushan, B., & Nayyar, A. (2021). *Recent trends in Social Engineering Scams and Case study of Gift Card Scam*. Research Gate.

Chuang, J.-Y. (2021). Romance Scams: Romantic Imagery and Transcranial Direct Current Stimulation. *Frontiers in Psychiatry*, *12*, 12. doi:10.3389/fpsyt.2021.738874 PMID:34707523

Commission, F. T. (2021). *Consumer Sentinel Network Data Book 2020*. Federal Trade Commission.

Criddle, C. (2020). *Facebook sued over Cambridge Analytica data scandal*. BBC.

Cross, C., & Holt, T. J. (2021). The Use of Military Profiles in Romance Fraud Schemes. *Victims & Offenders An International Journal of Evidence-based Research. Policy & Practice, 16*(3), 385–406.

Cross, C., & Layt, R. (2021). I Suspect That the Pictures Are Stolen": Romance Fraud, Identity Crime, and Responding to Suspicions of Inauthentic Identities. *Social Science Computer Review*, 1–19.

Faizal, M. M., Yahya, S., & Faisal Adham, A. S. (2019). A Review of Phone Scam Activities in Malaysia. *2019 IEEE 9th International Conference on System Engineering and Technology (ICSET)*. IEEE.

FBI. (2020). *Internet Crime Report 2020*. FBI.

Fletcher, E. (2019). *Older adults hardest hit by tech support scams*. Federal Trade Commission. www.ftc.gov

Habiba, S. U., Islam, M. K., & Tasnim, F. (2021). A Comparative Study on Fake Job Post Prediction Using Different Data mining Techniques. *2021 2nd International Conference on Robotics, Electrical and Signal Processing Techniques (ICREST)*. IEEE.

Haenschen, K., Frischmann, B., & Ellenbogen, P. (2021). Manipulating Facebook's Notification System to Provide Evidence of Techno-Social Engineering. *Social Science Computer Review*.

IBM. (2021). *Cost of a Data Breach Report 2021*. IBM. internetlivestats. https://www.internetlivestats.com. www.internetlivestats.com

Isaak, J., & Hanna, M. J. (2018). User Data Privacy: Facebook, Cambridge Analytica, and Privacy Protection. *Computer, 51*(8), 56–59. doi:10.1109/MC.2018.3191268

Lekati, C. (2018). Complexities in Investigating Cases of Social Engineering. *11th International Conference on IT Security Incident Management & IT Forensics* (pp. 107-109). IEEE.

Leonov, P. Y., Vorobyev, A. V., Ezhova, A. A., Kotelyanets, O. S., Zavalishina, A. K., & Morozov, N. V. (2021). The Main Social Engineering Techniques Aimed at Hacking Information Systems. *2021 Ural Symposium on Biomedical Engineering, Radioelectronics and Information Technology (USBEREIT)*. IEEE. 10.1109/USBEREIT51232.2021.9455031

Li, Y., Yu, Y., Susilo, W., Hong, Z., & Guizani, M. (2021). Security and Privacy for Edge Intelligence in 5G and Beyond Networks: Challenges and Solutions. *IEEE Wireless Communications, 28*(2), 63–69. doi:10.1109/MWC.001.2000318

Manocha, T., & Sharma, V. (202). Essential Awareness of Social Engineering Attacks for Digital Security. *Journal of Applied Management- Jidnyasa, 13*(1), 25-40.

Mehboob, A., & Malik, M. I. (2020). Smart Fraud Detection Framework for Job Recruitments. *Arabian Journal for Science and Engineering*, 46.

Mehmedov, R. (2021). *Automated classification of pet scam websites.*

Miramirkhani, N., Starov, O., & Nikiforakis, N. (2016). *Dial One for Scam: Analyzing and Detecting Technical Support Scams.* arXiv.

Nguyen, C., Jensen, M. L., Durcikova, A., & Wright, R. T. (2021). A comparison of features in a crowdsourced. *Information Systems Journal, 31*(3), 473–513. doi:10.1111/isj.12318

Norrman, K., Näslund, M., & Dubrova, E. (2016). Protecting IMSI and User Privacy in 5G Networks. *9th EAI International Conference on Mobile Multimedia Communications.* EUDL. 10.4108/eai.18-6-2016.2264114

Odeh, N. A., Eleyan, D., & Eleyan, A. (2021). A survey of social engineering attacks: detection and prevention tools. *Journal of Theoretical and Applied Information Technology, 99*(18), 4375–4386.

Payne, B. K. (2020). Criminals Work from Home during Pandemics Too: A Public Health Approach to Respond to Fraud and Crimes against those 50 and above. *American Journal of Criminal Justice, 45*(4), 563–577. doi:10.100712103-020-09532-6 PMID:32837151

Salahdine, F., & Kaabouch, N. (2019). Social Engineering Attacks: A Survey. *Future Internet, 11* (4).

Schneble, C. O., Elger, B. S., & Shaw, D. (2018). The Cambridge Analytica affair and Internet-mediated research. *EMBO Reports, 19*(8). doi:10.15252/embr.201846579 PMID:29967224

Schotte, T., & Abdalla, M. (2021). *The impact of the COVID-19 pandemic on the serious and organised crime landscape. Collection of Contributions to the CEPOL Online Research & Science Conference.* Pandemic Effects on Law Enforcement Training and Practice.

Schrade, M. J. (2021). *Tech support scams adapt and persist in 2021, per new Microsoft research.* Microsoft.

Shahrom, M. F., Maarop, N., Samy, G. N., Hassan, N. H., Rahim, F. A., Magalingam, P., et al. (2021). A Pilot Analysis of Factors Affecting Defense. *Open International Journal of Informatics (OIJI), 9*(1), 53-64.

Soomro, T. R., & Hussain, M. (2019). Social Media-Related Cybercrimes and Techniques for Their Prevention. *Applied Computer Systems, 24*(1), 9–17. doi:10.2478/acss-2019-0002

SophosLabs. (2021). *Sophos 2021 Threat Report*. SophosLabs.

Srinivasan, B., Kountouras, A., Miramirkhani, N., Alam, M., Nikiforakis, N., & Antonakakis, M. (2018). Exposing Search and Advertisement Abuse Tactics and Infrastructure of Technical Support Scammers. *Proceedings of the 2018 World Wide Web Conference*, (pp. 319-328). ACM. 10.1145/3178876.3186098

Statista. (2021). *Forecast number of mobile 5G subscriptions worldwide by region from 2019 to 2026*. statista. .

Statista. (2021). *Global digital population as of January 2021*. Statista

Syed, A. M. (2021). *Social engineering: Concepts, Techniques and*. ArXiv.

Telford, T. (2019). Thousands of Disney Plus accounts were hacked and sold online for as little as $3. *Washington post*.

Thapar, A. (2022). *Social Engineering An Attack vector Most intricate to tackle*. www.infosecwriters.com

Vishwakarma, R. K., Chaturvedi, P., & Yadav, A. K. (2021). Ascertaining Various Perceived Risks and Its impact on Customer's Purchase Intentions to Online Platforms. *Journal of Xi'an Shiyou University, Natural Science Edition, 17* (7).

worldpopulationreview. (2021). *GDP Ranked by Country 2021*. worldpopulationreview. com. www.nobelpeaceprize.org. *Alfred Nobel*. www.nobelpeaceprize.org

Zhang, P., Oest, A., Cho, H., Sun, Z., Johnson, R., & Wardman, B. (2021). CrawlPhish: Large-scale Analysis of Client-side Cloaking Techniques in Phishing. *IEEE Symposium on Security and Privacy*. IEEE. 10.1109/SP40001.2021.00021

ADDITIONAL READINGS

Aridor, G., Che, Y.-K., & Salz, T. (2020). The Economic Consequences of Data Privacy Regulation: Empirical Evidence from GDPR. SSRN *Electronic Journal*. doi:10.2139/ssrn.3522845

Badawi, E., Jourdan, G.-V., Bochmann, G., & Onut, I.-V. (2020). Automatic Detection and Analysis of the "Game Hack" Scam. [JWE]. *Journal of Web Engineering, 18*(8), 729–760. doi:10.13052/jwe1540-9589.1881

Basit, A., Zafar, M., Liu, X., Javed, A. R., Jalil, Z., & Kifayat, K. (2021). A comprehensive survey of AI-enabled phishing attacks detection techniques. *Telecommunication Systems, 76*(1), 139–154. doi:10.100711235-020-00733-2 PMID:33110340

Habiba, S. U., Islam, M. K., & Tasnim, F. (2021). A Comparative Study on Fake Job Post Prediction Using Different Data mining Techniques. *2021 2nd International Conference on Robotics, Electrical and Signal Processing Techniques (ICREST)*. IEEE.

Islam, N., & Shaikh, Z. A. (2013). Security issues in mobile ad hoc network. *Wireless networks and security*, 49-80.

Imran, M., Faisal, M., & Islam, N. 2019, November. Problems and Vulnerabilities of Ethical Hacking in Pakistan. In *2019 Second International Conference on Latest trends in Electrical Engineering and Computing Technologies (INTELLECT)* (pp. 1-6). IEEE. 10.1109/INTELLECT47034.2019.8955459

Norrman, K., Näslund, M., & Dubrova, E. (2016). Protecting IMSI and User Privacy in 5G Networks. *9th EAI International Conference on Mobile Multimedia Communications*. EUDL. 10.4108/eai.18-6-2016.2264114

Soomro, T. R., & Hussain, M. (2019). Social Media-Related Cybercrimes and Techniques for Their Prevention. *Applied Computer Systems, 24*(1), 9–17. doi:10.2478/acss-2019-0002

Vishwakarma, R. K., Chaturvedi, P., & Yadav, A. K. (2021). Ascertaining Various Perceived Risks and Its impact on Customer's Purchase Intentions to Online Platforms. *Journal of Xi'an Shiyou University, Natural Science Edition, 17* (7).

KEY TERMS AND DEFINITIONS

Baiting: Alluring someone to click on a link to get free products or money, asking to provide personal information and then use the information for malicious activity

Cybersecurity: The practice of defending network, devices, data and infrastructure from malicious users ensuring the security objectives such as confidentiality, integrity, privacy and non-repudiation

Eavesdropping: The practice of passively listening to someone's conversation such as via wiretapping

Holiday Scam: A type of scam generally proliferate on holiday with lucrative deals, most of the mare never delivered or executed, and victims looses their money

Honeypot: An alternate controlled environment created besides the working environment to observe the hacker's behavior and identify the possible threat to the environment

Phishing: Sending email to someone, pretending as reputable company, alluring him to disclose their personal information such as their keys, password or other personal information

Scam: A dishonest scheme or ploy to gain some one's information or money via deceptive means

Social Engineering: The use of deception to let someone disclose their personal/ confidential information that may be used later for malicious intent

Chapter 11
Relevance of Cybersecurity in the Business Models

Aysha Abdulla
Ibn Rushd College For Management Sciences, Saudi Arabia

ABSTRACT

As cyberattacks have become common due to ubiquitous hyperconnectivity of devices, modern business is highly susceptible to data breaches. This chapter aims to investigate the relevance of cyber security in business models. It explains the business impact of cyber security and the various types of cyber threats that has devastating effects on businesses. It further elaborates the various layers of business models. The major security provisioning scenarios that can be effectively applied to them are deduced and the chapter henceforth advances into the explanation of various technological concepts of cyber security. By integrating the security provisioning scenarios with the help of various cyber security technologies and the different layers of business model, an integrated framework of business model options including the most opportunistic model is developed. This research finding provides pragmatic solutions for building lucrative business model options in cyber security with optimum performance.

INTRODUCTION

In this era of technological advancement, as the network connections are intricate, the businesses are highly susceptible to impersonation via cyberattacks. Cyber Security is a growing concern for businesses like defense, healthcare, financial services and online social media. From a technical perspective, substantial research has been done in the field of Cyber Security in recent years. However, there are also grave

DOI: 10.4018/978-1-6684-6581-3.ch011

deficits in how modern networks significantly impact the security of management organizations. A world submerged in cutting edge innovations, swathes of information exchange and high speed demands an increased level of security. There would be alternative ways of arranging the prevalent technologies that render security. It is worth considering here that if the security service is monetizable, it will result in higher number of businesses catering secure services to their customers by investing in it.

The theory of business models as a boundary-spanning unit of analysis (C. Zott et al., 2011) is applied to build the basis for security business. The business model concept relates abstract strategies to the practicality of decisions and actions within the unpredictability of modern business models (A. Afuah, 2004; R. Alt and H. Zimmermann, 2001; H. Chesbrough and R. S. Rosenbloom, 2002; J. Richardson, 2008; S. M. Shafer et al., 2005). Business models are crucial for various technological businesses. A mediocre technology with a well-structured business model is bound to succeed, however a high end technology may fail due to a weak business model (H. Chesbrough, 2010). This is more significant for cyber security businesses, as failure could cause serious implications beyond monetary losses. Business model is defined as an architectural (P. Timmers, 1998) system of interrelated activities (C. Zott and R. Amit, 2010) and interdependent set of logic and strategic decision variables (S. M. Shafer et al., 2005; M. Morris et al., 2005), explaining transaction content, transaction governance and transaction relationship structure (R. Amit and C. Zott, 2001; P. Weill and M. Vitale, 2002) for maximum value creation and value capture (C. Zott and R. Amit, 2010).

The aim of this chapter is to elucidate the business impacts of cyber security in order to create awareness and underscore the significance of business models. It begins with a discussion of cybersecurity business by explaining the different types and costs of cyber threats. The next section discusses the business aspects of cyber security by exposing the theoretical concepts of business models. It elaborates how business opportunities emanate through the 4C framework of the business model. The chapter further delves into explaining the business perspective of cybersecurity. It depicts the four security provisioning scenarios. Furthermore, the various technical concepts of cybersecurity are explained. The chapter concludes by illustrating an integrated business model framework for cyber security businesses and identifying the most opportunistic businesses in the framework, leveraging the various technical concepts of cyber security.

Cyber Security Businesses

Cyber security is rendered as a third- party service or a product or as a combination of service and product that aids organizations and individuals to safeguard their digital assets. Based on this perspective, organizations can be broadly classified into two types. The first type of organizations directly or indirectly provides security solutions as a service or integrated with some other service or product. The second type of organizations are digitalized businesses that are compromised due to data breaches via cyberattacks. As we live in an insecure era, any cyberattack will have a significant impact on the business of these organizations. Thus, we explain various means to categorize security and generate monetary benefits from them. Here, the business impact of the cyber security phenomenon is first explained, moving further to the types of cyber threats and its related costs. Cyber threats can be defined as a risk or exploitation of vulnerabilities by attackers resulting in total disruption of an organizations' operations, the loss or capture of organization's assets (M. Lehto, 2015). Since time immemorial, it was known that catastrophes, device failures or indeliberate flaws of employees posed undesirable challenges to the organization's infrastructure and intelligent data. However, the conspired attacks that wreak havoc on the organizations incites interest in the reader.

Types of Cyber Threats

Cyber threats have a myriad of definitions in text, but the most widely used definition categorizes cyber threats in five groups based on the motivational instincts of the threat agents (Lehto, 2015; Bodeau et al., 2010); cyber activism, cyber- crime, cyber espionage, cyber terrorism and cyber warfare as depicted in Table 1.

The first type of threat is cyber activism, wherein the hacker embarrasses an organization. The hacker's motive is not to inflict any damage to an organization but to convey a political message to an organization. Hacktivists are groups or individuals who hack public websites and overload email servers with a political protest message (Lehto, 2015; Vatis, 2002).

Cybercrime involves exploiting the vulnerabilities of a victim's infrastructure through the use of network and information systems of the adversary. This can be executed by individuals or terrorist groups, insiders or spammers. The underlying reason for this attack could be data theft, or rendering an organization dysfunctional for monetary gain. (Vatis, 2002; R. McCusker, 2006). Cybercrime can be classified into three groups (Lehto, 2015), employing ICT to commit breaches and forgery; digital publication of illegal material and the exploitation of network vulnerabilities.

The third type of threat is cyber espionage. As the word espionage suggests, it is the extraction of secret information from organizations and governments for political or financial gain through the use of illegal means on the internet or networks, computers or programs (Lehto, 2015; Liaropoulus, 2012).It is executed by intelligent agents, individuals or groups who exploit the weaknesses in their adversary's system to obtain sensitive information. Cyber espionage is used by nations and their states to elicit intelligent information of their enemies (Bodeau, 2010; Vatis, 2002). It doesn't only pertain to political espionage but also extends to economic avenues. Professional agents can hack stealthily into an adversary's business system and steal their proprietary trade secrets.

Table 1. Features of different types of cyberattacks

Cyber activism	Cyber crime	Cyber espionage	Cyber terrorism	Cyber warfare
Hacking done that doesn't cause damage	Criminal activities	Illegal access to networks to gain intelligent information	Directed towards intimidating the government	War in the cyberspace
Used to embarrass an organization or send a political message	Can be executed by individuals, group, terrorist and insiders	Can be done by nation states	Initiated by terrorist groups	Threat elements are military, Intelligence services, organized insurgent groups ad terrorists
Example: Anonymous, Chaos computing cloud, Team Poison	Steals sensitive information and disrupts operations for financial gain.	It is employed for political espionage or financial cause	Sophisticated IT weapons are used by hackers	Executed as a multitude of attacks

The next level of threat is cyber terrorism. It is to commit cyberattacks directed towards crucial government infrastructure or private organizations aimed at intimidating a government or evoke panic amongst civilians (Vatis, 2002). The attack is initiated by terrorist groups who are focused to attract national or international attention (Beggs, 2006). These attackers wield offensive weapons alone or together with other ways of attack (Lehto, 2015). For instance, in 2011, the Canadian government reported a massive attack on its Defense research and development Canada agencies. The paramount economic agencies of Canada like the Defense Research and Development Canada were compelled to disconnect from the internet due to cyber terrorism (NATO, 2013).

Cyber warfare is the last level of cyber threat and it involves warfare in the cyberspace virtually (Lehto, 2015). The conventional threat agents are military and their intelligence services, terrorists or insurgent groups. The aim of this attack is to immobilize the critical infrastructure of the adversary by the use of malware like viruses, worms or denial of service attacks (DOS). Cyber warfare is not an isolated strategy, it is used in combination with other strategies for an offensive or defensive purpose (Bodeau et al., 2010). For instance, the Estonian government confronted severe cyberattacks against its websites and banks' websites causing a halt in online banking transactions. This apprehensive incident occurred when the government decided to relocate Soviet Union memorial (S. Herzog, 2011).

The aforementioned discussion is based on the various types and complexity of cyber threats. The threat can originate from several sources like nation states, organizations, individuals, groups, terrorists and insurgent groups. The motive of these agents may be to boost their ego or have illegitimate authority to promote a political cause, for financial benefit, in order to gain access to sensitive information for a future cause, to make people apprehensive or to compel a government to adopt or revoke a certain decision. The robustness of these attacks may differ from one another and the motive may be to cause minimal or optimum damage. Under all circumstances, a cyberattack results in some form of loss, such as, data theft, financial bankruptcy, infrastructure damage and loss of reputation. The following section discusses the costs of cyberattacks incurred on businesses.

Cost of Cyber Attacks

The incidents of cyberattacks are soaring high with an augmented cost to businesses and governments. The accurate cost of this is difficult to calculate, however various studies have given an estimated cost (Ulsch, 2014). The US chamber of commerce has reported that the monetary loss resulting from cyber crime alone ranges between US$ 24 billion and US$ 120 billion and the global loss is reported to be US$ 1 trillion (U. S. Chamber of Commerce, 2015). Also, the Intellectual Property Commission has reported that US losses approximately US$ 300 billion annually via intellectual property theft. A recent survey of 58 US organizations has revealed that the average cost of cyber crime to these organizations was US$ 15 million. There was an increase of 14% since the 2019 figures (Ponemon Institute, 2015).

According to a previous study the cost of cyber attack can be divided into preventive cost and post attack cost (Ulsch, 2014). The preventive cost is to invest in the infrastructure in order to increase the robustness of the organization, this eventually hinders any kind of intrusion or counters a breach. Although these measures are expensive, it is comparatively cheaper than the post attack remedies. The post attack costs are inclusive of the actual amount lost and the cost of remedies to mend the vandalized infrastructure; cost of activities for reacquisition of customers; cost of digital forensics, reports of systems and installation, incident response and crisis management, and communication of the incident to the stakeholders (Ponemon Institute, 2015).

Business Model Approach

The business model approach bridges the gap between abstract strategies and the decisions amidst the unpredictable modern business context (Afuah, 2004; Alt & Zimmermann, 2001; Chesbrough and Rosenbloom, 2002; Richardson, 2008; Shafer et al., 2005). Zott and Amit (2010) conceive business model as a boundary spanning set of activities directed at creating business value. Business model is conceptualized as a group of decisions related to venture strategy, architecture, value creation and capture that need to be created for sustainable competitive benefit in the selected markets (Morris et al., 2005). Zott and Amit (2010) argue that a business model operates to exploit a business opportunity. As a concept, the business model spans a variety of topics and there are numerous theories available in literature. The major issues in these concepts can be illustrated in figure 1. An opportunity centric business model comprises of the when, what, how, why, and where questionnaire to create and capture value when exploring and exploiting business opportunities (Ahokangas et al., 2016). Thus, this points at the prospective implementation of the business model to create optimum value for customers and in return discover means to capture value from the market.

Figure 1. Business model definition

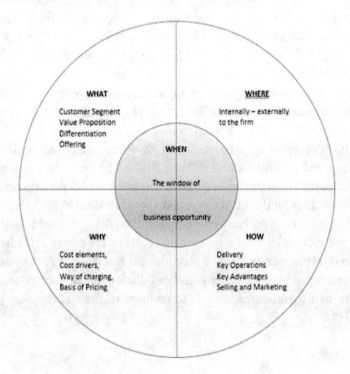

The business model approach addresses the organizational issues through various business aspects. The widely scripted business concepts in this discipline include value creation, value proposition, value capture, partners/suppliers, customers, customer relationships, value chain, revenue, cost drivers, pricing, capabilities and technology infrastructure (Zott, 2011; Shafer et al., 2005; Morris et al., 2005; Onetti et al., 2012).

As a boundary -spanning unit of analysis business model (Zott et al., 2011) links an organization with its business environment, partner organizations, customers and the society (Teece, 2010). Since the business model concept includes a myriad of partner organizational elements, it facilitates analysis of the business environment.

Integrating business models with cybersecurity poses two major woes. Firstly, as all the businesses operating digitally are vulnerable to cyberattacks, can the current business models aid the organizations counter such attacks. Secondly, can the security provision be incorporated in the business models to drive monetary gain in the future.

The ICT Business Model

With the advent of mobile telecommunications, business models have been adapted to shift the organizational boundaries with this industry vertically and horizontally via the integration of the business and complex provision of new services (Ballon, 2007). This integration of the business model with the ICT sector resulted in vertical business models focused in value creation implemented by infrastructure and technology providers and horizontal business models focused in value capture implemented mainly by service providers (Ballon, 2007; Ahokangas, 2015).

Writz et al. (2010) defined four business models for Internet specific business models. They built Web 2.0 business models on the basis of connection, content, context and commerce. Yrjola et al. (2015) explained these as a layered 4C-model, where more lower level technical layer is required for the higher level to exist. These layers can be identified as business opportunities where value creation and capture can be done parallelly. This model can be employed to examine a single layer element or an element that is active in all layers (Yrjölä et al., 2015). Thus, the following figure 4C -model, Figure 2 depicts a business model integrated in the ICT industry.

The first layer is based on the business model related to connections, here the connection related services are provided by the stakeholder (Ahokangas, 2016). The second layer pertains to the business model concerned with monetizing content. At this layer all kinds of online content are categorized and conveniently accessed by the end user. For instance, video streaming can be relevant, up to date and interesting. This includes user - oriented content (personal content), web content (information storage) and educational and entertainment content (audio, video, text etc.). The purpose of this layer is to define the owner of the content who can drive monetary benefit or free access to the users as is the case of advertisement content.

Figure 2. The 4C Business model for ICT business

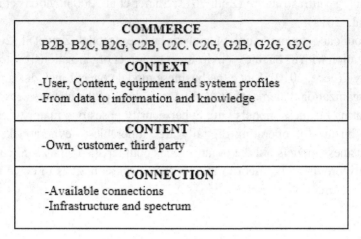

COMMERCE B2B, B2C, B2G, C2B, C2C. C2G, G2B, G2G, G2C
CONTEXT -User, Content, equipment and system profiles -From data to information and knowledge
CONTENT -Own, customer, third party
CONNECTION -Available connections -Infrastructure and spectrum

The third layer that is the context layer is related to the creation of value capture from the user, content, equipment and convert big data into meaningful information and knowledge. The information that is prevalent on the Internet can be aggregated for the simplicity of the navigation services, for instance google and provide relevant context for the underlying content. The user can identify his required content, thus resulting in evident business strategies. With the advent of the 5G networks agile business transactions will be executed on mobile devices with a variety of services offered to the user based on his profile, time, place and history. The context layer will furnish information about the network, device and user profile.

The last layer is based on commerce and it deals with monetizing the resources linked to connection, content or context and the activities related to the ongoing communications. This layer clearly identifies the communication between various entities like business (B), consumer (C) and government (G) (Mitola et al., 2014). Thus B2B, B2C, B2G, C2B, C2C, C2G or G2B, G2Cand G2G transactions are monetized at this layer.

Cyber Preparedness for Business Models

Businesses today are aware that they are prone to cyberattacks. Yet some take action only when they are attacked (Pinto, 2013). Other businesses that are proactive protect their IT infrastructure by assigning this task to their security managers (T. Scully,

2014). Consequently, this managerial approach exposes the businesses to cyber-attacks and its immediate consequences (Earnst & Young, 2016).

Cyber preparedness is the field of cybersecurity that deals with proactive preventive measures against the cyber- attacks and vulnerabilities detected in the organization's infrastructure. It is an organizational policy that finds its inception at the leadership and moves down to the entire organization. Bodeau et al., (2010) built a cyber preparedness framework that has a four stage methodology. Gomes et al. (2016) further enhanced the framework by including broader business, organizational and management perspective.

In the first stage, the leadership audits the organization's vulnerabilities, the related threats and the current security risk management framework to formulate a strategic plan. In the next stage, leadership assesses its cyber preparedness according to the threats detected. The various cyber preparedness levels are, perimeter defense, critical information protection, response awareness, architectural resilience, and pervasive agility (Bodeau, 2010). In the third stage, the organization evaluates the severity of the threat it faces and the its operational, technical and process capabilities to counter the threat. The final stage pertains integrating the cyber preparedness policy into the strategic plan.

In order to ease the cyber preparedness policy of an organization Gomes et al., (2016) combined various managerial elements with the business model. The vast theory of business model explains elements like customers, channels, customer relationship, partners, competitors, complementors, resources (human, non - human, technical and non-technical) among many other elements. The aim is that business model can facilitate the managers undermine the cyber security risks by analyzing the what, how, when and why elements of a business model. These elements are located either within or outside the periphery of an organization.

Pinto (2013) stated that the prevalent security technologies are excellent. However, the challenge is to be able to monetize cyber security so as to generate revenue for the business. Business models are conventionally employed in order to discover newer means of revenue generation. Considering the cyber security aspect of most businesses, it can make them more competitive by utilizing the business model as a boundary-spanning unit of analysis. Pinto (2013) further stated that cybersecurity cost should be included in the product development stage of an organization, thus securing the system and also boost business benefit and opportunities.

Cybersecurity from a Business Perspective

The field of cyber security has a profound effect on two types of organization. The first type of organizations are the ones which secure others against cyber threats by providing security solutions. The second type of organizations include all the others that are digitalized and hence vulnerable to cyber- attacks.

The customer base of companies offering cyber security solutions are broadly classified into two types. The largest customer group have been the Business to Business (B2B) customers or Business to Government (B2G) customers mentioned in the business discipline. These customers have invested highly in cyber security to sustain a secure business solution. Since these organizations are quite vigilant about their digitalization, there has been a growing business demand in this area. The second largest customer group is of individual customers, also known as Business to customer (B2C). It has been difficult to access this group since the value of private data or information on internet and other networks is dispensed solely by the individuals themselves.

The second type of companies whose business is impacted by cyber security are the ones who implement cyber security as a crucial part of their business. It is inclusive of all types of organizations globally, with each organization subjected to varying levels of cyber threats. However, there are certain organizations who do not realize the significance of securing their digital assets and eventually fail to invest sufficient amount.

As there is an imperative need for cyber security, organizations invest in security services as a measure to prepare themselves against prospective attacks (Gomes et al., 2016). This strategy of investing in security has shown competitive advantage for several organizations, however organizations that are unable to draw estimates for the need of security have witnessed immense failure. The inability to generate revenue results in the disinterest of organizations investing in cyber space.

The above figure depicts the relation between security level and revenue generation. In order to secure any digital asset, it is imperative for the organizations to make a higher investment. For a business to be lucrative, it has to generate new revenues for every investment. The interest of the organizations in investing in security solutions would be multifold, if they could find ways to generate new revenue from these security solutions. It could be further debated that investments in security may not lead to revenue generation directly, if there is a lack in the need for security. Thus, organizations should improve the security level as per the need for security by meticulously analyzing it.

Figure 3 explains the various cases of new revenue generation and security level for different technological eras. The four different cases are plotted as A, B, C, and D for the various eras beginning from no security at its inception to full-fledged security for the highly demanding digital companies in the future. At the inception of the digital era, when cyber - attack theory was not known to the world, several organizations were lucrative enough without any secure solutions. This is depicted by A in the graph. As time elapsed security services became more prominent, thus resulting in the trough of the graph, denoting a low level of revenue generation marked as B. However, recently the technology service providers have realized the need for security solutions and thus its implementation. This is depicted as C in the figure, where it shows a rising level both in the security level as well as new revenue generation. As for the future era marked by D, organizations need to provide highly secured services for new revenue generation.

Figure 3. Relation between security level and revenue generation

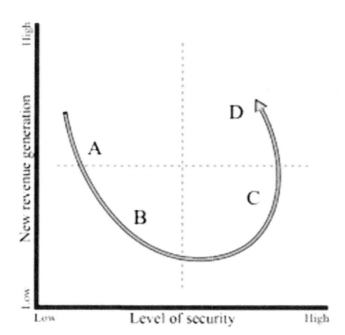

Users and Issues in the Cybersecurity Era

With the sophistication of networks and the intricately connected devices, there is a mammoth of information flowing across them. The number of IOT devices tripled the world population by 2016 and was expected to surpass fifty billion by 2020 (Statista, 2016). While, considering cybersecurity in this era, it is crucial to identify the impact of security level on the users and vice versa. The users can be broadly classified into two groups, as human users and other Devices and Machines. The major issues will pertain to Identification, experience of human users and quality of services of devices and machines. Privacy and safety is the common issue confronting both humans and machines.

To elaborate this further, if there is security for human users, it requires secured personal identification and also competitive user experience. They need to also ensure personal privacy and other safety measures. On the other hand, if we consider security services for machine users, the unique identification of the devices needs to be constantly secured. The quality of service also needs to be competitive with other devices. The novel cybersecurity phenomenon should be able to provide security beyond the conventional security techniques. Eventually, this will lead to an increase in the number of businesses inclined towards offering secured services to their customers and thus generate monetary gain.

Major Security Provisioning Scenarios

Looking at the broader picture of security provisioning, it is important to understand the interaction between the industry and the different types of security services. Thus, the following diagram Figure 4 illustrates four major security drivers for the future to create new businesses.

Figure 4. Security drivers with four major security provisioning scenarios

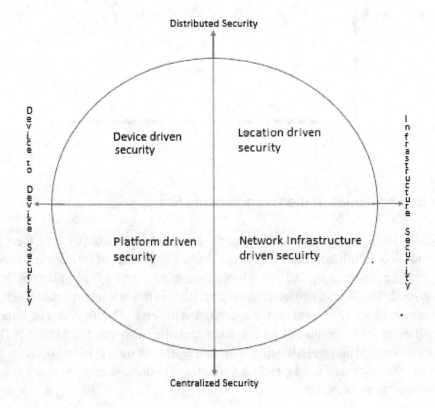

Security provisioning is widely divided into four schemes. They are device to device security, infrastructure security, distributed security and centralized security. Due to a wide demarcation between distributed and centralized security, they are polarized at the opposite ends of an axis. Similarly, there is also a broad distinction in D2D security and infrastructure security, thus they are placed on the opposite ends of the other axis.

This leads to four main security drivers that emanate with new business opportunities. Device driven security is inclusive of distributed and D2D security techniques. Platform driven security comprises of centralized and infrastructure security methods. Finally, location driven security leverages distributed and infrastructure security.

Technological Concepts of Cybersecurity

Authentication

AAA servers allows users to identify themselves by means of three steps; Authentication, implies who a user is; Authorization, implies what a user can do, and Accounting implies what a user did. It allows users to enter their usernames and identify themselves by entering a password after which they may be allowed to access protected resources. When authentication is successful, users; login is associated with the host from which he identified himself and all IP packets that originate from it for a duration specified by the user. Authentication is broadly categorized into three types; Authentication for accessing device; authentication for accessing internet data or resources; Authentication for accessing data via VPN tunnel, IPsec, or SSL VPN.

Data Confidentiality

Data confidentiality is achieved if only the intended receiver receives the sent message. The process of encryption and decryption is used for data confidentiality. The sender encrypts the data and only the receiver can decrypt it using the shared password. Encryption transforms information in clear text into cipher text which is not readable by unauthorized users. Decryption transforms ciphertext back into clear text with the help of a shared secret key making it readable by authorized users. Popular encryption algorithms include, DES, 3DES and AES.

There are two types of encryption: symmetric encryption and asymmetric encryption. In symmetric encryption the same key is used to encrypt and decrypt data. The key needs to be first exchanged before sending the encrypted data. Symmetric encryption is fast, less secure as key is shared. It is used for large amount of data.

In asymmetric encryption, each user has a pair of passwords that is public and private key. The public key is shared between the users and data is always encrypted using the recipient's public key so that the receiver can decrypt it using its private key. Once the password is exchanged the encrypted data is sent. Hence, it is more secure as the key exchange is robust. However, it is slow and is used to send a small amount of data.

In real time we use a combination of both asymmetric and symmetric encryption. The initial key exchange is done using asymmetric encryption followed by symmetric encryption to send data. This ensures optimum security and performance.

Data Integrity

Data Integrity ensures there is no modification in the sent message. It is achieved using hash algorithm. The sender sends the generated hash value of the file also to the receiver. The receiver on reception also generates a hash value to verify if the file is not tampered. If the hash value is the same as the one generated the sender, the receiver is assured that the file is not altered.

Thus, when data is sent over internet, only the authorized receiver should be able to view it. It should not be modified and the receiver should know that the sender is only sending it.

VPN (Virtual Private Network)

VPN provides security when you send the data via internet. Data is sent via internet to make it cost effective compared to leased lines that were dedicated lines from head office to branch office. A VPN provides the same network connectivity over a public infrastructure as they would have over a private network. The various services of VPN are; Data Confidentiality, Data Integrity, Data Authentication and Replay Protection.

There are two types of VPN, Site to site VPN and Remote access VPN. In site to site VPN the firewalls on branch office and head office does the encryption, hashing, authentication respectively. However, in remote access VPN, the VPN client software is installed on the remote access user computer does the encryption, hashing and authentication. The head office firewall does the decryption, de-hashing etc. VPN uses IPsec (Internet Protocol security) which is a secure IP protocol. It is defined as a framework of open standards developed by the IETF to create a secure tunnel at the network IP layer.

NAT (Network Address Translation)

The concept of NAT is used to save IP addresses and hide internal IP address. It is broadly classified into four types; Static NAT, Dynamic NAT, PAT (Port Address Translation), Redirect NAT.

Static NAT does one to one mapping of a private IP to a public IP. It is used to host public servers that are accessible from the internet. For a public network, there should be a network address and a broadcast network. For instance if an organization wants to host two servers three public IP addresses are wasted, two server and one broadcast address. Thus, public IP addresses are not used on public servers and Static Nat is configured to host public web servers accessible from the internet.

Dynamic NAT is used to configure many private to many public mapping, however it is not a one to one mapping. For instance, if there are hundred private IP addresses, they can be mapped to ten public IP addresses. It is configured for Lan users browsing internet. If the LAN users want to access internet, they are assigned a public IP address from the pool of public IP addresses available. In case all the public addresses are assigned to the LAN users, then the next LAN user will be assigned a public IP when one of the users disconnects from the internet. The user can obtain any public IP address based on availability. For the same user public IP may be different based on availability. It is only supported by cisco devices and the main benefit was giving good bandwidth in the early internet days when internet bandwidth was slow.

PAT (Port Address Translation) does many to one mapping. It maps many private IP addresses to one public IP address. All LAN user computers are mapped to one public IP address. In this type of address translation, all users can browse internet simultaneously and maximum public IPs are saved here. The main purpose of this is to allow all Lan users to access internet simultaneously using a single IP. Practically, all users of organizations, home use PAT while browsing internet. Every time, a Lan user sends a request, its address is translated to a public IP address plus a unique port number. When the reply comes, it checks the port number and accordingly directs it to the respective Lan computer. Port numbers in PAT are dynamically assigned, they are not fixed. If a computer sends a request using a particular port number and receives a reply on the respective port number, then for the next request send another port number may be assigned and the first port number used may be freely available for use by another computer on the same Lan. PAT is most widely used in an organization and it is a mandatory configuration.

Redirect NAT is mainly used if an organization is small and wants to host multiple servers with one public IP address. If an organization wants to host multiple web servers using redirect NAT, it can do it by changing the public port number.

Business Models for Cybersecurity

In this section, the concept of business models for ICT industry is integrated with the four security provisioning scenarios with CS technologies to build a 4x4 matrix having the 4C layers of the ICT business model on the y dimension and the four security provisions with CS technologies on the x dimension. This results in business models in multiple layers of 4C for each scenario envisioned. On the contrary, there are certain layers of 4C that are not included in every scenario.

Table 2 illustrates various business models for cyber security. The dark boxes in the figure reveal key business opportunities. Furthermore, every security driver has multiple business models.

Table 2. Business models for cyber security

Security drivers with cyber security technologies/ Business Models	Infra structure security using encryption, hashing and authentication	Platform driven security using encryption, hashing, authentication and VPN	Location driven security using encryption, hashing, authentication and Network Address Translation (NAT)	Device driven security using encryption, hashing, authentication and VPN
Commerce		Big Data Analytics	Value added location specific secure services	Secure devices for commercial purposes
Context	Mobile infrastructures for mass events	Secure IOT platform	Indoor location for providing secure access. Hospital, factories etc.	Secure devices for contextual purposes like military
Content		Content security on platforms like VPN, Uber	Location specific proprietary secure content	Device to device secure calls, data transmission and messages
Connectivity	Secure connections like in MNOs, NIVs and carriers			Secure vehicle to vehicle mesh networks

From the network infrastructure perspective, the highest business opportunities are for Mobile network operators (MNO), Network Infrastructure Vendors (NIV) and other carriers for providing secure connectivity in the connectivity layer. Moreover, there could be new business opportunities by providing secure connectivity using mobile infrastructure for mass events like sport events, voting banks, exhibitions, concerts etc. The various cyber security technologies that can be applied to this security provisioning scenario is encryption, hashing, authentication.

As for platform driven security, securing contents on the digital platform, gives rise to major businesses. Business models in this dimension are secure digital platforms, VPN providers who secure data transmission for user by altering location data. The platforms that have an inherent payment option also needs to be secured.

For instance, Uber needs to be secured for intra platform payments. Another example for the business model of the context layer is secure IoT platform. Thus, these secure platforms can generate revenue by creating big data analytics from the data they create in the commerce layer. The security techniques implemented here range from encryption, authentication, hashing and advanced concepts of VPN.

In case of location driven security, the most lucrative business model should fall in the context layer. Indoor locations can harness small cell base stations. Locations like hospitals, universities, production factories, sports arenas can function as micro-operator. These micro- operators can add a location specific service package referred to as PMSE in the commerce layer. Micro operators are defined by Ahokangas et al (2016) as an entity that provides mobile connectivity with specific local services, spatially confined to either its premises or to a specific area of operation; it is dependent on suitable available spectrum resources. Major business partners for micro- operators will be MNOs and NIVs. With respect to the content layer, the most opportunistic business is related to location specific proprietary secure contents which is accessible by authorized employee in that specific location. For instance, relaying video content during a sports event in a stadium. Encryption, authentication, and the theory of NAT is leveraged in this business opportunity.

For device driven security, the major opportunistic businesses are observed at the commerce layer. At this layer revenue can be generated by providing secure devices for commercial purposes. Examples of devices can range from secure mobile devices to secure IOT devices. Moreover, businesses in commerce layer can vary from encryption software, applications, and VPN providers which secure devices and contents. Also, secure devices can create business in the context layer if they can secure specific contexts like military context. There is prospective business in the connectivity layer pertaining to device driven security for the self-driving vehicles where vehicle to vehicle communication will exist. Thus, device driven security can be implemented in these contexts for mesh networks to secure vehicle to vehicle communication. Some of the security concepts implemented here are encryption, authentication and VPN.

The above discussion of business model options for cyber security should not be considered exhaustive rather as an inception to designing more business models with higher revenue generation. For creating security provisioning business model is used as a boundary spanning unit of analysis (Zott et al., 2011; Zott & Amit, 2010; Amit & Zott, 2001).

An organization that has a business opportunity and is also able to establish a required level of security by investing an additional amount, can serve as a business model framework for prospective revenue generating business models. The cybersecurity business models is an integration of the 4C business model [33,34] and the four major security provisioning scenarios. The 4C typology of ICT business models, aids us in creating market players and also explains where the highest opportunity for more players is. From a business perspective, this business model framework can be very helpful for recognizing viable opportunity and subsequently design organization specific business models.

CONCLUSION

This chapter entails the concept of cybersecurity and its dire need to the businesses today. It elucidates the various business models and provides an integrated system of the various business models, the security provisioning and the various cybersecurity technologies that can be leveraged for an optimum business performance. Security issues are not only a concern confronted by the businesses offering security solutions, however cyber threats are a challenge for any device connected to internet as they are vulnerable to attack. The development of ICT has made hyperconnectivity ubiquitous that has made cyber security imperative for any business operations. However, it is not just a technical challenge but also undermines what kind of business model exists with the provisioning of security. Thus, the business model approach can aid companies in unleashing the opportunistic business avenues and eventually acquire monetary gains.

REFERENCES

Afuah, A. (2004). *Business Models: A Strategic Management Approach*. McGraw-Hill/Irwin.

Liaropoulus, A. (2012). War and ethics in cyberspace: Cyber-conflict and just war theory. In Leading Issues in Information Warfare and Security Research, (2nd ed.), pp. 121-134. Good news digital books.

Onetti, A., Zucchella, A., Jones, M. V., & McDougall-Covin, P. P. (2012). Internationalization, innovation and entrepreneurship: Business models for new technology-based firms. *The Journal of Management and Governance*, *16*(3), 337–368. doi:10.100710997-010-9154-1

B. W. Wirtz, O. Schilke and S. Ullrich. (2010). Strategic Development of Business Models: Implications of the Web 2.0 for Creating Value on the Internet. *Long Range Plann.*, *43*, 272-290.

Beggs, C. (2006). Proposed risk minimization measures for cyber-terrorism and SCADA networks in australia. In *Proceedings of the 5th European Conference on Information Warfare and Security*, pp. 9.

Zott, C., Amit, R., & Massa, L. (2011). The business model: Recent developments and future research. *Long Range Planning*, *37*, 1019–1042.

Zott, C. & Amit, R. (2010). Business Model Design: An Activity System Perspective. *Long Range Plann., 43*, 216-226.

Bodeau, D. J., Graubart, R., & Fabius-Greene, J. (2010). Improving cyber security and mission assurance via cyber preparedness (cyber prep) levels. In *2010 IEEE Second International Conference on Social Computing*, (pp. 1147-1152). IEEE. 10.1109/SocialCom.2010.170

Teece, D. J. (2010). Business Models, Business Strategy and Innovation. *Long Range Plann., 43*, 172-194.

Earnst & Young. (2016). *Cyber preparedness: the next step for boards*. EY. https://www.ey.com/gl/en/issues/governance-and-reporting/eycyber-preparedness-the-next-step-for-boards

Chesbrough, H., & Rosenbloom, R. S. (2002, June 01). The role of the business model in capturing value from innovation: Evidence from Xerox Corporation's technology spin-off companies. *Industrial and Corporate Change*, *11*(3), 529–555. doi:10.1093/icc/11.3.529

Chesbrough, H. (2010). Business Model Innovation: Opportunities and Barriers. *Long Range Plann., 43,* 354-363.

Dobrian, J. (2015). Are you sitting on a cyber security bombshell? *Journal of Property Management*, *80*, 8–12.

Gomes, J. F., Ahokangas, G., & Owusu, K. A. (2016). Business modeling facilitated cyber preparedness. Conference Proceedings from European Wireless, (pp. 1-12).

Gomes, J. F., Ahokangas, P., & Moqaddamerad, S. (2016). Business modeling options for distributed network functions virtualization: Operator perspective. In *Conference Proceedings from European Wireless 2016*, (pp. 37).

Mitola, J., Guerci, J., Reed, J., Yao, Y. D., Chen, Y., Clancy, T. C., Dwyer, J., Li, H., Man, H., McGwier, R., & Guo, Y. (2014). Accelerating 5G QoE via public- private spectrum sharing. *IEEE Communications Magazine*, *52*(5), 77–85. doi:10.1109/MCOM.2014.6815896

Richardson, J. (2008). The business model: An integrative framework for strategy execution. *Strategic Change, 17*(5-6), 133–144. doi:10.1002/jsc.821

Lehto, M. (2015). *"Phenomena in the cyber world," in Cyber Security: Analytics, Technology and Automation*. Springer International Publishing. doi:10.1007/978-3-319-18302-2

Morris, M., Schindehutte, M., & Allen, J. (2005). The entrepreneur's business model: toward a unified perspective. *Journal of Business Research, 58*, 726-735.

Vatis, M. (2002). *Cyber attacks: Protecting America's security against digital threats*. Harvard Kennedy School.

NATO. (2013). The history of cyber attacks - a timeline. NATO. https://www.nato.int/docu/review/2013/cyber/timeline/EN/index.htm

Ulsch, N. M. (2014). *Cyber Threat!: How to Manage the Growing Risk of Cyber Attacks*. John Wiley & Sons. doi:10.1002/9781118915028

Ahokangas, P. (2015, January 29). Vertical, horizontal and oblique business models (Blog). *Technology & Business & Strategy & Internationalization & Futures*. http://techbusstratintfutures.blogspot.fi/

Ahokangas, P. Moqaddamerad, S. Matinmikko, M. Abouzeid, A. Atkova, I Gomes, J. F., & Iivari, M. (2016). *Future micro operators business models in 5G*, 143-149.

Ballon, P. (2007). Business modelling revisited: The configuration of control and value. *Info, 9*(5), 6–19. doi:10.1108/14636690710816417

Timmers, P. (1998). Business Models for Electronic Markets. *Electronic Markets, 8*, 3-8.

Weill, P Vitale, M. (2002). What it infrastructure capabilities are needed to implement e-business models? MIS Quarterly, 1, 17. .

Ponemon Institute. (2015). *2015 cost of data breach study: Global analysis*. Ponemon Institute, LLC.

Alt, R., & Zimmermann, H. (2001). Introduction to Special Section - Business Models. *Electronic Markets, 11*, 1019.

Amit, R., & Zott, C. (2001). Value creation in E-business. *Strategic Management Journal, 22*(6-7), 493–520. doi:10.1002mj.187

McCusker, R. (2006). Transnational organised cyber crime: Distinguishing threat from reality. *Crime, Law, and Social Change*, *46*(4-5), 257–273. doi:10.100710611-007-9059-3

Herzog, S. (2011). Revisiting the Estonian Cyber Attacks: Digital Threats and Multinational Responses. *Journal of Strategic Security, 4*, 49-60.

Shafer, S. M., Smith, H. J., & Linder, J. C. (2005). The power of business models. *Business Horizons*, *48*(3), 199–207. doi:10.1016/j.bushor.2004.10.014

Yrjölä, S., Ahokangas, P., & Matinmikko, M. (2015) Evaluation of recent spectrum sharing concepts from business model scalability point of view. In *2015 IEEE International Symposium on Dynamic Spectrum Access Networks (DySPAN)*, (pp. 241-250). 10.1109/DySPAN.2015.7343907

Statista, (2016). Internet of Things (IoT): number of connected devices worldwide from 2012 to 2020 (in billions). *Statista*: https://www.statista.com/statistics/471264/iot-number-of-connected-devices-worldwide/

Scully, T. (2014). The cyber security threat stops in the boardroom. *Journal of Business Continuity & Emergency Planning*, *7*, 138–148. PMID:24457325

U. S. Chamber of Commerce. (2015). *The case for enhanced protection of trade secrets in the trans-pacific partnership agreement.* US Chamber of Commerce.

Pinto, Z. (2013, March 13). Cyber Security - product of service? *Automation World*: http://www.automationworld.com/security/cyber-security-productor-service

Chapter 12
Implementation of Big Data in Modern Business:
Fraud Detection and Prevention Techniques

Arshiya Begum Mohammed
King Khalid University, Saudi Arabia

Asfia Sabahath
King Khalid University, Saudi Arabia

ABSTRACT

The term big data was started in the year of 2012 and since then it has emerged as one of the top trends in the business and technology world. Big data is referred to as massive amounts of data or information in business and technology. Many organizations are collecting, storing, and analyzing vast amounts of data in today's world. This data is commonly referred to as big data due to its volume, velocity, and variety of forms it takes. Businesses are recognizing the potentiality of big data and processing it to analyze the business. The development of big data tools has a significant impact on managerial decision-making in modern business. The key to success in big data implementation includes a clear business objective, a strong data infrastructure, skilled people, a strong decision-making team, and the correct analytical tools. The main objective of this chapter is to find the challenges, and implementation of big data, and how big data revolutionizes fraud detection and prevention methods in modern business.

DOI: 10.4018/978-1-6684-6581-3.ch012

INTRODUCTION

We are living in the era of big data (BD) and as a result, big data is appearing in almost all organizations including meteorology, genomics, physics simulations, biological and environmental research, finance, business, and healthcare. Big data research typically defines in terms of four characteristics: volume, variety, velocity, and veracity (Wiener et al., n.d.). Volume is the amount of data captured or processed, variety is the range of data sources and types, velocity is the speed or frequency with which data are recorded and analyzed, and veracity is the reliability of the captured data.

Figure 1. Trends of Big Data (Google, 2014)

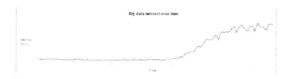

In figure 1, Google trends reveal the emerging interest in big data since 2012. This interest predicts the significance big data is believed to have on our society soon. Suppose that big data may change how people live their everyday lives, their work, and how their homes are connected. Probably one of the most discussed big data technologies in the civil world is Google's self-driving car, which is an excellent example of how big data technology might change the way we used to do everyday activities, like driving a car. Like the computer, there are indicators that big data will shape our lives and the business world as the first personal computers did at the end of the 20th century.

Organizations that utilize data are the innovators working with this technology due to their business model. Well-known companies like Amazon, Google, and Teradata and large conglomerate corporations like GE have not only invested heavily in big data but are already using it in their operations. This development will likely spread to other more traditional business sectors. especially in logistics, E-Commerce, Insurance, and Healthcare, big data has already started playing an important role and is transforming businesses.

Scholars and researchers acknowledge the importance of strategic business in big data (Yin & Kaynak, 2015), highlighting big data as "new oil" (Agarwal & Dhar, 2014; Babiceanu & Seker, 2016; Brynjolfsson et al., 2011; Constantiou & Kallinikos, 2015; George et al., 2014). For example (Samuel, 2016) the BD offers unknown opportunities to rise competitive advantages, thus considering it, "one of the most significant technology disruptions for businesses since the meteoric rise of the Internet and the digital economy". This point of view is supported by observed findings, which have suggested that organizations using BD performs well than those that do not use it in terms of productivity and profitability (Agarwal, n.d.).

Analogous, the business model concept has risen, increasing attention from both practice and research since the dot com revolution in the year 1990(Hartmann et al., 2016). The business Model describes the rationale of how an organization creates, delivers, and captures value, in economic, social, cultural, or other contexts. To prepare their business model for the future of their organizations are increasingly trying to use new methods and technologies in the business model such as wearable mini sensors and the Industrial Internet of Things (Chen et al., 2017), giving rise to the phenomena known as the big data business model (Sawy & Pereira, 2013).

The rise of business data business management systems (BDBMs) explains that business data and related technologies should not be seen as simple assets or resources but had to be set as strategic capabilities that can support organizational value creation and capture (Ehret & Wirtz, 2017; Marabelli & Markus, 2017; Osterwalder et al., 2005; Woerner & Wixom, 2015; Zuboff, 2015). The rise of business data can also entail the consequences such as those who recently experienced Facebook over data privacy.

The Vs of Big Data

The term big data is used in a variety of contexts, to define better its technologies and characteristics, it is necessary to first focus on its key characteristics.

Big Data is characterized by a collection of vast data sets (and with a great diversity of data types (Volume), generated very rapidly (Variety). The original Velocity) three Vs (Volume, Velocity, and Variety) were introduced in the year of 2001 by Doug Laney from Metagroup. Those days, Laney did not use the term 'Big Data, but he visualized that e-commerce accelerated data generation with incompatible formats and structures pushing traditional data management principles to their limits (Laney, 2001). Because of the massive amount of data and the variety of its sources, another characteristic of Big Data is the inherent error, noise, and induced bias of erratic data (Veracity) (Akter et al., 2016; Bharadwaj et al., 2016; Bhimani, 2015; Gupta & George, 2016; Loebbecke & Picot, 2015; Schroeder, 2016). This type of data is difficult to process by traditional data processing platforms, such as relational databases, and difficult to analyze with traditional techniques, such as data mining. Big Data refers to technologies that involve data that are too huge, diverse, and fast-changing to be processed efficiently with conventional techniques. The combination of the original three Vs and this fourth characteristic of Big Data is generally adopted as the Big Data Vs, depicted in Figure 2 and presented in Table 1.

Figure 2. The four V's of Big Data

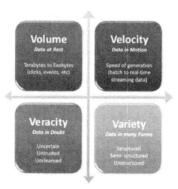

Table 1. The four V's of Big Data

Characteristics	Description
Volume	How much data: the amount of data that organizations try to harness to improve decision-making across the enterprise
Velocity	How fast data are created: How quickly the data can be available for analysis.
Variety	The various types of data: the different types of structured and unstructured data that can be collected by any organization, in terms of text, audio, or video
Veracity	How accurate data can be: The trust in data might be impaired by the data being uncertain or unpredictable, like the originality of the data source, trust

Recently more Vs have been proposed such as variability, which refers to constantly changing (Hilbert, 2015). Variability, which refers to data whose meaning is Variability gives the temporal dimension to the mentioned four Vs and thus could also be viewed as a property of the data itself.

One important part of Big Data is its value (Chen, 2014). The value of Big Data is multiple. Its inherent value of data in terms of the information contained and its worth in money (e.g., for reselling purposes). Processing Big Data and looking for correlations, predicting consumer behaviors, financial risk, and sentiment analysis lead to huge potentials in terms of e.g., dollar savings, market penetration analysis, or user satisfaction improvement.

The Business Importance of Big Data

The volume of data generated, stored, and mined for insights has now become economically relevant to businesses, governments, and consumers. The use of Big Data is now becoming an important way for raising organizations to outperform their peers. According to Wikibon Executive Summary 2015 (Hilbert, 2015; Mikalef et al., 2017; Schroeder, 2016; Wikibon, n.d.), the growth of the Big Data market started to slow down in 2014 (see Figure 3), although it remains significantly faster than other IT markets. According to Wikibon, in the period 2011-2026, the Big Data market growth will reach up to 17%.

Figure 3. Big data market growth expectations

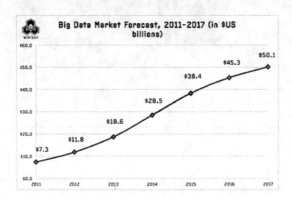

Big Data can help in business and industry by building new applications that were not possible before, developing competitiveness, and improving customer satisfaction by reducing costs, better segmenting customers to precisely customize the products and services, designing next-generation products, and reducing their time to the market.

Practical implementations of Big Data

In general, big data enables organizations and governments to acquire new insights into their environment. The possibilities are countless and will grow soon. It will help organizations comprehend business from different angles and unveil issues or occurrences that could not be revealed before. Probably one of the most interesting characteristics of big data is the ability to predict future scenarios with very high accuracy. This might be in near future, having an impact on business, prototype systems already today are using predictive analytics, for instance, predicting areas in a municipality where crimes are likely to happen at every moment (IBM, 2014). The same technology also uses Google's self-driving car to expect the next move of other drivers in the traffic and adjust its moves accordingly. The core of predictive analytics is the assumption that everything follows certain schemes. With enough data available the data scientist and ultimately their databases can recognize schemes out of millions of petabytes worth of data.

Analytics Methods

Big data and its analysis can be comprised of multiple very different methods of analysis. Some of the methods have been utilized already for decades in business, however, along with big data technology they have become more accurate, and analysis can consider a higher variety of parameters. The different analysis methods focus on different information that can be found within the data. The same data may be used as the basis for all different analysis methods, however, the results of the analysis may show a different picture, even though the same data was used.

Descriptive Analytics

Descriptive analytics is the use of historic data to describe mostly past events and describe a given situation. In a business case, this may be the analysis of past marketing events, campaigns, or demographics of a population. The intention is to understand and built a clear aspect of past events.

Diagnostic Analytics

Diagnostic analytics help to discover correlations, mostly using visual tools. These correlations may trigger further investigation. As mentioned before, the results are mostly presented visually and do not aim to give a too accurate picture of a given situation. The major aspect is to unveil hidden correlations that may affect e.g., a market. This may be interesting in marketing, where diagnostic analytics can help to identify micro markets or certain patterns in customer behavior.

Predictive Analytics/ Data Analytics

Predictive analytics is the most popular analytics in the field of big data analytics. The curiosity possibly derives from the fact that predictive analytics can predict a future scenario with very high accuracy. Predictive analytics is often used to predict sales figures and forecasts of a different kind (Payandeh, 2013). However, they may also be used in robotics. Theoretically, an industrial robot or mechanism with access to predictive analytics may be very useful in the prevention of accidents, e.g., in the automotive industry. The possibilities here are very vast and leave a lot of space for imagination because this is one of the latest developments in big data technology

Prescriptive Analytics

Prescriptive analysis is the automated analysis of data that creates predictions and suggests decision options (Evans, 2012). This sort of analytics can mostly be found in industrial operations or inventory management. Prescriptive analytics follows clear schemes and offers a few decision options. This sort of analysis has been used for a long time already; however, with increasing amounts of data, the offered options by the analysis are more comprehensive and able to consider a greater number of parameters, thus making the information more accurate.

Big Data Challenges

Big data creates challenges not only in its implementation but also challenges lawmakers to find new appropriate limitations to this new use of data. Organizations will struggle in the starting years of implementation of big data to define roles and encourage the use of big data in organizations. Data quality is one of the biggest challenges in data management and utilization of data quality. To gain valuable information from data, the data need to be of good quality. In the era of big data, with huge amounts of data, organizations face challenges in maintaining a sufficient level of data quality. An entire industry that deals with data management and quality assurance have emerged from this important need to assure the highest level of data quality (Forbes, 2014).

In this section, we will look at the theoretical requirements of data and the steps that organizations have taken to maintain a high degree of data quality. The prerequisite for accurate data is that the data collection must be set up correctly as per the technology configured for data collection. Good data quality is expressed mainly by the data's availability for its purpose. Only sufficient data quality can allow analytical departments of an organization, like Business Intelligence or Business Analytics, to conduct reliable analyses and reports. Speaking about big data quality, the terms volume, variety, and velocity of data are crucial elements of reliable and appropriate data. Apart from these, the availability of data, cleanliness, and correct data contribute significantly to the value and usability of data. especially the cleanliness of data represents a major challenge (Int. Assoc. for Information and Data Quality, 2013).

To achieve a good level of quality data Master Data Management can manually work in small systems. Big data, however, is in volume simply too vast to be under manual surveillance. Systematic solutions, provided by major players in the data industry like Teradata or IBM have developed solutions to tackle this problem (IBM, 2014). In general, data quality is more dependent on the business culture, rather than the IT systems. Inadequate data quality is often the result of poor data entry. Therefore, it is important to promote a detail-oriented approach within the organization to assure a high and consistent level of data quality. IT solutions to a certain extent, systematically improve data errors. In many organizations, this can already be achieved by limiting the scope of manual data input. The implementation of a Master Data Management team can help to minimize fluctuations in data quality as well as create a central reference and maintenance point for data issues (Microsoft, 2006).

As mentioned earlier, the industry has already recognized the challenges of data quality. Standards, for example, ISO 8000 have been developed to create guidelines and assure a robust minimum of quality. For years, quality management has been an important part of operations. In the last few years, quality management has also reached the data management of the business. The exponentially growing amount of data has made it challenging for organizations to maintain their current approach to data and quality. The realization that new approaches are required in the future is making it slowly into organizations and has reached a stage of 17 early adopters. It is a process of transition. The easier part is the implementation of the required IT. Significantly more difficult is the work that change management has to do in terms of changing the company culture and educating a literacy in data treatment.

BIG DATA IN MODERN BUSINESS MARKETING

Today Consumers have changed. They have put down the newspaper in favor of skimming through TV commercials and unsolicited emails. Consumers now have new options that better suit their digital lifestyle. New school marketers (Michael Minelli et al., 2013) deliver what today's consumers want relevant interactive communication across the top digital power channels, including email, mobile, social, display, and the web. Big data and analytics have become part of marketing strategies that offer benefits for various marketing activities (Palmatier & Martin, n.d.). To understand this, we begin with the marketing environment, Precision Targeting, and big data's role in value creation, communication, and delivery.

Understanding the Marketing Environment

A marketing environment is vast and diverse, with factors that are both controllable and uncontrollable. A good grasp of the marketing environment helps to identify opportunities, identify threats, and manage changes to maintain growth in a dynamic economy. Big data and analytics are used to understand the marketing environment that can benefit the firm's operations (Palmatier & Martin, n.d.). Marketers who have access to data and analytics can identify issues when customers interact directly with environmental factors and decide how to align themselves accordingly. As result, big data and analytics are critical tools for a company in which customers freely provide personal information about sensitive issues that are accessible via social media analytics and information (Merrill, 2016).

Precision Targeting

Marketers have learned that the customer's data can help them understand and navigate the situation by revealing customer beliefs and ideologies (Palmatier & Martin, n.d.). This data enables them to segment specific markets and target the desirable customer groups with great precision. Understanding the characteristics of the customer such as age, gender, and geography allows marketers to deploy their resources more effectively and reach the customer more strategically. Such a precise understanding of customers and the ability to target them with products and services is the key promise of big data.

Big Data's Role in Value Creation, Communication, and Delivery

Big data and analytics can improve the way marketing is carried out; they assist the marketer in creating value more successfully through enhanced offerings and customer experiences (Palmatier & Martin, n.d.). Analytics allow for real-time changes that reflect the customer's interaction with various features and attributes. Companies like Ford Motor Company, Nike, and Julep Cosmetics (Post, 2014; Underwood, 2014) use big data and real-time customer feedback to improve their products. Similarly, marketers can use data analytics to test pricing strategies, such as dynamic pricing applications, which allow marketers to change prices in real-time in response to customer demand. This logic underpins Uber's surge pricing mechanic, which adjusts fees to reflect peak demand times and destination (Kedmey, 2014), as well as airlines, which charge different customers different fares for identical flights (Rizzo, 2018).

Value communication to customers involves targeted advertising in which the customer is reached through the media they use, describing products and services that are ideally tailored to them, representing an ideal form of big data marketing (Palmatier & Martin, n.d.). New approaches to highly targeted ads enable researchers to determine the need for companies to be more transparent in their uses, grant customers control over the personal settings that lead to a suggestion for a specific ad, and provide a clear justification for using communication methods (John et al., 2018). An alternative to the targeted approach to customer communication is a real-time promotion in their geographic proximity, which combines the benefits of big data for both value communication and value delivery (Palmatier & Martin, n.d.). Value delivery using big data has evolved in getting the product and services to customers in the desired form and at a time convenient to the customer.

Proactive Customer Service

Big data has revolutionized customer service by allowing businesses to anticipate their customers' needs before they even express them. This type of proactive customer service will transform businesses that want to distinguish themselves with superior customer service. Big data analysis could enable representatives to contact customers proactively on accounts where predictive analysis indicates that the customer may have an issue in the future (Business, n.d.).

Customer-Responsive Products

Big data not only improves customer service by being more proactive, but it also enables businesses to create customer-responsive products. Product design meets the needs of customers in ways that were previously never possible. Instead of relying on customers to know what they want in a product, data analytics can be used to predict the information. Customers' data is shared with their preferences, allowing for a more accurate picture of what a future product should be (Business, n.d.).

Improvements in Operational Efficiency

Big data is a massive amount of information about every product and process, and industrial engineers are focused on analyzing big data to improve the efficiency of processes. Big data analysis works with constraints, where the data makes constraints easier to recognize and identify. The binding constraint can result in a significant increase in performance and throughput for the business (Business, n.d.).

Reduced Costs

Customers' information is now being used by modern businesses to identify trends and accurately predict future events in their respective industries. Knowing when something is likely to occur improves forecasting and planning, allowing planners to determine what to produce, how to produce it, and how much inventory to keep on hand (Business, n.d.).

Bringing Bigdata into Modern Businesses Marketing

When integrating big data into modern business, there are a few principles to follow for any size business (Glass & Callahan, 2015).

Customer Need

The businesses put their attention on their customers and use data to better understand them, which helps them understand prospects. When analyzing a customer, it is important to determine what traits they share, where to find more of them, what behaviors indicate a customer is likely to switch to a competitor, and what steps can be taken to retain them.

It's Big Data, but Start Small

When integrating big data into processes, the amount of data that the business has is collected through its website where each website visitor is, a company could collect data based on its visitor demographic, could determine whether the customer is a repeat visitor, could track her onsite behavior, and could analyze what drove her to the site with the help of many other pieces of information.

For several reasons, starting small makes sense. It won't strain the technology budget, to start. Second, it makes it possible to build the big data process in a controlled manner, and third, it allows for small data wins that can ultimately lead to budget allocation and buy-in from the decision-makers (Glass & Callahan, 2015).

Technology

Technology is an integral part of marketing. Choosing the right technology, to begin with integrating the data management platform to analyze the needs of the customer, the buyer's journey, and the company culture. Transforming the traditional marketing strategies with marketing and business analysis in the era of big data is shown in figure 4 where different consumers have different consumption purposes with various consumers (Hu, 2018).

Conduct a Data Audit

Many businesses collect a large amount of data but fail to effectively use it. A data audit assists in identifying what data they have access to and provides a better understanding of what data they require to increase revenue and profit (Glass & Callahan, 2015). Customer service has a separate database from sales, which has different data than marketing, which has different data than the e-commerce platform, which has different data than an advertising agency. Many marketers consolidate this database into a single database that provides a comprehensive view of the customer.

Figure 4. From Database to BI

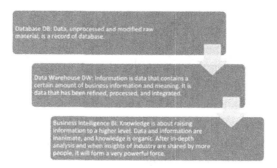

Practice Good Data Hygiene

Databases are essential in the digital age, and they must be kept up to date. The quality of a database has an unprecedented impact on the success of modern marketing campaigns. To ensure these databases are productive, marketers must maintain good data hygiene. To keep data accurate, the data entry team plays a critical role, and customer data must be updated regularly by requesting updated contact information. Use appropriate software to speed up the process of cleansing, correcting, and appending email and postal addresses (Glass & Callahan, 2015).

LITERATURE REVIEW

This research is based on literature from various sources. The research features books from well-known opinion leaders in the field of technology and big data, scientific journal articles, blog entries of established authors in the field of big data, and various online materials maintained by well-known publishers.

Over the last few years, the world of business involved in various technologies and business advancements worldwide which results in an effect on consumers, businesses, and organizations. Data usage increased; "Big Data" became a very important part of business as it refers to large data sets that cannot be captured, stored, managed, and analyzed by traditional tools (Hilbert, 2015; Mikalef et al., 2017; Schroeder, 2016; Wikibon, n.d.).

The Big Data Journal is entirely dedicated to the new business trend which gives more specific insights into the role big data will play in organizations and is presenting findings from a data science perspective. This rather new discipline, which is most likely the area that will host big data as an academic field, points out the benefits big data can have on business decisions. It however also points out that big data is only at a very early stage of its development (Schroeder, 2016). The authors demand that big data must find a way and establish itself as an academic discipline, which will help organizations and schools provide the skills that big data will require to be used efficiently. This is following an article in the Ivey Business Journal titled "Why big data is the new competitive advantage (2012) (Academia.edu, n.d.; Research Gate, n.d.). Since big data is a topic with high relevance to business, but the core development happens in IT, a general understanding of the technology behind big data is beneficial to the reader. Jeffrey Needham has a series of books with a big data focus. "Disruptive Possibilities: How Big Data Changes Everything (2013)", outlines the basis of the technical issues related to big data and provides fundamentals to understand big data as a technology.

Most published works and opinion leaders have a positive attitude toward big data and its development. Neil Richards and Jonathan King however approached big data from neither a technological nor a business perspective (Blasiak, 2014). In a Stanford Law Review paper titled" Three Paradoxes of Big Data" (2013) both voiced a critical opinion towards big data and its impact on privacy and security. The benefits for the business may be tremendous, but big data has also the capability of being one of the biggest threats to privacy in recent years. (Blasaik, 2014; Blasiak, 2014)

In Big data Creating Value from the Data Cycle, Dr. Veera Mani (Happiest Minds, n.d.; IBM Big Data Hub, n.d.) discussed Business in the era of big data, the scope for every sector and every field to make great use of Big Data in enabling better lives for users. To make it understand the concept more precisely he gave examples for deeper levels of understanding and targeting customers in the largest US retailer, optimizing business processes, driving smarter machines and devices, and smarter financial trading to name a few. He also discussed the data lifecycle phases and their challenges. The end-to-end lifecycle of data involves multiple phases as represented below, with challenges at each phase. Big Data needs contextual management from a haphazard, heterogeneous mix. There is also a question of credibility, uncertainty, and error in understanding the relevance of data. This management of data requires smart systems and better human collaboration for user interaction. A lot of debate on Big Data is focused on the technology aspect. (Happiest Minds, n.d.; IBM Big Data Hub, n.d.) However, there is also much more than the technology required to set up the fundamental basis for managing data analysis. It doesn't reckon to throw away existing structures, warehouses, and analytics. Instead, needs to build upon existing capabilities in data quality, Master Data Management, and data protection frameworks. Data Management needs to be seen from a business perspective, by prioritizing business needs and taking realistic actions.

McKinsey Global Institute May 2011 (Manyika et al., 2011) (Academia.edu, n.d.) report includes five domains for the potential of big data: health care (United States), public sector administration (European Union), retail (United States), manufacturing (global), and personal location data (global). Retail, manufacturing, and personal location data have the potential for business and marketing management areas. On the other hand, Wamba et al. (2015) examines big data-related publications and summarize the distribution of industries. They include that technology, service, and healthcare industries are the main industries for big data publications. As Erevelles et al. (2016) imply companies that do not effectively manage big data processes will have challenges related to competitive advantage and survival of the big data revolution. According to Dijcks (2013), enterprises that combine big data with traditional enterprise data and use it together could reach a better understanding of business. This better understanding ends up with; i) enhanced productivity, ii) greater innovation and iii) a better competitive position. In addition, the big data concept includes many opportunities for marketing decision-making, as consumers are important actors in the market or data environment. Therefore, managing big data and related processes is crucial for new marketing decision-making.

BIG DATA COMPARATIVE ANALYSIS

Big Data Market Analysis

The three main drivers of analytics, Big Data, and Business Intelligence (BI) expenditures today are improving operational performance, putting more emphasis on critical activities that lead to entering new markets and developing new business models, and enhancing consumer attention. Enterprises now have the chance to compete and advance in areas where they had little visibility before thanks to the insights concealed in unstructured data that are being released. The intricacy of B2B selling and service interactions, healthcare services, and maintenance, repair, and overhaul (MRO) of complicated machinery are a few examples of these fields. p-ISSN: 2395-0072 Predictive analytics will draw 40% of firms' net new investment in Business Intelligence and Analytics by 2020, according to the Roundup of Analytics, Big Data & BI decision-making Market Estimates for 2016. (Nadkarni & Vesset, 2016).

Big Data Analytics

Huge amounts of data that can't be processed efficiently by current standard applications are referred to as "big data." The first step in the processing of big data is to analyze the raw data. Big data and predictive analytics have a significant, transformative, and very visible business value. Statistical, Data Mining, Machine Learning, and Deep Learning models are some examples of predictive analytics techniques that analyze data to forecast unknowable future events. Today's models can quickly predict the future using millions of data records and hundreds of predictive variables once the data has been retrieved, categorized, and prepared. Pattern recognition is a specialty of machine learning techniques, and cognitive AI models (using deep learning or neural network approaches) function as decision-making agents that can track, process, and react more quickly than humans (Nadkarni & Vesset, 2016).

Important conclusions from IDC regarding the market for Big Data products and services from 2016 to 2020. The market for Big Data technologies and services is anticipated to develop at a compound annual growth rate (CAGR) of 22.6% from 2015 to 2020 and reach $58.9 billion in that year. According to estimates, revenue for Big Data infrastructure will increase at a CAGR of 20.3% from 2015 to 2020 and will total $27.7 billion in that year. According to estimates, revenue for big data software will increase at a CAGR of 25.7% from 2015 to 2020 and will total $15.9 billion in that year. Big Data services, which include professional and support services, are anticipated to generate $15.2 billion in revenue in 2020, growing at a CAGR of 23.9% from 2015 to that year.

(Columbus, 2016) "The Big Data technology and services industry will demonstrate significant momentum through 2020, thanks to aggressive DX activities," stated Ashish Nadkarni, program director, Worldwide Infrastructure, and co-lead of Big Data market research at IDC. As the market matures and develops into a section of the larger business analytics market as a whole, it is predicted that year-over-year growth will significantly slow down. to IDC. unaggregated data that is frequently challenging to automate. Big Data, a phrase for enormous amounts of data that are both structured and unstructured, inundates businesses on a daily basis. Big Data can be utilized to analyze insights that can help with decision-making and strategic business actions (Data Science vs. Big Data vs. Data Analytics, 2018).

According to Gartner, "Big Data is high-volume, high-velocity, and/or high-variety information assets that necessitate new, cost-effective methods of information processing to enable improved insight, decision making, and workflow." Large volumes of data are analyzed using big data analytics to find undiscovered patterns, correlations, and other insights. With today's technology, you can analyze your data and get answers from it practically instantaneously; this is feasible because more conventional business intelligence solutions are slower and less effective (Big Data Analytics, n.d.).

Big Data analytics may assist businesses in better understanding the information that resides inside their data and in identifying the data that will be most useful for current and upcoming business decisions. Big Data analysts frequently seek the information that results from data analysis (Vangie Beal, 2018). Tom Davenport, IIA Director of Research, spoke with more than 50 companies for his paper Big Data in Big Companies to better understand how they employed big data. He discovered that they benefited in the following ways.

Big Data technologies such as Hadoop and cloud-based analytics bring significant cost advantages when it comes to storing large amounts of data – plus they can identify more efficient ways of doing business (Big Data Analytics, n.d.). Big data and business analytics worldwide revenues will grow from nearly $122B in 2015 to more than $187B in 2019, an increase of more than 50% over the five-year forecast period. The industries that present the largest revenue opportunities are Discrete Manufacturing ($22.8B in 2019), Banking ($22.1B), and Process Manufacturing ($16.4B). Source: Worldwide Big Data and Business Analytics Revenues Forecast to Reach $187 Billion in 2019, According to Markets and Markets, the global predictive analytics market is expected to grow from $3.85 billion in 2016 to $12.41 billion by 2022 or a CAGR of 22.1%.

Similar growth rates are predicted by Zion Market Research. In its August issue, Faster, Better Decision Making, Forbes writes from a somewhat different angle. Businesses are able to evaluate information promptly and make decisions based on what they have learned thanks to the speed of Hadoop and in-memory analytics, as well as the ability to examine new sources of data (Big Data Analytics, n.d.). brand-new goods and services. Giving customers what they want is made possible by the capacity to use analytics to determine their demands and levels of satisfaction.

Davenport notes that more businesses are developing new goods to satisfy consumer demand thanks to big data analytics (Big Data Analytics, n.d.). Big Data Analytics often makes use of specialist software tools and applications for predictive analytics, data mining, text mining, forecasting, and data optimization to evaluate such a massive amount of data. These procedures work together as distinct but tightly interwoven components of high-performance analytics. By processing extraordinarily huge volumes of data that a company has gathered, an organization can use Big Data tools and software to identify which data is valuable and can be studied to lead to better business decisions in the future.

FRAUDS IN MODERN BUSINESS

Fraud involves significant financial risks that can adversely impact a business's profitability and the image of economic activity (Bănărescu, 2015). Fraud detection powered by big data analytics is used by 75% of respondents who have implemented AI and machine learning in their risk management strategies (Infopulse, n.d.). According to a Thomson Reuters report, financial crime cost businesses an estimated loss of $ 1.45 trillion, and 40.3 people are victims of modern-day slavery (Thomson Reuters, n.d.). Most financial crimes are committed in an effort to commit fraud or other illegal acts, as shown in figure 5 (Thomson Reuters, n.d.).

Modern businesses are using prevailing technology and big data analytics tools to combat economic fraud. Big data analytics use the system to identify patterns and behaviors, allowing fraud to be identified accurately and efficiently. Numerous studies and investigations provide a wide range of different methods for detecting fraud. The majority of the studies focused on internal and external fraudulent activities and proposed various data mining techniques to detect these fraudulent activities.

Fraudulent activities are not limited to specific filed they relate to all the domains, including insurance, healthcare, and network as shown in Figure 6 (Abbassi et al., 2021). Big data is used by financial organizations to reduce operational risk, and combat fraud while significantly alleviating information asymmetry problems and achieving regulatory and compliance objectives.

5.1 Insurance Fraud: With the rapid changes in technology, society, culture, politics, and economics, the insurance industry is playing an increasingly important role in modern economies. Because of the globalization of markets and the ongoing chaining of the business environment, risk and complexity management strategies for individuals, social groups, and businesses all need to include insurance (Al-Rawashdeh & Al Singlawi, 2016).

Insurance companies continuously deal with various risks associated with their services as well as other risks like committing fraud. The goal of an act of insurance fraud is to obtain a fraudulent outcome from the insurance process (Al-Rawashdeh & Al Singlawi, 2016).

Insurance fraud is a significant issue for the industry (Clarke, 1989); it is a real crime that jeopardizes the entire system and affects insurers, customers, businesses, society, and the economy. To obtain an unjustified benefit, insurance fraud can be committed in a variety of ways, including falsifying the preparation of insurance contracts, providing false or omitted information in insurance claims, filing claims for damages under the wrong conditions, inflating the value of the insured property, and fabricating injuries sustained in accidents.

Figure 5. Internal Vs External Perpetrators

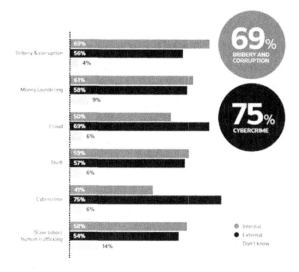

Figure 6. Fraud Domains

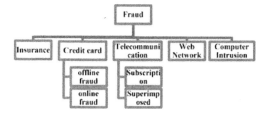

5.2 Credit Card Fraud: Fraud in credit card transactions is the unauthorized use of a user account by someone other than the account owner. It is necessary to put an end to such fraudulent practices to lessen and protect against similar occurrences in the future (Maniraj et al., 2019). Credit card Fraud detection involves monitoring the activities of the user to estimate, perceive or avoid objectionable behavior of fraud, intrusion, and defaulting. This type of fraud can occur in a variety of ways such as offline where the physical card will be stolen and online where the fraud is committed through the web or mobile device (Abbassi et al., 2021).

Telecommunication Fraud

Telecommunication fraud has caused several financial losses to telecommunication customers in modern business. The advancement of the internet, which allows people to access a variety of services at their fingertips, has resulted in the leakage of personal data (Zhao et al., 2018). Telecommunication fraud is the illegal use of telecommunication services to obtain money from a communication service provider or a customer. (Abbassi et al., 2021). It is classified into two types: i) Subscription fraud where the fraudster uses a stolen identity to get services without the intention to pay. ii) Superimposed fraud is a legal account taken by fraudsters (Kou et al., 2004).

5.4 Computer Intrusion: An intrusion is an action that threatens to violate the credibility, security, or availability of resources such as file systems, and user accounts (Abbassi et al., 2021). The evolution of malicious software has become more sophisticated, making it difficult to detect intrusions accurately. Failure to prevent intrusions could degrade the security services, data confidentiality, integrity, and availability (Khraisat et al., 2019). Computer intrusion is traditionally classified into two categories: i) Misuse intrusions catch intrusions in terms of characteristics of known attacks or system vulnerability; this action conforms the attacks against the known weak spots in a system such as denial of service attacks, malicious use of data, etc. ii) Anomaly intrusions is based on the normal behavior of a subject; any action that significantly deviates from the normal behavior.

5.5 Web Network Fraud: Web fraud is defined as the use of network resources or Internet-accessible applications to defraud or exploit victims. It includes (Abbassi et al., 2021)

i. Advertising fraud is a growing concern in the online advertising industry, where web advertising network fraud, is a go-between for internet publishers and advertisers.
ii. Online auction has led to a rise in deception and online criminal activity It involves the misrepresentation or non-delivery of a commodity available for sale.

Fraudulent activities have a negative impact on the reputation of the organization as well as financial losses.

RESEARCH METHODOLOGY

Traditional Fraud Detection Methods

Traditional fraud detection methods used humans, structured data, and discrete analysis as shown in figure 7. Investigators manually reviewed suspicious behavior detected by a rule-based algorithm. Time, human error, and the inability to detect irregular and unusual patterns of behavior that could lead to fraud are the main drawbacks of this method.

Figure 7. Discrete Analysis

The rule-based algorithm is based on the rules set by the expert where the algorithm would not be able to recognize the hidden patterns and predict fraud. The traditional fraud detection method can only analyze structured data like CRM, product silos, and security information, which is stored in an appropriate format.

Endpoint Centric: Secure the Points of Access

Endpoint-centric incorporates authentication for the customer access channels such as a combination of hardware or software ID and the personal identification number (PIN) or a user ID and Password with two-factor authentication. For higher-risk scenarios, three-factor authentication is more secure but also more inconvenient, whereas out-of-band authentication requires separate information channels for authentication and access (Barta & Stewart, n.d.).

Navigation-Centric: Compare Website Behavior with What is Expected

It includes the real-time, dynamic capture of the customer and accounts online activity, which is used to build a customer profile to determine the activity of the customer. The profile of the customer is the rich data store of the customer/account used for real-time decisions (Barta & Stewart, n.d.).

Channel Centric: Understand User and Account by Channel

The Channel Centric has End-to-end enterprise platforms that can address a specific channel and provide extensibility across channels. A strict channel-centric system would detect anomalies at the account level (Barta & Stewart, n.d.).

Novel Fraud Detection Techniques Leveraging Big Data

Digital transformation has transformed the massive volumes of unstructured real-time data of customer engagement and interactions moved online. This has become the biggest security crack for modern business where AI and machine learning algorithms have allowed for the evolution of fraud detection techniques as shown in figure 8 that leverage Big Data to analyze huge data sets and prevent security breaches listed below.

Figure 8. Novel Fraud detection

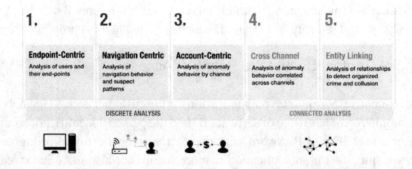

Ad-Hoc Analysis and Sampling

Ad-hoc testing checks transactions for potentially malicious behavior to uncover specific information about its application domain. Using a hypothesis as a starting point, this technique examines the transactions for possible fraud. Ad-hoc testing is labor-intensive and time-consuming because it is based on formulas and queries.

Sampling techniques operate effectively on small data sets but not on overwhelming data volumes. It is a complement to an ad-hoc analysis by providing samples of transactions with fraud risks with highlighting deviations.

Predictive Analysis

Predictive analysis plays an important role in the decision support system where it uses advanced mathematical formulas, statistical algorithms, IT tools, and services to identify dependencies, relationships, and patterns in the datasets and reduces their complexity (Dinov, 2018). Predictive analytics aims to build a model that can predict future events based on historical data using a Machine learning algorithm.

Connected Analysis

Modern data is unstructured, with numbers, text, voice, and gyro sensor readings, and a massive amount of information is hidden in the constant stream of data that represents the pattern of customer behavior. The traditional method's analysis capacity is insufficient to analyze the data, which is where connected data analysis comes in handy. This method provides the linked behaviors and relationships between subjects that aid in the detection of fraudulent activities. The connected analysis consists of Cross-product, Cross Channel, and Entity Link Analysis (Barta & Stewart, n.d.).

i. **Cross-Product, Cross-Channel-Correlate Activity and Alerts by Entity:** It takes the cross-channel approach to score transactions and entities across multiple accounts, products, and channels (Barta & Stewart, n.d.). The real-time fraud decision system for credit and debit cards has added cross-channel detection where the organization monitors the payments to credit card accounts made through phone banking.
ii. Entity Link Analysis-Gain Holistic Perspective of Related Customers

It analyzes the activities and relationships within a network of related entities for the customers who share the demographic data or transactions. Entity link analysis helps in detect and prevent fraud (Barta & Stewart, n.d.)

- By Identifying the pattern of behavior that appears suspicious when viewed across related accounts or entities.
- By discovering the networks associated with an identified suspicious account, entity, or individual to determine if a case is limited to an individual or part of a criminal conspiracy.

Continuous Analysis

It monitors transaction and user activities continuously using an algorithm that processes the data and revises its patterns in real time. Continuous analytics, as opposed to the traditional rule-based approach, offer the chance for new insights based on its findings where consistency is the key to fraud detection.

Social Network Analysis (SNA)

A social network analysis examines the relationships to describe individuals and groups as parts of a social structure. Individuals interact with each other, and these interactions provide insight into the individual involved (Barta & Stewart, n.d.). The relationship enables the information flow across a network enabling one individual to influence another. It expands the scope of valuable data by extracting additional value from the relationships.

Advanced Behavioral and Cognitive Analytics

Big data technology transforms structured and unstructured data into data storage with Operational Data Lakes (ODL). Open-source frameworks are provided by well-known big data processing platforms like Apache Hadoop, Apache Storm, Google BigQuery, and others. These platforms enable parallel processing by distributing enormous data sets across many servers and have opened novel approaches to data processing. The Deep analytics technique represents an evolution where it analyzes the behavioral patterns of each customer (Spending, transaction patterns, average balance, geolocation, etc.) can detect anomalies, and identify potentially fraudulent activity. It searches for patterns and connections between similar attacks and develops real-time algorithms for detecting suspicious activity.

AVOIDING FINANCIAL LOSSES WITH BIG DATA AND MACHINE LEARNING

Risk measurement is a top priority for any financial institution. When dealing with millions of sensitive personal files, identifying a potential threat possibly becomes a primary goal of any modern business. A fraud detection solution powered by big data is a possible solution to address global cybersecurity threats. When combined with machine learning and cloud computing, such solutions make real-time processing and analysis of massive amounts of streaming data possible. Fraud detection plays a major role in contributing to the company's information security and protection from external and internal threats. In recent years, internal fraud is more among society and is similar to that credit card fraud where the fraudulent collects data from telephone conversations, website visits, employee transactions, and other work-related activities. These data allow for the creation of patterns that helps in prevention of the internal fraudulent activities.

How Big Data and Machine Learning Works Together

Big data analytics using machine learning algorithms is a logical next step for businesses trying to optimize the potential value of their data. Machine learning tools examine data sets using data-driven algorithms and statistical models, then draw conclusions from found patterns or make predictions based on them. As they operate against the data, the algorithms learn from it, as opposed to conventional rule-based analytics systems that execute explicit instructions.

Big data analytics is the process of exploring and analyzing large amounts of data. It combines data mining, predictive modeling, statistical analysis, and machine learning. The cornerstone of modern AI applications, machine learning provides considerable value to organizations by deriving higher-level insights from big data than other types of analytics can deliver.

Without explicitly obeying predefined instructions or preprogrammed code, machine learning systems are capable of learning from data over time and adapting. In the past, businesses created intricate, rules-based systems for a wide variety of analytics and reporting functions, but they were frequently fragile and unable to manage continuously shifting business requirements. Companies are now better positioned to continuously enhance their decision-making, business processes, and predictive analytics capabilities thanks to machine learning.

Machine learning and big data are not necessarily exclusive or antagonistic ideas. On the contrary, they offer the chance to achieve some amazing effects when combined. In reality, handling all the V's of big data effectively contributes to improving the precision and power of machine learning models. Effective big data management strategies help machine learning by providing analytics teams with the vast amounts of relevant, high-quality data they need to properly construct those models.

The effectiveness of big data analytics augmented by machine learning has already been recognized by numerous enterprises. For instance, Netflix makes better recommendations by using machine learning algorithms to comprehend each user's viewing interests and help them stay on the streaming service longer. Similarly, to this, Google employs machine learning to give consumers a better-tailored experience. This applies not only to search but also to email predictive text and Google Maps users' optimized instructions.

The rate of data generation keeps increasing at an incredible rate. IDC, a market research company, projects that in 2025, 180 zettabytes of data would be produced and copied globally, nearly double the 64.2 zettabytes it estimated for 2020. Enterprises will only be able to make sense of the massive amounts of data they will inevitably keep and analyze without the aid of machine learning (Tech Target, 2021).

More businesses are combining big data, machine learning, and data visualization tools to power predictive and prescriptive analytics applications that aid business leaders in making better decisions, thanks to the work of data scientists, machine learning engineers, and other data management and analytics professionals. It won't come as a surprise if businesses that don't combine big data and machine learning fall behind rivals that do in the coming years (Tech Target, 2021).

DISCUSSION AND CONCLUSION

In this chapter, we have shown how big data in modern business helps in the detection and prevention of fraud using Big data analytics. Big data analytics is a potent tool that helps to both identify and prevent security risks and fraudulent activity. Data is the most valuable asset in a modern-day business where the consumers play an important role in the economy of the business and are sensitive when it comes to their security. Fraud detection is not only essential in the financial term but also regarding customer retention.

Big data are being used in fraud detection by a financial institution for client onboarding and KYC checks, anti-money laundering and terrorist financial screening on a shared platform, and detection of suspicious activities during ongoing monitoring.

In Modern business, Data is not just an IT asset; it is an essential component of the banking and financial sector's digital transformation. The latter calls for a high level of cybersecurity, which businesses can ensure by relying on cutting-edge, Big Data-powered fraud detection tools.

REFERENCES

Abbassi, El Alaoui, & Gahi. (2021). Fraud Detection Techniques in the Big Data Era. Proceedings of the 2nd International Conference on Big Data, Modelling and Machine Learning (BML 2021), 161-170.

Academia.edu. (n.d.). https://www.academia.edu/76334718/Big_data_the_management_revolution

Agarwal & Dhar. (n.d.). Editorial—Big Data, Data Science, and Analytics: The Opportunity and Challenge for IS Research. doi:10.1287/isre.2014.0546

Agarwal, R., & Dhar, V. (2014). Big data, data science, and analytics: The opportunity and challenge for IS research. *Information Systems Research*, *25*(3), 443–448. doi:10.1287/isre.2014.0546

Akter, S., Wamba, S. F., Gunasekaran, A., Dubey, R., & Childe, S. J. (2016). How to improve firm performance using big data analytics capability and business strategy alignment? *International Journal of Production Economics*, *182*, 113–131. doi:10.1016/j.ijpe.2016.08.018

Al-Rawashdeh, F., & Al Singlawi, O. (2016). The Existence of Fraud Indicators in Insurance Industry: Case of Jordan. *International Journal of Economics and Financial Issues*, *6*(S5), 168–176.

Anandkumar, R., Dinesh, K., & Ahmed, J. (2022). Securing e-Health application of cloud computing using hyperchaotic image encryption framework, Computers and Electrical Engineering, 100. doi:10.1016/j.compeleceng.2022.107860

Babiceanu, R. F., & Seker, R. (2016). Big data and virtualization for manufacturing cyber-physical systems: A survey of the current status and future outlook. *Computers in Industry*, *81*, 128–137. doi:10.1016/j.compind.2016.02.004

Bănărescu, A. (2015). Emerging Markets Queries in Finance and Business Detecting and preventing fraud with data analytics. *Procedia Economics and Finance*, *32*, 1827–1836. doi:10.1016/S2212-5671(15)01485-9

Barta & Stewart. (n.d.). A Layered Approach to Fraud Detection and Prevention Increasing Investigator Efficiency Using Network Analytics.

Bharadwaj, A. S., El Sawy, O. A., Pavlou, P. A., & Venkatraman, N. (2016). Digital business strategy: Toward a next generation of insights. *Management Information Systems Quarterly*, *37*(2), 471–482. doi:10.25300/MISQ/2013/37:2.3

Bhimani, A. (2015). Exploring big data's strategic consequences. *Journal of Information Technology*, *30*(1), 66–69. doi:10.1057/jit.2014.29

Big Data Analytics What it is and why it matters. (n.d.). SAS. https://www.sas.com/en_us/insights/analytics/bigdata-analytics.html

Blasaik. (2014). Big Data A Management Revolution Emerging role of big data in business.

Blasiak, K. (2014). Big Data; A Management Revolution: The emerging role of big data in businesses. https://urn.fi/URN:NBN:fi:amk-201405127199

Brynjolfsson, E., Hitt, L. M., & Kim, H. H. (2011). Strength in numbers: How does data-driven decision making affect firm performance? Working paper, MIT Sloan School of management, Cambridge, MA.

Business. (n.d.). https://www.business.com/articles/reinventing-business-intelligence-ways-big-data-is-changing-business/

Chen, A., Lu, Y., & Wang, B. (2017, December). Customers' purchase decision-making process in social commerce: A social learning perspective. *International Journal of Information Management*, *37*(6), 627–638. doi:10.1016/j.ijinfomgt.2017.05.001

Clarke, M. (1989). Insurance fraud. *British Journal of Criminology*, *29*(1), 1–20. doi:10.1093/oxfordjournals.bjc.a047785

Columbus, L. (2016). Roundup Of Analytics, Big Data & BI Forecasts And Market Estimates, 2016, accessed 14 May 2018, https://www.forbes.com/sites/louiscolumbus/2016/0 8/20/roundup-of-analytics-big-data-bi-forecasts-andmarket-estimates-2016/#27e44faf6f21

Constantiou, I. D., & Kallinikos, J. (2015). New games, new rules: Big data and the changing context of strategy. *Journal of Information Technology*, *30*(1), 44–57. doi:10.1057/jit.2014.17

Data Science vs. Big Data vs. Data Analytics. (2018). Simplilearn. accessed 14 May 2018, https://www.simplilearn.com/data-science-vs-bigdata-vs-data-analytics-article

Dinov I. D. (2018). Data Science and Predictive Analytics: Biomedical and Health Applications using R Data Science and Predictive Analytics: Biomedical and Health Applications Using R.

Ehret, M., & Wirtz, J. (2017). Unlocking value from machines: Business models and the Industrial Internet of Things. *Journal of Marketing Management*, *33*(1–2), 111–130. doi:10.1080/0267257X.2016.1248041

George, G., Haas, M. R., & Pentland, A. (2014). Big data and management. *Academy of Management Journal*, *57*(2), 321–326. doi:10.5465/amj.2014.4002

Glass, & Callahan. (2015). The Big Data Driven Business.

Gupta, M., & George, J. F. (2016). Toward the development of a big data analytics capability. *Information & Management*, *53*(8), 1049–1064. doi:10.1016/j.im.2016.07.004

Happiest Minds. (n.d.). https://www.happiestminds.com/whitepapers/Big-Data-101-Creating-Real-Value-from-the-Data-Lifecycle

Hartmann, P. M., Zaki, M., Feldmann, N., & Neely, A. (2016). Capturing value from big data – a taxonomy of data-driven business models used by start-up firms.

Hilbert. (2015). Quantifying the data deluge and the drought.

Hu. (2018). Marketing and Business Analysis in the Era of Big Data. American Journal of Industrial and Business Management, 8(7).

IBM Big Data Hub. (n.d.). https://www.ibmbigdatahub.com/blog/10-big-dataimplementation-best-practices

Infopulse. (n.d.). https://www.infopulse.com/blog/financial-fraud-detection-powered-by-big-data

John, L. K., Kim, T., & Barasz, K. (2018). Ads That Don't Overstep. *Harvard Business Review*. Available at https://hbr.org/2018/01/adsthat-Don't-overstep

Kedmey, D. (2014). This Is How Uber's 'Surge Pricing' Works. *Time*. Available at https://time.com/3633469/uber-surge-pricing/

Khraisat, Gondal, Vamplew, & Kamruzzaman. (2019). Survey of intrusion detection systems:techniques, datasets and challenges. doi:10.1186/s42400-019-0038-7

Kou, Y., Lu, C.-T., Sirwongwattana, S., & Huang, Y. P. (2004). Survey of fraud detection techniques. *IEEE International Conference on Networking, Sensing and Control*, 2, 749–754. 10.1109/ICNSC.2004.1297040

Loebbecke, C., & Picot, A. (2015). Reflections on societal and business model transformation arising from digitization and big data analytics: A research agenda. *The Journal of Strategic Information Systems*, *24*(3), 149–157. doi:10.1016/j.jsis.2015.08.002

Maniraj, Saini, & Ahmed. (2019). Credit Card Fraud Detection using Machine Learning and Data Science. International Journal of Engineering Research & Technology, 8(9).

Manyika, J. (2011). *Big Data: The Next Frontier for Innovation, Competition, and Productivity.* San Francisco, McKinsey Global Institute.

Marabelli, M., & Markus, M. L. (2017) Researching big data research: Ethical implications for IS scholars. *Proceedings of the 23rd Americas conference on information systems.*

Merrill, J. B. (2016). Liberal, Moderate or Conservative: See How Facebook Labels You. *New York Times.* Available at https://www.nytimes.com/2016/08/24/ us/politics/ facebook-ads-politics.html

Mikalef, P., Pappas, I. O., & Pavlou, P. A. (2017). Big data analytics and business value. *Information & Management.*

Nadkarni, A., & Vesset, D. (2016). Worldwide Big Data Technology and Services Forecast, 2016–2020, DEC 2016 - MARKET FORECAST - DOC # US40803116, accessed 14 May 2018, https://www.idc.com/getdoc.jsp?containerId=US40803116

Naim & Malik. (2022). Competitive Trends and Technologies in Business Management. doi:10.52305/VIXO9830

Naim, A., & Kautish, S. K. (Eds.). (2022). *Building a Brand Image Through Electronic Customer Relationship Management.* IGI Global, doi:10.4018/978-1-6684-5386-5

Osterwalder, Pigneur, Y., & Tucci, C. L. (2005). Clarifying business models: origins, present, and future of the concept. *Communications of the Association for Information Systems, 16*, 1–25. doi:10.17705/1CAIS.01601

Palmatier & Martin. (n.d.). The Intelligent Marketer's Guide to Data Privacy The Impact of Big Data on Customer trust. doi:10.1007/978-3-030-03724-6

Post, R. (2014). Ford and Nike Use Big Data to Make Smarter Sustainable Design. The G Design. *The Guardian.* Available at https://www.theguardian.com/ sustainablebusiness/ford-Nike-big-data-smart-sustainable-design

Research Gate. (n.d.). https://www.researchgate.net/publication/337483095_Big_ data_in_marketing_literature_A_Bibliometric_Analysis

Rizzo, C. (2018). Airlines Want to Start Charging Customers Based on Who They Are—And It Means Everyone Could Be Paying Drastically Different Prices. *Business Insider*. Available at https://www.businessinsider.com/airlines-charging-different-fares-for-different-people-2018-2

Samuel. (2016). How to improve firm performance using big data analytics capability and business strategy alignment? International Journal of Production Economics, 182, 113-131. doi:10.1016/j.ijpe.2016.08.018

Sawy, O.A., & Pereira, F. (2013). Business Modelling in the Dynamic Digital Space: An Ecosystem Approach. Springer.

Schroeder, R. (2016). Big data business models: Challenges and opportunities. *Cogent Social Sciences*, 2(1), 1166924. doi:10.1080/23311886.2016.1166924

Singh, Sobti, Malik, Shrestha, Singh, & Ghafoor. (2022). IoT-Driven Model for Weather and Soil Conditions Based on Precision. doi:10.1155/2022/7283975

Singh, D. K., Sobti, R., Jain, A., Malik, P. K., & Le, D.-N. (2022). LoRa based intelligent soil and Irrigation Using Machine Learning", Security and Communication Networks, vol. weather condition monitoring with internet of things for precision agriculture in smart cities. *IET Communications*, *16*, 604–618. doi:10.1049/cmu2.12352

Tech Target. (2021). https://www.techtarget.com/searchbusinessanalytics/tip/Big-data-vs-machine-learning-How-they-differ-and-relate

Thomson Reuters. (n.d.). https://www.thomsonreuters.com/en/press-releases/2018/may/almost-50-percent-of-companies-have-been-victims-of-financial-crime-according-to-new-thomson-reuters-report.html

Underwood, R. (2014). Putting Data in Design. *Inc*. Available at https://www.inc.com/magazine/201312/ryan-underwood/internet-companies-using data-for-design.html

Vangie Beal. (2018). Big Data Analytics, accessed 10 May 2018, https://www.webopedia.com/TERM/B/big_data_analy tics.html

Wiener, Saunders, & Marabelli. (n.d.). Big-data business models: A critical literature review and multiperspective research framework. doi:10.1177/02683962198968

Wikibon. (n.d.). https://wikibon.com/2015-big-data-market-shares/

Woerner, S. L., & Wixom, B. H. (2015). Big data: Extending the business strategy toolbox. *Journal of Information Technology*, *30*(1), 60–62. doi:10.1057/jit.2014.31

Yin & Kaynak. (2015). Big Data for Modern Industry: Challenges and Trends. Proceedings of the IEEE. 10.1109/JPROC.2015.2388958

Zhao, Chen, Li, Yang, & Wang. (2018). Detecting telecommunication fraud by understanding the contents of a call. doi:10.1186/s42400-018-0008-5

Zuboff, S. (2015). Big other: Surveillance capitalism and the prospects of an information civilization. *Journal of Information Technology*, *30*(1), 75–89. doi:10.1057/jit.2015.5

Compilation of References

Fezari, M., & Dahoud, A A. (2019). *Internet of Things Using Raspberry Pi.* WSN Applications. https://www.researchgate.net/publication/330513589_Internet_of_Things_IOT_Using_Raspberry_Pi

Hartmann, P. M., Zaki, M., Feldmann, N., & Neely, A. (2016). Capturing value from big data – a taxonomy of data-driven business models used by start-up firms.

Naim, A. (2022b). Neuro-Marketing Techniques for Proposing Information Driven Framework for Decision Making. *International Journal of Innovative Analyses and Emerging Technology*, *2*(2), 87–94.

Peres, S. C., Pham, T., & Phillips, R. (2013). Validation of the system usability scale (sus): Sus in the wild. *Proc. Hum. Factors Ergon. Soc*, *57*(1), 192–196. doi:10.1177/1541931213571043

Chen, A., Lu, Y., & Wang, B. (2017, December). Customers' purchase decision-making process in social commerce: A social learning perspective. *International Journal of Information Management*, *37*(6), 627–638. doi:10.1016/j.ijinfomgt.2017.05.001

Cowley, A. W. (2006). IUPS—a retrospective. *The Physiologist*, *49*(3), 171–173. PMID:16805368

Martin, K. D., & Murphy, P. E. (2017). The role of data privacy in marketing. *Journal of the Academy of Marketing Science*, *45*(2), 135–155. doi:10.100711747-016-0495-4

Tech A Team. (2017). *Top 6 Programing Languages for IoT Projects.* Tech Ahead Corp. https://www.techaheadcorp.com/blog/top-6-programming-languages-for-iot-projects/

https://www.google.com/role-of-Python-in-iot-development

Malik, H. A. M., Abdulhafeez, M., Aqeel, S., & Amin, A. (n.d.). The Impact of Social Media on the Personality Trait of Under-graduates students: A Descriptive Analytical Approach.

Putra, R. M., Maulida, M., & Rizki, M. R. (2020). The Moderating Role of Data Privacy and Protection Security on Service Quality, Brand Equity, and Tariff towards Firm Performance. In Conference Series (Vol. 3, No. 1, pp. 280-293).

Sawy, O.A., & Pereira, F. (2013). Business Modelling in the Dynamic Digital Space: An Ecosystem Approach. Springer.

Esteve, A. (2017). The business of personal data: Google, Facebook, and privacy issues in the EU and the USA. *International Data Privacy Law*, 7(1), 36–47. doi:10.1093/idpl/ipw026

Jupyter. (2022). *Introducing Functions*. NB Viewer. Https://nbviewer.jupyter.org/github/ehmatthes/intro_programming/blob/master/notebooks/introducing_functions.ipynb

Osterwalder, Pigneur, Y., & Tucci, C. L. (2005). Clarifying business models: origins, present, and future of the concept. *Communications of the Association for Information Systems*, 16, 1–25. doi:10.17705/1CAIS.01601

Tabassam, S., Shah, H., Alghamdi, K., & Badshah, A. (2019). *"Social Networks and Digital Security," 2019 International Con-ference on Electrical, Communication, and Computer Engineering*. ICECCE. doi:10.1109/ICECCE47252.2019.8940808

Appelbaum, D., Kogan, A., Vasarhelyi, M., & Yan, Z. (2017). Impact of business analytics and enterprise systems on managerial accounting. *International Journal of Accounting Information Systems*, 25, 29–44. doi:10.1016/j.accinf.2017.03.003

Ehret, M., & Wirtz, J. (2017). Unlocking value from machines: Business models and the Industrial Internet of Things. *Journal of Marketing Management*, 33(1–2), 111–130. doi:10.1080/02672 57X.2016.1248041

Mester, T. (2018). Python Libraries and Packages for Data Scientists (the 5 Most Important Ones). *Data36*. Https://data36.com/Python-libraries-packages-data-scienTists/

Tabassam, S., Hassan, O., Al-Qahtnae, E., & Al-Ahmary, N. (2019). Goal Question Metrics and Its Application to Process Man-agement and Improvement. International Journal on Engineering Applications (IREA), 7(2), 52-58. doi:10.15866/irea.v7i2.17013

Marabelli, M., & Markus, M. L. (2017) Researching big data research: Ethical implications for IS scholars. *Proceedings of the 23rd Americas conference on information systems.*

Singh, A. K. (2020). *IoT for Automation Clustering to Detect Power losses with Efficiency of Energy Consumption and survey of defense machinery against attacks*. CRC Press.https://www.routledge.com/Applied-Soft-Computing-and-Embedded-System-Applications-in-Solar-Energy/Pachauri-Pandey-Sharmu-Nautiyal-Ram/p/book/9780367625122

Tabassam, S., Al-Saeed, W., Almughram, O., Alghamdi, K. (2019). Scalable Data Analysis and Query Processing. *International Journal on Engineering Applications,* 7(3), 81-87. doi:10.15866/irea.v7i3.17012

Pavoine, S., Vallet, J., Dufour, A. B., Gachet, S., & Daniel, H. (2009). On the challenge of treating various types of variables: Application for improving the measurement of functional diversity. *Oikos*, 118(3), 391–402. doi:10.1111/j.1600-0706.2008.16668.x

Rajab, Aqeel, Al Reshan, Ashraf, Almakdi, & Rajab. (n.d.). Cryptography based Techniques of Encryption for Security of Data in Cloud Computing Paradigm. International Journal of Engineering Trends and Technology, 69(10), 1-6.

Singh, A. K. (2021). Machine Learning in OpenFlow Network: Comparative Analysis of DDoS Detection Techniques. *The International Arab Journal of Information Technology, 18*(2), 221-226. . https://iajit.org/PDF/Vol%2018,%20No.%202/19667.pdf doi:10.34028/iajit/18/2/11

Woerner, S. L., & Wixom, B. H. (2015). Big data: Extending the business strategy toolbox. *Journal of Information Technology, 30*(1), 60–62. doi:10.1057/jit.2014.31

Muniasamy, A., Tabassam, S., Hussain, M. A., Sultana, H., Muniasamy, V., Bhatnagar, R., & 2019). Deep Learning for Predictive Analytics in Healthcare. In *The International Conference on Advanced Machine Learning Tech-nologies and Applications (AMLTA2019)*. Springer International Publishing.

Naim, A. (2021). Green Business Process Management. *International Journal of Innovative Analyses and Emerging Technology, 1*(6), 125–134. https://openaccessjournals.eu/index.php/ijiaet/article/view/651

Singh, A. K. (2020). Digital Era in the Kingdom of Saudi Arabia: Novel Strategies of the Telecom Service Providers Companies. *Webology, 17*(1), 227-245. http://www.webology.org/issue.php?volume=1&issue=1&page=2 doi:10.14704/WEB/V17I1/a219

Zuboff, S. (2015). Big other: Surveillance capitalism and the prospects of an information civilization. *Journal of Information Technology, 30*(1), 75–89. doi:10.1057/jit.2015.5

Chatterjee, S., Chaudhuri, R., & Vrontis, D. (2021). Examining the global retail apocalypse during the COVID-19 pandemic using strategic omnichannel management: A consumer' data privacy and data security perspective. *Journal of Strategic Marketing, 29*(7), 617–632. doi:10.1080/0965254X.2021.1936132

Jenni, K. (2013). *Improve the Performance of Clustering Using Combination of Multiple Clustering Algorithms. International Journal of Data Mining Techniques and Applications.*

Schroeder, R. (2016). Big data business models: Challenges and opportunities. *Cogent Social Sciences, 2*(1), 1166924. doi:10.1080/23311886.2016.1166924

Singh, A. K. (2019). High performance computing (HPC) data center for information as a service (IaaS) security checklist: cloud data supremacy. *Webology, 16*(2), 83-96. , http://www.webology.org/issue.php?volume=2&issue=3 doi:10.14704/WEB/V16I2/a192

Akter, S., Wamba, S. F., Gunasekaran, A., Dubey, R., & Childe, S. J. (2016). How to improve firm performance using big data analytics capability and business strategy alignment? *International Journal of Production Economics, 182*, 113–131. doi:10.1016/j.ijpe.2016.08.018

Aqeel, S. (2017). *Study on Enhancement on Software Quality by Scheduling Techniques of Real Time Systems. European Journal of Advances in Engineering and Technology, 4*(3), 201–208.

Morse, E. A., Raval, V., & Wingender Jr, J. R. (2011). Market price effects of data security breaches. *Information Security Journal: A Global Perspective, 20*(6), 263-273.

Singh, A. K. (2019). An Intelligent Reallocation of Load for Cluster Cloud Environment. *International Journal of Innovative Technology and Exploring Engineering (IJITEE), 8*(8). https://www.ijitee.org/download/volume-8-issue-8/

Aljifri, H. A., Pons, A., & Collins, D. (2003). Global e-commerce: A framework for understanding and overcoming the trust barrier. *Information Management & Computer Security, 11*(2–3), 130–138. doi:10.1108/09685220310480417

Muiru, R. (2021). Python in IoT. *Top Coder.* https://www.topcoder.com/thrive/articles/Python-in-iot-internet-of-things

Raab, G., Ajami, R. A., & Goddard, G. J. (2016). *Customer relationship management: A global perspective.* CRC Press. doi:10.4324/9781315575636

Wiener, Saunders, & Marabelli. (n.d.). Big-data business models: A critical literature review and multiperspective research framework. doi:10.1177/02683962198968

Bharadwaj, A. S., El Sawy, O. A., Pavlou, P. A., & Venkatraman, N. (2016). Digital business strategy: Toward a next generation of insights. *Management Information Systems Quarterly, 37*(2), 471–482. doi:10.25300/MISQ/2013/37:2.3

Naim, A. (2022c). Mapping of Social Customer Relationship Management with Electronic Customer Relationship Management. *European Journal of Interdisciplinary Research and Development, 2*, 14–25. https://ejird.journalspark.org/index.php/ejird/article/view/10

Singh, A. K. (2019). Texture-based Real-Time Character Extraction and Recognition in Natural Images. *International Journal of Innovative Technology and Exploring Engineering (IJITEE), 8*(8). https://www.ijitee.org/download/volume-8-issue-8/

Tabassam, S., & Al-Qahtane, E. (2019). Comparative Analysis on Requirement Engineering Modelling Techniques Case Study of Personal Al-Haj E-Guide. 2019 2nd International Conference on Computer Applications & Information Security (ICCAIS), 1-8. 10.1109/CAIS.2019.8769549

Aqeel, S., Khan, A. S., Ahmad, Z., & Abdullah, J. (2021). *A comprehensive study on DNA based Security scheme Using Deep Learning in Healthcare.* EDPACS. doi:10.1080/07366981.2021.1958742

Bhimani, A. (2015). Exploring big data's strategic consequences. *Journal of Information Technology, 30*(1), 66–69. doi:10.1057/jit.2014.29

Shey, H., Mak, K., Balaouras, S., & Luu, B. (2013). Understand the state of data security and privacy: 2013 to 2014. *Forrester Research Inc, 1.*

Singh, A. K. (2019). A Wireless Networks Flexible Adoptive Modulation and Coding Technique in advanced 4G LTE. *International Journal of Information Technology, 11*(1), 55-66. doi:10.1007/s41870-018-0173-5 https://link.springer.com/article/10.1007/s41870-018-0173-5 doi:10.1007/s41870-018-0173-5

Gupta, M., & George, J. F. (2016). Toward the development of a big data analytics capability. *Information & Management*, *53*(8), 1049–1064. doi:10.1016/j.im.2016.07.004

Naim, A. (2022d). Understanding The Customer Centric Approach To Add Value To Social Ecrm (Secrm). *British Journal of Global Ecology and Sustainable Development*, *4*, 1–17. https://journalzone.org/index.php/bjgesd/article/view/45

Singh, A. K. (2017). The Active Impact of Human Computer Interaction (HCI) on Economic, Cultural, and Social Life. *IIOAB Journal, 8*(2), 141-146. https://www.iioab.org/vol8n2

Kaiser, R., Spiegel, P. B., Henderson, A. K., & Gerber, M. L. (2003). The application of geographic information systems and global positioning systems in humanitarian emergencies: Lessons learned, programme implications and future research. *Disasters*, *27*(2), 127–140. doi:10.1111/1467-7717.00224 PMID:12825436

Loebbecke, C., & Picot, A. (2015). Reflections on societal and business model transformation arising from digitization and big data analytics: A research agenda. *The Journal of Strategic Information Systems*, *24*(3), 149–157. doi:10.1016/j.jsis.2015.08.002

Singh, A. K. (2017). Security and Management in Network: Security of Network Management versus Management of Network Security (SNM Vs MNS). *International Journal of Computer Science and Network Security (IJCSNS), 17*(5), 166-173. http://search.ijcsns.org/07_book/2017_05.htm

Mikalef, P., Pappas, I. O., & Pavlou, P. A. (2017). Big data analytics and business value. *Information & Management*.

O'Brien, J. A., & Marakas, G. M. (2005). *Introduction to information systems* (Vol. 13). McGraw-Hill/Irwin.

Singh, A. K. (2017). Persona Of Social Networking In Computing And Informatics Era. *International Journal of Computer Science and Network Security (IJCSNS), 17*(4), 95-101. http://search.ijcsns.org/07_book/2017_04.h

Arnott, D. (2004). Decision support systems evolution: Framework, case study and research agenda. *European Journal of Information Systems*, *13*(4), 247–259. doi:10.1057/palgrave.ejis.3000509

Hilbert. (2015). Quantifying the data deluge and the drought.

Watson, H. J. (2018). Revisiting Ralph Sprague's framework for developing decision support systems. *Communications of the Association for Information Systems, 42*(1), 13. doi:10.17705/1CAIS.04213

Aronson, J. E., Liang, T. P., & MacCarthy, R. V. (2005). *Decision support systems and intelligent systems* (Vol. 4). Pearson Prentice-Hall.

Wikibon. (n.d.). https://wikibon.com/2015-big-data-market-shares/

Manyika, J. (2011). *Big Data: The Next Frontier for Innovation, Competition, and Productivity*. San Francisco, McKinsey Global Institute.

Naim, A., & Khan, M. F. (2021). Measuring the Psychological Behavior of Consumers for Medical Services. Zien Journal of Social Sciences and Humanities, 2, 119–131. Retrieved from https://zienjournals.com/index.php/zjssh/article/view/316

Academia.edu. (n.d.). https://www.academia.edu/76334718/Big_data_the_management_revolution

Sharkey, U., & Acton, T. (2012). Innovations in information systems from transaction processing to expert systems.

Peppers, D., & Rogers, M. (2004). *Managing customer relationships: A strategic framework*. John Wiley & Sons.

Tsai, P. (1996). A Survey of Empirical Usability Evaluation Methods. A Surv. Empir. usability Eval. Methods.

W3Schools. (2022). *Machine Learning- Linear Regression*. W3Schools. https://www.w3schools.com/Python/Python_ml_linear_regression.asp

Yin & Kaynak. (2015). Big Data for Modern Industry: Challenges and Trends. Proceedings of the IEEE. 10.1109/JPROC.2015.2388958

Naim, A., Hussain, M. R., Naveed, Q. N., Ahmad, N., Qamar, S., Khan, N., & Hweij, T. A. (2019, April). Ensuring interoperability of e-learning and quality development in education. In *2019 IEEE Jordan International Joint Conference on Electrical Engineering and Information Technology (JEEIT)* (pp. 736-741). IEEE. 10.1109/JEEIT.2019.8717431

Research Gate. (n.d.). https://www.researchgate.net/publication/337483095_Big_data_in_marketing_literature_A_Bibliometric_Analysis

Blasiak, K. (2014). Big Data; A Management Revolution: The emerging role of big data in businesses. https://urn.fi/URN:NBN:fi:amk-201405127199

Polkowski, L., Tsumoto, S., & Lin, T. Y. (Eds.). (2012). *Rough set methods and applications: new developments in knowledge discovery in information systems* (Vol. 56). Physica.

Blasaik. (2014). Big Data A Management Revolution Emerging role of big data in business.

Jia, P., Cheng, X., Xue, H., & Wang, Y. (2017). Applications of geographic information systems (GIS) data and methods in obesity-related research. *Obesity Reviews*, *18*(4), 400–411. doi:10.1111/obr.12495 PMID:28165656

Happiest Minds. (n.d.). https://www.happiestminds.com/whitepapers/Big-Data-101-Creating-Real-Value-from-the-Data-Lifecycle

Sigala, M. (2018). Implementing social customer relationship management. *International Journal of Contemporary Hospitality Management*, *30*(7), 2698–2726. doi:10.1108/IJCHM-10-2015-0536

IBM Big Data Hub. (n.d.). https://www.ibmbigdatahub.com/blog/10-big-dataimplementation-best-practices

Watanabe, C., & Hobo, M. (2004). Co-evolution between internal motivation and external expectation as a source of firm self-propagating function creation. *Technovation*, *24*(2), 109–120. doi:10.1016/S0166-4972(02)00043-3

Glass, & Callahan. (2015). The Big Data Driven Business.

Naim, A. (2021). Applications of MIS in building Electronic Relationship with customers: A case-based study. Periodica Journal of Modern Philosophy. *Social Sciences and Humanities*, *1*, 1–8.

Alt, R., & Puschmann, T. (2004, January). Successful practices in customer relationship management. In 37th Annual Hawaii International Conference on System Sciences, 2004. Proceedings of the (pp. 9-pp). IEEE. 10.1109/HICSS.2004.1265415

Merrill, J. B. (2016). Liberal, Moderate or Conservative: See How Facebook Labels You. *New York Times*. Available at https://www.nytimes.com/2016/08/24/ us/politics/facebook-ads-politics.html

Naim, A., Khan, M. F., Hussain, M. R., & Khan, N. (2019). "Virtual Doctor" Management Technique in the Diagnosis of ENT Diseases. *JOE*, *15*(9), 88. doi:10.3991/ijoe.v15i09.10665

Delone, W. H., & McLean, E. R. (2003). The DeLone and McLean model of information systems success: A ten-year update. *Journal of Management Information Systems*, *19*(4), 9–30. doi:10.1080/07421222.2003.11045748

Post, R. (2014). Ford and Nike Use Big Data to Make Smarter Sustainable Design. The G Design. *The Guardian*. Available at https://www.theguardian.com/sustainablebusiness/ford-Nike-big-data-smart-sustainable-design

Underwood, R. (2014). Putting Data in Design. *Inc*. Available at https:// www.inc.com/ magazine/201312/ryan-underwood/internet-companies-using data-for-design.html

Naim, A., Alahmari, F., & Rahim, A. (2021). Role of Artificial Intelligence in Market Development and Vehicular Communication. Smart Antennas. *Recent Trends in Design and Applications*, *2*, 28–39. doi:10.2174/9781681088594121020006

Scipy. (2022). *Image Manipulation and processing Using Numpy and Scipy*. Scipy Lectures. https://scipy-lectures.org/advanced/image_processing/

Standard, I. (1998). *Iso 9241-11*.

Foss, B., Stone, M., & Ekinci, Y. (2008). What makes for CRM system success—Or failure? *Journal of Database Marketing & Customer Strategy Management*, *15*(2), 68–78. doi:10.1057/dbm.2008.5

Kedmey, D. (2014). This Is How Uber's 'Surge Pricing' Works. *Time*. Available at https://time.com/3633469/uber-surge-pricing/

Cuthbertson, R., & Laine, A. (2003). The role of CRM within retail loyalty marketing. Journal of Targeting. *Measurement and Analysis for Marketing*, *12*(3), 290–304. doi:10.1057/palgrave.jt.5740116

Rizzo, C. (2018). Airlines Want to Start Charging Customers Based on Who They Are—And It Means Everyone Could Be Paying Drastically Different Prices. *Business Insider*. Available at https://www.businessinsider.com/airlines-charging-different-fares-for-different-people-2018-2

Collins, K. (2001). *Analytical CRM: Driving Profitable Customer Relationships*. Strategic Planning.

John, L. K., Kim, T., & Barasz, K. (2018). Ads That Don't Overstep. *Harvard Business Review*. Available at https://hbr.org/2018/01/adsthat-Don't-overstep

Business. (n.d.). https://www.business.com/articles/reinventing-business-intelligence-ways-big-data-is-changing-business/

Friday, D., Ryan, S., Sridharan, R., & Collins, D. (2018). Collaborative risk management: A systematic literature review. *International Journal of Physical Distribution & Logistics Management*, *48*(3), 231–253. doi:10.1108/IJPDLM-01-2017-0035

Bănărescu, A. (2015). Emerging Markets Queries in Finance and Business Detecting and preventing fraud with data analytics. *Procedia Economics and Finance*, *32*, 1827–1836. doi:10.1016/S2212-5671(15)01485-9

Eom, S. (2020, May). DSS, BI, and Data Analytics Research: Current State and Emerging Trends (2015–2019). In *International Conference on Decision Support System Technology* (pp. 167-179). Springer. 10.1007/978-3-030-46224-6_13

Infopulse. (n.d.). https://www.infopulse.com/blog/financial-fraud-detection-powered-by-big-data

Naim, A., & Alahmari, F. (2020). Reference model of e-learning and quality to establish interoperability in higher education systems. *International Journal of Emerging Technologies in Learning*, *15*(2), 15–28. doi:10.3991/ijet.v15i02.11605

Rupnik, R., & Kukar, M. (2007). Decision support system to support decision processes with data mining. *Journal of Information and Organizational Sciences*, *31*(1), 217–232.

Thomson Reuters. (n.d.). https://www.thomsonreuters.com/en/press-releases/2018/may/almost-50-percent-of-companies-have-been-victims-of-financial-crime-according-to-new-thomson-reuters-report.html

Abbassi, El Alaoui, & Gahi. (2021). Fraud Detection Techniques in the Big Data Era. Proceedings of the 2nd International Conference on Big Data, Modelling and Machine Learning (BML 2021), 161-170.

Edwards, C. J., Bendickson, J. S., Baker, B. L., & Solomon, S. J. (2020). Entrepreneurship within the history of marketing. *Journal of Business Research*, *108*, 259–267. doi:10.1016/j.jbusres.2019.10.040

Balmer, J. M., & Burghausen, M. (2019). Marketing, the past and corporate heritage. *Marketing Theory*, *19*(2), 217–227. doi:10.1177/1470593118790636

Hu. (2018). Marketing and Business Analysis in the Era of Big Data. *American Journal of Industrial and Business Management, 8*(7).

Al-Rawashdeh, F., & Al Singlawi, O. (2016). The Existence of Fraud Indicators in Insurance Industry: Case of Jordan. *International Journal of Economics and Financial Issues, 6*(S5), 168–176.

Naim, A. (2022e). Measurement of Electronic Commerce Effectiveness. *Neo Science Peer Reviewed Journal, 1*, 1–10. Retrieved from https://neojournals.com/index.php/nsprj/article/view/6

Babiceanu, R. F., & Seker, R. (2016). Big data and virtualization for manufacturing cyber-physical systems: A survey of the current status and future outlook. *Computers in Industry, 81*, 128–137. doi:10.1016/j.compind.2016.02.004

Bangor, A., Kortum, P. T., & Miller, J. T. (2008). An empirical evaluation of the system usability scale. *International Journal of Human-Computer Interaction, 24*(6), 574–594. doi:10.1080/10447310802205776

Chan, S. L., & Ip, W. H. (2011). A dynamic decision support system to predict the value of customer for new product development. *Decision Support Systems, 52*(1), 178–188. doi:10.1016/j.dss.2011.07.002

Jordan, M. I., & Mitchell, T. M. (2015). Machine learning: Trends, perspectives, and prospects. *Science, 349*(6245), 255–260. doi:10.1126cience.aaa8415 PMID:26185243

Asemi, A., Safari, A., & Zavareh, A. A. (2011). The role of management information system (MIS) and Decision support system (DSS) for manager's decision making process. *International Journal of Business and Management, 6*(7), 164–173. doi:10.5539/ijbm.v6n7p164

Clarke, M. (1989). Insurance fraud. *British Journal of Criminology, 29*(1), 1–20. doi:10.1093/oxfordjournals.bjc.a047785

Maniraj, Saini, & Ahmed. (2019). Credit Card Fraud Detection using Machine Learning and Data Science. International Journal of Engineering Research & Technology, 8(9).

Xu, H., Guo, S., Haislip, J. Z., & Pinsker, R. E. (2019). Earnings management in firms with data security breaches. *Journal of Information Systems, 33*(3), 267–284. doi:10.2308/isys-52480

Zhao, Chen, Li, Yang, & Wang. (2018). Detecting telecommunication fraud by understanding the contents of a call. doi:10.1186/s42400-018-0008-5

Kou, Y., Lu, C.-T., Sirwongwattana, S., & Huang, Y. P. (2004). Survey of fraud detection techniques. *IEEE International Conference on Networking, Sensing and Control, 2*, 749–754. 10.1109/ICNSC.2004.1297040

Naim, A. (2022f). Factors of Consumer Behaviour of youth from middle-east when purchasing Organic Food. Global Scientific Review, 3, 1–7. Retrieved from http://www.scienticreview.com/index.php/gsr/article/view/13

Khraisat, Gondal, Vamplew, & Kamruzzaman. (2019). Survey of intrusion detection systems:techniques, datasets and challenges. doi:10.1186/s42400-019-0038-7

Paryasto, M., Alamsyah, A., & Rahardjo, B. (2014, May). Big-data security management issues. In *2014 2nd International Conference on Information and Communication Technology (ICoICT)* (pp. 59-63). IEEE. 10.1109/ICoICT.2014.6914040

Naim, A. (2022g). Role of Artificial Intelligence in Business Risk Management. American Journal of Business Management. *Economics and Banking, 1*, 55–66.

Barta & Stewart. (n.d.). A Layered Approach to Fraud Detection and Prevention Increasing Investigator Efficiency Using Network Analytics.

Shao, X. F., Li, Y., Suseno, Y., Li, R. Y. M., Gouliamos, K., Yue, X. G., & Luo, Y. (2021). How does facial recognition as an urban safety technology affect firm performance? The moderating role of the home country's government subsidies. *Safety Science, 143*, 105434. doi:10.1016/j.ssci.2021.105434

Dinov I. D. (2018). Data Science and Predictive Analytics: Biomedical and Health Applications using R Data Science and Predictive Analytics: Biomedical and Health Applications Using R.

Popescul, D., & Genete, L. D. (2016). Data security in smart cities: challenges and solutions. *Informatica Economică, 20*(1).

Naim, A. (2022h). Cost Trend: Meaning and Importance Of Cost Trend in Public Enterprises. *American Journal of Technology and Applied Sciences, 1*, 37–46. https://americanjournal.org/index.php/ajtas/article/view/11

Tech Target. (2021). https://www.techtarget.com/searchbusinessanalytics/tip/Big-data-vs-machine-learning-How-they-differ-and-relate

Balachandar, S., & Chinnaiyan, R. (2019). Centralized reliability and security management of data in internet of things (IoT) with rule builder. In *International Conference on Computer Networks and Communication Technologies* (pp. 193-201). Springer. 10.1007/978-981-10-8681-6_19

Nadkarni, A., & Vesset, D. (2016). Worldwide Big Data Technology and Services Forecast, 2016–2020, DEC 2016 - MARKET FORECAST - DOC # US4080316, accessed 14 May 2018, https://www.idc.com/getdoc.jsp?containerId=US4080 3116

Astani, M., & Elhindi, M. A. (2008). an Empirical Study of University Websites. *Issues in Information Systems, 9*(2), 460–465.

Brynjolfsson, E., Hitt, L. M., & Kim, H. H. (2011). Strength in numbers: How does data-driven decision making affect firm performance? Working paper, MIT Sloan School of management, Cambridge, MA.

Grover, V., Chiang, R. H., Liang, T. P., & Zhang, D. (2018). Creating strategic business value from big data analytics: A research framework. *Journal of Management Information Systems, 35*(2), 388–423. doi:10.1080/07421222.2018.1451951

Le Cun, Y., Bengio, Y., & Hinton, G. (2015). Deep learning. *Nature*, *521*(7553), 436–444. doi:10.1038/nature14539 PMID:26017442

Columbus, L. (2016). Roundup Of Analytics, Big Data & BI Forecasts And Market Estimates, 2016, accessed 14 May 2018, https://www.forbes.com/sites/louiscolumbus/2016/08/20/roundup-of-analytics-big-data-bi-forecasts-andmarket-estimates-2016/#27e44faf6f21

Leonard, P. (2014). Customer data analytics: Privacy settings for 'Big Data' business. *International Data Privacy Law, 4*(1), 53-68.

Data Science vs. Big Data vs. Data Analytics. (2018). Simplilearn. accessed 14 May 2018, https://www.simplilearn.com/data-science-vs-bigdata-vs-data-analytics-article

Naim & Malik. (2022). Competitive Trends and Technologies in Business Management. doi:10.52305/VIXO9830

Anandkumar, R., Dinesh, K., & Ahmed, J. (2022). Securing e-Health application of cloud computing using hyperchaotic image encryption framework. Computers and Electrical Engineering, 100. doi:10.1016/j.compeleceng.2022.107860

Big Data Analytics What it is and why it matters. (n.d.). SAS. https://www.sas.com/en_us/insights/analytics/bigdata-analytics.html

Singh, D. K., Sobti, R., Jain, A., Malik, P. K., & Le, D.-N. (2022). LoRa based intelligent soil and Irrigation Using Machine Learning", Security and Communication Networks, vol. weather condition monitoring with internet of things for precision agriculture in smart cities. *IET Communications*, *16*, 604–618. doi:10.1049/cmu2.12352

Vangie Beal. (2018). Big Data Analytics, accessed 10 May 2018, https://www.webopedia.com/TERM/B/big_data_analy tics.html

Singh, Sobti, Malik, Shrestha, Singh, & Ghafoor. (2022). IoT-Driven Model for Weather and Soil Conditions Based on Precision. doi:10.1155/2022/7283975

Naim, A., & Kautish, S. K. (Eds.). (2022). *Building a Brand Image Through Electronic Customer Relationship Management*. IGI Global., doi:10.4018/978-1-6684-5386-5

Constantiou, I. D., & Kallinikos, J. (2015). New games, new rules: Big data and the changing context of strategy. *Journal of Information Technology*, *30*(1), 44–57. doi:10.1057/jit.2014.17

Holzinger, A., Dehmer, M., & Jurisica, I. (2014). Knowledge discovery and interactive data mining in bioinformatics - state-of-the-art, future challenges and research direc-tions. *BMC Bioinformatics*, *15*(S6), I1. doi:10.1186/1471-2105-15-S6-I1 PMID:25078282

Kostaras, N., Kostaras, N., Xenos, M., & Xenos, M. (2007). Assessing Educational Web-site Usability using Heuristic Evaluation Rules. *Evaluation*, (May), 543–550.

Naim, A. (2022a). Measurement Consumer Mood and Emotions for Fast Moving Consumer Goods. *International Journal of Innovative Analyses and Emerging Technology*, *2*(2), 83–86.

George, G., Haas, M. R., & Pentland, A. (2014). Big data and management. *Academy of Management Journal*, *57*(2), 321–326. doi:10.5465/amj.2014.4002

Naim, A. (2021). Applications of Marketing Framework in Business Practices. *Journal of Marketing and Emerging Economics*, *1*(6), 55–70.

Sheikh, J. A., Abbas, A., & Mehmood, Z. (2015). Design Consideration of Online Shopping Website to Reach Women in Pakistan. Procedia Manuf., 3, 6298–6304. doi:10.1016/j.promfg.2015.07.942

Wolfram, S. (1991). *Mathematica: A System for Doing Mathematics by Computer*. Addison Wesley Longman Publishing Co., Inc.

Engblom, S., & Lukarski, D. (2016). Fast MATLAB compatible sparse assembly on multicore computers. *Parallel Computing*, *56*, 1–17. https://www.researchgate.net/publication/330513589_Internet_of_Things_IOT_Using_Raspberry_Pi. doi:10.1016/j.parco.2016.04.001

Filip, F. G. (2020). DSS—*A Class of Evolving Information Systems*. In *Data Science: New Issues, Challenges and Applications* (pp. 253–277). Springer. doi:10.1007/978-3-030-39250-5_14

Hvannberg, E. T., Law, E. L. C., & Lárusdóttir, M. K. (2007). Heuristic evaluation: Comparing ways of finding and reporting usability problems. *Interacting with Computers*, *19*(2), 225–240. doi:10.1016/j.intcom.2006.10.001

Agarwal & Dhar. (n.d.). Editorial—Big Data, Data Science, and Analytics: The Opportunity and Challenge for IS Research. doi:10.1287/isre.2014.0546

Nielsen, J. (1994). *Human Factors Computing Systems: Enhancing the Explanatory Power of Usability Heuristics*. Hum. Factors Comput. Syst.

Palmatier, R. W., & Martin, K. D. (2019). *The intelligent marketer's guide to data privacy: The impact of big data on customer trust*. Springer International Publishing. doi:10.1007/978-3-030-03724-6

Abdel-Aziz, A. A., Abdel-Salam, H., & El-Sayad, Z. (2016). The role of ICTs in creating the new social public place of the digital era. *Alexandria Engineering Journal*, *55*(1), 487–493. doi:10.1016/j.aej.2015.12.019

Abdul-Jabbar, S., Aldujaili, A., Mohammed, S. G., & Saeed, H. S. (2020). Integrity and Security in Cloud Computing Environment: A Review. *Journal of Southwest Jiaotong University*, *55*(1), 1–15. doi:10.35741/issn.0258-2724.55.1.11

Abouelmehdi, K., Beni-Hessane, A., & Khaloufi, H. (2018). Big healthcare data: Preserving security and privacy. *Journal of Big Data*, *5*(1), 1. doi:10.118640537-017-0110-7

Abuabara, L., & Paucar-Caceres, A. (2021). Surveying applications of Strategic Options Development and Analysis (SODA) from 1989 to 2018. *European Journal of Operational Research*, *292*(3), 1051–1065. doi:10.1016/j.ejor.2020.11.032

Afuah, A. (2004). *Business Models: A Strategic Management Approach*. McGraw-Hill/Irwin.

Ahokangas, P. (2015, January 29). Vertical, horizontal and oblique business models (Blog). *Technology & Business & Strategy & Internationalization & Futures.* http://techbusstratintfutures. blogspot.fi/

Ahokangas, P. Moqaddamerad, S. Matinmikko, M. Abouzeid, A. Atkova, I Gomes, J. F., & Iivari, M. (2016). *Future micro operators business models in 5G,* 143-149.

Alarabi, S., Almuzeri, S., Alaradi, S., & Innab, N. (2018, April). Two Level Based Privacy Protection Approach for internet of things Users in Cloud Computing. In *2018 21st Saudi Computer Society National Computer Conference (NCC)* (pp. 1-6). IEEE.

Aldawood, H., & Skinner, G. (2019). Reviewing cyber security social engineering training and awareness programs—Pitfalls and ongoing issues. *Future Internet, 11*(3), 73. doi:10.3390/fi11030073

Al-Juaid, N., & Gutub, A. (2018). Combining rsa and audio steganography on personal computers for enhancing security. *SN Applied Sciences, 1*(8), 830.

Alkhurayyif, Y., & Weir, G. R. S. (2017). Readability as a Basis for Information Security Policy Assessment. *Seventh International Conference on Emerging Security Technologies (EST),* (pp. 114–121). IEEE. 10.1109/EST.2017.8090409

Almeida, F., Santos, J. D., & Monteiro, J. (2020). The Challenges and Opportunities in the Digitalization of Companies in a Post-COVID-19 World. *IEEE Engineering Management Review, 48*(3), 97–103. doi:10.1109/EMR.2020.3013206

Almeida, V. A., Doneda, D., & Monteiro, M. (2015). Governance challenges for the internet of things. *IEEE Internet Computing, 19*(4), 56–59. doi:10.1109/MIC.2015.86

Alshamari, M. (2016). A Review of Gaps between Usability and Security/Privacy. *International Journal of Communications, Network and Systems Sciences, 9*(10), 413–429. doi:10.4236/ijcns.2016.910034

Alt, R., & Zimmermann, H. (2001). Introduction to Special Section - Business Models. *Electronic Markets, 11,* 1019.

Amit, R., & Zott, C. (2001). Value creation in E-business. *Strategic Management Journal, 22*(6-7), 493–520. doi:10.1002mj.187

Ananda, D., Taqiyyuddin, T. A., Faqih, I. N., Badrahadipura, R., & Pravitasari, A. A. (2021, October). Application of Bidirectional Gated Recurrent Unit (BiGRU) in Sentiment Analysis of Tokopedia Application Users. In *2021 International Conference on Artificial Intelligence and Big Data Analytics* (pp. 1-4). IEEE.

Andoni, M., Robu, V., Flynn, D., Abram, S., Geach, D., Jenkins, D., McCallum, P., & Peacock, A. (2019). Blockchain technology in the energy sector: A systematic review of challenges and opportunities. *Renewable & Sustainable Energy Reviews, 100,* 143–174. doi:10.1016/j.rser.2018.10.014

Andrade, V. (2020). Assim se vê a força da PME [This is how you can see the strength of the PME]. *Expresso*. https://expresso.pt/economia/2020-06-27-Assim-se-ve-a-forca-da-PME

Annansingh, F. (2021). Bring your own device to work: How serious is the risk? *The Journal of Business Strategy, 42*(6), 392–398. doi:10.1108/JBS-04-2020-0069

Anusree, K., & Binnu, G. S. (2014). *Biometric Privacy using Visual Cryptography Halftoning and Watermarking for Multiple Secrets*. IEEE. doi:10.1109/NCCSN.2014.7001156

Anwar, F., & Shamim, A. (2011). Barriers in Adoption of Health Information Technology in Developing Societies. Food Chemistry -. *Food Chemistry, 2*(8). doi:10.14569/IJACSA.2011.020808

Argaw, S. T., Troncoso-Pastoriza, J. R., Lacey, D., Florin, M.-V., Calcavecchia, F., Anderson, D., Burleson, W., Vogel, J.-M., O'Leary, C., Eshaya-Chauvin, B., & Flahault, A. (2020). Cybersecurity of Hospitals: Discussing the challenges and working towards mitigating the risks. *BMC Medical Informatics and Decision Making, 20*(146), 146. doi:10.118612911-020-01161-7 PMID:32620167

Aridor, G., Che, Y.-K., & Salz, T. (2020). The Economic Consequences of Data Privacy Regulation: Empirical Evidence from GDPR. SSRN *Electronic Journal*. doi:10.2139/ssrn.3522845

Arisenta, R., Suharjito, & Sukmandhani, A. A. (2020). Evaluation Model of Success Change Management in Banking Institution Based on ITIL V3 (Case Study). *2020 International Conference on Information Management and Technology (ICIMTech)*, (pp. 470–475). IEEE. 10.1109/ICIMTech50083.2020.9211191

Assa-Agyei, K., Olajide, F., & Lotfi, A. (2022). Security and Privacy Issues in IoT Healthcare Application for Disabled Users in Developing Economies [JITST]. *Journal of Internet Technology and Secured Transactions, 10*(1), 770–779. doi:10.20533/jitst.2046.3723.2022.0095

Axelos (2022). *ITIL® 4: the framework for the management of IT-enabled services*. Axelos. https://www.axelos.com/certifications/itil-service-management

B. W. Wirtz, O. Schilke and S. Ullrich. (2010). Strategic Development of Business Models: Implications of the Web 2.0 for Creating Value on the Internet. *Long Range Plann., 43*, 272-290.

Badawi, E., Jourdan, G.-V., Bochmann, G., & Onut, I.-V. (2020). Automatic Detection and Analysis of the "Game Hack" Scam. [JWE]. *Journal of Web Engineering, 18*(8), 729–760. doi:10.13052/jwe1540-9589.1881

Badawi, E., Jourdan, G.-V., Bochmann, G., Onut, I.-V., & Flood, J. (2019). The "Game Hack" Scam. *International Conference on Web Engineering*. Daejeon, Korea.

Baik, J. S. (2020). Data privacy against innovation or against discrimination?: The case of the California Consumer Privacy Act (CCPA). *Telematics and Informatics, 52*, 52. doi:10.1016/j.tele.2020.101431

Ballon, P. (2007). Business modelling revisited: The configuration of control and value. *Info, 9*(5), 6–19. doi:10.1108/14636690710816417

Balogun, A. O., Adewole, K. S., Raheem, M. O., Akande, O. N., Usman-Hamza, F. E., Mabayoje, M. A., Akintola, A. G., Asaju-Gbolagade, A. W., Jimoh, M. K., Jimoh, R. G., & Adeyemo, V. E. (2021). Improving the phishing website detection using empirical analysis of Function Tree and its variants. *Heliyon*, 7(7), e07437. doi:10.1016/j.heliyon.2021.e07437 PMID:34278030

Basit, A., Zafar, M., Liu, X., Javed, A. R., Jalil, Z., & Kifayat, K. (2021). A comprehensive survey of AI-enabled phishing attacks detection techniques. *Telecommunication Systems*, 76(1), 139–154. doi:10.100711235-020-00733-2 PMID:33110340

Beggs, C. (2006). Proposed risk minimization measures for cyber-terrorism and SCADA networks in australia. In *Proceedings of the 5th European Conference on Information Warfare and Security*, pp. 9.

Bekker, E. (2021). *2021 Data Breaches*. IdentityForce.

Benhayoun, L., Ayala, N. F., & Le Dain, M. A. (2021). SMEs innovating in collaborative networks: How does absorptive capacity matter for innovation performance in times of good partnership quality? *Journal of Manufacturing Technology Management*, 32(8), 1578–1598. doi:10.1108/JMTM-11-2020-0439

Berger, B. (2017). The Small and Medium Business' False Sense of Cybersecurity. *Security Magazine*. https://www.securitymagazine.com/blogs/14-security-blog/post/88373-the-small-and-medium-business-false-sense-of-cybersecurity

Berger, D., Shashidhar, N., & Varol, C. (2020). Using ITIL 4 in Security Management. *8th International Symposium on Digital Forensics and Security (ISDFS)*, (pp. 1–6). IEEE. 10.1109/ISDFS49300.2020.9116257

Bhatti, B. M., Mubarak, S., & Nagalingam, S. (2021). Information Security Risk Management in IT Outsourcing – A Quarter-Century Systematic Literature Review. *Journal of Global Information Technology Management*, 24(4), 259–298. doi:10.1080/1097198X.2021.1993725

Bischoff, P. (2020). *Social media data broker exposes nearly 235 million profiles scraped from Instagram, TikTok, and Youtube*. CompariTech.

Biswas, S., Sharif, K., Li, F., Nour, B., & Wang, Y. (2018). A scalable blockchain framework for secure transactions in IoT. *IEEE Internet of Things Journal*, 6(3), 4650–4659. doi:10.1109/JIOT.2018.2874095

Blanchard, A., Kosmatov, N., & Loulergue, F. (2018). Tutorial: Secure Your Things: Secure Development of IoT Software with Frama-C. *2018 IEEE Cybersecurity Development (SecDev)*, 126-127.

Bodeau, D. J., Graubart, R., & Fabius-Greene, J. (2010). Improving cyber security and mission assurance via cyber preparedness (cyber prep) levels. In *2010 IEEE Second International Conference on Social Computing*, (pp. 1147-1152). IEEE. 10.1109/SocialCom.2010.170

Bodó, B., Gervais, D., & Quintais, J. P. (2018). Blockchain and smart contracts: The missing link in copyright licensing? *International Journal of Law and Information Technology*, *26*(4), 311–336. doi:10.1093/ijlit/eay014

Bogavac, M., Prigoda, L., & Cekerevac, Z. P. (2020). SMEs Digitalization and the Sharing Economy. *MEST Journal*, *8*(1), 36–47. doi:10.12709/mest.08.08.01.05

Bourgeois, D., & Bourgeois, D. T. (2014). *Information Systems Security*. Information Systems for Business and Beyond.

Bowcut, S. (2021). Cybersecurity guide for small business. *Cybersecurity Guide*. https://cybersecurityguide.org/resources/small-business/

Braa, J., Hanseth, O., Heywood, A., Mohammed, W., & Shaw, V. (2007). Developing Health Information Systems in Developing Countries: The Flexible Standards Strategy. *Management Information Systems Quarterly*, *31*(2), 381–402. doi:10.2307/25148796

Braun, V., & Clarke, V. (2006). Using thematic analysis in psychology. *Qualitative Research in Psychology*, *3*(2), 77–101. doi:10.1191/1478088706qp063oa

Braz, C., Seffah, A., & M'Raihi, D. (2007). Designing a Trade-Off Between Usability and Security: A Metrics Based-Model. *Lecture Notes in Computer Science Human-Computer Interaction – INTERACT 2007*, (pp. 114-126). Springer. doi:10.1007/978-3-540-74800-7_9

Brooks, C. (2022). Cybersecurity in 2022 – A Fresh Look at Some Very Alarming Stats. *Forbes*. https://www.forbes.com/sites/chuckbrooks/2022/01/21/cybersecurity-in-2022--a-fresh-look-at-some-very-alarming-stats/?sh=1c40f4406b61

Brumfitt, H. A., Askwith, B., & Zhou, B. (2015, October). Protecting Future Personal Computing: Challenging Traditional Network Security Models. In *2015 IEEE International Conference on Computer and Information Technology; Ubiquitous Computing and Communications; Dependable, Autonomic and Secure Computing; Pervasive Intelligence and Computing* (pp. 1772-1779). IEEE.

Burton, L. C., Anderson, G. F., & Kues, I. W. (2004). Using electronic health records to help coordinate care. *The Milbank Quarterly*, *82*(3), 457–481. doi:10.1111/j.0887-378X.2004.00318.x PMID:15330973

Cai, Z., Du, C., Gan, Y., Zhang, J., & Huang, W. (2018). Research and development of blockchain security. *International Journal of Performability Engineering*, *14*(9), 2040.

Calvo-Manzano, J. A., Lema-Moreta, L., Arcilla-Cabián, M., & Rubio-Sánchez, J. L. (2015). How small and medium enterprises can begin their implementation of ITIL? *Revista Facultad de Ingenieria Universidad de Antioquia (Medellín)*, *77*(77), 127–136. doi:10.17533/udea.redin.n77a15

Castelluccio, M. (2021). *Phishing During Covid*. sfmagazine.com.

CBI. (2022). *Blockchain technology for agricultural ingredients*. CBI. https://www.cbi.eu/market-information/natural-ingredients-health-products/blockchain-technology-agricultural#limitations-of-blockchain

Chaganti, R., Bhushan, B., & Nayyar, A. (2021). *Recent trends in Social Engineering Scams and Case study of Gift Card Scam.* Research Gate.

Chesbrough, H. (2010). Business Model Innovation: Opportunities and Barriers. *Long Range Plann., 43,* 354-363.

Chesbrough, H., & Rosenbloom, R. S. (2002, June 01). The role of the business model in capturing value from innovation: Evidence from Xerox Corporation's technology spin-off companies. *Industrial and Corporate Change, 11*(3), 529–555. doi:10.1093/icc/11.3.529

Chin, W. Y., & Chua, H. N. (2021). Using the Theory of Interpersonal Behavior to Predict Information Security Policy Compliance. *Eighth International Conference on eDemocracy & eGovernment (ICEDEG),* (pp. 80–87). IEEE. 10.1109/ICEDEG52154.2021.9530849

Chowdhury, M., Jahan, S., Islam, R., & Gao, J. (2018). Malware Detection for Healthcare Data Security. In R. Beyah, B. Chang, Y. Li, & S. Zhu (Eds.), *Security and Privacy in Communication Networks. SecureComm 2018. Lecture Notes of the Institute for Computer Sciences, Social Informatics and Telecommunications Engineering* (Vol. 255). Springer.

Chuang, J.-Y. (2021). Romance Scams: Romantic Imagery and Transcranial Direct Current Stimulation. *Frontiers in Psychiatry, 12,* 12. doi:10.3389/fpsyt.2021.738874 PMID:34707523

Chung, K., Boutaba, R., & Hariri, S. (2016). Knowledge based decision support system. *Information Technology Management, 17*(1), 1–3. doi:10.100710799-015-0251-3

Clarke, M. (2021). *ITIL Incident Management: What Are Best Practices? CIO Insight.* N.PAG-N. PAG.

Commission, F. T. (2021). *Consumer Sentinel Network Data Book 2020.* Federal Trade Commission.

Corallo, A., Lazoi, M., & Lezzi, M. (2020). Cybersecurity in the context of industry 4.0: A structured classification of critical assets and business impacts. *Computers in Industry, 114,* 103165. doi:10.1016/j.compind.2019.103165

Cranor, L. F., & Garfinkel, S. (2005). In F. L. Cranor & S. Garfinkel (Eds.), *Security and usability: Designing secure systems that people can use* (p. 21). O'Reilly Media.

Cresitello-Dittmar, B. (2016). *Application of the blockchain for authentication and verification of identity.* Tufts University. http://www.cs.tufts.edu/comp/116/archive/fall2016/bcresitellodittmar.pdf

Criddle, C. (2020). *Facebook sued over Cambridge Analytica data scandal.* BBC.

Cronholm, S., & Persson, L. (2016). Best Practice in IT Service Management: Experienced Strengths and Weaknesses of Using ITIL. *Proceedings of the European Conference on Management, Leadership & Governance,* (pp. 60–67). IEEE.

Crosby, M. Nachiappan, P. P., Verma, S., & Kalyanaraman, V. (2015, October 16). *Blockchain: Beyond Bitcoin—UC Berkeley Sutardja Center*. Berkeley College. https://scet.berkeley.edu/reports/blockchain/

Cross, C., & Holt, T. J. (2021). The Use of Military Profiles in Romance Fraud Schemes. *Victims & Offenders-An International Journal of Evidence-based Research. Policy & Practice*, *16*(3), 385–406.

Cross, C., & Layt, R. (2021). I Suspect That the Pictures Are Stolen": Romance Fraud, Identity Crime, and Responding to Suspicions of Inauthentic Identities. *Social Science Computer Review*, 1–19.

Cusick, J. (2018). Organizational Design and Change Management for IT Transformation: A Case Study. *Journal of Computer Science and Information Technology*, *6*, 10–25. doi:10.15640/jcsit.v6n1a2

D'Arcy, J., & Lowry, P. B. (2019). Cognitive-affective Drivers of Employees' Daily Compliance with Information Security Policies: A Multilevel, Longitudinal Study. *Information Systems Journal*, *29*(1), 43–69. doi:10.1111/isj.12173

da Cunha, P. R., Soja, P., & Themistocleous, M. (2021). Blockchain for development: A guiding framework. []. Taylor & Francis.]. *Information Technology for Development*, *27*(3), 417–438. doi:10.1080/02681102.2021.1935453

Dalpiaz, F., Paja, E., & Giorgini, P. (2016). *Security requirements engineering: Designing secure socio-technical systems*. The MIT Press.

Dapp, M., & Lyons, T. (2021, December 14). Privacy in the era of cryptocurrencies. *Bitcoin Suisse*. https://www.bitcoinsuisse.com/research/theme/privacy-in-the-era-of-cryptocurrencies

Dávila, A., Janampa, R., Angeleri, P., & Melendez, K. (2020). ITSM model for very small organisation: An empirical validation. *IET Software*, *14*(2), 138–144. doi:10.1049/iet-sen.2019.0034

de Leon, D. C., Stalick, A. Q., Jillepalli, A. A., Haney, M. A., & Sheldon, F. T. (2017). *Blockchain: Properties and misconceptions*. Asia Pacific Journal of Innovation and Entrepreneurship.

Deane, J. K., Goldberg, D. M., Rakes, T. R., & Rees, L. P. (2020). The effect of information security certification announcements on the market value of the firm. *Information Technology Management*, *20*(3), 107–121. doi:10.100710799-018-00297-3

Deloitte. (2022, May 19). *When Two Chains Combine Supply Chain Meets Blockchain*. Deloitte Turkey. https://www2.deloitte.com/tr/en/pages/technology/articles/when-two-chains-combine.html

Dinçer, H., & Yüksel, S. (2018). *Handbook of research on managerial thinking in global business economics*. IGI Global.

Dobrian, J. (2015). Are you sitting on a cyber security bombshell? *Journal of Property Management*, *80*, 8–12.

Dokuchaev, V. A., Maklachkova, V. V., & Statev, V. Y. (2020). Classification of personal data security threats in information systems. *T-Comm-Телекоммуникации и Транспорт, 14*(1), 56–60. doi:10.36724/2072-8735-2020-14-1-56-60

Dresch, A., Lacerda, D. P., & Antunes, J. A. V. (2015). Design science research. In *Design science research* (pp. 67–102). Springer. doi:10.1007/978-3-319-07374-3_4

Drescher, D. (2017). *Blockchain basics: A non-technical introduction in 25 steps.* Apress, Frankfurt-am-Mein. doi:10.1007/978-1-4842-2604-9

Du, W., Li, A., Zhou, P., Xu, Z., Wang, X., Jiang, H., & Wu, D. (2020). Approximate to be great: Communication efficient and privacy-preserving large-scale distributed deep learning in internet of things. *IEEE internet of things Journal, 7*(12), 11678-11692.

Earnst & Young. (2016). *Cyber preparedness: the next step for boards.* EY. https://www.ey.com/gl/en/issues/governance-and-reporting/eycyber-preparedness-the-next-step-for-boards

Eikebrokk, T. R., & Iden, J. (2017). Strategising IT Service Management through ITIL Implementation: Model and Empirical Test. *Total Quality Management & Business Excellence, 28*(3-4), 238–265. doi:10.1080/14783363.2015.1075872

El Yamami, A., Mansouri, K., Qbadou, M., & Illoussamen, E. H. (2018). Introducing ITIL Framework in Small Enterprises: Tailoring ITSM Practices to the Size of Company. *International Journal of Information Technologies and Systems Approach, 12*(1), 1–19. doi:10.4018/IJITSA.2019010101

Eling, M., McShane, M., & Nguyen, T. (2021). Cyber risk management: History and future research directions. *Risk Management & Insurance Review, 24*(1), 93–125. doi:10.1111/rmir.12169

Ellström, D., Holtström, J., Berg, E., & Josefsson, C. (2021). Dynamic capabilities for digital transformation. *Journal of Strategy and Management, 15*(2), 272–286. doi:10.1108/JSMA-04-2021-0089

Etzion, D., & Aragon-Correa, J. A. (2016). Big Data, Management, and Sustainability: Strategic Opportunities Ahead. *Organization & Environment, 29*(2), 147–155. doi:10.1177/1086026616650437

European Commission. (2022). *Internal Market, Industry, Entrepreneurship and SMEs.* European Commission. https://ec.europa.eu/growth/smes/sme-definition_pt

Evans R. S. (2016). Electronic Health Records: Then, Now, and in the Future. *Yearbook of medical informatics, Suppl 1*(Suppl 1), S48–S61. doi:10.15265/IYS-2016-s006

Eysenbach, G. (2001). What is e-health? *Journal of Medical Internet Research, 3*(2), E20. doi:10.2196/jmir.3.2.e20 PMID:11720962

Fabiano, N. (2017, June) of things and blockchain: Legal issues and privacy. The challenge for a privacy standard. In *2017 IEEE International Conference on internet of things (iThings) and IEEE Green Computing and Communications (GreenCom) and IEEE Cyber, Physical and Social Computing (CPSCom) and IEEE Smart Data (SmartData)* (pp. 727-734). IEEE.

Faizal, M. M., Yahya, S., & Faisal Adham, A. S. (2019). A Review of Phone Scam Activities in Malaysia. *2019 IEEE 9th International Conference on System Engineering and Technology (ICSET)*. IEEE.

Fanning, K., & Centers, D. P. (2016). Blockchain and its coming impact on financial services. *Journal of Corporate Accounting & Finance*, *27*(5), 53–57. doi:10.1002/jcaf.22179

Farhadi, M., Ismail, R., & Fooladi, M. (2012). Information and communication technology use and economic growth. *PLoS One*, *7*(11), e48903. doi:10.1371/journal.pone.0048903 PMID:23152817

Faroze, D. S. (2018). Block chain & internet of things: Security, challenges, research issues. *International Journal of Computer Science Trends and Technology*, *6*(5), 35–38.

FBI. (2020). *Internet Crime Report 2020*. FBI.

Fernández-Alemán, J. L., Señor, I. C., Lozoya, P. Á., & Toval, A. (2013). Security and privacy in electronic health records: A systematic literature review. *Journal of Biomedical Informatics*, *46*(3), 541–562. doi:10.1016/j.jbi.2012.12.003 PMID:23305810

Fernández-Caramés, T. M., & Fraga-Lamas, P. (2018). A Review on the Use of Blockchain for the Internet of Things. *IEEE Access: Practical Innovations, Open Solutions*, *6*, 32979–33001. doi:10.1109/ACCESS.2018.2842685

Fletcher, E. (2019). *Older adults hardest hit by tech support scams*. Federal Trade Commission. www.ftc.gov

Fortes, N., & Rita, P. (2016). Privacy concerns and online purchasing behaviour: Towards an integrated model. *European Research on Management and Business Economics*, *22*(3), 167–176. doi:10.1016/j.iedeen.2016.04.002

Gad, A. G., Mosa, D. T., Abualigah, L., & Abohany, A. A. (2022). Emerging Trends in Blockchain Technology and Applications: A Review and Outlook. *Journal of King Saud University-Computer and Information Sciences*.

Galup, S., Dattero, R., & Quan, J. (2020). What Do Agile, Lean, and ITIL Mean to DevOps? *Communications of the ACM*, *63*(10), 48–53. doi:10.1145/3372114

Gausdal, A. H., Czachorowski, K. V., & Solesvik, M. Z. (2018). Applying blockchain technology: Evidence from Norwegian companies. *Sustainability*, *10*(6), 1985. doi:10.3390u10061985

Gayathri, R., & Nagarajan, V. (2015). Secure data hiding using Steganographic technique with Visual Cryptography and Watermarking Scheme. IEEE ICCSP conference, (pp. 0118-0123). IEEE. doi:10.1109/ICCSP.2015.7322691

Ghosh, S., De Sayandip, S. P. M., & Rahaman, H. (2015). A Novel Dual Purpose Spatial Domain Algorithm for Digital Image Watermarking and Cryptography Using Extended Hamming Code. *IEEE Proceedings of International Conference on Electrical Information and Communication Technology (EICT 2015)*, (pp. 167-172). IEEE.

Giansanti, D. (2021). Cybersecurity and the Digital-Health: The Challenge of This Millennium. *Health Care*, *9*(62), 62. doi:10.3390/healthcare9010062 PMID:33440612

Gil-Gómez, H., Oltra-badenes, R., & Adarme-Jaimes, W. (2014). Service quality management based on the application of the ITIL standard. *Dyna*, *81*(186), 1–6. doi:10.15446/dyna.v81n186.37953

Glaspie, H. W., & Karwowski, W. (2018). Human Factors in Information Security Culture: A Literature Review. In *International Conference on Applied Human Factors and Ergonomics* (pp. 269-280). Springer. 10.1007/978-3-319-60585-2_25

Gomes, J. F., Ahokangas, G., & Owusu, K. A. (2016). Business modeling facilitated cyber preparedness. Conference Proceedings from European Wireless, (pp. 1-12).

Gomes, J. F., Ahokangas, P., & Moqaddamerad, S. (2016). Business modeling options for distributed network functions virtualization: Operator perspective. In *Conference Proceedings from European Wireless 2016*, (pp. 37).

Gordon, W. J., & Catalini, C. (2018). Blockchain technology for healthcare: Facilitating the transition to patient-driven interoperability. *Computational and Structural Biotechnology Journal*, *16*, 224–230. doi:10.1016/j.csbj.2018.06.003 PMID:30069284

Grander, G., da Silva, L. F., & Gonzalez, E. D. R. S. (2021). Big data as a value generator in decision support systems: A literature review. *Rev. Gest.*, *28*(3), 205–222. doi:10.1108/REGE-03-2020-0014

Grandi, A. P., Sarri, A., & Paggio, V. (2021). What Europe's SMEs need to do for a cyber-secure future. *We Forum.* https://www.weforum.org/agenda/2021/06/cybersecurity-for-smes-europe/

Granulo, A., & Tanovic, A. (2020). The Advantage of Using SWOT Analysis for Companies with Implemented ITIL Framework Processes. *43rd International Convention on Information, Communication and Electronic Technology (MIPRO)*, (pp. 1656–1661). IEEE, 10.23919/MIPRO48935.2020.9245393

Guin, U., Cui, P., & Skjellum, A. (2018). Ensuring proof-of-authenticity of IoT edge devices using blockchain technology. *2018 IEEE International Conference on Internet of Things (IThings) and IEEE Green Computing and Communications (GreenCom) and IEEE Cyber, Physical and Social Computing (CPSCom) and IEEE Smart Data (SmartData)*, (pp. 1042–1049). IEEE. 10.1109/Cybermatics_2018.2018.00193

Gunavathy, S., & Meena, C. (2019). A Survey: Data Security In Cloud Using Cryptography And Steganography. *International Research Journal of Engineering and Technology*, *6*(5), 6792–6797.

Gupta, A., & Walia, N. K. (2014). Cryptography Algorithms: A Review. *International Journal Of Engineering Development And Research*, *2*(2), 1667–1672.

Gupta, M. P., & Dubey, A. (2016). E-commerce-study of privacy, trust and security from consumer's perspective. *Transactions*, *37*, 38.

Habiba, S. U., Islam, M. K., & Tasnim, F. (2021). A Comparative Study on Fake Job Post Prediction Using Different Data mining Techniques. *2021 2nd International Conference on Robotics, Electrical and Signal Processing Techniques (ICREST)*. IEEE.

Haenschen, K., Frischmann, B., & Ellenbogen, P. (2021). Manipulating Facebook's Notification System to Provide Evidence of Techno-Social Engineering. *Social Science Computer Review*.

Hameed, M. A., & Arachchilage, N. A. G. (2019). On the impact of perceived vulnerability in the adoption of information systems security innovations. *International Journal of Computer Network and Information Security*, 4(4), 9–18. doi:10.5815/ijcnis.2019.04.02

Han, Y., He, W., Shuai, J., & Qing, L. (2014). A Digital Watermarking Algorithm of Colour Image based on Visual Cryptography and Discrete Cosine Transform. *IEEE Ninth International Conference on P2P,* (pp. 527-530). IEEE.

Harman, L., Flite, C., & Bond, K. (2012).. *The Virtual Mentor*, 14(9), 712–719. doi:10.1001/virtualmentor.2012.14.9.stas1-1209

Henry, R., Herzberg, A., & Kate, A. (2018). Blockchain access privacy: Challenges and directions. *IEEE Security and Privacy*, 16(4), 38–45. doi:10.1109/MSP.2018.3111245

Herzog, S. (2011). Revisiting the Estonian Cyber Attacks: Digital Threats and Multinational Responses. *Journal of Strategic Security, 4,* 49-60.

Higgins, M. (2021, November 8). Blockchain In Supply Chain. *Forbes.* https://www.forbes.com/sites/forbestechcouncil/2021/11/08/blockchain-in-supply-chain/?sh=183f62404e1a

Hina, S., & Dominic, D. D. (2017). Need for Information Security Policies Compliance: A Perspective in Higher Education Institutions. *International Conference on Research and Innovation in Information Systems (ICRIIS)*, (pp. 1–6). IEEE. 10.1109/ICRIIS.2017.8002439

Hiranandani, V. (2011). Privacy and security in the digital age: Contemporary challenges and future directions. *International Journal of Human Rights*, 15(7), 1091–1106. doi:10.1080/13642987.2010.493360

Hiter, S. (2021). CIO vs CISO: What are the 5 Big Differences? *Coin Insight.* https://www.cioinsight.com/it-management/cio-vs-ciso/

Hof, H. J. (2012). *User-Centric IT Security - How to Design Usable Security Mechanisms.* Cornell University.

Hof, H.-J. (2015). *User-Centric IT Security - How to Design Usable Security Mechanisms.* Cornell University. https://arxiv.org/abs/1506.07167

Hof, Hans-Joachim. (2013). Towards Enhanced Usability of IT Security Mechanisms-How to Design Usable IT Security Mechanisms Using the Example of Email Encryption. *International Journal on Advances in Security. 6.*

Holvast, J. (2009) History of Privacy. In Donaldson MS, Lohr KN, (eds.) *Health Data in the Information Age: Use, Disclosure, and Privacy*. National Academies Press. https://www.ncbi.nlm.nih.gov/books/NBK236546/

Hooper, M. (2018, February 22). Top five blockchain benefits transforming your industry. *IBM Supply Chain and Blockchain Blog*. https://www.ibm.com/blogs/blockchain/2018/02/top-five-blockchain-benefits-transforming-your-industry/

Horton, J., Macve, R., & Struyven, G. (2004). Chapter 20 - Qualitative Research: Experiences in Using Semi-Structured Interviews. The Real Life Guide to Accounting Research, 339-357. doi:10.1016/B978-008043972-3/50022-0

IBM. (2021). *Cost of a Data Breach Report 2021*. IBM. internetlivestats. https://www.internetlivestats.com. www.internetlivestats.com

Institute of Medicine. (2009). Committee on Health Research and the Privacy of Health Information. In Nass SJ, Levit LA, Gostin LO, (eds.) *Beyond the HIPAA Privacy Rule: Enhancing Privacy, Improving Health Through Research*. National Academies Press. https://www.ncbi.nlm.nih.gov/books/NBK9579/

International Organization for Standardization. (2013). *ISO/IEC 27001:2013*. ISO. https://www.iso.org/cms/render/live/en/sites/isoorg/contents/data/standard/05/45/54534.html

International Security, Trust, and Privacy Alliance (ISTPA) (2001). *The ISTPA Privacy Framework*. Columbia law. http://emoglen.law.columbia.edu/LIS/archive/privacy-legis/ISTPA-FrameworkWhitePaper013101.pdf

Isaak, J., & Hanna, M. J. (2018). User Data Privacy: Facebook, Cambridge Analytica, and Privacy Protection. *Computer*, *51*(8), 56–59. doi:10.1109/MC.2018.3191268

Ismail, W. B. W., Widyarto, S., Ahmad, R. A. T. R., & Ghani, K. A. A. (2017). Generic Framework for Information Security Policy Development. *4th International Conference on Electrical Engineering, Computer Science and Informatics (EECSI)*, (pp. 1–6). IEEE. 10.1109/EECSI.2017.8239132

ISO-9241-11. (2018). Ergonomic of Human-system interaction - Part 11:Usabililty: Definitions and concepts. ISO 9241-11:2018.

Izquierdo, R. (2022). A Beginner's Guide to the ITIL Framework. *The Ascent*. https://www.fool.com/the-blueprint/itil-framework/

Jagadeesh, G., Balakumar, P., & Inamdar, M. (2013). The Critical Steps for Successful Research: The Research Proposal and Scientific Writing. *Journal of Pharmacology & Pharmacotherapeutics*, *4*(2), 130. doi:10.4103/0976-500x.110895

Jang-Jaccard, J., & Nepal, S. (2014). A survey of emerging threats in cybersecurity. *Journal of Computer and System Sciences*, *80*(5), 973–993. doi:10.1016/j.jcss.2014.02.005

Jäntti, M., & Cater-Steel, A. (2017). Proactive Management of IT Operations to Improve IT Services. *Journal of Information Systems and Technology Management*, *14*(2), 191–218. doi:10.4301/S1807-17752017000200004

Jassim, N. A., Al-Zahir, B. A. M., & Khazraji, A. H. M. (2022). Diagnosing the Current Information Systems Security Department in the Information Technology Department According to the International Standard (Iso/Iec 27001: 2013). *Journal of Management Information & Decision Sciences*, *25*, 1–8.

Jesus, E. F., Chicarino, V. R., De Albuquerque, C. V., & Rocha, A. A. de A. (2018). A survey of how to use blockchain to secure internet of things and the stalker attack. *Security and Communication Networks*, *2018*, 2018. doi:10.1155/2018/9675050

Jha, P., Baranwal, R., & Tiwari, N. K. (2022, February). Protection of User's Data in IOT. In *2022 Second International Conference on Artificial Intelligence and Smart Energy (ICAIS)* (pp. 1292-1297). IEEE. 10.1109/ICAIS53314.2022.9742970

Jia, L. (2020). Research on Information Security of Large Enterprises. *IEEE 8th International Conference on Information, Communication and Networks (ICICN)*, (pp. 219–223). IEEE. 10.1109/ICICN51133.2020.9205077

Kabanda, S., Tanner, M., & Kent, C. (2018). Exploring SME cybersecurity practices in developing countries. *Journal of Organizational Computing and Electronic Commerce*, *28*(3), 269–282. doi:10.1080/10919392.2018.1484598

Kang, J. J., Dibaei, M., Luo, G., Yang, W., & Zheng, X. (2020, December). A privacy-preserving data inference framework for internet of health things networks. In *2020 IEEE 19th International Conference on Trust, Security and Privacy in Computing and Communications (TrustCom)* (pp. 1209-1214). IEEE.

Kaplunovich, A. (2021, December). COVID-19 Multi-Modal Data Analysis with Alexa Voice and Conversational AI Applications: Voice First System Tracking Novel Coronavirus. In *2021 IEEE International Conference on Big Data (Big Data)* (pp. 4514-4517). IEEE.

Karakış, R., Güler, İ., Çapraz, İ., & Bilir, E. (2015, December). A novel fuzzy logic-based image steganography method to ensure medical data security. *Computers in Biology and Medicine*, *67*, 172–183. doi:10.1016/j.compbiomed.2015.10.011 PMID:26555746

Karame, G., & Capkun, S. (2018). Blockchain security and privacy. *IEEE Security and Privacy*, *16*(04), 11–12. doi:10.1109/MSP.2018.3111241

Karanja, E. (2017). The role of the chief information security officer in the management of IT security. *Information and Computer Security*, *25*(3), 300–329. doi:10.1108/ICS-02-2016-0013

Kashinath, S. A., Mostafa, S. A., Mustapha, A., Mahdin, H., Lim, D., Mahmoud, M. A., Mohammed, M. A., Al-Rimy, B. A. S., Fudzee, M. F. M., & Yang, T. J. (2021). Review of data fusion methods for real-time and multi-sensor traffic flow analysis. *IEEE Access: Practical Innovations, Open Solutions*, *9*, 51258–51276. doi:10.1109/ACCESS.2021.3069770

Khalaf, B. A., Mostafa, S. A., Mustapha, A., Mohammed, M. A., Mahmoud, M. A., Al-Rimy, B. A. S., Abd Razak, S., Elhoseny, M., & Marks, A. (2021). An adaptive protection of flooding attacks model for complex network environments. *Security and Communication Networks*. doi:10.1155/2021/5542919

Kim, D. J., Hwang, I. H., & Kim, J. S. (2016). A Study on Employee's Compliance Behavior towards Information Security Policy: A Modified Triandis Model. *Journal of Digital Convergence*, *14*(4), 209–220. doi:10.14400/JDC.2016.14.4.209

Kim, D., & Solomon, M. G. (2021). *Fundamentals of Information Systems Security*. Jones & Bartlett Learning.

Kirlappos, I., & Sasse, M. A. (2014). What Usable Security Means: Trusting and Engaging Users. *Lecture Notes in Computer Science Human Aspects of Information Security, Privacy, and Trust*, (pp. 69-78). doi:10.1007/978-3-319-07620-1_7

Kitsios, F., Chatzidimitriou, E., & Kamariotou, M. (2022). Developing a Risk Analysis Strategy Framework for Impact Assessment in Information Security Management Systems: A Case Study in IT Consulting Industry. *Sustainability*, *14*(3), 1269. doi:10.3390u14031269

Kotzé. (2013). *Paula & Adebesin, Funmi & Greunen, Darelle & Foster, Rosemary*. Barriers and Challenges to the Adoption of E-Health Standards in Africa.

Kraus, S., Durst, S., Ferreira, J. J., Veiga, P., Kailer, N., & Weinmann, A. (2022). Digital transformation in business and management research: An overview of the current status quo. *International Journal of Information Management*, *63*, 1–18. doi:10.1016/j.ijinfomgt.2021.102466

Kruse, C. S., Smith, B., Vanderlinden, H., & Nealand, A. (2017). Security Techniques for the Electronic Health Records. *Journal of Medical Systems*, *41*(8), 127. https://doi.org/10.1007/s10916-017-0778-4

Ksibi, S., Jaidi, F., & Bouhoula, A. (2022). *A Comprehensive Study of Security and Cyber-Security Risk Management within e-Health Systems: Synthesis, Analysis and a Novel Quantified Approach; Mobile Networks and Applications*. Springer. doi:10.1007/s11036-022-02042-1

Kulkarni, R. (2018). *Mitigating Security Issues While Improving Usability* [Thesis or Dissertation, University of Ohio, USA]. https://etd.ohiolink.edu/

Kumar, N. M., & Mallick, P. K. (2018). Blockchain technology for security issues and challenges in IoT. *Procedia Computer Science*, *132*, 1815–1823. doi:10.1016/j.procs.2018.05.140

Kurtinaityte, L. (2007). E-Health – The Usage of ICT Developing Health Care System : Multiple-Case Study of European Countries Denmark and Lithuania [Dissertation, Högskolan i Halmstad/Sektionen för Ekonomi och Teknik (SET), Sweden]. http://urn.kb.se/resolve?urn=urn:nbn:se:hh:diva-779

Lampson, B. (2009). Privacy and Security, Usable security. *Communications of the ACM*, *52*(11), 25–27. doi:10.1145/1592761.1592773

Lau, F., & Kuziemsky, C. (2016). Handbook of eHealth evaluation: An evidence-based approach. University of Victoria.

Lee, R., Jang, R. Y., Park, M., Jeon, G. Y., Kim, J. K., & Lee, S. H. (2020, February). Making IoT data ready for smart city applications. In *2020 IEEE International Conference on Big Data and Smart Computing (BigComp)* (pp. 605-608). IEEE.

Lehto, M. (2015). *"Phenomena in the cyber world," in Cyber Security: Analytics, Technology and Automation*. Springer International Publishing. doi:10.1007/978-3-319-18302-2

Lei, J., & Huang, G. (2021, June). Smart Management System of Employment in Universities Based on Big Data Collection and Intelligent Analysis. In *2021 5th International Conference on Trends in Electronics and Informatics (ICOEI)* (pp. 1110-1113). IEEE.

Leite, L., dos Santos, D. R., & Almeida, F. (2022). The impact of general data protection regulation on software engineering practices. *Information and Computer Security*, *30*(1), 79–96. doi:10.1108/ICS-03-2020-0043

Lekati, C. (2018). Complexities in Investigating Cases of Social Engineering. *11th International Conference on IT Security Incident Management & IT Forensics* (pp. 107-109). IEEE.

Leonov, P. Y., Vorobyev, A. V., Ezhova, A. A., Kotelyanets, O. S., Zavalishina, A. K., & Morozov, N. V. (2021). The Main Social Engineering Techniques Aimed at Hacking Information Systems. *2021 Ural Symposium on Biomedical Engineering, Radioelectronics and Information Technology (USBEREIT)*. IEEE. 10.1109/USBEREIT51232.2021.9455031

Levstek, A., Pucihar, A., & Hovelja, T. (2022). Towards an Adaptive Strategic IT Governance Model for SMEs. *Journal of Theoretical and Applied Electronic Commerce Research*, *17*(1), 230–252. doi:10.3390/jtaer17010012

Li, C., & Palanisamy, B. (2018). Privacy in internet of things: From principles to technologies. *IEEE internet of things Journal, 6*(1), 488-505.

Li, D., Gong, Y., Tang, G., & Huang, Q. (2020, May). Research and design of mineral resource management system based on big data and GIS technology. In *2020 5th IEEE International Conference on Big Data Analytics (ICBDA)* (pp. 52-56). IEEE.

Li, Y., Nakasone, T., Ohta, K., & Sakiyama, K. (2014, January). Privacy-mode switching: Toward flexible privacy protection for RFID tags in internet of things. In *2014 IEEE 11th Consumer Communications and Networking Conference (CCNC)* (pp. 519-520). IEEE.

Liang, T. (2020, October). Design and Implementation of Big Data Visual Statistical Analysis Platform. In *2020 2nd International Conference on Machine Learning, Big Data and Business Intelligence (MLBDBI)* (pp. 287-291). IEEE.

Liaropoulus, A. (2012). War and ethics in cyberspace: Cyber-conflict and just war theory. In Leading Issues in Information Warfare and Security Research, (2nd ed.), pp. 121-134. Good news digital books.

Lima, I., Pedrosa, I., & Rito, S. (2020). Information Security on Portuguese Statutory Auditors Firms. *15th Iberian Conference on Information Systems and Technologies (CISTI)*, (pp. 1–6). IEEE. 10.23919/CISTI49556.2020.9140820

Liu, L., Liu, P., Luo, J., & Zhao, S. (2021, July). Big Data-Based Dynamic Decision-Making Algorithm for Power Enterprise Operation Risk Management. *In 2021 International Conference on Big Data and Intelligent Decision Making (BDIDM)* (pp. 70-74). IEEE.

Liu, S. (2018, January). Business management system and information analysis platform for economic innovation projects. In *2018 International Conference on Intelligent Transportation, Big Data & Smart City (ICITBS)* (pp. 408-411). IEEE.

Liu, X., & Liu, C. (2020, August). An Empirical Analysis of Applied Statistics and Probability Statistics based on Computer Software. In *2020 International Conference on Big Data and Social Sciences (ICBDSS)* (pp. 69-71). IEEE.

Li, Y., Yu, Y., Susilo, W., Hong, Z., & Guizani, M. (2021). Security and Privacy for Edge Intelligence in 5G and Beyond Networks: Challenges and Solutions. *IEEE Wireless Communications*, *28*(2), 63–69. doi:10.1109/MWC.001.2000318

Longnecker, J. G., Petty, W. J., Palich, L. E., & Moore, C. W. (2010). *Small business management: Launching & growing entrepreneurial ventures*. South-Western Cengage Learning.

Lopes, S. F. (2021). The Importance of the ITIL Framework in Managing Information and Communication Technology Services. *International Journal of Advanced Engineering Research and Science*, *8*(5), 292–296. doi:10.22161/ijaers.85.35

Lopez-Leyva, J. A., Kanter-Ramirez, C. A., & Morales-Martinez, J. P. (2020). Customized Diagnostic Tool for The Security Maturity Level of The Enterprise Information Based on ISO/IEC 27001. *8th International Conference in Software Engineering Research and Innovation (CONISOFT)*, (pp. 147–153). IEEE. 10.1109/CONISOFT50191.2020.00030

Lu, X., Li, Q., Qu, Z., & Hui, P. (2014, October). Privacy information security classification study in internet of things. In *2014 International Conference on Identification, Information and Knowledge in the internet of things* (pp. 162-165). IEEE. 10.1109/IIKI.2014.40

Mahalle, A., Yong, J., & Tao, X. (2020). ITIL Process Management to Mitigate Operations Risk in Cloud Architecture Infrastructure for Banking and Financial Services Industry. *Web Intell.*, *18*(3), 229–238. doi:10.3233/WEB-200444

Mairiza, D., Zowghi, D., & Nurmuliani, N. (2010). An investigation into the notion of non-functional requirements. *Proceedings of the ACM Symposium on Applied Computing* (pp. 311-317). ACM. doi:10.1145/1774088.1774153

Makris, C. (2021). Why enterprises are massively subcontracting cybersecurity work. *Venture Beat.* https://venturebeat.com/2021/10/13/why-enterprises-are-massively-subcontracting-cybersecurity-work/

Mallett, R., Hagen-Zanker, J., Slater, R., & Duvendack, M. (2012). The benefits and challenges of using systematic reviews in international development research. *Journal of Development Effectiveness, 4*(3), 445–455. doi:10.1080/19439342.2012.711342

Malonia, M. & Kumar, A. S. (2016). Digital Image Watermarking using Discrete Wavelet Transform and Arithmetic Progression. *IEEE Students's Conference on Electrical.* IEEE.

Manocha, T., & Sharma, V. (202). Essential Awareness of Social Engineering Attacks for Digital Security. *Journal of Applied Management- Jidnyasa, 13*(1), 25-40.

Marrone, M., & Kolbe, L. M. (2011). Impact of IT Service Management Frameworks on the IT Organization. *Business & Information Systems Engineering, 3*(1), 5–18. doi:10.100712599-010-0141-5

Mathur, N., Mathur, H., & Pandya, T. (2015). Risk management in information system of organisation: A conceptual framework. *International Journal of Novel Research in Computer Science and Software Engineering, 2,* 82–88.

McCusker, R. (2006). Transnational organised cyber crime: Distinguishing threat from reality. *Crime, Law, and Social Change, 46*(4-5), 257–273. doi:10.100710611-007-9059-3

Mehboob, A., & Malik, M. I. (2020). Smart Fraud Detection Framework for Job Recruitments. *Arabian Journal for Science and Engineering, 46.*

Mehmedov, R. (2021). *Automated classification of pet scam websites.*

Mehrtak, M. (2021). Security challenges and solutions using healthcare cloud computing. *Journal of Medicine and Life, 14*(4).

Mei, J., Chen, Y., Ye, T., Huang, C., & Ye, H. (2020, June). Research on User Behavior Analysis Model of Financial Industry in Big Data Environment. In *2020 IEEE International Conference on Artificial Intelligence and Computer Applications (ICAICA)* (pp. 1237-1240). IEEE.

Metalidou, E., Marinagi, C., Trivellas, P., Eberhagen, N., Skourlas, C., & Giannakopoulos, G. (2014). The Human Factor of Information Security: Unintentional Damage Perspective. *Procedia: Social and Behavioral Sciences, 147,* 424–428. doi:10.1016/j.sbspro.2014.07.133

Miramirkhani, N., Starov, O., & Nikiforakis, N. (2016). *Dial One for Scam: Analyzing and Detecting Technical Support Scams.* arXiv.

Mitola, J., Guerci, J., Reed, J., Yao, Y. D., Chen, Y., Clancy, T. C., Dwyer, J., Li, H., Man, H., McGwier, R., & Guo, Y. (2014). Accelerating 5G QoE via public- private spectrum sharing. *IEEE Communications Magazine, 52*(5), 77–85. doi:10.1109/MCOM.2014.6815896

Mohammad, A., & Zeki, A. M., Chebil, J., & Gunawan, T. S. (2013). Properties of Digital Image Watermarking. IEEE 9th International Colloquium on Signal processing and its Applications, (pp. 8-10). IEEE.

Monica, R., Henry, Q., & Estela, M. (2020). Why Implement Continuity Plans in Organizations? Approach of a Prospective Study Based on ITIL. *2020 International Conference on Intelligent Systems and Computer Vision (ISCV)*, (pp. 1–5). IEEE. 10.1109/ISCV49265.2020.9204335

Moniruzzaman, Hawlader, A. K., & Hossain, F. (2014). Wavelet Based Watermarking Approach of Hiding Patient Information in Medical Image for Medical Image Authentication. *IEEE 17th International Conference on Computer and Information Technology (ICCIT)*, (pp. 374-378). IEEE.

Morris, M., Schindehutte, M., & Allen, J. (2005). The entrepreneur's business model: toward a unified perspective. *Journal of Business Research, 58*, 726-735.

Mowbray, T. J. (2013). *Cybersecurity: Managing systems, conducting testing, and investigating intrusions*. John Wiley & Sons.

Müller, S. D., & de Lichtenberg, C. G. (2018). The Culture of ITIL: Values and Implementation Challenges. *Information Systems Management, 35*(1), 49–61. doi:10.1080/10580530.2017.1416946

NATO. (2013). The history of cyber attacks - a timeline. NATO. https://www.nato.int/docu/review/2013/cyber/timeline/EN/index.htm

Neisse, R., Steri, G., & Baldini, G. (2014, October). Enforcement of security policy rules for the internet of things. In *2014 IEEE 10th international conference on wireless and mobile computing, networking and communications (WiMob)* (pp. 165-172). IEEE.

Nguyen, C., Jensen, M. L., Durcikova, A., & Wright, R. T. (2021). A comparison of features in a crowdsourced. *Information Systems Journal, 31*(3), 473–513. doi:10.1111/isj.12318

Nielsen, J. (1994). How to Conduct a Heuristic Evaluation. *Nielsen Norman Group*. https://nngroup.com/articles/ten-usability-heuristics/

Norrman, K., Näslund, M., & Dubrova, E. (2016). Protecting IMSI and User Privacy in 5G Networks. *9th EAI International Conference on Mobile Multimedia Communications*. EUDL. 10.4108/eai.18-6-2016.2264114

Nwokedi, Ugochi, Amunga, Beverly, & Rad, Bashari, Babak. (2016). Usability and Security in User Interface Design: A Systematic Literature Review. *International Journal of Information Technology and Computer Science., 8*, 72–80. doi:10.5815/ijitcs.2016.05.08

Nyre-Yu, M., Gutzwiller, R. S., & Caldwell, B. S. (2019). Observing Cyber Security Incident Response: Qualitative Themes From Field Research. *Proceedings of the Human Factors and Ergonomics Society Annual Meeting, 63*(1), 437–441. doi:10.1177/1071181319631016

Odeh, N. A., Eleyan, D., & Eleyan, A. (2021). A survey of social engineering attacks: detection and prevention tools. *Journal of Theoretical and Applied Information Technology, 99*(18), 4375–4386.

Oliveira, D. L., Paula, E. C., & Lovo, O. A. (2017). IT outsourcing in small business: A view of risk and mitigating actions. *Sistemas e Gestão, 12*, 328–340. doi:10.20985/1980-5160.2017.v12n3.1078

Onetti, A., Zucchella, A., Jones, M. V., & McDougall-Covin, P. P. (2012). Internationalization, innovation and entrepreneurship: Business models for new technology-based firms. *The Journal of Management and Governance*, *16*(3), 337–368. doi:10.100710997-010-9154-1

Ormond, D., Warkentin, M., & Crossler, R. E. (2019). Integrating Cognition with an Affective Lens to Better Understand Information Security Policy Compliance. *Journal of the Association for Information Systems*, *20*, 1794–1843. doi:10.17705/1jais.00586

Paananen, H., Lapke, M., & Siponen, M. (2020). State of the Art in Information Security Policy Development. *Computers & Security*, *88*, 101608. doi:10.1016/j.cose.2019.101608

Park, J. H., & Park, J. H. (2017). Blockchain security in cloud computing: Use cases, challenges, and solutions. *Symmetry*, *9*(8), 164. doi:10.3390ym9080164

Patil, D. D. Y. (2021, December 31). *Blockchain Technology*. DPU. https://engg.dypvp.edu.in/blogs/blockchain-technology

Payne, B. K. (2020). Criminals Work from Home during Pandemics Too: A Public Health Approach to Respond to Fraud and Crimes against those 50 and above. *American Journal of Criminal Justice*, *45*(4), 563–577. doi:10.100712103-020-09532-6 PMID:32837151

Pelosi, M., Poudel, N., Lamichhane, P., Lam, D., Kessler, G., & Mac-Monagle, J. (2018). *Positive identification of lsb image steganography using cover image comparisons*. ADFSL.

Percivall, G. (2010). The application of open standards to enhance the interoperability of geoscience information. *International Journal of Digital Earth*, *3*(sup1), 14–30. doi:10.1080/17538941003792751

Pereira, G. V., Virkar, S., & Vignoli, M. (2018). Exploring the political, social and cultural challenges and possibilities associated with trading data: The case of data market Austria (DMA). *Proceedings of the 19th Annual International Conference on Digital Government Research: Governance in the Data Age*, (pp. 1–2).

Phillips-Wren, G., Daly, M., & Burstein, F. (2021). Reconciling business intelligence, analytics and decision support systems: More data, deeper insight. *Decision Support Systems*, *146*, 1–13. doi:10.1016/j.dss.2021.113560

Pinto, Z. (2013, March 13). Cyber Security - product of service? *Automation World*: http://www.automationworld.com/security/cyber-security-productor-service

pixelplex.io. (2022, September 14). *Blockchain Security: Everything You Need to Know*. PixelPlex. https://pixelplex.io/blog/everything-you-need-to-know-about-blockchain-security/

Ponemon Institute. (2015). *2015 cost of data breach study: Global analysis*. Ponemon Institute, LLC.

Prabhjot, N. S., & Kaur, H. (2017). A Review of Information Security using Cryptography Technique. *International Journal of Advanced Research in Computer Science, 8*, pp. 323-326, 2017

Pradhan, A., Sahu, A. K., Swain, G., & Sekhar, K. R. (2016). Performance evaluation parameters of image steganography techniques. *2016 International Conference on Research Advances in Integrated Navigation Systems (RAINS)*, (pp. 1-8). IEEE. 10.1109/RAINS.2016.7764399

Punchoojit, L., & Hongwarittorrn, N. (2017). Usability Studies on Mobile User Interface Design Patterns: A Systematic Literature Review. *Advances in Human-Computer Interaction, 2017*, 1–22. doi:10.1155/2017/6787504

Purtill, C. (2018, September 9). Equifax data breach: A year later, no punishment for the company. *Quartz*. https://qz.com/1383810/equifax-data-breach-one-year-later-no-punishment-for-the-company/

Qadir, S., & Quadri, S. (2016). Information Availability: An Insight into the Most Important Attribute of Information Security. *Journal of Information Security, 7*(03), 185–194. doi:10.4236/jis.2016.73014

Quader, F., & Janeja, V. P. (2021). Insights into Organizational Security Readiness: Lessons Learned from Cyber-Attack Case Studies. *Journal of Cybersecurity and Privacy, 1*(4), 638–659. doi:10.3390/jcp1040032

Qu, Z., Cheng, Z., Liu, W., & Wang, X. (2019, April). A novel quantum image steganography algorithm based on exploiting modification direction. *Multimedia Tools and Applications, 78*(7), 7981–8001. doi:10.100711042-018-6476-5

Rabah, K. (2004, March). Steganography—The art of hiding data. *Information Technology Journal, 3*(3), 245–269. doi:10.3923/itj.2004.245.269

Rahmadika, S., & Rhee, K.-H. (2018). Blockchain technology for providing an architecture model of decentralized personal health information. *International Journal of Engineering Business Management, 10*, 1847979018790589. doi:10.1177/1847979018790589

Rajawat, M., & Tomar, D. S. (2015). A Secure Watermarking and Tampering detection technique on RGB Image using 2 Level DWT. *IEEE Fifth International Conference on Communication Systems and Network Technologies*, (pp. 638-642). IEEE. 10.1109/CSNT.2015.245

Ramirez-Asis, H., Silva-Zapata, M., Ramirez-Asis, E., Sharma, T., Durga, S., & Pant, B. (2022, April). A Conceptual Analysis on the Impact of Big Data Analytics Toward on Digital Marketing Transformation. In *2022 2nd International Conference on Advance Computing and Innovative Technologies in Engineering (ICACITE)* (pp. 1651-1655). IEEE.

Rani, P. & Arora, A. (2015). Image security system using encryption and steganography. *IJIRSET, 4*(6).

Rantao, T., & Njenga, K. (2020). Predicting Communication Constructs towards Determining Information Security Policies Compliance. *South African Journal of Information Management, 22*(1), 1–10. doi:10.4102ajim.v22i1.1211

Rao, A. (2018, May 29). How to Secure your Personal Data using blockchain? *Coinmonks*. https://medium.com/coinmonks/guarantee-your-patients-privacy-today-securing-sensitive-data-with-blockchain-fcb179f1302c

Rashid, Y., Rashid, A., Warraich, M. A., Sabir, S. S., & Waseem, A. (2019). Case Study Method: A Step-by-Step Guide for Business Researchers. *International Journal of Qualitative Methods*, *18*, 1–13. doi:10.1177/1609406919862424

Reiter, M., & Miklošík, A. (2020). Digital Transformation of Organisations in the Context of ITIL® 4. *Mark. Ident.*, *1*, 522–536.

Reyna, A., Martín, C., Chen, J., Soler, E., & Díaz, M. (2018). On blockchain and its integration with IoT. Challenges and opportunities. *Future Generation Computer Systems*, *88*, 173–190. doi:10.1016/j.future.2018.05.046

Riasetiawan, M., Ashari, A., & Prastowo, B. N. (2021, November). 360Degree Data Analysis and Visualization for COVID-19 Mitigation in Indonesia. In *2021 International Conference on Data Science, Artificial Intelligence, and Business Analytics (DATABIA)* (pp. 7-12). IEEE.

Richardson, J. (2008). The business model: An integrative framework for strategy execution. *Strategic Change*, *17*(5-6), 133–144. doi:10.1002/jsc.821

Rid, T., & Buchanan, B. (2014). Attributing cyber attacks. *The Journal of Strategic Studies*, *38*(1-2), 4–37. doi:10.1080/01402390.2014.977382

Rieke, R., Repp, J., Zhdanova, M., & Eichler, J. (2014). Monitoring Security Compliance of Critical Processes. *22nd Euromicro International Conference on Parallel, Distributed, and Network-Based Processing*, (pp. 552-560). https://doi.irg/10.1109/PDP.2014.106

Rios, O. K. L., Filho, J. G. A. T., & Rios, V. P. S. (2017). Melhores Práticas Do COBIT, ITIL e ISO/IEC 27002 Para Implantação de Política de Segurança da Informação em Instituições Federais do Ensino Superior. *Revista Gestão & Tecnologia*, *17*(1), 130–154. doi:10.20397/2177-6652/2017.v17i1.1084

Rivera, D., García, A., Martín-Ruiz, M. L., Alarcos, B., Velasco, J. R., & Oliva, A. G. (2019). Secure communications and protected data for a internet of things smart toy platform. *IEEE internet of things Journal*, *6*(2), 3785–3795. doi:10.1109/JIOT.2019.2891103

Romano, D., & Schmid, G. (2021). Beyond Bitcoin: Recent Trends and Perspectives in Distributed Ledger Technology. *Cryptography*, *5*(4), 36. doi:10.3390/cryptography5040036

Ross, J., Stevenson, F., & Lau, R. (2016). Factors that influence the implementation of e-health: A systematic review of systematic reviews (an update). *Implementation Science; IS*, *11*, 146. https://doi.org/10.1186/s13012-016-0510-7

Ross, R. (2018). *Risk Management Framework for Information Systems and Organizations: A System Life Cycle Approach for Security and Privacy*. National Institute of Standards and Technology. doi:10.6028/NIST.SP.800-37r2

Sabbagh, P., Pourmohamad, R., Elveny, M., Beheshti, M., Davarpanah, A., Metwally, A. S. M., Ali, S., & Mohammed, A. S. (2021). Evaluation and Classification Risks of Implementing Blockchain in the Drug Supply Chain with a New Hybrid Sorting Method. *Sustainability*, *13*(20), 11466. doi:10.3390u132011466

Sahu, A. K., & Swain, G. (2019). A novel n-Rightmost bit replacement image steganography technique. *3D Res. 10*(1), 2.

Sahu, A. K., & Swain, G. (2019, September). an optimal information hiding approach based on pixel value differencing and modulus function. *Wireless Personal Communications*, *108*(1), 159–174. doi:10.100711277-019-06393-z

Salahdine, F., & Kaabouch, N. (2019). Social Engineering Attacks: A Survey. *Future Internet, 11* (4).

Saleh, M. E., Aly, A. A., & Omara, F. A. (2016). Data security using cryptography and steganography techniques. *International Journal of Advanced Computer Science and Applications*, *7*(6), 390–397.

Sanjay, K., & Ambar, D. (2016). A Novel Spatial Domain Technique for Digital Image Watermarking Using Block Entropy. *IEEE Fifth International Conference on Recent Trends in Information Technology*. IEEE.

Sarala, R., Zayaraz, G., & Aravindanne, S. (2015). Prediction of Insider Threats for Effective Information Security Risk Assessment. *International Journal of Applied Engineering*, *10*, 19033–19036.

Sasse, M. A., Brostoff, S., & Weirich, D. (2001). *BT Technology Journal*, *19*(3), 122–131.

Sasse, M. A., & Flechais, I. (2005). Usable Security: Why Do We Need It? How Do We Get It? In L. F. Cranor & S. Garfinkel (Eds.), *Security and Usability: Designing secure systems that people can use. (13 - 30)*. O'Reilly.

Sausalito, C. (2021). Cybercrime to Cost the World $10.5 Trillion Annually By 2025. *Cyber Security Ventures*. https://cybersecurityventures.com/cybercrime-damages-6-trillion-by-2021/

Schinagl, S., & Shahim, A. (2020). What do we know about information security governance? "From the basement to the boardroom": Towards digital security governance. *Information and Computer Security*, *28*(2), 261–292. doi:10.1108/ICS-02-2019-0033

Schneble, C. O., Elger, B. S., & Shaw, D. (2018). The Cambridge Analytica affair and Internet-mediated research. *EMBO Reports*, *19*(8). doi:10.15252/embr.201846579 PMID:29967224

Schotte, T., & Abdalla, M. (2021). *The impact of the COVID-19 pandemic on the serious and organised crime landscape. Collection of Contributions to the CEPOL Online Research & Science Conference*. Pandemic Effects on Law Enforcement Training and Practice.

Schrade, M. J. (2021). *Tech support scams adapt and persist in 2021, per new Microsoft research*. Microsoft.

Scully, T. (2014). The cyber security threat stops in the boardroom. *Journal of Business Continuity & Emergency Planning*, 7, 138–148. PMID:24457325

Serban, R. A. (2017). The impact of big data, sustainability, and digitalization on company performance. *Studies in Business and Economics*, *12*(3), 181–189. doi:10.1515be-2017-0045

Shackelford, S. J., & Myers, S. (2017). Block-by-block: Leveraging the power of blockchain technology to build trust and promote cyber peace. *Yale JL & Tech.*, *19*, 334.

Shafer, S. M., Smith, H. J., & Linder, J. C. (2005). The power of business models. *Business Horizons*, *48*(3), 199–207. doi:10.1016/j.bushor.2004.10.014

Shahrom, M. F., Maarop, N., Samy, G. N., Hassan, N. H., Rahim, F. A., Magalingam, P., et al. (2021). A Pilot Analysis of Factors Affecting Defense. *Open International Journal of Informatics (OIJI)*, *9*(1), 53-64.

Shao, P., & Yao, L. (2021, October). Empirical analysis on textile industry big data using computer mathematical statistics and double difference method. In *2021 IEEE International Conference on Data Science and Computer Application (ICDSCA)* (pp. 224-227). IEEE.

Shi, H., Zhang, X.-Y., Wang, S., Fu, G., & Tang, J. (2019). Synchronized detection and recovery of steganographic messages with adversarial learning. *Proc. Int. Conf. Comput. Sci*, (pp. 31-43). 10.1007/978-3-030-22741-8_3

Shojaifar, A., & Jarvinen, H. (2021). Classifying SMEs for Approaching Cybersecurity Competence and Awareness. *The 16th International Conference on Availability, Reliability and Security*, (pp. 1-7). IEEE. 10.1145/3465481.3469200

Silva, T. S., Carvalho, H., & Torres, C. B. (2003). *Segurança dos Sistemas de Informação*. Famalicão: Centro Atlântico.

Singh, J., Hasan K., & and Kumar, R. (2015). Enhance security for image encryption and decryption by applying hybrid techniques using MATLAB. *IJIRCCE*, *3*(7).

Sittig, D. F., Belmont, E., & Singh, H. (2018). Improving the safety of health information technology requires shared responsibility: It is time we all step up. *Health Care*, *6*(1), 7–12. doi:10.1016/j.hjdsi.2017.06.004

Sivaraman, V. (2019). Security Management at the National Institute of Management: To Outsource or Insource? Cases (A) and (B). *Vikalpa*, *44*(2), 95–96. doi:10.1177/0256090919854813

SK., W. H., Singh, S. P., & Johri, P. (2021, August). A Comprehensive Review on Securities and Privacy Preservation in IOT Healthcare Application for Diabetics. In *2021 Second International Conference on Electronics and Sustainable Communication Systems (ICESC)* (pp. 706-711). IEEE.

Smith, J. (2010). Web Page Design: Heuristic Evaluation vs. User Testing. *International Journal of Industrial Ergonomics*.

Smith, T. L. (2018a, March 23). The 6 Limitations of Blockchain Technology. *Everything Blockchain.* https://medium.com/everything-blockchain/the-6-limitations-of-blockchain-technology-2d1b686c0293

Smith, L. (2019). *Fordney's Medical Insurance - E-Book - Ch2 Privacy, Security.* And HIPPA.

Soomro, T. R., & Hussain, M. (2019). Social Media-Related Cybercrimes and Techniques for Their Prevention. *Applied Computer Systems*, *24*(1), 9–17. doi:10.2478/acss-2019-0002

Soomro, T. R., & Wahba, H. Y. (2011). Role of Information Technology Infrastructure Library in Data Warehouses. *American Journal of Applied Sciences*, *8*(12), 1384–1387. doi:10.3844/ajassp.2011.1384.1387

SophosLabs. (2021). *Sophos 2021 Threat Report.* SophosLabs.

Spasic, B., & Markovic, A. (2013). Information and Communication Technology Unit Service Management in a Non-Profit Organization Using ITIL Standards. *Management*, *18*(66), 39–70. doi:10.7595/management.fon.2013.0005

Squillace, J., & Bantan, M. (2022, June). A Taxonomy of Privacy, Trust, and Security Breach Incidents of Internet-of-Things Linked to F (M). AANG Corporations. In *2022 IEEE World AI IoT Congress (AIIoT)* (pp. 591-596). IEEE.

Srinivasan, B., Kountouras, A., Miramirkhani, N., Alam, M., Nikiforakis, N., & Antonakakis, M. (2018). Exposing Search and Advertisement Abuse Tactics and Infrastructure of Technical Support Scammers. *Proceedings of the 2018 World Wide Web Conference*, (pp. 319-328). ACM. 10.1145/3178876.3186098

Srivastava, V. (2022, January 23). *Limitations of Blockchain Technology.* Include Help. https://www.includehelp.com/blockchain/limitations-of-blockchain-technology.aspx

Statista, (2016). Internet of Things (IoT): number of connected devices worldwide from 2012 to 2020 (in billions). *Statista*: https://www.statista.com/statistics/471264/iot-number-of-connected-devices-worldwide/

Statista. (2021). *Forecast number of mobile 5G subscriptions worldwide by region from 2019 to 2026.* statista. .

Statista. (2021). *Global digital population as of January 2021.* Statista

Stepenko, V., Dreval, L., Chernov, S., & Shestak, V. (2022). EU Personal Data Protection Standards and Regulatory Framework. *J Journal of Applied Security Research*, *17*(2), 190–207. doi:10.1080/19361610.2020.1868928

Stoneburner, G., Goguen, A., & Feringa, A. (2002). *Risk management guide for information technology systems.* Springer. doi:10.1023/a:1011902718709

Stuurman, K., & Kamara, I. (2016, August). IoT Standardization-The Approach in the Field of Data Protection as a Model for Ensuring Compliance of IoT Applications? In *2016 IEEE 4th International Conference on Future internet of things and Cloud Workshops (FiCloudW)* (pp. 336-341). IEEE.

Sulaiman, R., Sharma, D., Ma, W., & Tran, D. (2008). A Security Architecture for e-Health Services. *International Conference on Advanced Communication Technology, ICACT. 2.* (pp. 999 – 1004). IEEE. doi:. doi:10.1109/ICACT.2008.4493935

Syed, A. M. (2021). *Social engineering: Concepts, Techniques and.* ArXiv.

Techtarget.com. (2021, September 9). *Using blockchain to improve security for IoT devices.* IoT Agenda. https://www.techtarget.com/iotagenda/post/Using-blockchain-to-improve-security-for-IoT-devices

Teece, D. J. (2010). Business Models, Business Strategy and Innovation. *Long Range Plann., 43,* 172-194.

Telford, T. (2019). Thousands of Disney Plus accounts were hacked and sold online for as little as $3. *Washington post.*

Thapar, A. (2022). *Social Engineering An Attack vector Most intricate to tackle.* www.infosecwriters.com

Timmers, P. (1998). Business Models for Electronic Markets. *Electronic Markets, 8,* 3-8.

Tong, S., Liu, Q., Huang, W., Hunag, Z., Chen, E., Liu, C., & Wang, S. (2020, November). Structure-based knowledge tracing: an influence propagation view. In *2020 IEEE International Conference on Data Mining (ICDM)* (pp. 541-550). IEEE.

Torre, I., Koceva, F., Sanchez, O. R., & Adorni, G. (2016, December). A framework for personal data protection in the IoT. In *2016 11th international conference for internet technology and secured transactions (ICITST)* (pp. 384-391). IEEE.

Treiblmaier, H. (2018). The impact of the blockchain on the supply chain: A theory-based research framework and a call for action. *Supply Chain Management, 23*(6), 545–559. doi:10.1108/SCM-01-2018-0029

U. S. Chamber of Commerce. (2015). *The case for enhanced protection of trade secrets in the trans-pacific partnership agreement.* US Chamber of Commerce.

Ulsch, N. M. (2014). *Cyber Threat!: How to Manage the Growing Risk of Cyber Attacks.* John Wiley & Sons. doi:10.1002/9781118915028

Uskenbayeva, R. K., Kuandykov, A. A., Kuatbayeva, A. A., Kassymova, A. B., Kuatbayeva, G. K., & Zhussipbek, B. K. (2021, September). Burn disease data analysis model in SAS UE. In *2021 IEEE 23rd Conference on Business Informatics (CBI)* (Vol. 2, pp. 197-201). IEEE.

Van der Kleij, R., Kleinhuis, G., & Young, H. (2017). Computer Security Incident Response Team Effectiveness: A Needs Assessment. *Frontiers in Psychology*, *8*, 1–8. doi:10.3389/fpsyg.2017.02179 PMID:29312051

Varadi, S., Varkonyi, G. G., & Kertész, A. (2018, April). Law and iot: How to see things clearly in the fog. In *2018 Third International Conference on Fog and Mobile Edge Computing (FMEC)* (pp. 233-238). IEEE. 10.1109/FMEC.2018.8364070

Vatis, M. (2002). *Cyber attacks: Protecting America's security against digital threats*. Harvard Kennedy School.

Ved, M., & Rizwanahmed, B. (2019, July). Big data analytics in telecommunication using state-of-the-art big data framework in a distributed computing environment: a case study. In *2019 IEEE 43rd Annual Computer Software and Applications Conference (COMPSAC)* (*Vol. 1*, pp. 411-416). IEEE.

Vermesan, O., & Bacquet, J. (2019). *Next generation Internet of Things: Distributed intelligence at the edge and human machine-to-machine cooperation*. River Publishers.

Vij, A., Saini, S., & Bathla, R. (2020, June). Big Data in Healthcare: Technologies, Need, Advantages, and Disadvantages. In *2020 8th International Conference on Reliability, Infocom Technologies and Optimization (Trends and Future Directions)(ICRITO)* (pp. 1301-1305). IEEE.

Virani, R. (2022). *Small businesses are most vulnerable to growing cybersecurity threats. Help Net Security*. https://www.helpnetsecurity.com/2022/01/11/small-businesses-vulnerable/

Vishwakarma, R. K., Chaturvedi, P., & Yadav, A. K. (2021). Ascertaining Various Perceived Risks and Its impact on Customer's Purchase Intentions to Online Platforms. *Journal of Xi'an Shiyou University, Natural Science Edition, 17* (7).

Visoottiviseth, V., Khengthong, T., Kesorn, K., & Patcharadechathorn, J. (2021, November). ASPAHI: Application for Security and Privacy Awareness Education for Home IoT Devices. In *2021 25th International Computer Science and Engineering Conference (ICSEC)* (pp. 388-393). IEEE.

Wang, X. (2021, June). Application of Big Data Technology in Economic Statistics. In *2021 International Wireless Communications and Mobile Computing (IWCMC)* (pp. 861-864). IEEE.

Wang, Z., Bin, W. U., Demeng, B. A. I., & Jiafeng, Q. I. N. (2018, December). Distributed big data mining platform for smart grid. In *2018 IEEE International Conference on Big Data (Big Data)* (pp. 2345-2354). IEEE.

Weill, PVitale, M. (2002). What it infrastructure capabilities are needed to implement e-business models? MIS Quarterly, 1, 17. .

Weng, X., Li, Y., Chi, L., & Mu, Y. (2019). Convolutional video steganography with temporal residual modeling. arXiv.

Whitman, M. E., & Mattord, H. J. (2017). *Principles of Information Security*. Cengage Learning.

Whitman, M. E., & Mattord, H. J. (2011). *Principles of Information Security* (4th ed.). Cengage Learning.

Whitten, D. (2008). The Chief Information Security Officer: An Analysis of the Skills Required for Success. *Journal of Computer Information Systems*, *48*, 15–19.

William, S. (2011). *Network Security Essentials: Applications and Standards (For VTU)*. Pearson Education India.

Woodside, J. M., Augustine, F. K. Jr, & Giberson, W. (2017). Blockchain technology adoption status and strategies. *Journal of International Technology and Information Management*, *26*(2), 65–93.

worldpopulationreview. (2021). *GDP Ranked by Country 2021*. worldpopulationreview.com. www.nobelpeaceprize.org. *Alfred Nobel.* www.nobelpeaceprize.org

Xiaochun, D., & Bing, W. (2018, June). Design and Application of Website Data Analysis Software in the Era of Big Data. In *2018 International Conference on Smart Grid and Electrical Automation (ICSGEA)* (pp. 334-337). IEEE.

Xiong, Z., Zhang, Y., Niyato, D., Wang, P., & Han, Z. (2018). When mobile blockchain meets edge computing. *IEEE Communications Magazine*, *56*(8), 33–39. doi:10.1109/MCOM.2018.1701095

Yaeger, K., Martini, M., Rasouli, J., & Costa, A. (2019). Emerging blockchain technology solutions for modern healthcare infrastructure. *Journal of Scientific Innovation in Medicine*, *2*(1), 1. doi:10.29024/jsim.7

Yaga, D., Mell, P., Roby, N., & Scarfone, K. (2018). *Blockchain Technology Overview*. NIST. https://nvlpubs.nist.gov/nistpubs/ir/2018/NIST.IR.8202.pdf

Yamakawa, P., Noriega, C. O., Linares, A. N., & Ramírez, W. V. (2012). Improving ITIL compliance using change management practices: A finance sector case study. *Business Process Management Journal*, *18*(6), 1020–1035. doi:10.1108/14637151211283393

Yang, M., & Wang, Q. (2018, May). Research on product development mode of network menswear brand based on big data statistics. In *2018 33rd Youth Academic Annual Conference of Chinese Association of Automation (YAC)* (pp. 694-700). IEEE.

Yang, G. (2018, August). Design of Performance Evaluation Model for Accurate Poverty Alleviation Projects Based on Big Data Analysis. In *2018 International Conference on Virtual Reality and Intelligent Systems (ICVRIS)* (pp. 102-105). IEEE.

Yang, Y., Wu, L., Yin, G., Li, L., & Zhao, H. (2017). A survey on security and privacy issues in Internet-of-Things. *IEEE Internet of Things Journal*, *4*(5), 1250–1258. doi:10.1109/JIOT.2017.2694844

Yee, C. K., & Zolkipli, M. F. (2021). Review on Confidentiality, Integrity and Availability in Information Security. *Journal of ICT in Education*, *8*(2), 34–42. doi:10.37134/jictie.vol8.2.4.2021

Yee, K.-P. (2004). Aligning security and usability. *Security & Privacy, IEEE.*, *2*, 48–55. doi:10.1109/MSP.2004.64

Yeoh, P. (2017). Regulatory issues in blockchain technology. *Journal of Financial Regulation and Compliance.*

Yiannas, F. (2018). A new era of food transparency powered by blockchain. *Innovations: Technology, Governance, Globalization*, *12*(1–2), 46–56. doi:10.1162/inov_a_00266

Yin, R. K. (2017). *Case Study Research and Applications: Design and Methods.* SAGE Publications.

Yli-Huumo, J., Ko, D., Choi, S., Park, S., & Smolander, K. (2016). Where is current research on blockchain technology? A systematic review. *PLoS One*, *11*(10), e0163477. doi:10.1371/journal. pone.0163477 PMID:27695049

Yrjölä, S., Ahokangas, P., & Matinmikko, M. (2015) Evaluation of recent spectrum sharing concepts from business model scalability point of view. In *2015 IEEE International Symposium on Dynamic Spectrum Access Networks (DySPAN)*, (pp. 241-250). 10.1109/DySPAN.2015.7343907

Yuan, Y., & Wang, F.-Y. (2018). Blockchain and cryptocurrencies: Model, techniques, and applications. *IEEE Transactions on Systems, Man, and Cybernetics. Systems*, *48*(9), 1421–1428. doi:10.1109/TSMC.2018.2854904

Zhang, H., Zhang, J., Tian, M., & Qiao, B. (2021, December). Design of Offline Analysis System for Remote Sensing Data Service Based on Hive. In *2021 International Conference on Digital Society and Intelligent Systems (DSInS)* (pp. 300-303). IEEE. 10.1109/DSInS54396.2021.9670605

Zhang, P., Oest, A., Cho, H., Sun, Z., Johnson, R., & Wardman, B. (2021). CrawlPhish: Large-scale Analysis of Client-side Cloaking Techniques in Phishing. *IEEE Symposium on Security and Privacy*. IEEE. 10.1109/SP40001.2021.00021

Zhou, X., Ma, Y., Zhang, Q., Mohammed, M. A., & Damaševičius, R. (2021). A reversible watermarking system for medical color images: Balancing capacity, imperceptibility, and robustness. *Electronics (Basel)*, *10*(9), 1024. doi:10.3390/electronics10091024

Ziegler, S., & Chochliouros, I. (2015, December). Privacy Flag-collective privacy protection scheme based on structured distributed risk assessment. In *2015 IEEE 2nd World Forum on internet of things (WF-IoT)* (pp. 430-434). IEEE.

Zott, C. & Amit, R. (2010). Business Model Design: An Activity System Perspective. *Long Range Plann.*, *43*, 216-226.

Zott, C., Amit, R., & Massa, L. (2011). The business model: Recent developments and future research. *Long Range Planning*, *37*, 1019–1042.

About the Contributors

Arshi Naim is an Associate Professor and Quality Programme head in Business Management, KSA She has completed her PHD in business management Singhania University Rajasthan, MBA in marketing management from HNB University and economics honours from AMU, Aligarh, India. Also, she has accomplished some certificates like QM peer reviewer and E-Learning expert from quality matters, US, ICDL from Australia and certificate on digital skills and digital marketing from UK. She is expert in curriculum and programme development, quality and accreditation process, E-learning and Quality Matters Peer Reviewer. She has research publications in Web of Sceince, IEEE, ACM, and Scopus Indexed Journals. She has also published books with Taylor and Francis, Nova Science Publications, IGI, and Springer. She is also closely associated with international and national universities for supervising PHD students.

* * *

Fernando Luís Almeida has a Ph.D. in Computer Science Engineering from the Faculty of Engineering of University of Porto (FEUP). He also holds an MSc in Innovation and Entrepreneurship and in Informatics Engineering from FEUP. He has around 10 years of teaching experience at higher education levels in the field of computer science and management. He has also worked for 15 years in several positions as a software engineer and project manager for large organizations and research centers like Critical Software, CICA/SEF, INESC TEC, and ISR Porto. He is a founder member of the International Association of Innovation Professionals and he is involved in the development of the US TAG group for ISO 56000 (Innovation Management). His current research areas include innovation policies, entrepreneurship, software development, and decision support systems.

Abdelmalek Amine received an engineering degree in Computer Science, a Magister diploma in Computational Science and PhD from Djillali Liabes University in collaboration with Joseph Fourier University of Grenoble. His research interests include big data, IoT, data mining, text mining, ontology, classification, clustering, neural networks, and biomimetic optimization methods. He participates in the program committees of several international conferences and on the editorial boards of international journals. Prof. Amine is the head of GeCoDe-knowledge management and complex data-laboratory at UTM University of Saida, Algeria; he also collaborates with the "knowledge base and database" team of TIMC laboratory at Joseph Fourier University of Grenoble.

Panem Charanarur has pursued his B.Tech (ECE), M.Tech (VLSI System Design). He has done his Ph.D. on Low Power VLSI and Advanced technologies in VLSI and Embedded systems. Published Nine Inter National Journal, Attended Three Inter National conference and three national level conference and two national level technical seminars, two national level workshops. Nine Professional Association member ships IAENG, CSIT, IACSIT. He has a review and Editorial, Advisory committee member in Eight International Journals. Now he is currently working as the Assistant Professor, Faculty of Computer Science and Technology, School of Cyber Security and Digital Forensic, National Forensic Sciences University, Curti, Ponda, Goa, India- 581301. His ORCID 0000-0002-7872-8902, E-mail: panem. charan@gmail.com

Panem Charanarur holds B.Tech & M.Tech degree in Electronics and Communication Engineering from JNTU Anantapuram, Andrapradesh, and Ph.D from Electronics in Data Communication from Goa University, Goa. He has more than 8 years of experience in teaching, institutional research, and the corporate environment. His Research Interests are Data Communication, MIMO Channel, SDR, Network on Chip(NoC), Cloud Computing, Artificial Intelligence and the Internet of Things, Cyber Security, and Digital Information Security. He has contributed to above 50 publications, publishers with houses like Elsevier, IOP, IEEE, Springer,Wiley etc and 11 patents, 6 Books, 12 Book Chapters. He invited speakers and guest lectures on emerging areas. He received five awards from reputed government agencies. He is currently working as an Assistant professor in the School of Cyber Security & Digital Forensics, National Forensic Sciences University (NFSU), Tripura Campus, Tripura, India email: panem.charan@gmail.com.

Antonyo George is a Business Solution Advisor at MSI Ethiopia Reproductive Choices, Ethiopia. He received his Master of Science Degree in Information Sciences and Systems (specializing in Information Systems) in 2020, from Addis Ababa University, Ethiopia. B.Sc. Degree in Management Information Systems in 2008, from Unity University, Ethiopia. His research interest is in the area of Usability in Information Security.

Srinivasa Rao Gundu has pursued his Bachelor of Science and Master of Computer Applications from Osmania University and Ph.D. in Computer Sciences from Dravidian University, India. Presently working as Faculty in the Department of Computer Science, Government Degree College Sitaphalmandi, Hyderabad-500 061. He is an Advisory Board Member of World Journal of Engineering Research and Technology (WJERT), Associate Member of the International Association of Innovation Professionals, Member of Institute of Mathematical Statistics, Institute of Mathematical Statistics, Computer Science Teachers Association Individual Basic Member USA, Internet Society Global Member and International Association of Engineers. His research work is focused on Load balancing in Cloud computing. His Research Interests are Cloud Computing, Artificial Intelligence and Internet of things. His publications are on current research-21, (Sci Indexed Journal -2, Web of Science -2 & Scopus Indexed (Springer nature -5), other journals -14 Papers, IEEE Conference Papers -2, Attended 13 Conferences. ORCID 0000-0001-7872-5114, His ORCID 0000-0001-7872-5114, Email:srinivasarao.gundu@gmail.com.

Mumtaz Hussain is a Computer Science graduate from SMI University, Karachi, Pakistan. He works as a freelance programmer and has a diverse work experience in IT Industry. He has been an active member of IEEE since 2018, currently volunteering as a Chair YP Karachi Section, and a member of the technical committee (Nanoscale Communications) of the IEEE Nanotechnology Council.

J. Vijaylaxmi has pursued her Ph.D. in Marine Sciences from School of Earth, Ocean and Atmospheric Sciences Goa University, Goa, India. Her study is focused on the Studies on the inter-tidal rocky shorecrabs (Decapoda: Crustacea: Brachyura) romGoa,Westcoast of India. Her research interests includes Marine Biology, Marine Ecology, Crustaceans Fisheries. She has many publications including Sci Indexed Journals ORCID 0000-0002-1419-0410. Her Email: luckyvj2012@gmail.com.

A. V. Senthil Kumar is working as a Director & Professor in the Department of Research and PG in Computer Applications, Hindusthan College of Arts and Science, Coimbatore since 05/03/2010. He has to his credit 11 Book Chapters, 265 papers in International and National Journals, 25 papers in International Conferences, 5 papers in National Conferences, and edited Nine books (IGI Global, USA). He is an Editor-in-Chief for various journals. Key Member for India, Machine Intelligence Research Lab (MIR Labs). He is an Editorial Board Member and Reviewer for various International Journals. He is also a Committee member for various International Conferences. He is a Life member of International Association of Engineers (IAENG), Systems Society of India (SSI), member of The Indian Science Congress Association, member of Internet Society (ISOC), International

Association of Computer Science and Information Technology (IACSIT), Indian Association for Research in Computing Science (IARCS), and committee member for various International Conferences

Lemma Lessa is an assistant professor of Information Systems at School of Information Science, Addis Ababa University, Ethiopia. He received his doctorate in Information Technology from Addis Ababa University in 2016. He has served over twenty years in the Ethiopian Higher education. His teaching interest is on the socio-technical aspects of Information Systems. His research interest is on e-Services, Information Systems Security Management, Enterprise Systems and IT Governance. He is member of Association for Information Systems (AIS) and current president of the Ethiopian chapter of AIS. He has authored or coauthored over twenty-five articles - four journal articles, and about twenty-one peer-reviewed conference papers. His articles have been presented and published in the International Journal of Leadership and Management, African Journal of Information Systems, proceedings of Americas Conference on Information Systems, International Conference on Theory and Practice of Electronic Governance, and European Conference of Information Systems among others. He also co-authored two peer-reviewed book chapters. He is serving as associate editor and/or PC member for African Journal of Information Systems, the International Conference on e-Democracy & e-Government, International Conference on Digital Transformations and Global Society, Hawaii International Conference on System Sciences, and International Conference on Electronic Governance and Open Society.

Mário Dias Lousã is a coordinator professor at Polytechnic Institute Gaya (ISPGaya), Portugal. He lectures courses on Computer Science. His primary area of research is information systems, as well as knowledge and organizational learning. He has participated in several national and international conferences and is the author and co-author of scientific publications in these fields. He is a reviewer in some international scientific journals with peer review and a consultant in information technologies. Furthermore, he has an MSc in Management Informatics from Portuguese Catholic University and a PhD in Technology and Information Systems from Minho University, Portugal.

Amir Manzoor holds a PhD in Management Sciences. He is a graduate of NED University, Pakistan, Lahore University of Management Sciences (LUMS), Pakistan and Bangor University, United Kingdom. He has more than 20 years of diverse professional and teaching experience working at many renowned national and internal organizations and higher education institutions. His research interests include E-commerce, Strategic Management, Enterprise Resource Planning (ERP),

Project Management,Supply Chain Management, Data Analysis, and Technology applications. Amir can be contacted at engr.dr.amir@gmail.com.

Abdul Hafeez Muhammad is an educationist with 20 years of experience working as Associate Professor in computer science department, Bahria University Islamabad, Pakistan, Lahore Campus. Author of more than 25 research articles in high impact factor journals.

Anandhavalli Muniasamy MCA, MPhil, Ph.D. is currently working as an Associate Professor, at the College of Computer Science, King Khalid University, Saudi Arabia. Her areas of interest are data mining, machine learning, and soft computing. She has published more than 30 research publications in highly reputed international journals and book chapters. She has attended and presented at more than 25 national & international conferences. She served as a principal investigator for the funded project from the All India Council for Technical Education (AICTE). She served as a manuscript reviewer for renowned international journals for the past 15 years, and Ph.D. thesis reviewer for several universities. She has been invited to give guest lectures and as an editorial board member for a few journals and conferences. She is a member of the International Association of Engineers, IEEE - Western Saudi Arabic Section, Computer Society of India, and the International Association of Computer Science and Information Technology.

Asfia Sabahath is currently working as a computer Science Lecturer in King Khalid University. Sabahath has 10+years of experience in educational field, and her hobbies are reading books.

Sergio Francisco Sargo Ferreria Lopes is a professor at Higher Polytechnic Institute Gaya (ISPGAYA), Researcher at Laboratory of Distance Education and e-Learning (LE@D - UID-FCT n° 4372) at Open University of Portugal, Trainer, and Manager of the ICT area, Ph.D. in Information Sciences (specialty Information Systems, Technologies, and Management), M.Sc in Teaching and Educational Management, MBA in ICT Management, Specialist in Higher Education Teaching and Bachelor in Information Systems. Reserve Officer of the Brazilian Army, having held the position of Manager of the Telecommunications and Information Technology area (Telematics). Decorated with the Patriarca da Independência medal, for relevant services rendered to the Brazilian Army. Certified IT professional by Microsoft, ISACA, and EXIN (Holland) in MIE, ITIL, COBIT, ISO/IEC 27002 (Information Security Management), and Green IT Citizen, working with

ITC department management and project management. Trainer accredited by the Scientific-Pedagogical Council of Continuous Training of the Ministry of Education (Portugal). Corresponding Associate Member of the Brazilian Association of Distance Education (ABED).

Arun Kumar Singh is working in the Mathematics and Computer Science, PNG University of Technology, Lae, PNG. He worked (2015-2021) in College of Computing and Informatics, Saudi Electronics University, Kingdom of Saudi Arabia (KSA). He received Ph.D. in CE/IT-2013 by the School of Computer Engineering/Information Technology, SU, Meerut, India, under the guidance of Dr. Neelam Srivastava (IET Lucknow) and Dr. R. P. Agarwal (IIT Roorkee), M.Tech. (IT-WCC) degree in 2005 from IIIT-Allahabad under the guidance of Prof. M. Radha Krishnan and B.E. (ECE) degree in 2002 from BSACET Mathura-Dr. B. R. Ambedkar University, Agra, India. His research interests are Machine Learning, IoT, AI, Big Data, Network Management, Wireless networking, Social Networking and Mobile computing

Index

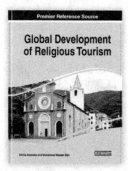

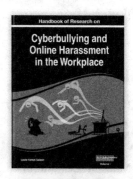

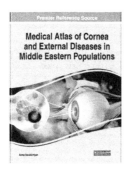
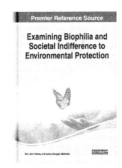
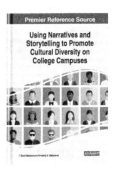

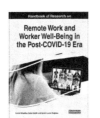

Printed in the United States
by Baker & Taylor Publisher Services